GO-BETWEENS FOR HITLER

Karina Urbach was a Kurt Hahn Scholar at the University of Cambridge, where she took her PhD. For her German Habilitation she was awarded the Bavarian Ministry of Culture prize. She has published on nineteenth and twentieth-century European history and is currently at the Institute for Advanced Study, Princeton. Urbach has worked as historical advisor on many BBC, PBS, and German TV documentaries. She is campaigning for the release of interwar material from the royal archives.

Praise for *Go-Betweens for Hitler*

'engrossing and well-researched'

—Richard J. Evans, *London Review of Books*

'A fascinating page-turner about Hitler's secret diplomacy in the 1930s, which was intended to secure British amity and then neutrality when he led Germany to war…Urbach combed her way through archives across Europe to construct this image of a decaying aristocracy using their connections in the cultivation of appeasers in Britain. They were not without influence.'

—Lawrence Goldman, Books of the Year 2015, *History Today*

'What Urbach offers in this gripping and highly readable account of go-betweens is a rare insight into the unofficial side of diplomacy.'

—Julie Gottlieb, *Journal of Contemporary History*

'To be sure, *Go-Betweens For Hitler* may essentially be based within the parameters of a scholarly undertaking, but it almost reads like that of a John le Carré or Robert Littell novel. In and of itself, this speaks volumes.'

—David Marx, *Book Reviews*

'From peace-feelers in the First World War to appeasers on the eve of the Second World War, this unique book makes fascinating reading'

—Coryne Hall, *European Royal History Journal*

'A fascinating and painstaking reconstruction of the real history of the go-between, so long shrouded in rumour and speculation. This really is a privileged journey behind the scenes of international diplomacy in the company of a cast of larger than life characters brought vividly to life.'

—Richard Overy, editor of *The Oxford Illustrated History of World War II*

'Karina Urbach's scintillating book illuminates a vital and heretofore neglected feature of twentieth-century diplomacy—the role of private intermediaries between governments. Through imaginative research in dozens of archives scattered across the European Continent, Urbach brings to life the hidden world of multilingual aristocrats in the era of the two world wars…As [she] demonstrates, such high born intermediaries, operating under the radar, helped solidify the Austro-German alliance before 1914 and enabled Hitler to influence the British upper classes in the 1930s. Urbach sketches personalities so vividly and writes so well that, in addition to its scholarly importance, this work reads like a mystery novel.'

—Stephen A. Schuker, University of Virginia

GO-BETWEENS FOR HITLER

KARINA URBACH

OXFORD
UNIVERSITY PRESS

Great Clarendon Street, Oxford, OX2 6DP,
United Kingdom

Oxford University Press is a department of the University of Oxford. It furthers the University's objective of excellence in research, scholarship, and education by publishing worldwide. Oxford is a registered trade mark of Oxford University Press in the UK and in certain other countries

First published 2015
First published in paperback 2017

Impression: 1

Published in the United States of America by Oxford University Press
198 Madison Avenue, New York, NY 10016, United States of America

British Library Cataloguing in Publication Data
Data available

Library of Congress Cataloging in Publication Data
Data available

ISBN 978–0–19–870366–2 (Hbk.)
ISBN 978–0–19–870367–9 (Pbk.)

Printed in Great Britain by
Clays Ltd, St Ives plc

Praise for Karina Urbach

Queen Victoria:

This clever and enlightening biography of Queen Victoria is a gripping read. With humour and psychological expertise Karina Urbach portrays—supported by a multitude of documents—an impressive portrait of this woman.

Christopher Clark, University of Cambridge

This short and readable biography of Queen Victoria is a remarkable achievement. First and foremost, it is a masterpiece of a biographical miniature, not in terms of its scholarliness, insight or intellectual power—all of which are by no means in short supply given its proportions. Rather, it manages to be readable, clear, interesting, witty and brief, and yet also important.... The failure of academic historians to consider Queen Victoria seriously has meant she has been enigmatic to date. A triumph of Karina Urbach's book is that, by its end, if anything, Victoria has become more seriously and urgently so.

John Davis, *Sehepunkte*

A little masterpiece

Andreas Rose, *Historische Zeitschrift*

Bismarck's Favourite Englishman:

Karina Urbach has managed to bring together an impressive amount of new evidence... She gives us a balanced, carefully researched and gracefully written account of personalities and policies.

James J. Sheehan, *Times Literary Supplement*

Karina Urbach has a light touch and a sharp eye. She provides vivid portraits of William I, Berlin in the 1870s and the great Bismarck, with whom Russell had a close relationship. Here is a work which is a sheer delight to read.

Jonathan Steinberg, University of Pennsylvania,
and author of *Bismarck: A Life*

Preface

Many of us have been go-betweens at one time or another in our lives. We may have conveyed messages between siblings, parents, or friends after a misunderstanding or argument. But go-betweens not only exist on a personal level, they are also employed in high politics, well hidden from the public eye. Right now they may be working where official channels have become stuck.

Go-betweens are not an invention of the twenty-first century, they have existed for a long time. Those in power who have launched go-between missions over the last century have done so regardless of the form of government. But a common thread existed when it came to choosing the ideal person for such missions: up to 1945 they were mainly members of the aristocracy from every corner of Europe. Only after the Second World War were these people replaced by international businessmen, secret servicemen, and journalists.

In the American television series *House of Cards*, the Vice-President snarls at a congressional inquiry: 'When a back channel becomes public, it defeats its purpose.' It has been my purpose for the last five years to highlight the role of the back channel in the first half of the twentieth century. This book uses new sources found in thirty archives in the United States, Britain, Germany, the Netherlands, and the Czech Republic.

It has been a pleasure writing this story because it gave me a chance to meet real life go-betweens. Following James Watson's advice 'avoid boring people', I have been spoilt with wonderful friends and colleagues. This is a, probably, incomplete list of them: Gerry Bradshaw, Christopher Clark, Matthew Cotton, Shawn Donnelley, Andreas Fahrmeir, Otto Feldbauer, Annegret and Peter Friedberg, Lothar Gall, Ulrike Grunewald, Klaus Hildebrand, Paul Hoser, Eva Klesse, Jeremy Noakes, Klaus Roser, Stephen Schuker, Jonathan Steinberg, the Stolzenbergs, Natascha Stöber, Miles Taylor, the Unholzers.

The Austrian novelist Thomas Bernhard coined the idea of *Lebensmensch*. I have had three such people in my life: my mother Wera Frydtberg (†2008), who was not just a great actress but also the most enchanting person I have ever met; my son Timothy, and my husband Jonathan Haslam, who have made me so happy.

London, June 2015

Contents

List of Illustrations

Introduction

In the summer of 1940 a bizarre incident occurred at the German–Italian border—the Brenner. In July the 83-year-old Duchess in Bavaria was refused permission to return to the German Reich. She was stuck in Italy and tried for months to get back to her home in Bavaria. Her aristocratic friends and relatives as well as the German embassy in Rome tried their best to help her. The ambassador Hans Georg von Mackensen explained the case of the displaced duchess to the German Foreign Ministry: she had travelled to Italy 'for the sole purpose of supporting her granddaughter, the Italian Crown Princess', during the last stages of her pregnancy.[1] This was required because the mother of the Crown Princess could not come to Italy herself. She was the Dowager Queen of the Belgians and had 'for understandable reasons' decided against such a trip.[2]

This family friendly explanation did not have much effect in Berlin, though. Because nothing was done in the following months, the visit of the duchess threatened to turn into a serious diplomatic incident between Germany and Italy. Only when the 'esteemed' Nazi Prince Philipp von Hessen intervened did things start moving again. Hessen used pragmatic arguments vis-à-vis Berlin: as long as the Bavarian duchess was stuck at the border, the Italian royal family had to pay for her costly maintenance. This financial burden was seen as a great nuisance. In October 1940 the displaced Duchess was allowed to re-enter Germany. It turned out that she was not the only member of the higher aristocracy who was in trouble at the border. Over the following years the embassy in Rome was kept busy trying to help other German aristocrats get home.

So what was the regime afraid of? This book will show that the Nazi leadership feared the higher aristocracy because it had *used* their international networks for years and it therefore knew of their great potential.

Members of the aristocracy had worked as go-betweens for Hitler and established useful contacts with the ruling elites of other countries. By 1940 the regime feared that these networks could also work against them.

So far research has focused on the support German aristocrats gave Hitler in gaining power *within* Germany. What has been neglected, however, is that there was also an important international dimension.

Aristocrats saw themselves as an international elite—with their marriages and friendships transcending national boundaries. These international ties were tested in the First World War when royal houses and aristocratic families were attacked as 'hybrids' and had to demonstrate national allegiance. But behind the scenes some aristocrats continued to use their international networks. As unofficial go-betweens for emperors and foreign ministries, British and German aristocrats conveyed peace feelers. This activity came to an end in 1918. But not for long. In the inter-war period a new common enemy appeared on the scene: Bolshevism. Fear of it was another bonding experience for the aristocracy. The British were alarmed lest the Empire should be undermined, the Hungarians feared a repeat of Bela Kun's red terror (1918), and the Germans were scared of their emerging communist party, the largest in Europe.

Encouraged by the Italian model—where Mussolini successfully incorporated the monarchy in his regime (1922)—they turned to a German version of the Duce: Hitler. In 1933 the Führer was short of international contacts and did not trust his own Foreign Ministry. He therefore used members of the German aristocracy for secret missions to Britain, Italy, Hungary, and Sweden. One of the most notorious was the Duke of Coburg—a grandson of Queen Victoria. Born in England and educated in Germany, Carl Eduard is an example of thorough re-education. Unfortunately it was a re-education in reverse—away from the constitutional monarchy he was reared in to dictatorship. This process could have remained a footnote in history. But Carl Eduard's determination to help the Nazi movement first clandestinely, later publicly, had an impact that, like many other go-between missions, has so far not been recognized. Coburg's importance to Hitler had been known by the British intelligence services for a long time. In April 1945 the code breakers at the Government Code and Cypher School, Bletchley Park, came across a telegram from Hitler. The contents intrigued them:

> Source saw a fragment which contained the following sentence: 'the Führer attaches importance to the President of the Red Cross, the Duke of Coburg, on no account falling into enemy hands'.[3]

Hitler was at this point encircled in the bunker. Since he was not known for his caring side it seems bizarre that he made the effort to give instructions about an obscure duke. His message could mean two things. Either Hitler wanted his old confidant, the Duke of Coburg, to be whisked to safety or this was a 'Nero order', i.e. he wanted him to be murdered before the enemy could get hold of him. One thing appeared certain: the secrets Hitler and the Duke shared seemed to be so important that they needed to be forever hidden from public view. This makes one wonder what role Coburg had played for Hitler. Had the Duke been entrusted with secret missions to Britain including one to his close relative Edward VIII, later the Duke of Windsor?

The aim of this book is not just to untangle Coburg's secret negotiations for Hitler, but to uncover several go-between missions, their origins, their significance, and their consequences. It will span the period from the First World War to the Second World War. Apart from the Duke of Coburg, it throws light on the work of many other go-betweens such as Prince Max Egon II Fürstenberg, Lady Barton, General Paget, Lady Paget, Prince Max von Baden, Prince Wilhelm von Hohenzollern-Sigmaringen, Princess Stephanie Hohenlohe-Waldenburg-Schillingfürst, and Prince Max Hohenlohe-Langenburg.

It will hopefully further refine our image of the manner in which diplomacy was conducted in the first half of the twentieth century and will cast new light on a dimension of Hitler's foreign policy tactics hitherto ignored.

PART I

Go-betweens *before* Hitler

I

What are Go-Betweens?

In L. P. Hartley's novel *The Go-Between*, a 12-year-old boy is used by two lovers as a go-between. The affair ends tragically for all parties, overshadowing the boy's later life.

Go-betweens do not necessarily have tragic fates. Far from it. In the modern academic sub-discipline of 'network analysis', for example, they are regarded as having certain inbuilt advantages: 'People whose network connections allow them to act as go-betweens in organizations, connecting otherwise disconnected individuals and groups, tend to garner many benefits.'[1]

It is of course exactly those benefits that attract them to the task. Historians and political scientists know everything about the *official* side of diplomacy, but rarely stray onto its unofficial side. There are many things which statesmen are reluctant to put into writing. The picture therefore gained by historians can be incomplete. Well hidden from the public eye, statesmen often want to send a message to their opposite numbers that can be very different from their public utterances; in some extreme cases, even the opposite. To achieve this balancing act, they have to use a go-between. But what exactly are political go-betweens?

So far there exists no proper definition. In Britain various terms are used to describe the phenomenon: they are called 'unofficial contacts' or 'backroom diplomats'. The Americans call them 'back channels' or 'track II diplomacy'.[2] In Germany their work is labelled as 'Substitutionsdiplomatie (substitute diplomacy)', 'personal diplomacy', or 'secret diplomacy'.

Since go-betweens have no defined job description and no official standing, it is easy to dismiss them as men and women of no importance. That they are overlooked is understandable. At the conclusion of treaties it is the politicians and diplomats who make the photo shoot and later get most of the attention from historians. However, a wider aperture can be useful.

Out of focus, in the shadows are other figures. It is these people, the camera-shy, who will be drawn to the centre of the stage in this book.

Go-betweens are not part of the government or parliament. They are not elected and they are never civil servants. They are off the books and everything they say is off the record. Because they are not part of a hierarchy they cannot be controlled. They only have to answer to one person—their employer, who is a high-ranking politician, the head of state, or the head of the government.

Though they have things in common, go-betweens are *not* lobbyists or mediators. Mediators have to be impartial, whereas go-betweens are used by one party and therefore represent the interests of that party. They are also not lobbyists. Lobbyists try to cultivate their 'target' because of a single issue they want to push. But go-betweens usually know 'their targets' already in a completely different context. They have history. As one modern day go-between explained: 'I knew XY well. When I approached him he was open because we had known each other for a long time in a different capacity.'

In some ways aristocratic go-betweens are a throwback to the old form of ad hoc diplomacy which had ended with Cardinal Richelieu institutionalizing the diplomatic service in 1626. Up to that date ambassadors had often been connected to sovereigns by blood (or the connection was made artificially, resulting in the expression Ambassador de Sang). With Richelieu a professionalization had set in. The new concept meant that one did not send diplomats on special occasions, but employed a permanent representative, showing continuity in one's relations with other countries.[3]

So are go-betweens just atavistic, a throw-back to the age before Richelieu?

Some want us to believe this. At the Munich security conference in 2007 Vladimir Putin expressed the opinion that the 'system of international relations is equal to mathematics. There are no personal dimensions.'[4]

Indeed, international relations are not like personal relations, as any politician confused on this point will find out at his peril. National or ideological interests always outweigh even the most loyal partners. But this does not mean that the personal element cannot play a part. Go-betweens symbolize and use that personal element. They think of international relations as their relations. With this simple approach they work in the antechambers of power, circumventing normal diplomatic channels.

Their work is based on the assumption that only in an ideal world do people act rationally all the time. Cultural and social backgrounds, peer group pressure, and emotions have an influence on decision-making processes. These are factors to which go-betweens can appeal.

Up to 1939 go-betweens were chosen from among people with high-level international contacts. Those who offered such contacts were traditionally members of the higher aristocracy (slowly joined by international businessmen and journalists). They were ideal because they were blood-related or connected by friendship to the elites of many other countries. It would indeed be wrong to assume that, with the rise of the middle classes in the nineteenth century, aristocratic spheres of influence were completely taken over by a new elite. A once powerful group does not just vanish into the night. When displaced, it finds new niches. One of them was go-between work. Their *international* network made them ideal for such work. It was a network that had grown organically over several generations and had gained them many advantages. Nobles had always been naturals for international relations. In the early modern period it had not been unusual for aristocrats to have different homelands at different stages of their lives. The Prince von Nassau-Siegen, for example, was the son of a German-Dutch family, born in 1743 in France. He became a grandee of Spain, married a Polish countess, and worked as a Russian admiral until 1794.[5] Aristocratic families had for centuries acted like a fund-manager who lays bets on different companies to diversify assets: they married off their children or put them in military service in different countries, hoping to open up new branches of the house. As a result many aristocrats had expert knowledge of countries that were seen at the time as rather 'obscure'. The German Prince Wilhelm of Hohenzollern-Sigmaringen (1864–1927), brother of the King of Romania, for example, knew Romanian society well. As will be shown, he was therefore used for unofficial contacts during the First World War. So was the Nazi go-between Prince Max Hohenlohe (1897–1968), twenty years later. Hohenlohe still thought of his family as truly international because they had produced: 'a German chancellor, a French Marshal, a Roman Catholic Cardinal, a number of Austro-Hungarian Field Marshals, Generals of Prussia and Baden, hereditary Marshals of Württemberg, and ADCs General to the Russian Tsar'.[6] Such international reach was clearly a source of considerable pride.

This genealogical and professional internationalism existed in the higher aristocracy more often than in any other class. Whereas in the eighteenth century most people never even left their own town or village, aristocrats already had the highest mobility rate in Europe. Before the term *Weltbürger* (citizen of the world) was invented, the 'aristocrat of the world' existed. The German novelist Thomas Mann was an admirer of this type. He described the most famous exponent of the 1920s—Richard Coudenhove-Kalergi—as a man who made 'the average German feel provincial'. Coudenhove's blood had been 'mixed by the international aristocracies of Europe, he was of genteel humanity, a man who was used to thinking in continents'.[7] Viscount Lymington made a similar observation in his memoirs of 1956: 'What was and still is, interesting is that there is a sort of international aristocratic family freemasonry which permeates Europe even now.'[8]

As a consequence integration into other countries remained easier for nobles than for any other social group. According to the Nazi Prince Rohan this was because: '[we] are united beyond all national passion by a common heritage, blood that has often mixed, a common social level and attitude to life's problems'.

As we will see aristocrats had languages—more than that, they had native instruction. Others had to learn what they knew already.[9] They answered to a decisive form of communication, which the up and coming middle classes could not copy: a common social code, based on an idealized medieval code of honour, courtesy rules, and a strong ancestral cult. They also shared a common European memory. The cornerstones of this memory were the threats of 1789, 1848, and 1917.

The details of an aristocratic lifestyle could vary from country to country, but everywhere in Europe the maxim was: aristocrats have access to other aristocrats.[10]

A further reason why easy access was obtainable not just to other aristocrats but, as we will see, to democratic politicians as well, was the power of their names. Marcel Proust demonstrated in his novel *À la recherche du temps perdu* the irresistible glamour of old names. They seem to have had their own aura and 'pull' over people—Hitler included. Someone with a 'big name', a name that evoked historical grandeur—a Habsburg, a Hohenzollern, a Coburg—was, well into the 1930s, much more easily received in the drawing rooms of power than somebody without such an illustrious family name.

Of course the question arises, why were diplomats not used for delicate missions since, well into the 1930s, they too were from aristocratic families?

Indeed, some diplomats and civil servants thought of go-betweens as unwelcome rivals. The Permanent Under Secretary at the Foreign Office Lord Hardinge of Penshurst wrote in 1917 about go-betweens:

> We have had considerable experience of unofficial action in these matters [peace feelers] and it generally contains an element of danger, however sound the motive.[11]

Diplomats warned of missions that were not run by diplomats. Naturally they feared commitments would be made behind their backs which could not be delivered (or, worse, had to be delivered).

But using diplomats had its drawbacks. It gave the missions an official character. Conversations were recorded in dispatches and eventually became public in the 'blue books' in Britain (or in the 'white books' in Germany). Formalities had to be observed and openness showed weakness. Indiscretions and leaks after talks were also more likely, because others were also involved in the process. The Austrian Foreign Minister v. Czernin believed that 'every political secret is known to one hundred people—the civil servants in the Foreign Ministry, the encipher clerks, the embassies, the envoys and the staff'.[12]

Go-betweens on the other hand hid behind face-to-face conversations and (usually) avoided leaving any written record. They could be much more creative at problem solving and float ideas. They could also make themselves 'invisible': unlike diplomats whose comings and goings are noticed, the sudden appearance of aristocratic go-betweens in other countries was not registered by the press. It was assumed that they were simply visiting relatives and friends. Also go-betweens did not fall under the scrutiny of parliament and could not be checked up on by a commission. When one wanted to keep talks unrecorded and secret it was therefore ideal to use a go-between.

Another reason for using 'outsiders' instead of 'in house people' can also be that the head of government does not trust his own diplomats. This was the case with Hitler who until 1938 suspected his own Foreign Ministry of not being fully 'nazified'.[13] Diplomacy in its traditional form was despised by him. He therefore preferred his chosen Nazi aristocrats to deliver important messages for him. Three of them, the Duke of Coburg, Princess Stephanie Hohenlohe, and Prince Max Hohenlohe, will be analysed in this book. But they are only the tip of a much bigger iceberg.

Guarding one's turf and distrust of one's own civil servants can also be the reason for using go-betweens in a democratic country. In the inter-war years, foreign affairs were an embattled field in democracies where players tried to establish their own backroom channels, independent of their Foreign Offices. Heads of governments often saw themselves as foreign affairs experts and they therefore used go-betweens to carry out their own policy. President F. D. Roosevelt preferred to use go-betweens to circumvent Cordell Hull at the State Department; John F. Kennedy employed a long-established go-between during the Cuban Missile Crisis. Such channels were also popular with US adviser on national security Henry Kissinger and German Chancellor Willy Brandt, neither of whom had sufficient confidence in their own diplomatic representatives but wished to sustain a public policy at variance with reality.[14] The British were not averse to this kind of tactic either. As will be seen, Chamberlain chose the go-between option for his appeasement policy. In history books he could find many examples for it. The Stuart King Charles II, for example, had learnt in exile to use the 'back stairs', people he trusted in untrustworthy times.[15]

Naturally not everyone who was well connected made a good go-between. To carry out missions go-betweens needed to have fairly stable characters, coping with stressful situations (particularly when they were employed during a war). Their work could be immensely frustrating, varying between times of high tension and total idleness.

They therefore needed a lot of patience and stamina. A study of peace negotiators in the twenty-first century stated: 'only vicars have to drink more tea in the course of their duty than peace mediators. Well tea or coffee or Coca Cola.'[16] Apart from Coca Cola, this was not so very different from a go-between in the first half of the twentieth century.

They also needed a very good memory. Since nobody wanted to commit anything to paper, go-betweens had to try to remember verbatim the arguments of the people involved. Of course this did not guarantee that they passed them on correctly. As in every conversation they could misinterpret the subtext or the tone of voice (threatening, consoling). They could be too eager to hear things that were not actually said. To please their 'employer' they could also raise hopes that were misplaced. Flattered by the mission, they could even oversell themselves to both sides. The better and longer they had known their opposite number, the higher the chance they understood the message. What one German go-between would call 'the study of people' (*Menschenbeobachtung*) was a prerequisite for the job. Nowadays it is quoted as the key to conflict resolution theory: 'the historical setting, the culture, the character of the people involved.'[17]

All of this is, of course, common sense. And that is another prerequisite for go-betweens. They had to understand emotions, they played to a certain degree the politics of emotions, 'Gefühlspolitik' as one German called it, but they could never get emotional themselves. Since aristocrats believe in *Affektkontrolle* (the control of one's emotions) they were well prepared for this.

They also needed to be good at lighting upon the right windows of opportunity, occasionally exclude controversial topics, and bring in new ideas at the right time. Consequently many of the people involved in secret negotiations were often good chess players, thinking strategically. They even used occasional chess language to explain their moves—one go-between was arguing the whole war should be ended and a 'partie remise' (replaying the game later) declared.

So why did aristocrats offer themselves as go-betweens?

First of all the human ego should never be underestimated. Even though these were clandestine missions, they could bring great prestige. Those in the know would remember what a go-between had achieved and compensate them in some form for it. This would not necessarily be financial. Go-between work was not lucrative work per se, but 'only for honour'. A major exception in this book is the go-between Stephanie Hohenlohe who made sure she received very expensive 'thank you' presents.

Another reason for undertaking this job was that many aristocrats thought of themselves as entitled to play a political role. Simply to be asked restored their political relevance.

So in which situations were these go-betweens actually used?

As the following chapters will show, there was a great difference between their work in peacetime and their work during wars. In peacetime go-betweens were mainly employed to solve misunderstandings between heads of states and governments or to establish a channel for future crisis situations.

In times of war, go-betweens could play an even more useful role. When embassies were closed down and every meeting between diplomats interpreted as a possible overture, go-betweens could put out peace feelers and work in an undetected way.

Yet, despite its important role, thus far no one has done any scholarly work on this phenomenon. One reason for this may well be that historians are usually middle class and do not make the connection. They may have been aware of the international networks of the aristocracy but they did not enquire what they were used for. Because no equivalent phenomenon exists among the middle classes, it was simply not looked for in other classes. Instead the aristocracy was dismissed as an anaemic group, entirely passé, which no longer constituted a relevant political and economic factor. Sir David Cannadine described the British aristocracy more or less gracefully vanishing into the historical background after 1918. He had no interest in international relations and also ignored their impressive survival techniques which have made them an economic and social success to this day. Only a few historians, like Arno Mayer, have believed in the longevity of aristocratic power, pointing out that they still played at least an economic and social role.[18]

Added to this class-determined narrow vision, the aristocracy and monarchies did not exactly make it easy for historians to find out more about them. They simply gave a stylized picture of themselves, cleansed of any political haut gout. To this day the private archives of many aristocratic families do not allow research on twentieth-century material. The most famous are the Royal Archives at Windsor. They have a strict embargo on royal correspondence for the inter-war years. Another problem has been that aristocratic go-betweens did not leave many traces behind. They did not write down their instructions and later did not 'confess' about them in a sensationalized autobiography. He (or in many cases she) was discreet and loyal. Since their work was not to be mentioned in any official documents, diplomatic historians could get a lopsided view. The Permanent Undersecretary of the Foreign Office, Sir Robert Vansittart, was well aware of this problem: 'It is perhaps difficult for the pure historian to write contemporary history. It cannot be written on documents only—above all on diplomatic ones. I know too much of what lies behind them, too much of what does not appear.'[19]

He meant the characters of the people involved and the unwritten assumptions. But he also meant back channels. Vansittart himself actually used go-betweens as will be shown in Chapter 6.

So how can one find out about such missions if there are no sources?

It is certainly not easy and most missions will probably never come to light. But one can reconstruct some by finding a way in by the backdoor. Traces, if they exist at all, can be found mainly among private papers. Occasionally missions are made public by new archival discoveries, e.g. files of the security services. They will therefore play an important part in this book. Even a failed mission can be invaluable to the historian. For instance, after the disastrous 'Sixtus' mission came to light in 1918 (of which more later), the people involved were eager to protest their innocence in their memoirs. The same was true for the go-betweens Hitler used, many of whom wanted to rewrite their life after 1945.

Just because it is difficult to research these missions does not mean one should ignore them. It would entail missing out an important dimension and just relying on official documents. This could easily turn into what E. H. Carr called 'documentary fetishism'. A historian who does not develop a feel for the gaps in the sources misses out on important connections. He might end up like the Pulitzer prize winner A. Scott Berg, who wrote a biography of Charles Lindbergh without apparently noticing that Lindbergh led a double life in Germany—including having several children.

When it comes to political double lives, go-betweens illuminate a hitherto well-hidden world.

A common language?

At the heart of this book is the question: 'what' did aristocratic go-betweens talk about? We should also have a brief look at *how* they talked. How did they use language to establish a closeness with their 'targets'? And what was their lingua franca? English, German, or French?

If one follows Ludwig Wittgenstein's conclusion that 'the limits of my language mean the limits of my world', then an analysis of the language spoken by aristocratic elites would yield not only an insight into their communication skills but also help us to understand their mentality. Of course, it has to be established first *how* aristocratic language differed from the language of other social groups.

Aristocrats were considered to have a particularly exclusive language.[20] Since medieval times, the ideal of knights and their chivalrous vocabulary had become part of how the aristocracy was seen. By the nineteenth century what was assumed to be an artificial mode of speech had become a special focus of attack. Particularly in Germany and France the aristocracy was ridiculed for its 'unnatural' discourse and effeminate gestures, which were seen as 'insincere'. Well into the 1950s a critic of the Austrian aristocracy commented on their 'bad German, which is littered with foreign words'.[21] This was not just an Austrian phenomenon. In Britain, the letters of the Mitford sisters show the peculiarity of aristocratic language in the twentieth century. To this day these aristocratic siblings are seen as odd because the two most beautiful of them, Diana and Unity, were infatuated with Hitler, whereas a less glamorous one, Jessica, chose Stalin. It was therefore no surprise that the eldest sister, Nancy Mitford, quite sensibly mined her family as material for her novels. But apart from indulging in extreme politics the Mitfords are also famous for communicating in their own special vocabulary. Today people think of their letters either as charming or highly obnoxious. Yet whatever the standpoint, these letters stood for much more than eccentricity.

Aristocratic women were cocooned in an insular world, usually tutored at home while their brothers went off to boarding schools, the army, or university. This upbringing made aristocratic women the guardians of an exclusive language. It was Nancy Mitford who wrote the decisive essay on the language of the British upper classes, which to this day has no German or French equivalent. Her essay was inspired by the linguist Alan S. C. Ross. He had written an article on U (upper-class) and non-U (non-upper-class) language. While for example 'toilet' or 'mirror' were non-upper-class words, 'loo' and 'looking-glass' were upper class. Together with other prominent contributors Ross and Mitford then published in 1956 *Noblesse Oblige: An Enquiry into the Identifiable Characteristics of the English Aristocracy*. It caused a furore, making many middle-class people change their vocabulary overnight.

Even though Mitford's analysis was delivered in an ironic tone, it is not an accident that a female member of the upper class helped Ross in his research. These women followed a strict policy of linguistic exclusion, thereby watching over their family's social contacts. Aristocratic and upper-class women also employed a special diction. This 'affected' pronunciation naturally upset members of other classes who felt excluded. When Nancy Mitford served in a firewatching unit in 1940, other watchers—from the middle and working class—wanted her fired.[22] They misunderstood her accent as mockery. Mockery was not her intention, but it was an accent so ingrained in female upper-class girls that even Nancy's rebellious sister Jessica Mitford never dropped it. She became a committed communist who sounded like a duchess.

Such artificial diction was less marked among aristocratic and upper-class men, though. Recordings of upper-class male voices well into the 1930s sounded relatively 'normal'. To have a local accent was also common for male aristocrats in Germany. Chancellor Otto von Bismarck identified with 'simple country people' for whom he could switch into a local dialect. Kaiser Wilhelm II often sounded like a Berliner. This was recounted in many anecdotes and is one reason for his surprising popularity.[23] His 'common touch' was intended to lessen social tensions. He tried to use language as a means of sustaining a sense of shared experience and became a master of the popular catchphrase. His 'soundbites' were unforgettable and often unforgivable. He famously described the Chinese as the 'yellow peril', advised women to stick to 'Children, kitchen, church' (*Kinder, Küche, Kirche*), and called socialists 'fellows without a fatherland' (*vaterlandslose Gesellen*). The fact that the Emperor delivered these soundbites in a manly Berlin accent appealed to the average German.

Even though aristocratic men belonged to a closed group, it would therefore be wrong to see them as socially autistic. Unlike female aristocrats, men often had a greater variety of interlocutors. They talked to members of reigning houses, their own peer group, professional elites (the local doctor, the lawyer), their staff, and farmers. Ideally an aristocrat had to react with different languages to these very different social groups. Indeed, many tried to become experts in varied forms of communication.

When it came to corresponding with monarchs, aristocrats used an extremely formal language. This was the case in Britain, but even more so in Austria-Hungary and Germany. Despite his 'common touch', when talking to his Berliners, the Kaiser expected an almost byzantine writing style from members of his court. His 'favourites', Prince Eulenburg and Prince Fürstenberg, managed to perfect this. Even relatives of the Kaiser had to follow this rule, as did the Kaiser's uncle, Chlodwig von Hohenlohe-Schillingsfürst, who became German Chancellor in 1894. Whereas he was addressed by Wilhelm II as 'uncle', he had to answer the Kaiser as 'your Majesty's humble, loyal servant'. Hohenlohe explained such servility with the words: 'one is not related to sovereigns.'[24]

However, between sovereigns there existed equality, even if one side came from a tiny state while the other was a British king. The reigning Prince Hohenzollern-Sigmaringen used the German 'Du' when he talked to King George V. The King, who had learnt German in Hesse, reciprocated and made statements to Hohenzollern-Sigmaringen that he would not have made to anyone outside this closed circle. On 24 May 1914 he said to Hohenzollern, for example: 'Du (you) will see that Grey will drag us into a disaster before long.'[25] He was probably referring to the problems in Ireland at the time. Yet the fact that the King distrusted Grey, his own Foreign Secretary, was quite a useful piece of information for Hohenzollern-Sigmaringen. It was one of many remarks he passed on to the German Foreign Ministry.

Equality also existed amongst the group that ranked below the reigning houses, the aristocrats. In the case of France, the sociologist Monique de

Saint Martin has shown that to this day there exists a tradition in the aristocratic French Jockey Club that 'two members sitting next to each other at dinner, who have never met before do not introduce themselves to each other. Since they belong to the same world, they have to act as if they had known each other all their lives.'[26]

A similar tradition exists in the Bavarian aristocracy where members address each other on a first name basis, even if they are not related or friends. It was this 'linguistic closeness' that would become useful for go-between missions. To be on first name terms with many of the people they had to approach naturally helped to make conversations more relaxed and open.

However, ladders were pulled up when it came to communication with the middle classes. To deter social climbers, the aristocracy used insider jokes and endless pet names. Today research in private archives is sometimes extremely frustrating because nobody can any longer identify the addressees of letters. Who was dear 'Mossy' or darling 'Dodi' who got 'tons of love from Rolly'? Many of these childhood pet names stuck for life. The youngest daughter of Alfred Duke of Saxe-Coburg and Gotha, for example, remained in the family correspondence the 'Baby'. As an old lady she signed off letters to her sister, the Queen of Romania, with 'love from your old baby'. This 'infantilization' of family members had several causes. Traditionally aristocratic families often used the same first names for their children. Consequently there might be an inflation of Victorias, Wilhelms, Franz, Heinrich, Ernst, or Louis in one house. To have such a popular first name, a *Leitname* as the Germans called it, was a sign of prestige and status within the family. By using pet names internally their holders could be identified more easily. Apart from this practical approach there was another important reason for pet names—it worked perfectly as a form of exclusion, as the writer and director Julian Fellowes has shown. Fellowes has written many screenplays about the aristocracy whose accuracy can be questioned, but he has identified correctly why pet names were vital:

> Everyone is 'Toffee' or 'Bobo' or 'Snook'. They themselves think the names imply a kind of playfulness, an eternal childhood, fragrant with memories of nanny and pyjamas warming by the nursery fire. But they are really a simple reaffirmation of insularity, a reminder of shared history that excludes more recent arrivals; yet another way of publicly displaying their intimacy with each other. Certainly the nicknames form an effective fence. A newcomer is often in the position of knowing someone too well to continue to call them Lady So-and-So but not nearly well enough to call them 'sausage', while to use their actual Christian name is a sure sign

within their circle that one doesn't really know them at all. And so the new arrival is forced back from the normal development of friendly intimacy that is customary among acquaintances in other classes.[27]

Pet names were therefore a useful strategy to avoid unwelcome advances from middle-class outsiders. Nancy Mitford described such advances as pure torture. She hated to be addressed as 'Nancy' by people she hardly knew.

Though the aversion to the social climbing middle classes was obvious among aristocratic and upper-class families, feelings towards the 'lower classes' could be very different. Mitford's essay on U and non-U language already gives an indication of this. The language of the upper classes in England was closer to that of the working classes. They shared much of the same traditional vocabulary. Furthermore, while the working classes had their cockney slang, their upper-class counterparts showed a similar preference, according to Ross: 'There seems no doubt that, in the nineties and at least up to 1914, U-speakers (particularly young ones) were rather addicted to slang.'[28] This is illustrated, for example, in P. G. Wodehouse's *Blandings Castle* where the son of Lord Emsworth constantly uses slang words and addresses his enraged father as 'guv'nor'.[29]

The relative closeness between the 'upper' and the 'lower classes' was not just an English phenomenon. In Germany many aristocrats lived during the first stages of their lives in the countryside; it was here that they learned dialects from the local staff (often to the horror of their middle-class nannies). In later life many male aristocrats actually preferred the company of 'common people' to mingling with the educated middle classes. This was something Prince Castell-Castell mused about in a letter to his wife. Like so many members of his peer group he experienced during the First World War a clash of classes at the front. Many of his officers were middle-class men and Castell-Castell came to the conclusion that aristocrats could get on much better with simple soldiers. 'Less educated people', as he called them, were more agreeable than bourgeois show-offs. Of course, one reason for this was that the middle-class officers were from urban centres and could not understand Prince Castell's rural world. He cared about issues like the latest harvest results and therefore had more to talk about with a farmhand turned soldier than with a dentist turned officer. The dentist had different subjects and vocabulary. Wolfgang Frühwald even claimed that the German middle classes developed their own 'educated dialect' in clear demarcation from the nobility *and* the 'common people'.[30]

The British middle classes were much less critical of their social superiors than their German counterparts. But even they had serious comprehension problems. In one of his short stories, Aldous Huxley satirized the erratic conversation techniques of the higher aristocracy: Lord Badgery, a member of an old family, constantly changes the subject during a disastrous dinner party. Such an associative conversation was seen as a sign of esprit by the aristocracy, but Badgery's middle-class guests cannot keep up with the pace.[31] Badgery in turn is deeply bored by their company. Long, educational monologues by professionals were perceived as an imposition. The aristocratic ideal was to be a dilettante in as many fields as possible (to them dilettante still had a positive meaning, stemming from the Latin word *delectare*, to delight). To their annoyance professional middle-class men did not want simply to delight, but rather to 'specialize'. At the end of the twentieth century, the Duke of Devonshire therefore saw it as courageous of his wife 'Debo' to sacrifice a whole day once a year talking to the local dignitaries. In his eyes they were far from interesting. Luckily, Debo was an unusual Mitford girl, not known for the famously sharp Mitford tongue. She was careful not to upset—as Lord Cecil of Chelwood had put it once—'the middle class monsters'.[32]

When it came to actual correspondence with the middle classes the aristocracy was in fact very careful to avoid any such thing. In Germany and in England, a polite, politically correct tone was used. This fastidiousness was characteristic of speeches in front of a 'mixed' audience. Prince Castell-Castell referred to his middle-class listeners in a church sermon as 'alongside people' (*Nebenmenschen*).

Apart from the court language, the internal peer group language, and the politically correct language for the middle classes, almost all members of the higher aristocracy also had foreign languages in common. In Germany the aforementioned Prince of Hohenzollern-Sigmaringen, for example, read newspapers in three languages: The *Illustrated London News*, *Indépendence romaine*, and the *Bukarester Tageblatt*. Language training started early. Prince Hans Pless had at the age of 8 to summarize articles from *The Times* and the *Figaro* for his father.[33] French governesses had groomed the Russian aristocracy and gentry from the time of the Empress Catherine and therefore French was still important, but English had become more fashionable by the later nineteenth century. Armies of British nannies invaded the Continent and left their mark:

> Before the war it would have been hard to exaggerate the sway of British nannies among some central European children; toes kept count of pigs going to market

before fingers learnt to bead and Three Blind Mice rushed in much earlier than inklings of the Trinity.[34]

By the beginning of the twentieth century it was seen as a social stain not to know about blind mice. The Dutch noblewoman Victoria Bentinck commented that her 'poor' niece Mechthild had married down linguistically: 'She made a marriage of convenience to a German Count. As he couldn't speak any other language but his own, he was rather a "fish out of water" in our family at Middachten, where four languages were constantly being spoken sometimes in the same breath. She was the sort of woman who ought to have married a diplomat instead of a country gentleman. In the diplomatic service she would have been in her element.'[35]

Indeed, Mechthild was not happy about her indolent German husband who had missed out on learning languages properly. The British born Daisy Pless made a similar mistake. She married in 1891 into one of the richest German aristocratic families and for forty years survived on a rather limited German vocabulary.[36] One reason for this was that all her German friends, Kaiser Wilhelm II included, insisted on talking English to her. In this regard she 'benefited' from the dominance of English as the new language of the aristocracy. But she should have listened to the advice of her friend King Edward VII, who had admonished her for not learning proper German. In British royal circles German was, until 1914, quite important. Edward VII made sure his older sons learnt it. His son George (later George V) was sent on a refresher course to Hesse when he became Prince of Wales.

Learning foreign languages remained an important way of keeping international friendships and family networks alive. It also demonstrated ubiquity. Royal houses were generally seen as the role model by aristocrats. The Emperor Franz Joseph spoke French, Italian, Czech and a bit of Hungarian, so he could talk to the majority of his subjects in their own languages.'

In Germany, the Pless children learnt Polish, because their father had Polish speaking tenants. Language skills were used as a tool to overcome ethnic differences within one's domain and to demonstrate rights to the land. To speak Polish or Czech showed allegiance to that region, too. By learning Polish, Prince Pless also wanted to defuse social and political tensions. He did not want to be seen as an 'alien element'. He knew that families who neglected such language skills could suffer. A former servant of the south German Prince Oettingen-Wallerstein commented on such a failure: 'the young Prince had a Czech teacher, but he did not want anything to do with

Czech ideas.'[37] To the disappointment of his parents Oettingen-Wallerstein never developed an interest in the family's Bohemian properties.

Prince Max Egon II zu Fürstenberg made no such mistake. He was brought up bilingually because his family had property in Czech speaking Bohemia and in Germany. When he became a member of the Austro-Hungarian upper house, his Czech language skills repeatedly helped him to sort out political discord.

However, as will be seen in Chapter 2, it was exactly this cosmopolitanism that came into collision with the German middle classes. In the nineteenth century they had been at the forefront of the nationalist movement and attacked the 'linguistic degeneracy' of the higher aristocracy. The German gentry (*niederer Adel*) agreed on this issue: Hans von Tresckow feared in 1907, like many members of the German gentry, a lack of national feeling among the aristocracy. A symptom seemed to be their mania for foreign languages:

> Count Maltzahn had invited me to breakfast with him in the Hotel Kaiserhof. I met there Prince Brion, Prince Schönaich-Karolath and a Polish Count Skorczewski—all members of the Prussian upper house, which is currently discussing the expropriation act aimed at the Poles. I sat at a separate table with Maltzahn, because these 'pillars' of the Prussian throne were conversing in French out of consideration for their Polish colleague, who by the way speaks German well. This is really the height of snobbery. The government is supporting a policy of germanisation and the worthy members of the upper house are talking in the German capital with a Prussian citizen of Polish descent, French. Maltzahn was outraged. He is a really good German, who isn't infected by the internationalism of the great families.[38]

The 'great families' had a lot of reasons not to give up their language skills. They helped them to keep their widespread property arrangements and their social networks going. And it was their multi-layered communication skills which would eventually make them ideal go-betweens.

Networks before 1914: the Protestant network

There existed two main networks in aristocratic and royal circles: a Protestant and a Catholic one. Both were based on faith and family. Both were competing for international connections. An overlap of networks was rare, as Prince Philip, the Duke of Edinburgh, explained in 2009:

> The princely families of Europe knew each other. They met each other a lot and it was all the way across. France being Roman Catholic, there were few matrimonial connections. There was some with Belgium, but that was fairly distant. Of course, there was Scandinavia. But the nearest other Protestant country that produced wives and husbands was Germany, so there was much more familial contact that way.[39]

While the Catholic network was dominated by the Habsburgs, the Protestant network had the British royal family at its centre. There were several reasons for this. For Protestant aristocrats all over Europe it had always been appealing to cultivate their British counterparts. Especially since the nineteenth century, Britain was an attractive model that was admired, envied, and copied.[40] British aristocrats seemed to have adapted best to the social challenges of the Industrial Revolution and profited well from it economically. Furthermore they had an empire at their disposal that offered investments and jobs for their second sons. They had brought their middle classes 'under control' by reforms and kept deference intact.

This was something a continental aristocrat wanted to be connected with. The best route to Britain was via the royal networks. Already the German wives of the Georges had brought in their relatives and so did Queen Victoria and Prince Albert. They were related to a variety of minor German princelings (most importantly the Coburgs, the Leiningens, and the Hohenlohes). Members of these families eventually became Anglo-German, effortlessly moving between the two countries. It was these families who would form the basis for many go-between missions in the twentieth century.

The Coburg network turned out to be the most successful one of them all because it was close-knit. In a secret memorandum Prince Albert's brother, Duke Ernst II of Coburg (1818–93), described how to keep it that way: most important was *Vertrauen*, trust, among family members. Above all: 'bitterness, irony, must be alien to us, as much as avarice and jealousy.' Ernst II appealed to comradeship. Picking up on Dumas's *The Three Musketeers*, a novel published in 1844, Ernst pointed out that his 'house' could achieve greatness as long as all the members stayed united—'one for all and all for one'.[41]

Of course there were many reasons why the members should respond to such an appeal. The family network was a perfect insurance system and for many poorer relatives a 'meal ticket'. To leave it could mean financial and social suicide. The name Coburg therefore offered its members what the sociologist Pierre Bourdieu has labelled as 'symbolic capital' (titles), 'cultural capital' (knowledge, education, taste), and 'social capital' (contacts).[42]

It was common sense to remain a part of and support such a network. But apart from the rational arguments there was also an irrational reason that kept the network together: the power of emotion. In fact, taken as a whole, aristocratic and royal families were experts at managing such emotion.

To this day there is bizarre disagreement about whether the aristocracy was capable of 'genuine' emotion or not. The one extreme of the debate is represented by media personalities like Julian Fellowes, of *Downton Abbey* fame, and the journalist Peregrine Worsthorne, who portray aristocrats as caring individuals who looked after family members and staff well. Their opponents at the other extreme see aristocrats and dynasties as emotionally autistic. Their counter-scenario reminds one of the Great Gatsby narrative. Like Scott Fitzgerald's portrayal of the super-rich they would agree that aristocrats are 'careless people (who) smashed up things and creatures and then retreated back into their money . . . and let other people clean up the mess they had made'.[43]

Both portrayals are naturally caricatures. Fellowes is clearly idealizing the aristocracy. On the other hand it is contradictory to accuse a class that is so obsessed with the idea of family of a lack of emotional bonding. The topos of the 'cold' ruling classes and their loveless family life was in fact used as a line of attack by the rising middle classes, as one historian has pointed out: 'the criticism of aristocratic family life by professional men was among the earliest forms of class consciousness.'[44] This was not just directed against the upper classes.[45] The working classes were also portrayed as dysfunctional and incapable of bringing up their children. Upper-class families, however, remained the worst culprits: they handed over children to nurses and married them off for material advantage and not for affection—apparently unlike middle-class people. According to this argument, only the middle classes married for love and looked after their family altruistically. Of course this was a completely idealized representation, but this class fight over emotion was continued by historians. Lawrence Stone, for example, was attacked by E. P. Thompson for his theory that the romantic ideal had started in the upper classes. According to Thompson other classes, including the working classes, also loved romantically. Who loved more or better remains subject to ideological dispute to this day.

For the early twentieth century we still do not know much about emotional bonding within aristocratic families. One reason is that the history of royal and aristocratic families is written by middle-class historians who have their own vantage point. They are also prevented from getting a better view, because royal and aristocratic families seldom afford access to their archives. As a result historians have to use aristocratic autobiographies. These are, however, heavily filtered. According to the mores of the times they don't mention the family much. Wives are only referred to *en passant* and usually described as 'good comrades'. This is deceptive, because *not* to talk about the family was part of the social articulation of feelings well into the 1950s. That feelings were kept private does not mean, however, that they did not exist. In fact the private letters by nobles that are accessible show a surprisingly egalitarian relationship between many members of the family network.

When Duke Ernst II wrote his Coburg memorandum he was aware of the fact that all families can rise or fall depending on how well emotion within the family was handled. The Coburgs invested a lot of time on this issue. Every aristocratic family needed its members to stay loyal to the house *because* it expected them to make great personal sacrifices. In general second sons had to give up their inheritance to first born brothers. This kept great estates intact, but could naturally cause enormous bitterness. Similar sacrifices were expected from daughters. They either had to be 'exported' abroad for an advantageous marriage and therefore leave their homes at a young age or they had to abstain from unsuitable marriages, to keep the family exclusive (after all social permeability had to be avoided at all costs).

Making such demands on one's family members meant that negative emotions had to be constantly managed. This was not an easy task and families therefore developed a double strategy. To keep everyone in line was first of all achieved by inheritance law and family contracts. But contracts were not enough. One had to offer family members more, as Duke Ernst had realized, and that was emotional attachment. Emotion in aristocratic families was fostered on two levels: First of all, children were indoctrinated with emotional stories about the family. It was usually the female members of the family who were in charge of this task. They recounted every turn in history connected to their own family history, they personalized and emotionalized history and adapted it according to the needs of the time. In their stories, there was usually a family hero, a martyr, and a black sheep—working as examples or warnings. Such stories made the family history a highly emotional business for its offspring. Impressionable children naturally wanted to follow in the footsteps of the worthy ancestors, taking enormous pride in the traditions of their house.[46] Strong emotions were also aroused by retelling stories of suffering. One example of this is the experience of Queen Victoria's German relatives, the Hohenlohes and the Leiningens. Both houses had lost their reigning status at the beginning of the nineteenth century. This was a trauma never forgotten. Such loss of status and prestige left a deep impression on the next generation. These were powerful emotions that bound one to the family.

There was another method of creating emotion: memorabilia. To this day on entering a country house one can spot which ancestor is positioned at the centre of the family's heritage. At the English country house Broadlands in Hampshire, for example, the focus is not on perhaps its most famous owner, the Prime Minister Lord Palmerston, but on an arguably less significant figure, the Duke of Edinburgh's uncle Lord Mountbatten. He made sure that Broadlands became a shrine to his success. His tennis and military trophies are on display and his private cinema shows clips from his exploits during the Second World War. Aristocratic children were surrounded by such family memorabilia to which highly charged emotions were attached: a sword that had been used by the courageous family founder or a helmet that was worn by the family's military hero who died selflessly on the battlefield.

Apart from managing the family through strong emotions, one also had to manage the wider network of relatives and friends. It was important to cultivate as many other families as possible. In aristocratic and royal circles the more international contacts a house had up to 1914, the higher their status within the peer group.

The cultivation of as many people as possible was achieved by constant communication—letter writing and regular visits. German aristocrats called it 'Schlössern', visiting each other's country houses and castles (*Schlösser*). Such visits could be expensive for the host as well as the guest, but they created a closeness and were a good social training ground for the children. They were also important for getting ahead at court where one needed contacts as well as good psychological skills.

A man who was brought up within this Protestant network and greatly benefited from its methods plays an important role in the following chapters: Duke Carl Eduard of Sachsen-Coburg und Gotha (Figure 1). He

Figure 1. The young Charles Edward, who would turn into Carl Eduard Duke of Coburg, with his sister Alice.

would interpret Ernst II's secret family motto 'one for all and all for one' in his own way. His interpretation would make it possible for him to survive at two courts—the court of Kaiser Wilhelm II as well as the court of Adolf Hitler.

If one wants to understand why the Duke of Coburg could become a go-between for the Nazis, one has to examine his early life.

Carl Eduard was born Charles Edward. His father Leopold Duke of Albany had been the most intellectual of Queen Victoria's children. He had studied properly at Oxford and became a friend of the author of *Alice in Wonderland*, Lewis Carroll.

Leopold suffered from haemophilia and nobody expected him to live a normal life, let alone father children. Yet in 1882 Queen Victoria managed to find a bride for him, Helene Friedericke Auguste zu Waldeck und Pyrmont. Helene was not informed about her husband's illness and her family was naturally pleased about the advantageous marriage. It lasted two years. In 1883 their daughter Alice was born, named after *Alice in Wonderland*, and a year later Charles Edward.

Leopold never saw his son; he died from a fall five months before Charles Edward's birth in 1884. Helene was a widow at 23 with two small children and reduced status. Her frustration about this situation and her closeness to her own family in Germany, the Waldeck Pyrmonts, would later have an indirect effect on Charles Edward's Nazi career.

While Leopold had been artistic and well read, his son Charles Edward inherited no intellectual curiosity. What he did inherit, though, was poor health. He was described as a highly nervous child who needed constant protection by his older sister Alice (a pattern that would continue to his death). Though Alice herself was extremely healthy, she was a carrier of haemophilia and would pass it on to her own sons.

As one of Queen Victoria's many grandsons, Charles Edward was expected to lead a privileged and unspectacular life. Had he stayed in England, he could have joined one of the fighting services, or he could have lived as a gentleman of leisure. But unforeseen circumstances changed the expected course of events. In 1899 after a family row his Coburg cousin Alfred committed suicide. Young Alfred was the only son of Alfred Duke of Coburg. The Duke himself had been unwell for some time and therefore a new heir had to be found quickly. The first reaction of the British royal family had been to order Queen Victoria's next son in line to take over the dukedoms. Yet the Duke of Connaught was a British general and German newspapers immediately criticized this idea. To them the British royal family were foreigners who had no understanding of Germany, let alone Coburg. They demanded a German Prince instead: 'How shameful for the people [of the dukedoms Coburg and Gotha] to be handed over into foreign hands, like some dead family heirloom.'[47] The *Leipziger Neueste Nachrichten* adopted the slogan 'German thrones for German Princes' and the *Berliner Tageblatt* added:

> The highest value that three bloody wars have given the German people is a newly awakened national consciousness. The first Chancellor [Bismarck] praised the reigning Princes as custodians and carers of the newly founded German Reich. They have to be German Princes. It is impossible to have two souls inside one's breast—a German and a foreign one.[48]

This reference to Goethe's *Faust* created a clichéd but effective picture. 'Being hybrid', having two 'souls', was seen as cancerous. The Faustian image stuck. Because of this personality split, the Duke of Connaught might side against Germany. A Cologne paper therefore came to the conclusion:

> The German Reich has a direct interest in preventing a foreigner whose spiritual life and interests are rooted abroad from succeeding to a German throne.... German unity cannot flourish if there is not complete trust between the German reigning houses... If one of them is a foreigner this important trust is violated.

For most German reigning families this must have sounded bizarre. Many had foreign blood and 'trust' for them was based on completely different criteria. They took the criticism extremely seriously, none the less.

Kaiser Wilhelm II, always sensitive to the press and therefore perpetually hurt, decided to intervene. He made it clear that compromises had to be found to satisfy national feelings. His grandmother Queen Victoria had her own agenda. According to Charles Edward's sister Alice '[grandmama] wrote a letter to Sir Robert Collins, mother's comptroller, informing him that Uncle Arthur [Connaught], who was her favourite, could not leave England owing to his military duties, and as his young son, Prince Arthur, could not go to Germany alone and be separated from his family, Charlie, being next in line would have to be trained for the dukedom.'[49]

In June 1899 Connaught was therefore obliged to 'decline' the dukedom of Coburg. The Kaiser, Queen Victoria, and the ailing Alfred Duke of Coburg settled on the 14-year-old Charles Edward instead. He was fatherless and still young enough to be turned into a 'proper German'. The local Coburg newspaper was pleased. After all Charles Edward's mother was already a 'proper' German and had agreed to live with her son permanently in Germany. His education would be German and he would serve in the German army.

Indeed, Charles Edward had become a test case. An increasingly self-confident public had asked openly whether international families were capable of 'genuine' national feelings. If there were doubts, the 'hybrids' were rejected. The Coburg case gave all internationally connected families of reigning houses as well as the higher aristocracy a foreboding of what was to come in 1914.

Although the Kaiser recognized the signs of the times, Queen Victoria was obviously out of touch with German affairs. To her, Coburg was still the charming little town her husband came from, a sort of fairytale place. She was not alone in seeing its harmless side. For the average British newspaper reader Coburg was a Pumpernickel dukedom with a few toy soldiers—politically negligible. These perceptions overlooked an important fact. The dukedom of Coburg was the most nationalist in Germany. If one wants to understand the growth of German nationalism, Coburg offers the ideal case study: it developed from a dukedom that supported national unity in the first half of the nineteenth century, into a highly chauvinistic place that would after the First World War become a refuge for radical right wing movements and eventually the first town in Germany to be governed by the Nazis.[50]

Once the decision had been taken to turn Charles Edward into the German Carl Eduard, the press hawkishly waited for the outcome of the experiment. The family was now under intensive observation and had to tread carefully. They did their best to avoid scandals. Even the smallest detail was taken care of. It would have been obvious to send Carl Eduard directly to Coburg. Duke Alfred was still alive at the time and wanted to 'train' his young successor. But the family turned Alfred down. To be associated with him was too risky. He was perceived as too British and on top of this suffered from alcoholism. Nobody gave him much longer to live anyway. The offer by Queen Victoria's daughter Vicky (Empress Frederick) to find a Frankfurt Gymnasium for Carl Eduard was rejected as well. The reason for this was anti-Semitism. Alice recorded in her memoir that her brother 'Charlie' (Carl Eduard) could hardly have gone to a school full of Jews:

> Aunt Vicky [Empress Frederick] who, although she was dying of cancer, was continually meddling, wanted Mother to send him [Charlie] to a school in Frankfurt which was supposed to be very modern but was mainly attended by the sons of rich Jews.[51]

Instead the Kaiser took over the education of his young cousin. He pledged to turn him into a Prussian officer—with the political views associated with the role. As a schoolboy, Carl Eduard's interest in politics had naturally been limited. His grandmother Queen Victoria was by then a supporter of the Conservative party and an ardent imperialist. However, she was wise enough to hide her views from the public. This was not the style of Carl Eduard's new mentor, Kaiser Wilhelm II. The Kaiser was at war with the two rising parties in Germany: the SPD (the German Socialist party) and the Zentrum (the Catholic Centre party). The resentment towards them and the *Reichstag* (parliament) in general was shared by many members of the Hohenzollern family. It was in this strained political atmosphere that the young Carl Eduard grew up. His mentor and cousin the Kaiser had no intention of bringing him up to respect the Reichstag. On the contrary Carl Eduard would learn to despise it. The Kaiser's political grooming would work in the most sinister way.

On his arrival Carl Eduard was 15, the ideal age for a guinea pig. To the Kaiser he became a 'seventh' son blending in with his own children. Since Wilhelm II himself famously suffered from a 'hybrid heritage' turning Carl Eduard into a German must have felt like correcting his own upbringing. This time it had to succeed. Carl Eduard was enrolled in a military academy, the Cadet school in Berlin Lichterfelde (a German equivalent to Sandhurst), and his mother and sister Alice were put up in a nearby villa. Alice later described their benefactor Kaiser Wilhelm as demanding but 'naturally kind and generous'. His wife and children in particular were 'delightful' and enabled them to become 'another brother and sister to them.' The only exception she made was the Kaiser's son, the Crown Prince Wilhelm: 'he was rather spoilt and conceited.'[52]

Since Carl Eduard's mother was a German princess, he did not have much of a language problem when he moved to Potsdam. His German essays were soon receiving higher marks than his English ones. The culture shock was also softened by visiting relatives he had known all his life. He spent the weekends at his mother's villa in Potsdam and the holidays visiting relatives in Germany and England. For a while he seemed to be safe from any further disruption. But when Alfred Duke of Coburg died, the situation became daunting. According to his relatives, Carl Eduard was utterly inconsolable at the funeral. His emotional outburst was probably not so much due to his love for a relatively distant uncle, but more to the challenges ahead. He was only 16 and far from ready to take over any responsibilities. To soften the blow, he was given five more years to finish his education. For a while his old life could continue. But he was missing Britain and when his exams come up in 1902 he wrote to his sister: 'You cannot imagine how awful it was to decide not to go to England.'[53] Though on the outside Carl Eduard had now turned into a German, on the inside he felt thoroughly English. When his sister announced her engagement in 1903 he wrote to her:

> Dearest Tigs,
>
> You cannot tell how awfully pleased I am about your engagement, although it separates us... You really can't understand how pleased I am that my brother in law is an Englishman, I can't help saying this although I ought not to. Algy always was a good friend of mine so I can only say I am really very happy that he should be your husband. I only hope he won't have to go to Africa.[54]

In Carl Eduard's eyes 'Algy' was an Englishman even though he had German roots. He was a Teck, the youngest brother of Queen Mary and therefore the same Anglo-German mixture as Carl Eduard. But because 'Algy' was based in England and was about to make an English career, Carl Eduard thought of him as an ideal brother-in-law. Algy lived the life he would have loved to have lived if the family had not ordered him to become German.

After finishing the *Abitur* (his results were never published) he spent some time in Berlin, being briefed at the Prussian Ministry of the Interior and the Ministry of Agriculture. In 1903 he was sent off to study law at Bonn—the university his grandfather Albert had attended. Unlike the studious Albert, Carl Eduard did not seem to receive much intellectual stimulation from this experience. During three terms at Bonn he was more interested in the non-academic life offered to aristocratic students—joining the Corps Borussia. Since his relationship with women seemed to be ambiguous, his family decided to marry him off as soon as possible. As ever Kaiser Wilhelm was eager to be the matchmaker. For Carl Eduard, he chose his wife's niece—Victoria Adelheid. Victoria was the daughter of the Duke of Schleswig-Holstein Sonderburg-Glücksburg and considered to be stable. Her loyalty to the Hohenzollerns combined with her maternal instincts seemed ideal to control an immature young man like Carl Eduard. He was ordered to propose and as usual he did as he was told. In 1905 he wrote to Alice that he was visiting his 'bride elect': 'Dearest Tigs, I am longing for the time when you will see Victoria, she is such a dear. I am sure you will appreciate my choice.'[55] Not that he had much of a choice.

Possessed of a German education, a German mother, and a German wife, Carl Eduard's credentials seemed to be unassailable by the time he finally took over the duchies in 1905. He was 21 years old and he knew that he had to create a formidable first family based on the Victoria and Albert model. He therefore quickly fathered an heir and a spare (as well as several daughters). He also joined almost every patriotic club available in Coburg and Gotha to prove his commitment. Yet despite all these efforts he did not become popular. This was particularly the case in Gotha, the poor twin of Coburg. The Dukedom of Gotha had been merged with the Duchy of Coburg in 1826. The merger had never been a success—for geographical as well as for human reasons. Geographically Coburg and Gotha were separated by 100 km, divided by the forests of Thuringia. Sandwiched in between was another territory, belonging to the house of Saxe-Meiningen.

If they did not have to travel for business reasons, the people of Coburg and Gotha avoided contact. A longstanding reason for this was also the antipathy of the Gotha population to their hostile 'takeover' in 1826.[56] Prince Albert's mother had been the heiress of Gotha when she married Duke Ernst I of Coburg. If she had remained Ernst I's wife, the people of Gotha might have accepted the subsequent merger, but her marriage collapsed and she was sent into exile. Afterwards the people of Gotha did not warm to Duke Ernst I, feeling like the neglected twin of the newly created dual duchies. Indeed Gotha and Coburg were economically and politically worlds apart. Rich Coburg was conservative and therefore naturally more attractive to the dukes than rebellious, chronically poor Gotha. During the ninety-two years of their union the dukedoms would therefore stay adamantly disunited. By 1905, Gotha was dominated by working-class families who supported the socialist party (SPD). To them it seemed bizarre that the new Duke Carl Eduard was indulging in an almost absolutist life at court. The Coburgers were more tolerant, yet they had also found him too aloof. They criticized the fact that on his walks around town Carl Eduard was always accompanied by a policeman. His Englishness in particular remained an issue. He continued to have an English accent and everyone agreed that there was something foreign about him.[57] He was even criticized for keeping Scotch terriers. Like it or not, Carl Eduard remained a stranger in his home. Ironically this 'stain' would eventually become an asset. It was his Anglo-German identity that would turn him into a successful go-between for Hitler.

The Catholic network: Prince Fürstenberg and Kaiser Wilhelm II

As we will see later, the Duke of Coburg's work as a go-between started after the First World War. But a member of the higher aristocracy was working as a go-between long before him—Prince Max Egon II zu Fürstenberg (1863 to 1941). Like Coburg he developed into an enthusiastic supporter of Hitler.

Before Fürstenberg turned to the Nazis, he was the closest friend of Kaiser Wilhelm II. This in itself was an impressive achievement. Fürstenberg was Catholic and Austrian, two attributes that made a friendship with Wilhelm II unusual. The Kaiser was fiercely Protestant and often wary of his alliance partner Austria-Hungary. It was Fürstenberg's brief to change this attitude. For almost twenty years he worked as a private channel between Vienna and Berlin trying to prop up the German-Austrian dual alliance. When Germany finally stood by Austria in the July crisis of 1914 his dreams seemed fulfilled.

His employers were the Habsburgs. Apart from Fürstenberg two other people who saw the Habsburgs as their role model will be central to this book later: Prince Max Hohenlohe-Langenburg (1879–1968) and Princess Stephanie Hohenlohe (1891–1972). Like Fürstenberg they grew up in the Habsburg monarchy and used the methods of the Habsburg network well into the 1930s.

The fabric of this network was old and close-meshed. It had started in the sixteenth century as a marriage network. At that time the Habsburgs could genuinely claim 'Bella gerant alii, tu felix Austria nube' ('Let others wage war: you, happy Austria, marry'). Yet for this concept one needed to produce plenty of marriage partners and by the mid-seventeenth century, inbreeding had resulted in a shortage of healthy children. As a consequence the Spanish branch of the Habsburg family died out. The Austrian branch, however, was saved by Empress Maria Theresia's impressive stamina. She gave birth to sixteen children, validating the phrase 'felix Austria nube' again. Her marriage network made it possible in 1914 for members of the Habsburg family to be still connected to all the royal houses in Catholic countries. This would play an important part in go-between missions during the First World War.

Like the Protestant network Carl Eduard Coburg belonged to, members of the Catholic network had many advantages—most importantly high status marriage partners and useful career opportunities. In return total submission was expected from all family members; the interests of the 'house' always outweighed the wishes of the individual member. Everyone was expected to do his or her bit. This naturally included go-between missions.

Max Egon Fürstenberg's family had served the Habsburg network as diplomats and military men for generations. It had been a beneficial arrangement for both sides and Fürstenberg was eager to continue the tradition. Unlike his brother, who became a diplomat, he chose to work mainly behind the scenes. It would make him much more effective.

To understand why Fürstenberg's go-between work before 1914 was so valuable to the Habsburgs, one has to understand the conflicted relationship between Germany and Austria-Hungary during the pre-war years. No one has captured this better than the Austrian novelist Robert Musil. In his masterpiece *The Man Without Qualities* he describes how a committee of patriotic Austrians in 1913 starts to plan festivities for their Emperor's platinum jubilee.[58] Their idea is to celebrate Emperor Franz Joseph's seventy years on the throne in bombastic style—outshining Kaiser Wilhelm II's upcoming thirty years jubilee. The committee members are determined that their festivities will be far superior, demonstrating Austria-Hungary's cultural and intellectual wealth over upstart Germany. Their only problem is finding a motto for the festivities. They are torn between 'The Austrian Peace Year 1918' or the 'Austrian *World* Peace Year 1918'. This fictitious scene in Musil's novel is not just an ironic comment on Austria-Hungary's pre-war society and its obsession with the octogenarian Emperor Franz Joseph, who would die in 1916. It also shows the competitiveness between Austria-Hungary and Germany. Musil's patriotic Austrians do not only get their timing wrong, they seem to live in a perpetual Camelot, far away from the realities of world politics, conveniently ignoring—among other things—that Austria is in an alliance with Germany. Prince Maximillian Egon II Fürstenberg never lost sight of its importance. His aim was to strengthen the Dual Alliance as much as possible. This was not an easy task for several reasons.

That Germany would stay with its alliance partner Austria-Hungary was far from clear when the alliance was formed in 1879. At the time, the German Chancellor Otto von Bismarck had intended to keep it alive only so long as it was useful to German interests. His successors, however, lacked the skills to build an alternative alliance system. Despite efforts to win over other countries, Germany remained 'stuck' with Austria-Hungary and later the capricious Italy, in the Triple Alliance. The diplomatic history of this alliance has been well researched.[59] Yet what has been neglected is a look behind the scenes—at the unofficial contacts. Who was supporting it? In other words, how much real 'life' existed behind the political facade?

At first glance the answer would be not very much. The Austro-Prussian war of 1866 naturally had a negative impact on mutual relations. Between 1867 and 1912, the postal services registered a decrease in communication between the two countries.[60] The relationship seemed to exemplify two countries divided by a common language.

Of course, an interest in Austria-Hungary still existed in Germany but it was difficult to quantify. Supporters were believed to be found among German Catholics of all social classes who felt close to Austria for religious reasons, and among German intellectuals who were drawn to Vienna because of its cultural vibrancy.

However, the main group which in this period unflinchingly sustained the Austro-German alliance were a handful of aristocrats. They were called 'greater Germans' (*grossdeutsch*) or Austro-Germans and advocated a close relationship with Germany.[61] Among them were leading Austro-German families like the Fürstenbergs, the Hohenlohes, the Thurn and Taxis, and the Oettingen-Wallersteins. They felt as much members of the Austrian as of the German higher aristocracy. The Thurn and Taxis for example, were not just connected to Austria-Hungary by marriage but also to Italy (and could therefore claim to be the personification of the Triple Alliance).

These families often identified more with Vienna and the Habsburgs than with Berlin and the Hohenzollerns. A look at the newspapers they took makes this clear. Prince Oettingen-Wallerstein's servant recorded in 1911 that his master was only reading 'papers and magazines from Vienna and Munich' (obviously not from Berlin).[62] Because these aristocrats were landowners in both countries, they were the subjects of two emperors. Reading their letters it is sometimes difficult to guess which emperor is being discussed. The context is clearer in 1916 when Princess Therese Waldburg-Zeil wrote: 'The death of the old Emperor is affecting me very much. For three generations he was the Emperor.'[63] Though she was living in Germany, 'her' Emperor remained the Austrian Kaiser Franz Joseph. Because of this mental map, it came naturally to Austro-Germans to support the alliance. It was also a way of staying politically relevant.

Fürstenberg had a great interest in staying relevant. From 1899 to 1918 he 'commuted' between Vienna and Berlin. What made him an ideal political go-between was his intimate friendship with Kaiser Wilhelm II (Figure 2).

To this day Fürstenberg's role in pre-war politics has been overlooked. There exists no biography of him and in articles he is usually portrayed as one of Wilhelm II's 'mates', a man who loved dirty jokes. In fact Max Egon Fürstenberg was much more than that, a homo politicus, who was eager to manipulate Austro-German affairs via the Kaiser.[64] His contemporaries guessed as much. Some of them saw the friendship of an Austrian aristocrat with the Kaiser as highly dangerous. The author of the contemporary book 'Around the Kaiser' certainly depicted Fürstenberg in this light:

> [Fürstenberg] this Austro-German grand seigneur and millionaire, is the power behind the German throne. No other man has the same influence, only very few have ever enjoyed Wilhelm's confidence in the same way. It is rumoured that the Kaiser, asked his plutocratic bosom friend, to become Chancellor and to trade in the part of the faithful friend to become the first adviser of the Crown.[65]

Figure 2. Wilhelm II (1859–1941) Emperor of Germany from 1888–1918, right, holding up a hunting trophy. The other figure is Max Egon zu Fürstenberg.

Though the last sentence was an exaggeration, Fürstenberg's role was not discussed just in sensational publications. He was also feared by members of diplomatic and court circles. In 1909 a Prussian diplomat reported from Baden, Fürstenberg's home in southern Germany:

> From various discriminating people I have heard recently that the special trust and the friendship with which his Majesty the Kaiser honours Prince Fürstenberg is not politically welcomed. One is of the opinion here that [Fürstenberg] influences our Emperor in a perhaps damaging way, he is too temperamental, often one-sided and not informed...only when it comes to our relationship with Austria has he, without a doubt, improved it for the better. I only know the Prince superficially and can therefore not give my opinion, but I would like to pass on in confidence this widely held impression, especially since the political influence of [Fürstenberg] is also often discussed in a negative light at court.[66]

That Fürstenberg was a dangerous factor was also the belief of the German Chancellor Bernhard von Bülow.[67] In his postwar memoirs he accused Catholics like Löwenstein and Fürstenberg of having relentlessly campaigned for Austro-Hungarian interests before 1914. Fürstenberg in particular had 'exploited' the Kaiser:

> Wilhelm II had in the second half of his reign a special preference for Prince Max Egon Fürstenberg, who, as a result of inheriting property, was domiciled in Baden, but by birth, in his nature, tradition and inclination was an Austrian. He paid a visit to Fürstenberg each year, took him with him on his travels and even took him to the German maneuvers. From the Austrian Fürstenberg the Kaiser had no secrets, either personal or political. He showed him confidential reports, made a jest of his own ministers and foreign potentates, let himself go completely in his presence. The Emperor Francis Joseph did not understand such intimacies. 'I can't be too astonished' he said once to another Austrian Prince who reported it to me, 'how the German Kaiser can treat, as he does, Max Fürstenberg who knows nothing and is not a serious person at all. Why does he admit only Max Fürstenberg to his intimacy? Of course it is all the same to me.'

Bülow was convinced that Fürstenberg did great harm politically 'as far as his intelligence and ability permitted, he did his best to promote Austrian interests...Thereby he influenced our relationship with Russia and Italy repeatedly and unfavourably.'[68] This character assassination was not surprising. Fürstenberg and Bülow had known and despised each other for years. As will be shown later Bülow rightly suspected that 'the Austrian' had played a role in his dismissal. Both men certainly had a lot in common. They had managed with traditional courtier tactics to get into the imperial orbit and once there shared an animal instinct to defend their patch. But was Bülow right about Fürstenberg's dangerous influence on Wilhelm?

That Fürstenberg managed to become Wilhelm's friend and a go-between, was due to several coincidences: an unexpected inheritance, his versatile character, and the Eulenburg scandal.

Fürstenberg had grown up in Bohemia, a part of the Austro-Hungarian Empire, speaking German and Czech. He had been sent to a German school in Prague and later studied law in Germany. At the age of 24 he was elected to the Bohemian parliament (Landtag) where he supported the German landowning party (Deutsche Verfassungstreue Großgrundbesitzerpartei). He had always been interested in closer links with Germany but when in 1896 his childless cousin Karl Egon Fürstenberg died, he inherited a vast property in Baden, southern Germany. This gave him an economic and social power base in Germany. He was already a wealthy landowner in

Bohemia but he now added 40,000 hectares of German land to his possessions.[69] A caricature of 1900 shows him as a man split in the middle: he sits erect on a chair, dressed in knight's armour, but wearing a top hat, the symbol of a well-to-do Bürger. It was quite a clever analysis: his head was ruled by the ideas of a middle-class industrialist, while his body (and heart) was still stuck in knight's 'armour'. This summed up well Fürstenberg's aim to be a mixture of modernity and tradition. As a great landowner his main income was farming and forestry, but he had already started to industrialize his property in Bohemia and he wanted to build a very modern portfolio. He called it the Princes Trust (Fürstenkonzern)—a big conglomerate of businesses which included shipping, luxury hotels, restaurants, shares in theatres, bus lines in Berlin and Hamburg, coal mines, as well as spas and gambling places in Madeira.

Apart from great wealth in two countries, Fürstenberg had also inherited political influence: seats in the upper houses of two south German states (Baden and Württemberg) and in the Prussian upper house. This meant that he had strong economic and political reasons to get involved in go-between missions. To show his commitment to both countries, he started to commute. He spent the winter with his family in Vienna, Berlin, and Prague and spring and summer in southern Germany, at his castle in Donaueschingen.[70]

To move regularly from one property to another was nothing unusual among members of the higher aristocracy. It kept boredom at bay, but it also demonstrated omnipresence. To the outside world Fürstenberg presented the image of a man who could run several estates simultaneously. Most importantly his often rather hectic movements between the two countries blurred his national affiliation. Which nation he actually called his 'home' confused even his peers. Prince Heinrich von Schönburg-Waldenburg wrote after a weekend trip to Fürstenberg's German castle Donaueschingen:

> Before Max inherited his German lands he had been an Austrian national. Now he was a Badener and therefore German. The Emperor had honoured him for this with the uniform of the garde du corps, though Fürstenberg was at the same time still in the [Austrian] Dragoner-Regiment. People were quite upset about this at the time, but it did not lead to a serious problem with our allies![71]

Despite his German inheritance, Fürstenberg would not necessarily have played an influential role in Austro-German politics. This became possible only through meeting Kaiser Wilhelm II. Like the unexpected inheritance, this friendship was also a coincidence. In 1906 the journalist Maximilian Harden had outed the Emperor's closest friends, including Prince Eulenburg, as homosexuals.[72] In the press Eulenburg was portrayed as a dangerous manipulator of Wilhelm II. The ensuing court case was not only traumatic for the people involved but also left a vacuum. The position of the Kaiser's 'favourite' was available and everyone knew that it was only a matter of time before it would be filled again. The candidate had to be entertaining and openly heterosexual—an ideal role for the masculine Fürstenberg. He was known to prefer women, including his wife. He had been trained at the Habsburg court and consequently was an expert in the flowery language expected of a courtier. He loved music and hunting and therefore combined the female and male elements Kaiser Wilhelm looked for in a companion. Fürstenberg was certainly ready to court the Kaiser. In fact it had been his ambition for some time. How hard he worked on this relationship can be seen from their correspondence. In 1906 a friendly postcard from Wilhelm II was enough to elicit Fürstenberg's devotion: 'I belong to you body and soul.'[73] In the crisis year 1908, the relationship had developed in depth and the letters grown in length. Fürstenberg was now giving psychological advice: 'On my knees I beg your Majesty with all the amazing energy which is yours, to fight your depression!'[74] Unofficially Fürstenberg was by 1908 the Kaiser's 'favourite'. Officially he had the ornamental court title of an Oberst-Marschall. Because he did not join any faction at court, he remained a lone fighter. This 'independence' made him useful for the Kaiser, but it could be strenuous for Fürstenberg. Other courtiers did their best to make his life difficult. They 'overlooked' inviting him to manoeuvres, or during cruises 'forgot' to inform him when the Kaiser went on shore. In 1912 Fürstenberg recorded one of these incidents: 'I ran to get my coat, in the meantime the Kaiser had taken off and the "charming mates" left me behind. Bastards! His Majesty was outraged that they had forgotten me!'[75]

The 'charming mates' were torn between the fear that Fürstenberg would become too influential and the need to cheer up the demanding Kaiser. Fürstenberg was certainly good at helping to control imperial mood swings and of those there were many—due to political as well as marital problems. An exhausted Fürstenberg wrote in 1908 that the Kaiser 'told me "[the Empress] is a good woman but awful". You can imagine how embarrassing this was. I did not know what to say to him. He poured his whole heart out to me and I really felt for him, the poor man.'[76]

The biographer of Kaiser Wilhelm II, John Röhl, has shown that the imperial marriage had indeed been claustrophobic from the beginning. The

Empress offered neither intellectual nor sexual stimulation for Wilhelm who found the former with his male friends and the latter with various ladies. Though he loved to project a harmonious family to the public, he spent most of his married life making excuses why he could not be with his wife. With the years Fürstenberg grew used to Wilhelm's marital woes and commented on the marriage rows with his usual sense of humour: 'Kaiser is cutting trees again, allegedly for a better view. He is particularly pleased about it because the Empress will be shocked!'[77]

Wilhelm II not only found his wife unbearable, he also thought his sons, particularly his heir, ungrateful. At family dinners Fürstenberg therefore had to work hard at improving the atmosphere. He was needed not only at family reunions. His expertise was mainly required when the Kaiser fell out with his ministers. In April 1912, for example, Wilhelm II had clashed with Chancellor Bethmann-Hollweg over the Haldane mission (a failed attempt to improve Anglo-German relations). After a heated discussion, they had to have dinner together. Fürstenberg wrote: 'I sat next to Bethmann and pumped at the conversation. After dinner there was a stiff mood and I used all my eloquence and humour to get a good atmosphere going. Everyone thanked me for it. They begged me not to travel home before the Chancellor has departed. They said it would simply not work without me.'[78]

Despite pretending to be superficial, Fürstenberg analysed his 'master' quite carefully. In his eyes Wilhelm II combined 'a great heart with hardness; [he is] an enigmatic character who will never be completely understood'.[79] He was, however, eager to study him for as long as possible. For this he was equipped with all the right character traits. He enjoyed analysing human behaviour, was good at self-presentation, controlled his emotions, and could ooze charm whenever needed. He also made the Kaiser's interests his own, expressing enthusiasm for whatever latest fashions Wilhelm II indulged in.

The symbiosis between the two men even went so far that Fürstenberg adapted his appearance to that of the Kaiser. Photos and film footage of the two men can be quite confusing. Like Siamese twins, they have the same haircut, the same moustache, and even the same walk. They also shared a few character traits: both could not be without company and both yearned for constant recognition. Like the Kaiser, Max loved to collect uniforms, medals, and honorary appointments. To achieve this he could be very persistent. According Wilhelm II's daughter, Fürstenberg was always around: '[he] visited my father too often, thinking he was indispensable. But . . . I am certain that he did not aim for political advantage or power.'[80] This was a pretty naive judgement for a princess. At court the private and the professional were one. However, to stay in a symbiosis with the restless Kaiser meant constant work and this could be tiring. In a letter to a friend Fürstenberg wrote: 'in a few days I am travelling... with His Majesty to Corfu. I won't have much peace, but that's the way it goes in my profession.'[81]

To be with and work on the Kaiser was indeed like a full-time profession. Fürstenberg was on standby and had to drop all his other engagements when Wilhelm felt like it. In 1907, for example, Fürstenberg had to cancel his attendance in the upper house of Baden at short notice: 'I was ready to attend... when an order of his Majesty arrived, telling me to come to England.'[82] As we will see, it would have been wiser to cancel that particular trip.

In many letters to his wife Fürstenberg openly complained about the tiring time with the Kaiser. Especially when it came to holiday cruises he was 'counting down the days' until his return. At one point he actually did leave early and was reprimanded by Wilhelm in the strongest terms: 'You left me last year, I don't want to experience something like that again my dear Oberstmarschall. Understood?!'

In shock Max Egon described the whole scene to his wife word for word. It was the first time he had become the victim of an imperial tirade. This was particularly inconvenient because he had secretly planned to leave early again. Now he feared the consequences:

> I was deeply shaken and told him how much work I had going on, but the Kaiser dismissed it with: 'yes, yes, excuses.' I was totally broken by this and now don't know what will happen to me because he said it in a very odd, serious voice, as if he wants to prevent me from doing a runner! I had not told a soul about my plans, but the Kaiser is sometimes spooky. He can see right inside you and seems to be able to read one's thoughts! I am really totally downbeat that I cannot leave earlier. There are limits![83]

The cruises with the hyperactive Kaiser were so exhausting that even a strong personality like Fürstenberg could only endure them in small doses.

So was it all worth it? What personal advantages did Fürstenberg actually have from the relationship? And at what point could he use it for his go-between work?

The rewards certainly outweighed the 'hardships'. To be a friend of the German Kaiser strengthened Max Egon's position in Austria and Germany. The House of Fürstenberg was always of high standing in Viennese society, but every generation had to add greater glory. To have a Fürstenberg close to the Kaiser had an impact on all members of the house. The career of Fürstenberg's younger brother, the diplomat Karl Emil, for one thing benefited from it.[84] Also, Fürstenberg's children would become quite successful on the aristocratic marriage market. After all, a connection with the Fürstenbergs was considered highly desirable. The closeness with Wilhelm II also gave Max Egon social leverage. When his Princes Trust collapsed, many people lost their life savings. Fürstenberg's main partner Prince Hohenlohe-Öhringen had to sell large parts of his property. Both men blamed each other for the disaster, yet socially and economically only Fürstenberg survived. He had greater funds than Hohenlohe to fall back on but, more importantly, he persuaded Kaiser Wilhelm that the main fault for the disaster lay with Hohenlohe-Öhringen. Wilhelm believed in his 'Max's' innocence and this meant that German society sided with Fürstenberg. His honour and reputation remained intact.

His friendship with the Kaiser also turned out to have another direct economic advantage. It helped to promote one of Fürstenberg's more successful enterprises—the Fürstenberg beer (a brand which is popular in southern Germany to this day). Fürstenberg had brought the recipe from Bohemia, a region famous for brewing good beer. To make the beer popular in Germany he used his imperial connections and advertised it as being drunk by his 'Majesty, the Kaiser and King'. This quickly made the beer into a fashionable beverage. When Fürstenberg claimed to love the Kaiser, he loved profitably.

Apart from the social and economic gains this imperial 'friendship' brought Fürstenberg, it also helped with his ambitious political aims. His ultimate hope was of course to use Wilhelm II to strengthen the Dual Alliance. Yet this was not an easy task.

The success of such work depended on the very basic question of how much influence the Kaiser actually had on foreign affairs. To this day this is a highly controversial issue amongst historians. For his contemporaries the Kaiser was the decisive figure in German politics: detested, admired, feared, or loved—depending on the circumstances—but certainly in charge. In reality the situation was much more complicated.

Germany was a constitutional monarchy, though the Kaiser was theoretically more powerful than his British counterpart. The German constitution has often been described as a 'structure of compromises'. In fact the Reichstag had legislative and budget powers which meant that every law needed to pass the Reichstag and the monarch had no veto rights—in contrast to the Belgian, Italian, and Romanian monarchies. There also did not exist much monarchical deference. On the contrary the Reichstag sessions between 1910 and 1914 show how professional and often critical of the Kaiser politicians had become. However, the counterweight to this increasingly confident parliament was the Chancellor. He was three people in one: Chancellor of the German Empire, Prime Minister of Prussia, and Foreign Minister of Prussia. On an international level German foreign policy was executed by the imperial state secretary for foreign affairs—a civil servant. This complicated system had been created by and for Chancellor Bismarck (who himself was never the leader of any political party) and it caused obvious problems for his successors. Since the Chancellor was elected not by the majority party, but chosen by the Kaiser, this meant he entirely depended on a good relationship with the Kaiser. He also needed to get on with parliament. Though the Chancellor could not be ousted by parliament, he could not rule against it for too long either. A chancellor who had no political majority and was not backed by the monarch, had no hope of survival.

The right to choose the Chancellor gave Wilhelm II a powerful tool. Another tool was his position as head of the army and navy—a decisive field of influence. John Röhl has shown that the Kaiser's court was a 'miniature state within the state', with its own civil, military, and naval cabinets—altogether 2,000 people. The military cabinet was in charge of postings and promotions. This gave it an enormous influence because military service was obligatory in Germany. Every family with a son therefore depended on the good will of this department.[85] Of course, having such powers did not necessarily mean that Wilhelm actually used them and Röhl has been criticized by Christopher Clark and Wolfgang Mommsen for overestimating 'the personal regime' of the Kaiser.[86] What emerges from these debates is a mixed picture. Röhl is right when he claims that despite his erratic behaviour Wilhelm's powers were substantial particularly in the early years of his regime. By 1906, when several scandals had hit the court, his influence, however, diminished considerably. One therefore has to look at each issue and instance to evaluate what Wilhelm's impact actually was. What was decisive was the different relationships he had with his chancellors—whereas for example, he dominated during the chancellorship of his uncle Chlodwig Hohenlohe-Schillingsfürst, he lost influence under the Chancellors Bülow and Bethmann-Hollweg who played him well.

Since the Kaiser was not capable of a full working day and was famous for erratic decisions, a cunning Chancellor could always outwit him. The same was true of Wilhelm's military and naval advisers. The influence

Admiral Tirpitz, for example, had over Wilhelm would play a devastating part in the Anglo-German naval race.

Apart from the power of his chancellors, another factor which restricted Wilhelm II in his decisions was the fact that German society had become a much more polycratic society, with many different power centres. The state was strong in Germany and enormous power was concentrated in the bureaucracy. Civil servants increasingly accrued these powers, and this also meant that ministries like the Ministry of Foreign Affairs were following their own particular agenda.

Despite these caveats, the Kaiser certainly liked to give the *impression* of being in charge. He often bragged that he drove Germany like a pony wagon with his ministers taking a backseat. Although many Germans liked the energy and vitality of his speeches, they did not translate well. Outside Germany his speeches were seen as insensitive and often aggressive—opening up a great cultural gap. What seemed to an assertive Berliner manly and hearty language had a thoroughly negative effect on the world. Since the international newspaper coverage mainly focused on Wilhelm and not his grey and fairly obscure ministers and chancellors, Germany's image was lopsided.

But it is clear that the Kaiser certainly wanted to dominate foreign affairs and often interfered. One method he used was to run his own private communication system, independent of the Chancellor. This was a parallel organization of contacts that could not be controlled by anyone else and it included Fürstenberg. It was not a new concept, of course. Early modern historians have shown that at courts there was an increase in 'favourites' (minions or protégés), as soon as a ruler feared his power might be reduced. To Kaiser Wilhelm, Fürstenberg was therefore turning into his 'man in Vienna'—a reliable communication channel to Austrian power centres—the court, the upper house, and the Austrian Foreign Ministry. This made sense, since in the Habsburg Empire the old elites still had a strong political position. Contemporaries knew that access to the Habsburg court could work only via key people. Nobody else but a native aristocrat could understand the refined signals and codes of this power centre. Even the most experienced foreign ambassadors found it difficult to find their way through the labyrinth of various cliques. A contemporary critic of the Viennese court, Robert Scheu, describes it as an 'unbelievable source of power.... A net of favours and sinecures, a secret language with codewords, in which everyone from early on secured his route and sinecure, where every relationship from the cot to the rot was cultivated to get to the cow's udder, and to be included in the secret club of the chosen ones... The whole population was permeated by court traditions and court interests. The masses were not aware that their opinions, judgements, their language and accents were all influenced by these traditions.'[87]

To understand the court properly could take up an entire lifetime.[88] Fürstenberg was born into it and would never have tired of it—if it had not come to an abrupt end in 1918. This made him ideal for Wilhelm II. The Kaiser made use of his friend as a channel to Austria and was in turn exploited by him. It was an ironic situation, with Fürstenberg's role rather like that of a character in Carlo Goldoni's classic eighteenth-century comedy a 'Servant of Two Masters'.

However, while Fürstenberg was aware of his duty to the Habsburgs, Wilhelm II ignored the fact that his friend might have divided loyalties. In 1908 he told Fürstenberg: 'Franz Thun [an Austrian aristocrat] reproached me for dragging you too close to me and therefore alienating you from Austrian political life. This would be a real pity because you are predestined to do great things in Austria. I replied to Thun "I don't care. In this I am an egotist, I want Max to myself".'[89]

But the idea that he had 'Max' to himself was an illusion. Fürstenberg's very first go-between mission in 1899 had, after all, been to improve the Austrian channel to Berlin. It was a banal but telling incident: The Austrian ambassador to Berlin, Count Szögyenyi-Marich, had asked Fürstenberg to resolve a misunderstanding between Archduke Franz Ferdinand and the Kaiser. Fürstenberg managed this easily and when a year later a more serious problem occurred between the two courts in connection with the Dreyfus affair, Fürstenberg was sent again to Berlin to mediate. A by-product of this second successful charm offensive was that in its aftermath Emperor Franz Joseph was persuaded to visit Berlin.[90] The Austrian politician Baernreither was aware of the connection: 'Because of his position in Germany and Austria, Fürstenberg is predestined to make important services for the alliance. The journey of our Emperor to Berlin is in great parts due thanks to Fürstenberg's mediation.'[91]

At the beginning, the issues Fürstenberg had to tackle were mainly about personal clashes between the courts. Since the Kaiser was very sensitive Fürstenberg would write letters like this:

> Despite everything I am convinced that his Imperial Highness [Archduke Franz Ferdinand's] odd behaviour is due to some misunderstanding.[92]

Such 'misunderstandings' could be triggered, for example, by a 'forgotten' invitation. In 1907 Wilhelm II complained to Fürstenberg that Archduke Franz Ferdinand had not invited him on a hunting trip.[93] At the time Wilhelm was particularly sensitive to his public image and his complaint was not really about a missed shoot. What he needed was a symbolic gesture by the Austrian court to improve his status. Fürstenberg was ideal in such cases. He could work as an early warning system detecting misunderstandings and resolving them without attracting public attention. His influence on the German side grew over the years because he established a good relationship with Archduke Franz Ferdinand. Since 1906 the Emperor Franz Joseph had been handing over more powers to his successor, the Archduke. Franz Ferdinand was now becoming a key player who increasingly tried to place his own choices within the military and the diplomatic service. To be close to him meant to be close to tomorrow's power broker. Yet to achieve such proximity was far from easy. The Archduke was not a people person and had a famously bad temper. Somehow Fürstenberg gained his trust. To stabilize and extend this decisive channel Fürstenberg used traditional lobbying techniques. Cultivating decision makers on both sides involved constant travel diplomacy. Tirelessly he kept commuting between the two courts and their attached power centres—the Wilhelmsstraße (the Ministry of Foreign Affairs in Berlin) and the Ballhausplatz (the Austrian Foreign Ministry). He cultivated diplomats and politicians and had unofficial meetings which were often a blend between the personal and the professional. Fürstenberg's go-between work sometimes turned into a game of Chinese whispers. In 1913 Baernreither noted in his diary: 'I related my conversation with Krobatin [the Austro-Hungarian Minister for War] to Max Fürstenberg. He reported it to the German Emperor, he told it to our [Austrian] ambassador in Berlin, who told Berchtold who told our Emperor, who sent for Krobatin' (who was naturally not happy at having his confidential information passed backwards and forwards between Vienna and Berlin).[94]

Fürstenberg's power base became quite impressive over the years: On the Austrian side his contacts included, apart from the imperial family, all Austrian foreign ministers up to 1918. On the German side he worked with Chancellor Bethmann-Hollweg and Foreign Minister Jagow and his successors. To keep Jagow on his side for example, Fürstenberg regularly informed him about his conversations with both emperors. By these means diplomats did not feel threatened, but saw him as a useful source. The following letter of 1913 from Fürstenberg to Jagow is one example:

> My dear friend,
>
> I wanted to inform you that SM [Kaiser Wilhelm II] again dropped hints that he wished to give me a letter to the heir apparent [Archduke Franz Ferdinand] to inform him about the situation. I think I was doing the right thing to dissuade him. He did not refer to it again. The moment I arrived [in Vienna], the heir apparent [Franz Ferdinand] wanted to talk to me urgently. I am now waiting for orders from him and will inform you about my audience.[95]

As usual Fürstenberg was careful not to put too many details on paper. In fact this particular audience focused on the question of Romania and Bulgaria. Franz Ferdinand informed the Germans via Fürstenberg that Austria would do its best not to alienate the Romanians. Bulgaria however posed a problem for Austria and Fürstenberg was of the opinion that this was another point Franz Ferdinand and Wilhelm II had in common:

> Franz Ferdinand hates the King of Bulgaria and hopes to do everything to make him less powerful. In this he fully agrees with the German Kaiser. The relationship between the two gentlemen is excellent. They correspond a lot with each other and talk about each other using the highest praise.[96]

Fürstenberg's mission was to keep it that way. He was aware of the fact that he was dealing with two highly strung men, whose vanity was easily injured. Since Fürstenberg had a relaxed, sunny disposition he could deal with this. Over the years he learnt to act pre-emptively. When in 1913, for example, the celebrations for Wilhelm's 25th jubilee got under way, Fürstenberg wanted to make sure that Franz Ferdinand was invited:

> he would be delighted [to be invited]. Otherwise he could get the wrong idea, since Wilhelm is meeting the King of Italy in July and before that the Russian Tsar and the English king.[97]

It was all a question of balance.

By then Fürstenberg's reports had high priority in the German Foreign Ministry and were often passed on to the Chancellor. When Fürstenberg was too busy to come to Berlin, he visited the German embassy in Vienna instead to pass on information. His reports were always colourful—a mixture of gossip and hard political facts. In April 1913, for example, the German ambassador reported about such a visit:

> Prince Fürstenberg had the honour today to be received in private audience by Emperor Franz Joseph. He told me the following in great confidence. His

Majesty the Emperor conducted a lively conversation. He showed he was informed about all social and political issues in detail and treated some of them with great humour.... The behaviour of the King of Montenegro, whom his Majesty called several times 'the wretch', was unbelievable. Now it was even being demanded of him that he pay the wretch money, this was despicable, the whole thing was a disgrace. But what could he do if he was being pressured from all sides. He had to admit it was better to give in to this odious measure, if the fall of the dynasty in Montenegro and a union of Serbia and Montenegro could thereby be prevented, since this could not be tolerated under any circumstances. Russia's approach was highly unreliable and ambivalent and this country could only be mistrusted.[98]

Of course, Franz Joseph wanted these opinions passed on to the German side unofficially and Fürstenberg could achieve this. His employers were the Habsburgs, but Wilhelm II continued to ignore this. In his conversations with Fürstenberg, the Kaiser simply expected 'his Max' to keep up the good work for Germany. The list of demands the Kaiser made on Fürstenberg is impressive. One of them was that 'Max' should do his utmost to enlarge the Austrian fleet. Fürstenberg commented in his diary: 'The good master sometimes has bizarre ideas of what one can achieve.'[99]

But Fürstenberg took the imperial orders seriously. He tried to engage more strongly with Austrian naval affairs. In 1908 he had become vice-president of the Austrian upper house. As with his seats in the German upper houses, this was more of an ornamental role, but he could use it to network even more. On his next trip with the German Emperor he was therefore well prepared: 'SM discusses the Austrian fleet with me, which is also going to build 3–4 Dreadnoughts. He is very busy with the whole affair and reads me a letter to Archduke Franz Ferdinand and shows me secret naval papers and drawings. Very interesting. He wants me to send the letter to Vienna, so that nobody knows about it.[100]

This back channel work had some results. The Austrian navy was extended in the following years and Fürstenberg and Wilhelm kept discussing future plans for Austria's fleet whenever they met.[101]

Today the Austrian Dreadnought programme is seen by historians as part of Austro-Italian naval rivalry. In the years 1909 to 1913 Austria tried to catch up with the Italians, who had built eighteen early model Dreadnoughts. What is ignored is the substantial German influence on this accelerated naval race. Although German naval experts had not much respect for the Italian navy, they developed a much greater one for the Austrian navy which they saw as 'capable'.[102]

Fürstenberg worked hard at improving the image of the Austrian navy. It was one way of making the Austro-German alliance attractive to Wilhelm II. Wilhelm's favourite tool became Fürstenberg's hobby as well. To show his commitment Fürstenberg and then Archduke Franz Ferdinand joined the Austrian naval club in 1908. Egged on by the Kaiser, Fürstenberg together with Archduke Franz Ferdinand gave every support he could to the Austrian navy. In 1911 he triumphantly celebrated the launching of the new Austrian Dreadnought in Trieste. He also made it possible for German and Austrian squadrons to meet on the high seas in 1911 during the Kaiser's Mediterranean cruise—it was a symbolic demonstration of their alliance. Fürstenberg noted proudly: 'I am very happy that I pushed it through!'[103] To Fürstenberg this showed how important Austro-German relations were after all, despite all the negative predictions he constantly had to deal with. He therefore gave his wife a blow-by-blow account of the encounter of the squadrons. He was standing next to the Kaiser on deck when it took place:

> We can see the Austrian squadron approaching, everyone is excited and well prepared for it. Emperor is on deck (they raised the Austrian flag), great atmosphere ...it was unforgettable and beautiful. I was speechless and really, really proud. Sunny—an unforgettable picture. SM (Wilhelm II) moved and deeply satisfied. He pressed my hand, said it was a memorable moment because for the first time an heir apparent of Austria was meeting the German Kaiser on the bridge of his ship! Then I drafted a thank you telegram to our old Emperor to which SM added with his own hand that he was moved by the beautiful, memorable sight which filled him with gratitude. You can imagine how deeply contented I was that I had achieved this.[104]

It was indeed his work that had made the whole encounter possible. For the people in the know this was a demonstration of what Fürstenberg could achieve. From the Kaiser's point of view it was meant as a political demonstration. After a long and exciting day Fürstenberg was ordered into the Kaiser's cabin again:

> Before bedtime, SM called me and handed over photos ...and a letter for Archduke Franz and for the Emperor (Franz Joseph). I'm reading the letter to the Archduke, it is very well written and refers to the impressive squadron encounter and says that the Austrian navy, which owes its impetus to the Archduke, must have been proud.[105]

The special relationship with 'Max' certainly had an effect on the Kaiser's view of Austria-Hungary. Despite his erratic behaviour Wilhelm II repeatedly supported the Austro-German alliance. This was mainly from necessity because Germany failed to find other allies, but it also had something to do with the personal relationships that 'Max' had helped to build between

German and Austro-Hungarian decision makers. For this he arranged meetings that first everyone could enjoy and secondly took place far away from the public eye. His German castle in Donaueschingen became a luxurious and more importantly a 'protected place' for an Austro-German tête-à-tête. Ostensibly the weekends in this charming hideaway were about hunting, accompanied by music, amateur theatre, and fireworks. Politics seemed not to be on the agenda, but in fact everyone present was obsessed with nothing else. Here Fürstenberg made sure that Wilhelm was introduced to his closest friends from Vienna, all political heavyweights: Joseph Baernreither (1848–1925), Erwein Graf Nostitz (1863–1931), Alain Rohan (1853–1914), and Ottokar Graf Czernin (1872–1932). All were members of the pro-German party in Austria-Hungary and got on swimmingly with the German Kaiser.

Another 'protected place' was the royal yacht *Hohenzollern*. On their Mediterranean cruises Fürstenberg and the Kaiser always talked politics. Wilhelm was more relaxed on the royal yacht, far away from his wife and Berlin society. Here he could create a sort of Peter Pan existence, surrounding himself with clubbable male friends and living a purely hedonistic lifestyle. On board politics turned into a parlour game and a good listener could pick up useful information. Though Fürstenberg often complained how stressful life with Wilhelm II could be, he was eager to be the ideal listener. On the surface he always acted as a helpful go-between who prevented any misunderstandings between the two nations. But this could involve working against many other nations. In fact Fürstenberg egged the Kaiser on when it came to Austria- Hungary's rivals. It may not have been a coincidence that Fürstenberg happened to be at the Kaiser's side during two anti-British incidents. Of course, it could be argued that the two men spent so much time together that Fürstenberg just happened to be around on these occasions. But even if this was true, he obviously did not have a calming effect on Wilhelm when it did not serve his own interests.

The first incident in which Fürstenberg seems to have played a malevolent role was during the *Daily Telegraph* affair. The Kaiser had been invited for a state visit to Britain in November 1907. At the time he was still recovering from the press revelations that members of his circle, including his closest confidant Eulenburg, had been outed as homosexuals. Wilhelm II had been hesitant to appear in public, but to his great surprise the visit to London turned out to be a success. This brought back momentarily his old enthusiasm for Britain and he spontaneously decided to stay on for a holiday. Fürstenberg was ordered to keep him company. The Kaiser rented for himself and his entourage Highcliffe Castle from Colonel Edward Montagu-Stuart-Wortley. The two men became close and Wilhelm, in his usual indiscreet way, had long conversations with his clubbable host. In Fürstenberg's presence he outlined all the British mistakes of the past years, adding how unpopular the English were in Germany and that he was the only friend Britain had at the moment. Fürstenberg and Stuart-Wortley did not object to any of this and the Kaiser left England thoroughly refreshed. For him the relationship with Stuart-Wortley was like a holiday romance, yet like many holiday romances it did not survive the return home. Stuart-Wortley turned their conversations into an article and asked the Kaiser whether he could be allowed to publish it. Back in Berlin, Wilhelm was not so sure any more. From this point onwards the affair got muddied with everyone blaming everyone else. The Kaiser followed the correct procedure and passed on the draft of the article to Chancellor Bülow asking him for approval. Bülow would later claim he never read the article and sent it to the Foreign Ministry instead. The Foreign Minister was away at the time, and lower ranking civil servants did not dare to criticize the contents of the article. In the end it was signed off for publication.

The press storm that erupted on both sides of the Channel was volcanic. To this day the article reminds one of a particularly incoherent rant over a liquid lunch. In it the Kaiser actually managed to insult everyone: the British, the French, the Russians, the Japanese, and even his own countrymen (he claimed he had helped the British in the Boer War, *against* German public opinion). Particularly confusing were the contradictions. Since the talks took place over several evenings, Wilhelm seems to have changed his mind every other day. Though he claimed to be the only friend Britain had, he then called the British all 'mad, mad, mad as March hares'. He also had plenty of patronizing advice for the British government. His explanation for the constant enlargement of the German navy was that it would be needed for the fight in the Pacific. One day Britain would be grateful to have Germany on its side. The interesting point about all these rambling talks, however, is that there was one country that the Kaiser did not attack: Austria-Hungary.

This certainly had something to do with Fürstenberg's presence. That Fürstenberg did not stop Wilhelm from attacking everyone else is also revealing. As a go-between for Austria-Hungary, Fürstenberg had no interest whatsoever in improving Anglo-German affairs.

Fürstenberg himself was anti-British for political and cultural reasons. Politically he wanted to strengthen the German-Austrian alliance and this meant preventing any closeness between Berlin and London. Personally, he did not like the British. He did not speak English well and felt uneasy in their company. They seemed rather hard to read and he was always irritated by the transformation the Kaiser underwent when he was in British company. In his diary Fürstenberg noted that whenever they visited a British ship, the Kaiser seemed to blossom, however 'the moment he is back home, he gets moody again'.[106]

Fürstenberg certainly had no interest in Wilhelm strengthening his British side. On the contrary, he must have done everything to make him forget it.

The damage done by the *Daily Telegraph* interview was twofold. In Germany the press attacked the Kaiser for weeks on end and a stormy parliamentary debate on the affair took place in December 1908. There was even talk of the Kaiser abdicating. Despite all the heated debates, at the end of the day no consequences followed in Germany. The impression the article made on the rest of the world was catastrophic. Since the Kaiser was seen as Germany's official mouthpiece, new anti-German feelings erupted. The result was that Germany became more isolated politically. This of course meant that it was becoming even more dependent on its ally Austria-Hungary—a development Fürstenberg naturally welcomed. He also welcomed the fact that during this affair Wilhelm fell out with his Chancellor von Bülow.

It has often been argued that Bülow had read the draft of the *Daily Telegraph* interview and knew full well the dynamite it contained. He may have deliberately let it be published to teach the Kaiser a lesson and make himself indispensable.[107] He certainly did nothing to defend Wilhelm II in the ensuing Reichstag debate, but concentrated on saving his own reputation. He also worsened the situation by encouraging the Kaiser to go on another hedonistic holiday with Fürstenberg. While the storm was blowing, Wilhelm spent seven days in Donaueschingen. Yet whenever he talked to Fürstenberg, he dissolved in tears. 'Max' propped him up and Wilhelm thanked him later: 'you were the balm for my soul, and gave me the strength and courage to believe in myself.'[108]

Amid the tears he indulged in the usual escapism at Donaueschingen. A fox hunt ensued, as did a Cabaret show that had been brought in from Frankfurt especially.[109] Unfortunately, during one of the performances the chief of Wilhelm's military cabinet died from a heart attack while dancing in a tutu. A cross-dressing scandal was of course the last thing the Kaiser needed. It leaked nonetheless. In the end Fürstenberg turned out to be the surprising winner of the crisis. The scandals of 1908 strengthened the relationship between him and Wilhelm. They turned Fürstenberg into the Kaiser's prime agony aunt. At Christmas 1908 Wilhelm thanked him for all his support:

My dear Max,

with the books I'm sending you for Christmas, I'm adding a few lines to thank you again with all my heart for everything you have been and done for me last autumn. After all the disappointments and sorrows other people have inflicted on me, you showed me what a real friend can do. God will repay you and Irma [Fürstenberg's wife], I will never forget it. I have really been shaken up. 1907 Kuno Moltke, Hoffmann and the whole year the Eulenburg affair which went on into spring 1908. 1908 the events we all know about! [the *Daily Telegraph* affair] That's a bit much for a sensitive soul.[110]

That Wilhelm described himself as sensitive would have surprised many. He certainly did not forgive Bülow his lack of loyalty. In this he was encouraged by Fürstenberg who was outraged about the Chancellor's 'treachery' and urged Wilhelm to get rid of him. Bülow became aware of this threat and tried hectic last minute overtures to charm Fürstenberg. Max resisted. He wrote to his wife that the Chancellor had even employed his old mother-in-law, the influential Donna Laura Manghetti, to win him over:

Sitting next to me [at dinner] was Donna Laura Manghetti, 82 years old, who said to me among other things: 'you must have been through difficult times with the poor Kaiser. Thank God he and Bernhard [Bülow] are on good terms again. Bernhard has told me repeatedly what a true friend you have been and how much he owes to you!'

Fürstenberg was annoyed: 'What a fraud, to train his mother-in-law to pass this on to me. I'm not fooled by the chap!'

On the contrary—he told the Kaiser at every opportunity to drop Bülow: '[I told the Kaiser] Bülow is not to be trusted. There is something fake in his eyes and he never looks one in the eye. He will easily forget all grace and forgiveness, because he has a cold and fake heart!'[111]

In the end Bülow was forced to resign in 1909 over an entirely different issue, yet everyone guessed the connection. Bülow certainly blamed his downfall on Fürstenberg. His memoirs quote a letter from the disgraced Philip Eulenburg (another enemy of Fürstenberg): 'a certain Max Fürstenberg is the person chiefly responsible for the present turn of events, in so far at they affect yourself [Bülow].'[112]

How much Fürstenberg's opposition to Bülow played a part in the end is difficult to verify, but it certainly gave a clear signal to the rest of the imperial entourage. From now on nobody dared to openly alienate Fürstenberg. Crucially nobody in the German Foreign Ministry wanted to cross swords with him. The new chancellor Bethmann-Hollweg and his Foreign Secretary Alfred von Kiderlen-Wächter made sure to regularly consult Fürstenberg on Austro-German issues, treating him with the utmost courtesy.

Despite being treated courteously Fürstenberg had no interest in supporting Bethmann-Hollweg in order to achieve a better understanding with London. He was fully informed about Wilhelm II's new naval plans, which he naturally supported. The naval race with Britain was from Fürstenberg's point of view highly welcome. So was the failure of the Haldane mission of 1912: while Chancellor Bethmann-Hollweg had tried to come to an understanding with London, Admiral von Tirpitz at the same time planned to enlarge the German navy. His plan endangered the negotiations. In the end Tirpitz and Wilhelm 'won' against Bethmann—the naval race continued and any understanding with Britain was dead.

To give his side of the argument, Wilhelm informed Fürstenberg about every detail. While they were staying at Corfu, Fürstenberg was handed a big file of top secret diplomatic dispatches. He could hardly believe his luck:

> The Kaiser received me on the patio and gave me secret files to read. They included the whole correspondence from early February to 21 March, the negotiations with Haldane, the fight with the Chancellor and Kiderlen regarding the Naval amendment. Terribly interesting. It is unbelievable how people gave the Kaiser a run-around! A historical document...One learns from it how right the Kaiser was. The English have behaved abominably and duped the Chancellor and Kiderlen and denied everything that they had promised. The agreement is buried! Shame, but one can see that it was never meant seriously, but was just a bluff to hinder us from bringing our army and navy up to scratch. Outrageous. SM is in a very serious mood and angry with the Chancellor.[113]

While Fürstenberg claimed here to see the mission from a German point of view, this was far from true. Had this mission been successful, Germany would certainly have neglected, perhaps even discarded its ally Austria-Hungary. It would have damaged Fürstenberg's work. Instead the Haldane mission turned out to be Germany's last chance to break free from its claustrophobic alliance system.

Fürstenberg also did his best to portray the Balkans as 'a German problem'. He knew that Wilhelm not only read articles prepared for him by civil servants and courtiers but also found his own alternatives. Fürstenberg therefore 'helped' pro-Austrian journalists. In 1913 he wrote enthusiastically to the author of an article in the *Frankfurter Zeitung*:

> Nobody knows better than I, how wrongly Balkan affairs are reported in Germany—especially the extent to which Germany should be interested in them. [Everyone thinks] the whole Balkan situation is a private affair of the Austrians that should not involve Germany. Your clear words and your logical analysis will educate people. Everyone who wishes the German-Austrian friendship well, should be grateful to you.[114]

Fürstenberg then went on to promise the article's author, Dr Rudolf Sieghahn, to help him influence the 'right' people in Berlin. This naturally included the Kaiser. Fürstenberg had every reason to worry about German support in the Balkans. At the beginning of 1913 Baernreither noted: 'Emperor Wilhelm expressly told Fürstenberg that he would, of course, be loyal to the alliance; but that he could not interpret the alliance to imply that he would allow his soldiers be shot to pieces for the sake of promoting Austria's Serbia plans.'[115] And in March 1913 the Emperor again stressed to Fürstenberg that 'he is reliably informed that were Austria to march upon Serbia, Russia would act at once, lest it lose prestige. To which Fürstenberg agreed.'[116] Both men therefore knew in 1913 that a war against Serbia could not be localized. The alliance seemed a brittle construct. The German ambassador in Vienna even in 1914 asked his superiors in Berlin 'whether it makes much sense for us to be connected to this Empire which is creaking in all its joints and whether we should continue all this hard work piggy-backing it'.[117]

Fürstenberg knew about such dangerous sentiments. He therefore increased his diplomatic commuting between Vienna and Berlin, connecting his own salon wagon to the fastest trains available. When Archduke Franz Ferdinand was killed in Sarajevo, Fürstenberg did not just lose a friend but also a cornerstone of his power base. The relationship with Franz Ferdinand had been instrumental for Fürstenberg's Austro-German go-between missions. Now the Archduke was dead, Fürstenberg's leverage seemed diminished. What was worse, his German pillar, the Kaiser, wobbled in the weeks following the assassination. After so many years of friendship, Fürstenberg knew that Wilhelm liked to sound firm but, when called upon to act, usually retreated. It was therefore far from clear whether the Kaiser would support Austria-Hungary in a war against Serbia. In the past Wilhelm had been cautious on this issue. He had previously advised the Austro-Hungarians to win over the Serbians with 'cash gifts'. When he had met Archduke Franz Ferdinand for—what turned out to be—the last time in June 1914 he had tried to avoid the subject of Serbia altogether. Though Wilhelm was now genuinely shocked about the brutal death of the Archduke, it was not clear what German policy on Serbia would be.

The July crisis of 1914 has been analysed at great length from almost every angle, including the monarchical. It is well known that the Kaiser made bold promises to the Austrians and was then sent away on his annual summer holidays. During the decisive days of the crisis he was therefore cut off from decisions. When Wilhelm finally aborted his cruise on 27 July, he was presented by his Chancellor with a fait accompli. By then it was obvious that the war could not be localized any more. Wilhelm's ensuing hectic correspondence with the Tsar did not change the course of events. He was aghast when he realized that the war he had helped to bring about had actually happened. Entirely in character, he crumbled when the enormity of the situation hit him. After a panic attack, he started to rage about the trickery of France, Russia, and Britain who had trapped and encircled Germany. This became the general line fed to the German public—encirclement by enemies—the war was therefore a matter of national survival.

Fürstenberg did not rage. The events of July 1914 had put an end to his greatest fear. The alliance did not break up. On the contrary, it became stronger than ever before. Germany sided with Austria-Hungary after all. Fürstenberg had every reason to be satisfied. But as Oscar Wilde has put it: 'In this world there are only two tragedies. One is not getting what one wants, and the other is getting it. The last is much the worse; the last is a real tragedy!'[118]

2

Go-Betweens in the Great War

In September 1914 the Bavarian aristocrat Prince zu Löwenstein-Wertheim-Rosenberg wrote a depressed letter from the front: 'the economic losses of this war will be enormous. It is as if a brewery owner picks a quarrel with a pub-owner and then kills him. He has won the fight, but nobody will be left to buy his beer.'[1] Such a rational verdict was only the more impressive since Löwenstein had been a friend of the murdered Archduke Franz Ferdinand.

He was also a friend of the English Duke of Portland, who had a similar opinion: 'The outlook is very bleak and Europe will not recover from this for two generations.'[2] Portland had relatives in the Netherlands and Germany. For him the war also meant that he had to cut off links with many of them.

Ideally royal and aristocratic families worked like a closed ecosystem. However, the ecosystem could get out of balance when separate elements broke off. Three main threats endangered the equilibrium: first biological failure (no male descendants); second, financial failure (bad investments); and third, unpredictable outside threats like revolutions, coups, or wars. This last threat appeared in 1914. Until then there were not many reasons to cut oneself off from the international network. It was literally a safety net. Up to 1914 it had also been in the interest of aristocratic families to extend their international contacts. The image of a wide family tree held its appeal. They were proud of the age of their tree—the older the better. But they were even keener that branches were 'growing' into different neighbourhoods, i.e. countries. The more branches abroad, the grander the family had become. It was blooming.

However, this was not a picture that appealed to ardent nationalists. A tree trunk that spread its branches into foreign territory was suspected of being rotten, diseased. It had to be axed to fit national demands.

In August 1914 the question for international families therefore was, did kinship rank before national loyalty? Up to this point it had been possible to juggle both.

Identities are not like hats: one can wear more than one at the same time.[3] European aristocrats had always done this. Increasingly, however, they encountered difficulties. They were truly international and therefore regarded as unpatriotic. Already in nineteenth-century Britain, the Queen's husband Prince Albert was repeatedly attacked for his German background and had his loyalties questioned. In Germany, criticism of dynasties and the higher aristocracy was even broader and fiercer. Here it was not just the German middle classes who attacked the higher aristocracy, but lower German nobles joined in too. They themselves rarely had international connections and resented the rich 'grand seigneurs'. The extreme nationalist and anti-Semitic historian Heinrich von Treitschke was one such critic.[4] In his eyes many members of the higher aristocracy were cultivating their English connections too much which in turn westernized them. Treitschke was not alone in fearing conflicts of loyalty, even potential treason. The German Chancellor Bernhard von Bülow criticized the higher aristocracy in Germany for their 'cosy' closeness to their 'foreign relatives'. The insinuation was that this closeness had resulted in them becoming politically unreliable. Bülow himself was married to an Italian noble and hypocritical to the core, but he absorbed the Zeitgeist. The *Deutsche Adelsblatt* (a German paper for the nobility) declared it as its major aim to create a homogeneous, national German nobility. International aristocrats no longer fitted into this concept.

By the end of the nineteenth century German aristocrats were therefore confronted with two threatening new movements: nationalism and democracy. Both seemed alien to them. As Prince Rohan explained in 1929, his peer group had to make a choice since opposing both movements seemed impossible:

> The formation of nationhood was naturally anti-aristocratic, it was the victory of the modern against the medieval world. Along with the national, the democratic idea, the older brother of the national, won power over Europe. The nobility faced the choice of siding with national or with democratic ideas. Since both had risen in the fight against the nobility, it had chosen the one that was easiest to adapt to its traditions.[5]

In other words aristocrats had to react pragmatically: Because the threat of democracy was so much greater—nationalism was the lesser evil. Prince

Rohan would take nationalism to its greatest extreme and become a dedicated Nazi.

Since many members of the higher aristocracy were international in their roots and way of life, they had to indigenize and sell themselves as home grown 'natives'. This was far from easy. Marie von Bunsen, for example, fretted about her 'double' identity for years. In the 1930s she described how much it had weighed her down: 'since my childhood I have clearly seen the disadvantages of my extraordinary existence. Later I fought internally against my double nationality and got it under control. I tried, without losing the values of England, to gain the calm, firm line of the German national community (*Volksgemeinschaft*).'[6]

A further problem was that aristocrats did not fit the racial categories. This had already started during the nineteenth century when racial theories and the idea of 'pure' blood began to circulate. Similar to the genome today, blood was used as an overriding explanation for human behaviour. It also developed a metaphysical meaning: there were things that one had had for 'generations in the blood' and predestined one for one's station in life.

The Queen of Romania, for example, wrote about herself and her sisters (Figure 3): 'we were a strong race—the mixture of Russian and English was a strange blend, setting us somewhat apart from others, as, having strong and dominating characters we could not follow, only lead.'[7] Others would not have agreed with such a positive interpretation. Their blood analysis of the higher aristocracy was far less benevolent. According to purists the 'international blood' which was common in dynasties and the higher aristocracy

Figure 3. Four Coburg sisters who would be divided by the First World War: Princess Beatrice (Spain), Princess Victoria Melita (Russia), Princess Alexandra (Germany), and Crown Princess Marie of Romania in 1900.

transferred negative qualities. Being 'mongrels', whether dogs or human beings, implied imperfection.

In Germany the mixed blood issue was combined by critics of the aristocracy with the old argument of their immoral behaviour. A Cologne newspaper, for example, reported in 1916 in great detail about the chaos in an 'international aristocratic home'.[8] A divorced American, a Miss Gould, had chosen to marry the Duke of Talleyrand-Périgord. Their resulting son would have been the heir to the Silesian property of his father. But because the dissolution of the first marriage of his mother had not been recognized by the Catholic Church, the son was seen as illegitimate. The journalist used this story to analyse the pedigrees of everyone involved. The divorced American lady got surprisingly high marks because her father had started off as a hard-working miner who had made his fortune by honest means. The aristocratic son-in-law Talleyrand-Périgord, however, was portrayed as a scoundrel who was frequently sent off by his family to countries 'where the ground was less hot than in France'. Because of his bad reputation, even his Silesian peer group refused to receive him. His son on the other hand offered hope for improvement and was recognized by the Silesian magnates. The main point of the article was not that the 'illegitimacy' of the boy was the problem. What was seen as shocking in 1916 was the fact that he and his immoral father were 'sujets mixtes', French-Germans who were allowed to live in both nations. Such 'sujets mixtes', were according to the newspaper:

> more common among the aristocracy than one realizes. With the strong national antagonism that has surfaced in the current war, legal questions about property held beyond borders will become even more acute. In their various homelands these mixed people will feel alien and won't fit in with the mores of their environment. This appears even less desirable with highly born people because ... the well being of their subjects depends on them.[9]

Suspicion towards cosmopolitan families was of course not just a British or German phenomenon and it was not just focused on the aristocracy. It went beyond class barriers. This became evident when war broke out. The Viennese writer Karl Kraus famously captured the jingoism that gripped Austria-Hungary in 1914 in his novel *The Last Days of Mankind*.[10] Similar outbreaks were recorded all over Europe. In Berlin, London, and Paris, foreigners were attacked on the streets. Families that had been naturalized for generations were suddenly under suspicion and proud old names became a liability. From France, the British ambassador Sir Frances Bertie reported that Princess Frederica of Hanover had been attacked at Biarritz because of her German sounding title. That she was a member of the British royal family was known only to genealogists; the average Frenchman did not care about such details.[11]

On the other side of the 'trenches' in Germany, the Dowager Duchess of Coburg did not dare to leave her apartments because she had been called a 'Russian spy' by angry Germans. In fact, it was even more confusing as she had changed her nationality twice. Born a Russian, she had married Queen Victoria's second son Alfred and become British. Once Alfred succeeded to the Dukedom of Coburg, she had turned into a German.

The Grand Duke of Hesse suffered from the same 'burden'. He was a German sovereign but close to his sister Alexandra, Tsarina of Russia, and his cousin the British King George V. Added to this, his residence, the little town of Darmstadt, was in the summer of 1914 full of Russian students who were now a major target. Most of them left just in time, but the angry Darmstädters went out on a witchhunt anyway, suspecting everyone of spying for Russia and even searching under nuns' habits. Also rumours circulated that cars were transporting gold from France via Germany to Russia, so every car in Darmstadt was being stopped by the Grand Duke's suspicious subjects.[12]

The Grand Duke was not at home at the time and returned immediately to restore some kind of order. In fact the outbreak of the war had caught many aristocrats on their holidays abroad. The British born Princess Daisy Pless was visiting relatives in England in the summer of 1914. Her German husband ordered the chauffeur to return but did not ask his wife to come home as well. She felt rather hurt about this oversight. The couple had been estranged for some time but Prince Pless tried to apologize in a clumsy way:

> I know that you are a good German in regard to your wish that we will win this war, because the future of your sons depends on it. But despite all this you will suffer from the tragedy which is looming over your old country and from which all your relatives and friends will suffer. There is no doubt that the war between England and Germany will be fought to the bitter end, and even you can only hope that the English will be vanquished decisively.[13]

Princess Pless could not follow her husband's argument. She returned to Germany but remained unhappy. In her memoirs she described her frustration:

> I had relatives and dear friends in England, Germany, Austria, Hungary, France, Spain, Russia, Sweden... How selfless they were, how well these best elements of

the fighting nations knew each other and despite this, they had to continue killing each other.[14]

Prince Max von Baden, later Chancellor of Germany, empathized with her. In 1916 he wrote to Daisy Pless:

I pity all these people who haven't been born in the country in which they live and now belong to one of the belligerent nations. It is a hard fate, especially during the war, which brings out all the bad emotions. Since my mother was Russian I can understand this especially.[15]

Baden did not mention to Daisy that he used his international contacts for clandestine negotiations. As will be shown later these negotiations were far from benign.

Thus birth into a 'multinational family' met a reversal of fortunes, became troublesome, even dangerous. This was particularly the case for aristocrats who were more visible than any other social group. After all their glamorous social engagements and international connections had been covered in the press over many years.

They soon realized they had to act if they did not want to be swallowed up by a wave of nationalism. To demonstrate loyalty seemed easier for aristocratic men than for women. Men could just put on a uniform which clearly demonstrated which country they belonged to. But even this simple act became a matter of soul searching. Some men simply did not know which army they should serve in. Even members of the famous military von Moltke family were slightly confused: 'Count Moltke, the Danish envoy in Berlin, had once served for a short time in the French army and was therefore distrusted by the Germans.'[16]

The aristocratic Bentincks, a Dutch, English, and German family, seriously believed that they could continue their commuting between the countries concerned. The German officer Wilhelm Bentinck, born in the Netherlands, asked Kaiser Wilhelm II not to have to fight against England, where most of his relatives lived. When this was denied Bentinck retired and returned to Holland. His Anglophile sister Victoria supported his decision: 'Some blame him for this . . . personally I am glad he acted in this way.'[17] She spent the war in Britain, but not all Bentincks decided on a pro-British stance. Some had not forgotten that the German Kaiser had graciously visited their Dutch family seat Middachten in 1909. One Bentinck daughter was married to Rudolphe Frederic van Heeckeren van Wassenaer (1858–1936) who sympathized with the Central Powers and even published a pro-German newspaper in Holland. Another Bentinck would in 1918 offer his home to the exiled Kaiser Wilhelm II.

Other international families also had trouble choosing an army. Queen Victoria had financed her German relatives the Leiningens for several generations. Now they joined the German army. Prince Emich Leiningen, born in Osborne House and socialized in England, got into a bizarre situation. He looked English and when he occupied a French village in 1914 the villagers took him for an Englishman. Leiningen felt deeply uncomfortable: 'I told them that I had been born in England but wasn't sure whether I was still English.'[18] For him this wasn't just a legal, but also an emotional question. Even though he would distance himself from his English side during the war, he thought it could still come in handy. To his soldier-son he wrote in 1917: 'If the English get you, don't forget that your grandfather was a British Admiral, they might treat you better then.'[19]

Yet once these aristocrats had decided on a uniform they had to prove that this was not some kind of camouflage. Pure mimicry was not sufficient. A full metamorphosis was expected of them. Aristocratic women tried to help. They did their best to prove themselves by focusing on medical and charitable fields. This had been an old tradition for the aristocracy and always brought popularity. Amongst many aristocratic women there started a real race to prove themselves the leading Florence Nightingale. The competition was fierce: the bigger your hospital, the better. In Germany they particularly fought over Red Cross medals; everyone wanted to receive the new status symbol. The role model for hospital work was the royal houses, whose members visited the wounded. In Britain this was famously demonstrated by the King and Queen, who embarked on endless hospital visits. It was far from easy for them. Queen Mary simply did not like sick people. Her relative Maria of Romania, who thought of herself as a competent nurse, was quite scathing on this point: 'Although she [Queen Mary] hates illness she is very kind to the sick and pays them stiff little visits and always sends messages of enquiry.'[20] Maria of Romania thought that overall the British royal couple did a pretty good job nonetheless: 'He [King George V] and she worked in such harmony. They were like a splendidly paired couple of first-class carriage horses, stepping exactly alike.'[21]

In spite of these good works, suspicion was not dispelled. Demonstrating commitment to the war effort was not enough.

Despite her charity work, the British/German Daisy Pless became a target. In 1916 her husband informed her that he had done his best to defend her reputation:

> A newspaper reported that on your birthday we had raised the English colours; it had to apologise. It was just the colours of the Wests [Daisy's British family] red and blue, which some idiot took for the English flag.[22]

The Pless family sued the newspaper. But Daisy's problems seemed relatively minor compared to the Duke of Coburg's.

Since his wartime experiences are essential for understanding how he developed into a go-between for Hitler, a brief look at his case will be illustrative. Coburg had spent the run-up to the war in England. On 28 June 1914 he was visiting his sister in London when he first heard about the assassination of Archduke Franz Ferdinand. Though it did not seem urgent at this point, he decided to return to Germany. Carl Eduard now lived in the castles of his ancestor Ernst II Duke of Coburg, who had once written that the secret motto of the Coburg family should be 'one for all and all for one'. But such a thought seemed to be outdated.

In retrospect Carl Eduard saw the events of August 1914 as the greatest disaster of his life. After the war he wrote to his sister Alice: 'the last time we parted [with] you going to Canada, the awful war broke out, breaking our happiness.'[23] Up to this point he had commuted effortlessly between Britain and Germany, paying visits to the royal family at Sandringham and the Kaiser in Berlin. Yet pleasing both camps was no longer possible. According to his sister Alice's memoirs, the war 'shattered his life, for he was denounced in Germany for being English and in England for being German. He told me once that had it not been for his wife and family he would have returned to England, had it been possible. He had to serve in the army, but refused to fight against England and was posted to the Russian front.'[24]

As usual, Alice was being economical with the truth. Coburg had two lives—a placid one before the war and a criminal one after the First World War.

Her recollection that he was sent to the Russian front is also incorrect. He was more or a less a chocolate soldier, who spent most of his time dining at various casinos behind the front and visiting 'his' Coburg troops. These trips were camouflaged as 'research trips' and always followed the same pattern. The VIP guests were shown around a trench, photos were taken, short conversations with a few 'ordinary soldiers' arranged, followed by dinner with the highest ranking officers. The next morning medals were handed out. Carl Eduard, always an ardent traveller, enjoyed these trips and decorated many a soldier. Unlike his relative the Grand Duke Ernst Ludwig of Hesse, Carl Eduard never felt any shame about this ornamental role. Hesse would later accuse his dynastic peer group of using the war more or less as a series of sightseeing trips—either visiting each other or the cities Germany had just occupied. Ernst Hesse felt ashamed of this voyeurism. When he met soldiers who had experienced combat, it 'made one feel very small'.[25]

Carl Eduard was not known for any such reflections. He also did not hesitate when it came to publicly distancing himself from his British relatives. This was an episode his sister Alice naturally did not mention in her memoirs. For Carl Eduard it was simply a priority to assure the survival of the *German* branch of the House of Sachsen-Coburg und Gotha. In 1914 he had announced: 'I hereby publicly declare that I have renounced my position as chief of the Seaforth-Highlanders regiment, because I cannot be…in charge of a regiment which belongs to a country that has attacked us in the most despicable way' ('dessen Land uns in schändlicher Weise überfallen hat').[26]

In March 1917 he went a step further and signed a bill declaring that 'members of the House of Sachsen-Coburg und Gotha who belong to foreign nations will lose the right of succession if their country is at war with Germany'. His advisers had phrased the document carefully. They could not exclude all 'foreign' members of the house because the King of Bulgaria was a Coburger—and Bulgaria was a German ally. However, the bill was a slap in the face for the British, Belgian, and Portuguese relatives. It also showed Carl Eduard's complete disregard for the dynastic principles he was reared in (and which he would five years later simply revert to when they became useful again). Furthermore it demonstrated indifference to his closest relative. His mother was living in London during the war and had every reason to fear reprisals. Like so many royal German relatives, she was taken in by Queen Mary and therefore elegantly removed from the public eye. Carl Eduard's sister does not mention the event at all in her memoirs. Instead she focuses on the way the British royals changed their names in July 1917. She was now turned from a Teck into a Countess of Athlone. For Alice this was an unwelcome imposition: 'Granpa [her husband] was furious, as he thought that kind of camouflage stupid and petty.'[27]

Alice does not elaborate on this point, though it would have been interesting to know what exactly she felt had to be camouflaged. George V certainly had every reason to change the family name. On 13 June 1917

German planes had attacked London and killed 160 people. Anti-German feelings were stronger than ever before.

Because of George V's 'Titles Deprivation Act' of 1917 and the confirmation of it in 1919, Carl Eduard lost the title Duke of Albany and all rights to the dukedom of Albany and other territories attached to the title. He was officially a traitor peer. His immediate reactions to this are unknown. It was not just the British connection that he had lost, his old mentor, the Kaiser, was also no comfort. Wilhelm II had been sidelined from the beginning of the war. After General von Moltke's nervous breakdown and General Falkenhayn's dismissal two new leaders emerged—Hindenburg and Ludendorff. Though Carl Eduard joined the Bund der Kaisertreuen (the Kaiser Loyalists Club) to demonstrate his allegiance to Wilhelm II, he was fully aware of Wilhelm's impotence and preferred Hindenburg. The admiration for Hindenburg crossed social and religious divides. Even Catholics developed the belief that this Protestant warrior could save Germany. Though Carl Eduard was unwell for periods of the war, the weaker he became physically, the tougher his political views were. For a while Hindenburg was his favourite but, as we will see later, he would soon be interested in much more radical options.

While Carl Eduard became an eager go-between in the inter-war years, he did not play such a role in the First World War. But other families with international connections were interested in such work. They wanted to turn their 'hybrid' background to advantage. This made sense at a time when official diplomatic relations between enemy states had ended. With the outbreak of war embassies had been closed down and a diplomatic blackout ensued. Representatives of neutral states were now employed to communicate on the most urgent issues between enemy countries. Yet they could not be trusted completely. They had to follow their own national interests and had to be careful not to endanger their country's neutrality. This diplomatic vacuum made the use of go-betweens a matter of urgency.

Prince Fürstenberg's mission

Fürstenberg was enormously satisfied that Germany had stood by its alliance partner Austria-Hungary. It was everything a good go-between could hope for. Yet, with the outbreak of war his grip on Wilhelm II started to slip.

This flabbergasted Fürstenberg who had hoped to play a key liaison role between the two countries. He also had expected to join the Kaiser at army headquarters. On 3 August he wrote in his diary:

> Audience with SM [Wilhelm II] who was so touchingly nice, but on Plessen's advice he does not want me at headquarters! It was a tough moment. He embraced me repeatedly.[28]

The Kaiser seemed to realize how upset his old friend was and sent him a warm telegram a few days later:

> In the spirit of our old friendship, I shake your hand. Even though duty separates us during these hard times, everything remains the same between us. Good bye in better times![29]

Hans Georg von Plessen, who was running the imperial headquarters, had cunningly told the Kaiser that for Fürstenberg surely 'the Austrian army was closer to his heart'. An invisible cordon sanitaire had been drawn around Wilhelm. To have an influential Austrian near the Kaiser was the last thing the courtiers and the German military wanted. From now on Wilhelm was shielded from the more unpleasant aspects of the war. The Kaiser's cousin, the Grand Duke of Hesse, later claimed that this was a mistake, that Wilhelm should have been forced to face the realities of the situation. But the Kaiser's mental state was already unbalanced. The man who had loved indulging in war games found reality unbearable.

Following Plessen's advice, the disappointed Fürstenberg joined the Austrian army, pretending not to care about the imperial snub. Always the bon vivant, he recovered quickly. His work for the Austro-German Alliance remained paramount and he hoped that eventually he would be able to continue it. His go-between work had always been driven by economic and political motives but by now it had also become an emotional concern. Among his papers he kept a sentimental poem from 1915:

> In all countries it will be admired in days to come:
> Alone two brothers stood, with the world at war.
> And while cities were burning and sank day by day,
> the brothers did not separate but stood firm,
> And fought without regret and treachery
> The Nibelungen-fidelity became reality!

Over the following years, the meaning of almost every line of this poem would be reversed.

Fürstenberg had welcomed the war enthusiastically and he certainly enjoyed the fighting. The adrenalin rush reminded him of his favourite sport—hunting. During these first months in the field he wrote home cheerful letters full of hunting metaphors. Yet the cheerfulness eventually subsided. By 1915 he had realized how badly the Austro-Hungarian military was doing in comparison with its German ally. This unevenness on the battlefield also had a negative effect on Austro-German diplomatic relations. The feelings of brotherhood Fürstenberg had hoped for had always been a fantasy. With the stresses of war, the artificiality of the alliance became more and more apparent. The whole construct had been based on necessity, not sympathy, often only covered by a thin veneer of politeness. Increasingly nervy diplomats had propped up the structure, helped by a very thin Austro-German elite of which Fürstenberg was a key member. The more strained everybody's nerves became, the more Fürstenberg was therefore needed back from the front. Like most members of his peer group he was more or less an 'ornamental soldier', commuting between the front and his post as vice-president of the Austrian upper house. He had kept in touch with Austro-German affairs and, as Wilhelm's closest friend, it seemed natural for the Kaiser to ask him to take up his old go-between work again. Fürstenberg accepted gladly. Yet to be a go-between in war would be a much more strenuous job than in peacetime. During the next four years the cheerful Fürstenberg aged rapidly.

To make his mission possible, Fürstenberg left the Austrian army at the end of 1915 and officially switched to the German army. This meant he could see the Kaiser twice a month.

How bad the communication channels between the Austrian and the German leadership had become by then can be seen by the bombardment of letters Fürstenberg now received. Though his private papers are uncatalogued one can wade through a mass of correspondence from his political friends in Austria who wanted him to act as a channel to Berlin. Fürstenberg was used to this and so far had enjoyed it. But he was not used to an avalanche. The Austrian minister Joseph Maria Baernreither's long memoranda, for example, were littered with points that Fürstenberg should make to the Kaiser. Fürstenberg's annotations illustrate that he did try to discuss these issues with Wilhelm, but he knew that this was not enough. He was well aware of the fact that the Kaiser's power had diminished and other decision makers had to be tackled. Fürstenberg therefore liaised mainly with members of the military and the German Foreign Ministry. These files indicate how often the Austrian government—via Fürstenberg—tried to convey its views to its German allies. Issues ranged from foreign policy subjects like a future kingdom of Poland to more pressing issues like food supplies.[30]

It was a delicate game for Fürstenberg. He had to work on two fronts—to negotiate with the German ally, and at the same time defend German policies in Vienna. He also had to please two very different courts. With the successor to the throne Franz Ferdinand gone, Fürstenberg had been without a key court contact in Vienna. He had never been close to Emperor Franz Joseph who allegedly found him too 'flippant'. Considering the advanced age of the Austrian monarch, Fürstenberg knew that he had to bide his time. By 1916 Franz Joseph was dead and Fürstenberg's influence at the Habsburg court improved. With his easy charm, he managed to develop a relationship with the new Emperor Karl. However, he never succeeded in becoming close to Karl's wife Empress Zita and her powerful family, the Bourbon-Parmas. This would later turn out to represent a dangerous disadvantage for his missions.

Apart from cajoling emperors, Fürstenberg also had to keep his peer group in the upper house content. How difficult this could be can be illustrated by a session of the Austrian upper house in 1917. During a debate, the Archbishop of Lemberg, Józef Bilczewski, had attacked Germany. Fürstenberg as vice-president of the upper house rebuked him and warned 'the Archbishop in sharp words, for which he was applauded by the whole house, even the Poles'. The Archbishop immediately played down his statements, saying that 'he had not meant to offend', and it was all a misunderstanding due to his inadequate German.[31] (This was a rather feeble excuse since the Archbishop had once studied in Vienna. In the long term it worked, though, Józef Bilczewski was canonized in 2005 by a German Pope).

Despite such backpaddling Bilczewski was certainly not alone in his distrust of German policies. Many saw Fürstenberg as a German puppet.

This was not the perception of the German side. Though the German Foreign Ministry was grateful when Fürstenberg stood up for Germany in public, in private he was far more critical. The longer the war dragged on, the more Fürstenberg's 'begging missions' irritated his German partners. One of Fürstenberg's constant campaigns was to alleviate the food shortages in Austria-Hungary. The German embassy in Vienna reported as early as November 1916 that Fürstenberg had stressed that a continuation of Austrian support for the war depended on adequate nutrition for the Austrian population. He insisted that Hindenburg should be informed about this problem—having obviously given up on the Kaiser.[32] It is therefore ironic that Fürstenberg's opponent Josef Redlich accused him of being entirely in the German camp, while the German side suspected Fürstenberg of dramatizing the situation in Austria and being a tool of Austrian Foreign Minister Count Czernin. In some ways this was the natural dilemma for a go-between.

The perception that Fürstenberg was close to Czernin, the new Austrian Foreign Secretary, was, however, correct. Czernin needed Fürstenberg's help. Both men had realized early on that the war was going badly for Austria-Hungary and that the only solution was a quick peace. Czernin was already arguing in 1916 that the war should be brought to an end. This was the only way in his opinion to stop the dissolution of the Habsburg Empire.

The main problem was that peace depended on Germany making territorial sacrifices. Czernin could not force Austria's ally to make such a commitment. The hope was that Fürstenberg might help with the persuading. He was willing to get involved and also to initiate peace feelers. After 1918 these feelers would become an embarrassment and Fürstenberg must have destroyed some of his private correspondence relating to them. Since his papers are in a chaotic state, it is hard to tell whether letters were 'displaced' on purpose or accidentally. However, one of the clues for his involvement is hidden in an envelope entitled 'Parliamentary life in 1916'.[33]

The contents of that envelope are intriguing: On 24 October 1916 a meeting took place in a Viennese flat owned by Max Egon Fürstenberg. He had invited pro-German aristocrats who were united by the wish to find a way out of the war. Present were Czernin, Baernreither, Clam-Martinic, and Nostitz. All of them would a month later be given key positions by the new Emperor Karl. At the meeting this 'band of brothers' entirely agreed that it was vital to convey to Germany, as Clam-Martinic put it, 'that we just can't go on anymore'. Once the message was understood, peace talks had to start. Fürstenberg himself considered the timing ideal. He argued that the Central Powers still had the largest amount of human resources and were not yet exhausted. If a peace deal was secured now they could recover quickly and 'pursue their plans at a later opportunity'. He never elaborated on what this 'later opportunity' meant and it was obvious that this was sheer face saving.

The next question was who would agree to start peace negotiations with the Central Powers. Russia and France were according to Czernin out of the question. Britain seemed easier to approach. Czernin stressed that one should try to impress the message on London that there would be no winners or losers in this war, but that one had played a 'partie remise' (a game postponed). His chess metaphor seemed flippant considering the exorbitant death rate, but none of his friends minded the language. Only Clam-Martinic, who would soon run Emperor Karl's cabinet, was pessimistic, believing that Germany would never agree to a key point on which the Entente Powers would insist, giving up territory. He conceded however that it was up to Austria's diplomatic skills to persuade its ally. The prospect of an international peace conference might impress Germany. In the end all agreed that the King of Spain, Alfonso XIII,[34] should be persuaded 'to propose a peace conference in Madrid or The Hague as a result of which all nations relinquish territory and any idea of compensation'. The aim of the congress would be to recover the *status quo ante bellum*.

It was important that the King of Spain made this suggestion and not Austria-Hungary, otherwise she would lose face and her bargaining capacity would be lowered. To keep the whole plan secret, the Austrian ambassador to Spain should not be informed. This was not without irony, since the ambassador was Karl Emil Fürstenberg, Max Egon Fürstenberg's younger brother. Though everyone trusted him, a leakage en route was always a possibility. Furthermore Karl Emil was not known for his acting qualities and by circumventing him he could react with genuine surprise, denying any knowledge of the offer. As Austrian ambassador he had to tread carefully in Madrid. While the Spanish King and the conservative party were considered to be pro-German, the Spanish Prime Minister Count Romanones was known to have pro-Entente sympathies.

Keeping Karl Emil Fürstenberg in the dark, however, posed another problem. If he was not used to deliver the details of the peace offers, the question arose how to get the message to the Spanish King. In the end it was decided to send a courier by submarine.[35]

Submarines had become the latest weapons of the war. Navigation with them was still a risky business and survival rates in battle were low. Still, the plan was successfully carried out. The U-boat surfaced in Cartagena and the letter it carried was for the King's eyes only. However, the appearance of a submarine caused the wildest speculations. Bizarre rumours now circulated about Spain's intention of giving up her neutrality. While Count Romanones was kept in the dark, the Spanish King enjoyed the rumours. His enthusiasm for secret games was one of the reasons he had been chosen by Fürstenberg and his friends. On a note during their meeting Baernreither had written:

> Why Spain? First of all because of the able representative Karl Emil and because the King is laid back.[36]

King Alfonso was indeed 'laid back', a man who seemed to adapt to every political turn. He had studied in Austria and England and knew both countries well. As the son of a Habsburg princess he was a member of the Catholic network, but he also had good British links. His wife Victoria Eugenie of Battenberg had been born in Balmoral in 1887, a granddaughter of Queen Victoria. In a rare move for members of the Protestant network, she had switched to Catholicism to marry Alfonso at the age of 18. Despite, or because of, the birth of seven children, the marriage had deteriorated quickly. Their temperaments were hardly compatible. Looking at photographs of Victoria and Alfonso, even their visual differences are striking. While she had an intelligent face with inquisitive eyes, her husband looked like the cliché of a shifty gigolo (a cliché he tried to live up to by producing a multitude of illegitimate children). One of his excuses seemed to be that his wife, a carrier of haemophilia, was responsible for their sons' illnesses.[37] Yet despite their marital estrangement Alfonso made use of Victoria's British contacts. Though he was a ruler only on the periphery, his Austrian/British links made him central to peace feelers, a centrality he very much enjoyed. Alfonso's dream had always been to bring Spain into closer contact with the major European powers.[38] From the start of the war he had therefore offered himself to all sides for peace talks. His motives were hardly altruistic. Parallel to supporting peace attempts, he kept trying to sell Spain's neutrality to the highest bidder. He started with this double agenda in September 1914 by first offering the French ambassador his mediation between France and Germany.[39] He also claimed that Germany had offered long-term compensation for Spain's neutrality: Tangier, Portugal, and Gibraltar.[40]

In the end Spain did not manage to sell itself to anyone and remained neutral throughout the war. According to the rather Freudian interpretation of the Italian ambassador this was due to the influence of Alfonso's mother. The Austrian Marie Christine apparently encouraged her son to stick to neutrality at all costs.

But even though Alfonso gambled with Spain's neutral status, he also wanted to help his Austrian friends. To this day the Spanish royal archives are closed and his secret modus operandi remains obscure. However, as will be shown later, Alfonso was also involved in Lady Paget's peace mission—which took place at the same time as the Fürstenberg one.

Despite the greatest efforts, the Austrian peace feelers via Spain suddenly stopped. Fürstenberg never forgot this failure and after the war tried to reconstruct why and by whom they had been terminated. In 1919 he had a conversation with the German General Consul in The Hague, Dr von Rosen. Rosen had been in Spain in 1916 and had conducted several conversations with the Spanish King. He confirmed that Alfonso XIII had wanted to help with the peace talks and via Rosen this message had been conveyed to Berlin. The Kaiser then 'agreed with it enthusiastically'. So why had the feelers failed? Fürstenberg and Rosen came to the conclusion that the German Foreign Ministry had vetoed the plan in the end. It might have feared that its Austrian ally could use this channel to come to a separate peace agreement with Britain. To Fürstenberg the whole story proved one thing: that his friend Wilhelm had been seriously seeking peace. This was an important conclusion for him, because by then the 'Hang the Kaiser movement' was in full swing and Fürstenberg needed arguments to defend the ex-Kaiser. But even though Wilhelm II had supported the Spanish mission, Fürstenberg's analysis had its flaws. The Kaiser's mood swings were as unpredictable as his influence on political decisions. He probably did hope for a good outcome via Spain, yet he also had a tendency to change his mind—according to the military situation—several times a day. Ignorant about the true nature of the war he vacillated between advocating a quick peace one day and dictating the strictest peace terms the next.

The Spanish peace feelers of 1916 and 1917 also failed because Austria-Hungary came with heavy German baggage. The British were by then only interested in a peace deal with Austria-Hungary alone, hoping to divide the Central Powers.

The failure of the Spanish peace initiative was just one of many frustrations the constant go-between Fürstenberg suffered during the war. By the beginning of 1918 he had become desperate. To his old friend Clam-Martinic, who was now military governor in Montenegro, he wrote:

> I could write you volumes about the situation here. Suffice it to say that I, a dedicated optimist, have started to wobble. One should suppress such feelings but I am sometimes getting really scared.

Viennese life depressed him: 'I am so fed up with the political life. A constant tilting at windmills.'[41]

The abilities of German politicians did not give him much hope either. In February 1918 German diplomats reported that Fürstenberg had harangued them:

Fürstenberg says that even in German circles [in Vienna] resentment against Germany is growing. The reason for this is the feeling that Austria is fighting only for German conquests and economic compromises and will in the end be left empty handed... On this basis it is no longer possible to operate. Even Emperor Karl can, despite the best of wills, no longer stand up to public opinion. The alliance is therefore standing at the crossroads.[42]

In fact the disintegration of the Austro-German alliance seemed unstoppable. It had been Fürstenberg's *raison d'être* and he saw it faltering before his eyes. Ironically, the last nail in the coffin of the alliance was a rival go-between mission that went tragically wrong: the infamous Sixtus affair. The mission

Figure 4. A mission that ended in scandal: Prince Sixtus of Bourbon-Parma, brother of the Austrian Empress Zita.

was set up unbeknown to Fürstenberg and would end up ruining everything he stood for. It is a well-documented affair, but it has never been seen in the wider context of go-between missions. However, it is very useful for understanding go-between work in general, because it illustrates the unpredictable dynamics of such work and the element of danger involved in them (Figure 4).

In the autumn of 1916 the Austrian Emperor Franz Joseph had died and Emperor Karl and his wife Zita succeeded him. Zita had two brothers, Sixtus and Xavier of Bourbon-Parma. The Parmas were considered to be a highly ambitious family, deeply rooted in the Catholic network. In August 1914, two years before Karl succeeded to the Habsburg throne, he had had a long conversation with Zita's brothers. The war had just begun, and Karl and Zita felt deeply ambivalent about their German ally. They agreed with Zita's brothers that the war could 'increase Prussian military power which would not only be a threat to French security but also to the independence of the Habsburg Empire'.[43]

When Karl succeeded to the throne, he (or his wife Zita) started to look for a back channel to the Parma brothers. They chose Princess Sarsina.[44] She was a member of the Habsburg network and would now start to act on behalf of Empress Zita.

Sarsina was living in Italy when war broke out. When Italy sided with the Entente powers in 1915 she moved to Switzerland in protest against 'Italian treason'. Living in the Swiss town of Fribourg also meant that she could stay in contact with both sides of her family—she had relatives in France, Italy, and in Austria-Hungary. Though she was born in France and married to an Italian, her loyalties were completely Austrian. She was a devout Catholic and particularly close to Maria Antonia of Parma, the mother of the new Austrian Empress Zita. Because of this background she seemed a natural for a go-between mission. But her work would not go unnoticed. Sir Hugh Whittal was working for MI6 in Switzerland. One of his best sources was the Swiss political department, which passed on intelligence to him. They were aware of the importance of Sarsina's work. In a memorandum about the 'Fribourg conversations' Whittal wrote:

> The central person of the whole affair is Princess Sarsina.... She is on friendly terms with the Dowager Duchess Maria Antonia of Parma (nee Princess of Braganza and Infanta of Portugal) who is the mother of the Empress Zita of Austria. Princess Sarsina is also on extremely friendly terms with the Empress Zita herself, with the Emperor Charles [Karl] and with many other important and influential persons at the Court of Vienna.... Princess Sarsina's house has been during the last

three years the scene of many meetings between various members of the various branches of the house of Bourbon and many Roman Catholic dignitaries and others who have been active pacifists.[45]

Most importantly the Swiss had seen (probably opened) a letter the Empress Zita had written to Princess Sarsina in early 1917: 'the Empress Zita's letter contained a reference to French rights in regard to Alsace-Lorraine. At the foot of this letter Emperor Charles [Karl] appended a word of greeting over his signature.'

From the intelligence report Zita emerges as the driving force. She wanted a quick peace: 'the Empress Zita's letter said that Austria did not desire to be ruined for the sake of saving Alsace-Lorraine for Germany.'

This was an entirely female network that only used men as a front. Behind the scenes women were dictating the agenda and the pace. That Zita and her mother were quite manipulative of the men they used even occurred to the intelligence agents: 'the Duchess of Parma (Zita's mother) in her great desire to bring about the conclusion of hostilities, may have misled the Emperor Charles regarding the strength of peace desires in France and Italy, and may have exaggerated the possibilities of success in bringing about a reconciliation between Vienna on the one hand and the Entente on the other.'

The Duchess of Bourbon-Parma saw negotiations with the Entente powers as a career chance for her sons, who were serving in the Belgian army. If Sixtus and Xavier could broker a peace between France and Austria-Hungary, their careers were secured. It was therefore the Duchess (with the help of Sarsina) who orchestrated a first 'peace feeler' meeting in Switzerland in January 1917. Everyone in this game naturally had their own complicated agendas. The Parma brothers' first trip to Switzerland was cleared by the King of the Belgians and the French government. They realized that Sixtus and Xavier Parma were ideally placed to get in contact with Emperor Karl. The French probably also hoped that the Sixtus mission could sow discord among the Central Powers. However, they had no clear idea how ambitious the plan of the Parma family actually was. In fact Sixtus did not simply want to deliver a message—he wanted to write the message. He and his mother hoped for a big 'scoop', for the glory of the House of Parma. At the first meeting between the Parma brothers and their mother in Switzerland they discussed a list of demands that should be fulfilled by Austria-Hungary. In return for a peace deal with the Entente, Austria-Hungary should agree to: first making Germany return Alsace-Lorraine to France, secondly Belgium becoming sovereign again, thirdly Austria-

Hungary relinquishing any interest in Constantinople, and finally giving Serbia its sovereignty back.

These demands were communicated to Emperor Karl's private envoy, Count Thomas Erdödy. In his first reaction Emperor Karl agreed to all points apart from the last one, in a second reaction he backpedalled. Sixtus, however, kept insisting that all points had to be fulfilled. This put Emperor Karl in a dilemma. He wanted an honourable peace (which would mean including his German ally) but if that was not possible he needed to drop his ally to save his crown. Up to this point he had planned to run the Sixtus go-between mission himself, but he now realized that he needed the support of his Foreign Secretary Czernin. Czernin had to help him put pressure on their German ally. On his own Emperor Karl saw no chance of persuading the Germans to cede Alsace-Lorraine. Though Czernin was now brought in, he was not informed about all the details of the Sixtus mission. Karl simply told his Foreign Secretary that he might have found a way for peace negotiations with the French. Czernin was therefore under the wrong impression that the French had approached the imperial family, not the other way round. In fact during the whole mission Emperor Karl did not give Czernin vital details. Sixtus was *his* go-between and he wanted to keep it that way. To inform Czernin only 'on a need-to-know basis' naturally carried the risk of misinterpretations. As events would show, it would have been wiser to keep Czernin either entirely in or out.

Since Czernin worked under a misapprehension about France's motives, he insisted on playing hardball. He wanted to achieve a peace that included Germany. Karl, pressured by his wife and the Parmas, was however now willing to drop his German ally if necessary. Since the outbreak of the Russian Revolution in March 1917, he had been in a state of panic. He kept asking his ministers the same question again and again 'is it possible here too?'[46] Czernin could not give him much assurance, and privately he confided to his friends that 'the Russian Revolution is having an influence. Our dynastic roots might be stronger, but in the last three years a new world has emerged.'[47]

On 24 March 1917 Karl gave Sixtus a letter for the French in which he promised to do his utmost to impress on his German allies the 'just' French demands on Alsace-Lorraine.[48] Furthermore, Belgium should be restored and be allowed to keep its African colonies. Serbia's sovereignty should also be restored. Karl did not want to comment on Russia, while the revolution was still ongoing.

This was good material for Sixtus to use back in France. The French President was interested in Emperor Karl's reply, yet he was also informed about Czernin's much less lenient stance. It was obvious to him that the Emperor had promised concessions he might not be able to deliver. Czernin and Emperor Karl now seemed to compete with each other in sending out go-betweens to France. For Emperor Karl it was important that his brother-in-law Sixtus was achieving results first. Knowing that his Foreign Secretary did not approve of a separate peace, he had every reason to keep Sixtus, i.e. his cards, close to his chest. Meanwhile it had dawned on Czernin that he was not being fully informed. He had met Sixtus but did not approve of using him as a go-between. In rivalry with the Parma brothers he therefore set up another channel to France—Count Mensdorff. Mensdorff was a former diplomat and, unlike Sixtus, had the complete trust of Czernin. To get him into the game, Czernin seized on an interesting new offer. It came from a woman. Alexandra Barton, a member of the rich Peel family, was an English lady living in Switzerland. In March 1917 she approached an Austro-Hungarian diplomat informing him that the French were interested in a meeting with a high ranking Austrian emissary. At the centre of their talks should be peace negotiations. Count Czernin quickly picked up on this offer.

Alexandra Barton-Peel seemed to be a serious go-between, well connected to British and French political circles. This made her a highly useful commodity. So far the Entente powers had never agreed jointly on one go-between. On the contrary they had been jealous and highly suspicious of any contact the other party had made. Barton, however, seemed to be trusted by both—the French and the British. That made a constructive outcome more likely. Though Czernin was satisfied with her credentials, it is not actually clear who her French contacts were. On the British side they included the former Foreign Secretary Grey and the leader of the opposition Asquith. Both men obviously hoped to achieve a political scoop that might bring them back to power.

Barton seemed too good an opportunity to miss and Mensdorff was sent on his way. Though he was not a diplomat any more he would still have attracted suspicion. Swiss hotels in Berne and Geneva were crowded with people who reported on each other. Mensdorff therefore used an appropriate cover—he claimed to be working for the Red Cross. Once established he made contact with Alexandra Barton. He was impressed by her. She was obviously not an attention seeker but highly intelligent and without a doubt employed by high ranking members of the Entente powers. But her offer was a disappointment for Mensdorff and Czernin, who still hoped to find a peace proposal that included Germany. Lady Barton kept repeating that Britain and France sought peace with Austria-Hungary alone. She explained that no one would dare to start negotiations with Germany, because the jingoistic mood in England would not allow for it. Britain aimed for a complete victory over Germany and was confident that this could be achieved.[49] Attitudes towards Austria-Hungary, however, were different. Nobody, Barton insisted, felt any hatred towards the Austrians; even Italy and Russia had no such feelings, while 'the whole world was filled with hatred' towards Germany. Mensdorff was taken aback by this and stressed that a separate peace with Austria-Hungary was impossible. In his memorandum to Czernin he summarized the impression Barton's arguments had made on him:

1. They want to separate us from Germany.
2. They are eager to humiliate Germany...but there might be a possibility for an overall peace agreement if Alsace-Lorraine was returned and Belgium restored.[50]

Barton must have given him a hint in this direction. Yet, by now Czernin knew that it was hopeless to get the Germans to cede Alsace-Lorraine. Mensdorff was however not willing to give up so easily. At a further meeting with Alexandra Barton on 4 April he floated a scenario in which Austria-Hungary, Italy, and Russia would drop out of the war and the fighting would be continued by Britain, France, and Germany.[51] It was blue-sky thinking, but must have encouraged the British not to give up on their Austrian contacts.

As we will see, Barton was not the only woman who carried out such clandestine negotiations. Like many other female go-betweens, she was discretion personified. It was only in her will that she gave an ironic hint of her work—a hint that so far seems to have gone unnoticed. In 1935 she bequeathed her house in Geneva—the Villa Barton and its extensive park—to the Swiss Confederation, so it could be turned into the Graduate Institute of International Studies.[52] Barton obviously saw her go-between work as a useful tool for international relations. Today's students are unaware that their benefactor had once tried to help such relations in her own way.

While Alexandra Barton stayed anonymous all her life, her rival go-between Sixtus of Parma was less lucky. During the whole Sixtus mission Emperor Karl had relied on the discretion of the people involved. This was a reasonable assumption, yet in times of war, 'trust' had become a rare commodity. Like so many other failed peace feelers the Sixtus one might have stayed secret, at least until the end of the war. Yet indiscretion—the greatest threat to all go-between missions—changed this overnight.

It was, of all people, the experienced diplomat Count Czernin who broke the rules. Though he knew all too well that mutual trust between parties involved in go-between missions was paramount, Czernin publicly announced that the French had made peace overtures to Austria-Hungary but that his government had stood by Germany. He must have known that the press would cover his statement at length. He also should have known that the French would retaliate. In fact Czernin had triggered a disaster. His speech was so completely out of character that nobody (including Czernin himself) could later understand the motive behind it. One explanation was that he was still under the misapprehension that the initial overture had been made by the French. He was also ignorant about the letters Karl had sent via Sixtus to the French. Another reason for his speech could have been his desire to show himself as a man who had tried everything to achieve a peace deal, indicating that this peace would have been possible if Germany had not stood in the way of resolving the Alsace-Lorraine problem. This might have been a coded hint to the German ally. Still, it does not justify the recklessness of his remarks. A more simple explanation for them is that he was not acting rationally. His mental state was by then fragile. The war had taken its toll on everyone, but Czernin had known for almost two years that it was lost. By 1918 he was completely overworked and close to a nervous breakdown. His concentration had suffered and this might have made him say things off the cuff. Whatever the reasons, the speech would become his personal suicide note.

The French were outraged and decided to return the compliment, by publishing Emperor Karl's incriminating letters ten days later. Czernin was naturally shocked. Emperor Karl then gave Czernin his 'word of honour' that no more letters existed. He also claimed he had never made any commitments in regard to Alsace-Lorraine. This was an obvious lie. It was now expected that Czernin would do the 'honourable thing' and shield the Emperor, taking sole responsibility and resign. He refused. As a consequence he was dismissed four days later.

Czernin's career was over and Emperor Karl's reputation tarnished. Fürstenberg, who had never liked Zita's 'awful family', the Bourbon-Parmas, was outraged. He agreed with many members of Austrian society that the Parma intrigues had been responsible for this blunder. While everyone discussed whether Karl had actually lied to his minister or not, one thing seemed clear to many now—the Habsburg dynasty was severely damaged and might not survive the war.

The Sixtus mission was a debacle on several levels. Most importantly it ended the chances for any more Franco-Austrian peace feelers. It also made Austria-Hungary even more dependent on Germany while at the same time poisoning their relationship irrevocably.

Fürstenberg's sentimental little poem about the two faithful brothers—Austria and Germany—seemed to mock him now:

> The brothers did not separate but stood firm,
> And fought without regret and treachery
> The Nibelungen-fidelity became reality!

There was no trace of 'Nibelungen-fidelity' left. It was obvious to everyone that Karl had wanted to achieve a quick peace settlement to rescue his crumbling empire, and that he would have sacrificed his German ally to achieve this.

Apart from bringing about the beginning of the end of the German–Austrian alliance, the Sixtus mission also changed the public's perception of their leaders. Censorship and propaganda had shielded people from the truth for four years. Now they saw an 'international clique' at work, which was acting outside the boundaries of government and the judicial system.

The American observer George D. Herron (1862–1925) saw the affair as a decisive turn. He wrote to the Secretary of the American Legation in Berne in May 1918: '[This scandal] seems to be the starting point for a new and searching examination of the psychology and the validity of the present modes of government.'

Herron was a theologian who had moved to Switzerland after the outbreak of war, explaining American policy to the Entente powers. Since 1917 his main role, had been to 'sell' President Woodrow Wilson's ideas for a peace agreement. Apart from this Herron also wrote private reports to Wilson about the situation in Europe. The President liked receiving information from semi-official channels and for a while Herron was one of them.[53] His take on the Sixtus mission was therefore important. He was well aware of how tired people had become of secret diplomacy and how much they yearned for more transparency. The Bolsheviks had by then published the secret treaties that tied the Entente together and the world had woken up to the fact that dubious negotiations had been concluded in the course of the war. The Tsar was out of action now, but the Austrian Emperor was very much in play. His handling of secret go-betweens and his lies showed how much the political classes had failed. Herron's conclusions about the public's outrage therefore just confirmed what Wilson had said only a few months previously. Number one of the President's fourteen points had been to end secret diplomacy. The Sixtus scandal confirmed this. It was truly ironic that of all people Sixtus, the ambitious aristocrat, triggered a cry for democracy.

The fallout from the Sixtus mission for the Dual Alliance now became Fürstenberg's problem. His go-between work continued, yet it had become pretty desperate. On 24 June 1918 he delivered Emperor Karl's letter to the Kaiser, announcing that Austria would soon seek for peace. Though the war dragged on, everyone knew the situation was irrevocable. On one of his last missions Fürstenberg was sent to Wilhelm II to 'beg' for food supplies for the starving Viennese. The old link worked one last time. The Kaiser ruled in favour of his old friend's country.

In October 1918 the German ambassador in Vienna reported that Fürstenberg had finally given up:

> Prince Fürstenberg regards his efforts for a firm unity between the allied monarchies as having failed und has given up his political work.[54]

From this moment onwards Fürstenberg was no longer a go-between. However he stayed by the Kaiser's side during the last days of his reign. In November 1918 he travelled to the German army headquarters and was shocked by the state of his old friend. Fürstenberg's short diary entries of November 1918 show how claustrophobic the situation had become, with the Kaiser going on endless walks and taking too many sleeping pills. In this bunker atmosphere, nobody among the imperial entourage plucked up the courage to tell Wilhelm to abdicate. Fürstenberg was not capable of it either and noted: 'I do not have the heart.' To the end he was complicit in sheltering his friend from reality.

Fürstenberg and Wilhelm never got over the Sixtus 'betrayal'. After the war, in 1921 Fürstenberg wrote a long letter to the depressed ex-Kaiser. To cheer him up he told him the story of another ex-emperor, Karl. Karl and his wife Zita seemed to live in much worse circumstances. They resided in the glorified Swiss 'castle' of Hartenstein, which apparently resembled more a 'run down' hotel than an imperial palace. Fürstenberg's brother had just visited them and reported back that the 'castle' was overflowing with members of Zita's pushy family, the Bourbon-Parmas:

> They all intrigue and agitate for their own ends. My brother was relieved to get out alive... He thinks no fruitful action can be taken as long as the Parmas maintain their influence. But it seems to be impossible for Emperor Karl to get rid off his horrid in-laws.[55]

Wilhelm II and Fürstenberg had of course good reason to despise the Parma family for their involvement in one of the most damaging go-between missions of the war. Yet Fürstenberg's fixation on the 'Parmas', i.e. Empress Zita and her mother, also shows that the aristocratic peer group often made wives responsible for the 'bad' decisions their husbands had taken during the war. While Empress Zita was condemned for dragging Emperor Karl into intrigues, in the case of Russia the Tsarina was posthumously made responsible for the downfall of the Romanovs while, as we will see, Queen Marie of Romania was accused of 'manipulating' her husband Ferdinand into war. All three women were portrayed in the manner of Lady Macbeth, employing rather doubtful methods for the survival of their house. Blaming the wives was a convenient way of exculpating the husbands. As in chess, sacrificing the Queen may be required to save the King. Consequently King Ferdinand's, Emperor Karl's, and Tsar Nicholas's legacies stayed fairly intact. At least, within their peer group, they could still be portrayed as following the aristocratic code of honour. This tactic was rather misogynistic, but it also reveals another point. Queen consorts were perceived as serious players. In many cases this was a correct analysis. They could gain power, even if it was only behind the scenes.

But who were these women?

Go-betweens for two queens

In 1916 Queen Marie of Romania wrote to her British cousin King George V: 'I never imagined that it would be the lot of our generation, we who were children together, to see this great war and in a way to have to remodel the face of Europe.'[56]

Though she was wildly exaggerating her role, the first part of her observation was of course correct.

Much has been written about the dilemma faced by the most prominent grandchildren of Queen Victoria in 1914: Wilhelm II, George V, and the Tsarina found themselves on opposite sides. But they were not the only royal grandchildren who had to cope with the break-up of their international family. Queen Victoria also had grandchildren living on the periphery of the war—in neutral countries. One of her granddaughters was the Queen consort of Romania, three others the Queen consorts of Spain, Greece, and Norway. All of these countries were neutral at the beginning of the war and therefore of great interest to the belligerent powers. Luring them out of their neutrality would have been a strategic as well as a propaganda success for each side.

It took Queen Victoria's grandchildren some time to understand the implications of their new role. They had been brought up to believe in a strong family unit. Many had made friends with their cousins who were now in the enemy camp. Belonging to a royal cohort that was born in the late nineteenth century, they had never encountered a major European war. Instead they had been reared in an extremely sheltered environment, surrounded by growth and prosperity. Many of them had been born at their grandmother's in Windsor, Osborne House, or Balmoral. Even their marriages had been influenced by Victoria's wishes. Whether they married into German, Russian, Spanish, or Romanian royal houses, their reference point had always remained Britain. Long after the First World War and by then scattered across the Continent, they would still reminisce about summer holidays in Balmoral. In their memories Britain became a synonym for the innocence of their youth.

These grandchildren had always been conformists. In 1914, however, they were faced with a situation that demanded a very different attitude. Some realized this earlier than others. Marie of Romania was a romantic pragmatist and her above-mentioned letter to cousin George showed that by 1916 she had adapted to the new war games. While she still reminded George of the memories of an idyllic childhood, she was also pursuing a new agenda. The 'remodelling plans' she mentioned to cousin George turned out to be demands for territorial gains. Romania would be willing to join the Entente, if a long shopping list of territorial concessions was agreed on. In the end Marie would be successful in using her family network to help remodel Romania. But the road to this remodelling process was an unusual one.

Officially Marie had no power. She was 'simply' a consort, who was expected to produce children and look beautiful. In her memoirs she wrote:

> My people always considered me pretty, and were proud of me, *notre belle reine*. In a way it was considered one of my royal duties to please their eyes, and yet it is the only duty for which I cannot be held responsible![57]

Technically Marie's husband was a very powerful monarch. In the First World War Romania was far from being a constitutional monarchy. In fact, King Ferdinand, together with his Prime Minister Bratianu, were the decision makers. Since Ferdinand was considered to be weak, people in the know turned to his wife Marie. She became the target of German and British go-betweens. That she was perceived by both sides as a potential ally was due to her 'hybrid' background.

Marie was born in England in 1875 and named after her mother the Russian Grand Duchess Marie, or Maria Alexandrovna. Her parents' marriage had been a mistake. At least this was the opinion of Marie's grandmother Queen Victoria. The Queen had not welcomed her second son Alfred marrying a Romanov. After the Franco-Prussian war Queen Victoria had given up the idea of playing politics by marrying off her children into foreign royal houses. Yet her son remained obstinate. He had already been forced to give up another marriage plan because of his mother's interference and was now determined to push this one through. He also claimed to be in love with Marie Alexandrovna, though his mother doubted that he was capable of any serious feelings. Victoria was in general critical of her children, but she did have good reasons for not supporting the Romanov project. The Crimean war had deepened distrust in British society towards Russia and the Queen shared this feeling wholeheartedly. Political clashes with St Petersburg seemed likely in the future and Victoria rightly feared that a Russian daughter-in-law could become a long-term liability. Privately she thought the Romanov family itself was arrogant and full of 'half oriental notions'.[58]

Victoria was proved right; the marriage was not very successful. But a son and four daughters were born before the couple became completely estranged. Whereas the son committed suicide, the daughters would play interesting parts during the First World War—three in the allied camp, one with the Central Powers. Like Chekhov's *Three Sisters*, these four daughters dreamed of nothing more than to get out into the world. One of them actually made it to Moscow—Victoria Melita ('Ducky')—another found a Spanish princeling, and Marie became Queen of Romania. Alexandra (Sandra) was 'only' married to Prince Ernst Hohenlohe-Langenburg, yet it would always be the unglamorous Hohenlohe the sisters turned to when unpleasantness had to be sorted out.

Growing up with her siblings in Britain and Malta, Marie thought of herself as of mixed blood—Russian and English. Her mother Marie

Alexandrovna was however suspicious of the English element. When Marie had the opportunity to marry 'back' into the royal family, her mother blocked it. She did not want her daughter to marry the second son of King Edward VII, George (later George V). Marie Alexandrovna favoured another offer. Over the years she would gain the reputation of marrying off her children young—a habit that Ernst Hohenlohe-Langenburg would call a 'mania'.[59] Following this mania, the 17-year-old Marie was quickly married to Ferdinand von Hohenzollern-Sigmaringen, the Crown Prince of Romania. She did not enjoy the privilege at first. To move from prosperous Britain to poor Romania turned out to be a severe culture shock. Yet over the years Marie did develop into an enthusiastic Romanian. It was this newfound patriotism for Romania that explains her political work during the war, using all the family networks available to her.

In fact her involvement with go-betweens is one of the few better-documented cases of the First World War. The reason for this is that Marie was refreshingly indiscreet. Her three-volume memoirs which she published in the 1930s are—despite their flowery language and obvious self-aggrandizement—a useful source. So are her letters to friends in America, in which she gives colourful portrayals of her international relatives.

When war broke out in 1914 Marie was not yet Queen consort. Her uncle King Carol I of Romania had still three more months to live. King Carol was originally a Prince of Hohenzollern-Sigmaringen, who loved his 'adopted country' Romania. Yet adoption processes can be an emotionally draining experience and countries were not necessarily as grateful as lonely children. To adopt a country turned out to be a mixed blessing for the Hohenzollern-Sigmaringen family.

As a member of the House of Hohenzollern-Sigmaringen King Carol had always been pro-German. Though he was resentful that his relative Kaiser Wilhelm II had never shown much interest in or even visited Romania, when war broke out he favoured siding with Germany. King Carol mainly felt bound by treaty obligations. Despite many differences with Austria-Hungary, Romania had renewed a secret understanding with the Triple Alliance in 1913 and was therefore an ally of Germany, Italy, and Austria-Hungary.[60]

However, Romania's ruling elite did not share the King's enthusiasm for Germany and traditionally felt pro-French. For informed circles it was consequently no surprise that a compromise was reached and Romania declared herself neutral in 1914. It was a wise decision, but a decision the other nations did not accept. From this point onwards, the Entente as well as the Central Powers hoped to lure Romania out of its neutrality. The country became a battlefield of a different kind, with weapons that varied from threats and financial bribes to promises and flattery.

When King Carol died in October 1914, the new royal couple, Ferdinand and Marie, became the main target of diplomatic pressure from the Entente and the Central Powers to join the war.

Since the royal couple were part of an international royal network it seemed appropriate to send to them, apart from diplomats, people to whom they were related and whom they trusted. George V sent a special confidant to Romania, General Paget. The Central Powers even tried out three different go-betweens to put pressure on the royal couple: first Marie's mother Marie Alexandrovna (by then dowager Duchess of Coburg), second, Marie's brother-in-law Ernst Hohenlohe Langenburg, and third, King Ferdinand's brother, Prince Wilhelm Hohenzollern-Sigmaringen.[61]

The German line was simple: the new royal couple should be reminded of their German roots and of all the money Germany had poured into Romania. Emotional blackmail should be used if appropriate. Such blackmail was best carried out by a mother. Marie of Romania's mother Marie Alexandrovna (dowager Duchess of Coburg) consequently demanded in her letters support for Germany. These were not simply the private letters of a controlling mother. They were commissioned by the German Foreign Minister von Jagow, who wrote happily in June 1915 that the correspondence was carried out satisfactorily.[62] But letter writing was not enough. Jagow also wanted Marie Alexandrovna to travel to Romania to increase the pressure on her daughter. Marie Alexandrovna felt too old for such a strenuous trip. She suggested to Jagow that one of her sons-in-law, Ernst Hohenlohe-Langenburg, should go to Bucharest instead. The Foreign Minister hesitated at first. The trip of a man like Hohenlohe would be much more visible than that of an old mother. In June 1915 Jagow therefore telegraphed to his envoy in Bucharest:

> Private. Strictly confidential. What influence has the brother-in-law of the Queen, Prince Hohenlohe on the royal couple? Would his visit be perhaps viewed favourably? Duchess of Coburg [Marie Alexandrovna], who does not want to go to Bucharest herself, seems to wish the visit to take place, but it could also be based on the wish to make her son-in-law play a political role.[63]

The reply of the German envoy was positive and Hohenlohe-Langenburg was dispatched to Bucharest.

While some members of the diplomatic service thought that one should avoid sending 'amateurs', others were more practical. One explanation for this was the mindset of civil servants in the German Foreign Ministry. They lived in a monarchy and were mainly aristocrats. Of the 550 diplomats who served in the German Foreign Ministry 70 per cent were members of the nobility. The decisive policy department in the Foreign Ministry, department IA, was until 1914 dominated by civil servants, 61 per cent of whom had an aristocratic background. Non-aristocratic civil servants were sidelined and ended up in less prestigious departments (economic, legal, or consular).[64] It was therefore no surprise that the aristocratic civil servants believed in the benefits that could be achieved by dynastic contacts with other countries. Since diplomats did not want such a delicate task to be carried out by anyone outside their trusted circle it seemed sensible to employ private individuals, their fellow aristocrats. After all, these 'amateurs' understood the cultural context and often knew the decision makers personally.[65]

Once approached, members of the higher aristocracy usually agreed. Ever since the outbreak of war, they had wanted to prove their relevance and their 'usefulness'. They had done this by getting involved in military and charitable projects. A semi-diplomatic role seemed even more prestigious.

As Jagow's telegram shows, however, he was somewhat suspicious of Prince Hohenlohe. Jagow knew that Hohenlohe had had political ambitions in the past and might be interested in securing a return to the Foreign Ministry. Being married to one of Queen Victoria's granddaughters, Hohenlohe was certainly well connected. In 1900 the family had created a job for him by appointing him Regent for the young Carl Eduard Duke of Coburg. Ernst 'reigned' for five years in Coburg and Gotha, a position he enjoyed tremendously. In this case his family connections had been useful, yet they hindered him five years later. His dreams of becoming German ambassador to Britain were rejected by King Edward VII for practical reasons: Hohenlohe and his wife were 'family' and would therefore have been entitled to precedence over the other ambassadors and their wives, something that could have caused endless rounds of embarrassment.[66] Hohenlohe had to accept this argument and turned to politics. He tried his luck as colonial secretary (1905/6) and became a member of the Reichstag. None of these experiments satisfied him and by 1913 he decided to run his estates full time.

It was the outbreak of war that helped him to reactivate his career again—not as a proper diplomat, but in a semi-official role. A successful go-between mission in Romania could have been his ticket back into the political arena. That such a success might be possible was the opinion of Prince Löwenstein. He wrote in 1915: 'It is funny, that Ernie Langenburg could never become ambassador because his wife is an English Princess. And now that we are at war with England, in critical negotiations with Romania and she has a sister sitting in Russia, all of a sudden it works. For negotiations with Romania he will perhaps be useful.'[67]

Jagow had come to the same conclusion in the end. Hohenlohe would be one of his go-betweens.

However, the most important prerequisite for a go-between mission was that it should stay secret and here secrecy was blown early on. Rumours soon circulated in the international diplomatic corps in Bucharest about the Hohenlohe visit. The German envoy in Romania reported that Prince Hohenlohe's arrival was not welcomed by the Romanian 'warmongers' and was being used for anti-German agitation.[68]

That his trip to Romania had become common knowledge was a blow for Hohenlohe. Officially he had been made a special envoy to Constantinople in 1915 and his 'stop over' in Bucharest had been portrayed as a family visit. But now that his cover was blown, pro-Entente circles were nervous. Marie of Romania, in particular, felt that Hohenlohe's visit was a serious threat to her own agenda. In her memoirs she wrote:

> I was hungry for news of everybody and everything at Coburg, and yet it was a difficult encounter, as Ernie sensed which way the tide was turning, and I well knew that his contact with Nando [her husband King Ferdinand] was not without danger. Ernie represented too evidently that German atmosphere dear and familiar to my husband, and it was but natural that Ernie should profit by his visit to further German interests; besides Ernie was a very sympathetic German agent.[69]

Her husband liked Hohenlohe because he confirmed what the King believed in: the 'invincibility' of the German army.[70] But King Ferdinand had been under constant pressure from Francophile Romanian circles, who doubted that he was acting as a 'good Romanian'.[71] The King had coped with these accusations badly and seemed close to a nervous breakdown. Hohenlohe's visit was now propping him up. Though Hohenlohe did not achieve spectacular results, at least Romania *stayed* neutral. In the eyes of Foreign Minister Jagow, Hohenlohe therefore remained a useful factor in German–Romanian relations.

Apart from Marie Alexandrovna and Hohenlohe, Jagow employed a further German go-between to King Ferdinand: Wilhelm Hohenzollern-

Sigmaringen (1864–1927). Wilhelm was Ferdinand's elder brother and the head of the house of Hohenzollern-Sigmaringen. Even though he lived in the sleepy little town of Sigmaringen, Wilhelm's mental map was much bigger. Politically and financially his family had interests in Prussia, the Rhineland, southern Germany, and Romania. Though the last one was a rather unusual affiliation, it added enormous honour to the House.[72]

Wilhelm had of course no powers comparable to those of his brother Ferdinand of Romania but he thought along traditional hierarchical lines. Since he was the head of the house and the elder brother, he felt he had to guide Ferdinand. Like the other two go-betweens he urged him to join the Central Powers. In long letters Wilhelm kept analysing the 'misguided politics' of Romania's Prime Minister Bratianu and painted the dark consequences for 'dynasty and the state' if Ferdinand joined the Entente. This, Wilhelm Hohenzollern-Sigmaringen argued, would be fatal for Romania and would lead to an 'awful break with your family and your old homeland'.[73]

Wilhelm Hohenzollern-Sigmaringen had a trustworthy source at the Romanian court, a secretary of the King named Baron Basset. Basset was born in Switzerland and by 1916 already 69 years old. But as the report stressed, he was agile and lucid. He had been a secretary to the deceased King Carol and was now working for his successor King Ferdinand.

Basset regularly visited Germany and informed Wilhelm about the King's state of mind. He assured him that Ferdinand was feeling German and had in 1915—when Italy joined the Entente Powers—condemned the 'treacherous betrayal by Italy of its treaty obligations in the sharpest way'.[74]

Basset always made sure to remind Ferdinand of the testament of King Carol and to advise him to visit his uncle's grave before making any decisions.

Hohenzollern-Sigmaringen was satisfied with such reports and so was Secretary of State Jagow. His Romanian back channels were so important to him by now that he thought of various elaborate ways of sending the letters. To make sure that they would not cause any suspicion: 'I have chosen to use the Romanian envoy to hand over [the letter] so as to avoid it looking like an official pro-German method of influencing them. This is better than the German envoy handing it over.'[75]

Jagow was of the opinion that every possible back channel should be used to keep control of the Romanian situation. He did not trust the Romanian Prime Minister Bratianu, whom he described as a 'blackmailer'.[76]

Indeed Bratianu had since 1914 played off both sides against each other. Jagow summed up the situation in June 1915:

> Romania doesn't want to commit, wants to wait and see, even hesitates to state precise wishes, and wants great concessions for simply remaining neutral.[77]

King Ferdinand was involved in this bargaining. He had written a private letter to the Kaiser trying to explain that in spite of his own personal feelings and sympathies, he was before all else 'one with his people, who were clamouring for the liberation of the Romanians living under the sway of the Hungarians'. In other words he wanted the German government to put pressure on Austria-Hungary to offer Transylvania.

The Germans supported this, but they could not make the decision alone. Their Austro-Hungarian ally would have to make the greatest territorial concessions to Romania. And they were far from willing. Queen Marie wrongly assumed it to be Germany's fault: 'The Kaiser paid little heed to his cousin's letter [Ferdinand's], and adopted a high-handed manner towards us, little conducive to encouraging good feelings.'[78]

The Germans guessed that it was difficult to win the Queen over. Though she loved flattery, she did not fall for the charms of Count Czernin or any other Austrian or German emissary sent to her. In her memoirs she would state: 'It is true that I had never felt German but English, though much of what was German was sympathetic to me, and that I was always eager to promote any understanding between England and Roumania; but England never showed any particular interest in my adopted country, which I often regretted.'[79] Despite all the money Germany poured into Romania, the Queen was of the opinion that the majority of the Romanian people favoured France. To achieve such a deal for Romania, Marie now used her family network:

> The Emperor of Russia and the King of England being both of them my first cousins, it was easy for me to keep in touch with them unofficially, and of course I was ready to serve my country in every way. Being entirely trusted by both the King and the Prime Minister, I was more initiated into State affairs and secrets than is usual for Queens. I was considered a valuable asset and therefore expected to do my share.[80]

Though she had missed out on the chance of marrying 'back into' the British royal family, she had maintained a close relationship with her cousin George V: 'George has always kept a special affection for me. I stimulate him, my uncrushable vitality makes the blood course more quickly through the veins.'[81] Emotionally they were worlds apart and the highly flamboyant Marie was very aware of this, 'he has no special personality... is stiff and conventional'.[82] But despite this accurate portrait, she hoped he might bring about a solution for Romania. In March 1915 she wrote a personal letter to George V signalling interest in an alliance:

> it is quite clear that public feeling is turning more and more towards the side where my heart really is.... I for one am of course delighted to see England at last take some interest in Roumania.[83]

In a second letter she described in detail what territorial gains Romania was hoping 'for its security and development.... The frontiers of the Danube to the Theiss, as well as that of the Pruth in Bucovina are essential conditions.' She went on for several pages, though she was sure her cousin George had problems in following her detailed description:

> In our youth, we had played 'geographical' games together under my Mamma's critical eyes. I knew that European geography had not been George's strong point. Mamma had been very withering in her criticisms of our ignorance... I could almost see George's wrinkled brow whilst labouring through it.[84]

The person who helped Marie of Romania to stay in touch with George was a British go-between. His name was General Sir Arthur Paget. Paget was a military man, who up to this point had had a rather mixed career. He was married to an American heiress and had served with great brutality during the Boer War and later in Ireland. In books on South Africa he is usually described as lazy and incompetent. He was known to despise politicians whom he called 'swine'. According to Victor Bonham-Carter, Sir Arthur was 'a stupid, arrogant, quick-tempered man'. This did not alienate him from the King, however. George V used him (most probably after consultation with the government) as a go-between with Romania. It was Paget who helped Marie of Romania and Prime Minister Bratianu to eventually get a deal struck with Britain. Paget delivered letters and probably also the verbatim replies by George V to Marie. Paget's role in all of this has never been written about; the only clue to it is an appreciatory remark by Marie. 'In March 1915, General Arthur Paget... came on a mission to our part of the world... to me it was a great relief to be able at last to speak to an Englishman, and I explained our difficult situation and also gave him a letter for King George.'[85] The episode sheds new light on the General—arrogant he might have been, but hardly stupid. As will be shown later there seems to have been a certain tradition within the Paget family to work as go-betweens. His relative Lady [Walburga] Paget tried her hand at it as well.

Marie did not only inform 'cousin George' about Romania's territorial wishes, she wrote a similar letter to the Tsar. Her relationship with 'Nicky' was, however, more complex. She had visited the Russian royal family in the spring of 1914, when there had been a vague plan for her eldest son to marry one of the Tsar's daughters (a plan Marie claimed to dread since it would bring haemophilia into her family).[86] She was fond of her Russian cousin though: 'from Nicky one never felt estranged, but neither did one get any nearer. He seemed to live in a sort of imperial mist.'[87] Such imperial mist was alien to Marie who was more down to earth. But she had been flattered when the Russian royal family paid a return visit to Romania in June 1914. It was the last time she saw them.

To contact the Tsar, she now used an intermediary from her female network, the Grand Duchess Vladimir. According to Marie, the Grand Duchess was ideal because she was 'very eager that we should come in on the Russian side'.[88]

The Grand Duchess Vladimir (1854–1920) was born in Germany as Marie of Mecklenburg-Schwerin. She had married the third son of Tsar Alexander II and was by 1914 the most influential hostess in St Petersburg. She was always trying to get involved in politics and had great ambitions for her son the Grand Duke Kirill. So had her daughter-in-law—Victoria Melita ('Ducky'). Ducky happened to be a sister of Marie of Romania and worked closely with the Grand Duchess Vladimir on the advancement of Kirill.

All three women—'Ducky', the Duchess Vladimir, and Marie of Romania now tried to help along a Romanian–Russian alliance. From autumn 1914 Marie used her correspondence with Ducky to signal interest in closer ties with Russia. In August 1915 she wrote to her: 'But I can only tell you one thing: here, in spite of German successes and the non-success of the Entente our people still have absolute confidence in the Entente's victory.'[89]

She quite rightly assumed that this would be passed on. Ducky and the Grand Duchess Vladimir did their best to 'help'. From 1915 onwards the Grand Duchess delivered Queen Marie's letters 'to the right people' and sent back the replies under her name.[90] She was not simply a glorified messenger. She also got involved herself. To Marie she wrote:

> after reading your letter I spoke to Sazonov [the Russian Foreign Minister] and pleaded your cause. I have the impression that both he and Nicky are sincerely willing to come to a good understanding with Romania, and to bring about a satisfactory alliance with you, making certain concessions.[91]

Marie's negotiations with the Entente were now increasingly successful and the German go-betweens fell behind. They were well aware of it.

In June 1916, shortly before Romania sided with the Entente, Jagow planned to try and influence King Ferdinand one last time. He wrote to Ernst Hohenlohe-Langenburg begging him to urge the King 'to stick it out'. Hohenlohe should use the advantageous military position of Germany as one argument. It was decisive now to warn Ferdinand 'not to be taken in by his dodgy ministers'.[92]

The pro-Russian atmosphere in Romanian society certainly alarmed the Germans. Basset reported to Hohenzollern-Sigmaringen that this atmosphere had affected the King, who had started to 'sway and lose energy'. Furthermore Queen Marie had managed to suppress all the pro-German voices at court. Basset described Marie of Romania quite rightly as the leader of a 'parallel government', which supported Bratianu's policy.

Despite these warnings from Basset, the events during the summer of 1916 came as a shock to everyone in Germany, including Hohenzollern-Sigmaringen. When on 27 August 1916 the arrival of his trusted intermediary Basset was announced, he suspected nothing serious:

> I thought the King [of Romania] might want me to talk to the Kaiser to get his support in case he had to maintain neutrality against the will of the Romanian government.[93]

Instead, Basset informed him that the situation had deteriorated and everything possible should be done to stop King Ferdinand from committing the 'mad deed'. Basset gave Hohenzollern-Sigmaringen a blow-by-blow account of what had happened during the recent days. On 24 August the King had suddenly asked Basset to deliver a letter to his brother in Sigmaringen. Basset thought it odd that shortly afterwards the Queen of Romania also wanted him to deliver a letter to her mother Marie Alexandrovna, the dowager Duchess of Coburg. Basset now handed over King Ferdinand's letter which Hohenzollern-Sigmaringen read immediately. It was an apology, saying that the King had to 'follow the will of his people' and side with the Entente. This meant that King Ferdinand had already decided to go to war on 24 August. Basset was of the opinion that the culprit for this was the 'old fox Bratianu who had bought the press. The main fault was with the Queen, who felt like an Englishwoman and had also become Russophile.' Basset thought that 80 per cent of the Romanian public was totally indifferent as to which side to fight on and that the Social Democratic Party in Romania was still in its infancy. The Romanian officers were in general 'pro-French, superficial and hedonistic'.[94]

Hohenzollern-Sigmaringen reacted immediately to this letter, still hoping to stop his brother. He drafted a telegram to Bucharest. Its contents were close to emotional blackmail. This telegram is an interesting source because it illustrates the psychological methods that were used in aristocratic and royal houses to keep family members in line. As we have seen earlier, to keep a house united meant to take emotional aspects into account. A manipulation of feelings was necessary so that everyone would fulfil their duty to the house. One method of keeping family members under control was to remind them constantly of their ancestors' heroism and sacrifices. Family honour was paramount and had to remain untarnished. Hohenzollern-Sigmaringen therefore used an amalgam of such arguments in his telegram to King Ferdinand:

> I want to warn you for the last time against complacency and fateful weakness, stay firm and strong in your belief in God. Rather follow the ultimate logic of your beliefs and abdicate instead of jumping hand in hand with Bratianu into the dark abyss. This would expose your house and your country to doom and ridicule. Think in these difficult moments of our deceased uncle [Ferdinand's predecessor King Carol I. of Romania] and loyal ancestors. Grandfather and father are looking down on you from heaven. I believe in your understanding and loyalty. May God be with you! Wilhelm.[95]

The telegram was never sent because the following morning, Romania declared war on Austria-Hungary.

In the early modern period family members who disobeyed the head of the house had to fear economic and social sanctions.[96] Wilhelm Hohenzollern-Sigmaringen acted in this tradition. He could hardly punish his brother financially, but he excluded him from the House of Hohenzollern-Sigmaringen. Other relatives reacted in a similar way; the dowager Duchess of Coburg terminated contact with her daughter, Marie of Romania.[97] So did Marie's German sister Alexandra.

The German press was outraged about the 'Romanian' betrayal. To be related to the Romanian royal family was now a social stigma and Wilhelm Hohenzollern-Sigmaringen was insulted in the streets as 'the brother of a traitor'. He silenced speculation about his patriotism by officially distancing himself from King Ferdinand in a press release.

However, the shock waves ran deeply through German aristocratic circles. Ernst Hohenlohe Langenburg had to cope with his upset mother-in-law and his scared wife Alexandra. In his diary he noted 'bad news' from Coburg. There had been agitation against the family, i.e. his mother-in-law and his wife.[98]

Hohenlohe's aunt Grand Duchess Luise von Baden was not personally attacked but felt outraged anyway. A Hohenzollern by birth, she could not comprehend how a fellow Hohenzollern like the King of Romania could bring such shame on his own house.[99] Ernst Hohenlohe tried to explain the events in a letter to her:

> How intensely I can identify with what you are feeling now. That a Hohenzollern is playing such a role one would never have thought possible in the old days. Even if he could not take the pressure any more, the only thinkable solution would have been abdication.... I can only assume that behind Nando's [King Ferdinand's] back Bratianu was silently working to join the Entente and at the last moment confronted Nando with a fait accompli. Since shortly before the declaration of war, Nando gave his assurances he would stay neutral, I cannot think that he was not telling the truth. He is not very intelligent and also weak but as far as I know he is not capable of such a lie. My poor mother in law [the dowager Duchess of Coburg Marie Alexandrovna] who in this war feels and thinks so much like a German Princess is outraged about this breach of loyalty.[100]

Out of tact, Ernst did not mention Queen Marie of Romania's role, he merely expressed grief that she had lost her youngest son at this time of crisis. Though Ernst tried to play down the role of Marie, over the following months the general line in Germany became that Marie of Romania was responsible for the 'mess': poor Ferdinand of Romania had acted under the influence of his 'dreadful wife' and could not be made responsible for his deed.

In defence, Ernst Hohenlohe quoted from a letter Marie had written to her mother shortly before Romania joined the war. In it she had expressed the 'sincere' wish that Romania would stay neutral but also stressed that the pressure on 'Nando' was immense. Hohenlohe therefore claimed that: 'this letter is upright and it confirms my belief that the accusations against my sister in law as a warmonger are unfounded. It was the Entente and Bratianu that forced poor Nando with bribery and promises into the war.'[101] He did not mention that he himself had once indulged in similar tactics to win over 'Nando'. He had other things to cope with now; his wife and mother-in-law were close to a nervous breakdown: 'they are suffering from it badly. Both reject the Romanian policy sharply. My mother-in- law has always warned in her letters to her daughter [Queen Marie] of the Entente intrigues and always begged and pleaded to her not be taken in by them. But even though she is outraged by Romania's stance the fate of her daughter who has just lost her youngest son, has been thrown out of her house and now faces an insecure future is affecting her heart.'[102]

After the events of August 1916 it would have been natural to assume that go-betweens like Hohenlohe and Prince Hohenzollern-Sigmaringen had lost their usefulness for the German Foreign Ministry. Yet even though their employer Jagow eventually resigned, Hohenzollern-Sigmaringen stayed an adviser on Romanian affairs. A secret memorandum about a conversation between Chancellor Bethmann-Hollweg and Hohenzollern-Sigmaringen from 5 October 1916 shows that the German government had not given up its dynastic schemes for Romania. They were now planning to 'save' the throne in the long term for the (so far) untarnished Romanian Crown Prince, Carol. Since surprisingly little was known in Germany about young Carol, the German Chancellor needed a character analysis by Hohenzollern-Sigmaringen and so he was called in. According to his summary, the conversation with Bethman-Hollweg became quite emotional:

> We talked about Romania's treason...and the future of Romania. In Berlin it had been expected that King Ferdinand would stick to the beliefs of King Carol, that he would stand up for neutrality and because of his German origins would never approve of Romania fighting against his 'old allies'. It had been thought that this breach of promise, this unfaithfulness, this shameful treason would mean the abdication of King Ferdinand. However, the fact that a Hohenzollern supports such a shameful policy, that [Ferdinand] has drawn his sword against his own fatherland against his own tribe of the Zollern, that has hurt and truly outraged the German Emperor and the government.

Chancellor Bethmann-Hollweg told Hohenzollern-Sigmaringen that Ferdinand:

> had brought disaster and shame to his country. The Oberste Heeresleitung [German High Command] is now determined to demonstrate to Romania what it means to provoke German anger. The Romanian crusade will be decided quickly. Of course Romania will suffer heavy losses. Romanians will awaken from their nice dream of an enlarged country and will sink low, politically and geographically. In a future Romania, King Ferdinand can of course no longer be a ruler. He and the 'power-crazed' and intriguing Queen Marie of Romania will have to leave forever.[103]

It was therefore 'natural' to turn to Crown Prince Carol as a successor. Hohenzollern-Sigmaringen fully supported this idea, thereby hoping to save the Romanian branch of his house. In the following days he had several conversations about the future of Romania and the idea came up that Hohenzollern-Sigmaringen should travel to the Romanian front and report his impressions back to Berlin.[104] He obeyed but found his trip to Romania emotionally upsetting:

> to step on Romanian soil under these circumstances, a soil that I had so often visited as a welcome guest, made a deep impression on me. Full of sorrow and tormented by pain I looked at this beautiful Romania which I had learnt to love. Wistfully I thought of the fate of the Hohenzollern dynasty.

It was a confusing situation. He still felt close to his brother but had to suppress such emotions and talk to his brother's new enemies—Falkenhayn and the Austrian heir presumptive Karl. He gave them general information about Romania, its army and society. And he had to volunteer ideas on how to overthrow Ferdinand.

The decision to side with the Entente would bring two years of turmoil to Romania. The country was quickly overrun by the Austro-Hungarian and German armies, and the Romanian royal family had to flee. By September 1916 Marie of Romania was desperate. To her cousin Nicky she wrote: 'It is as a woman and as a Queen that I make my appeal to you, to the man and to the Emperor! Send us the help we ask for at once.'[105]

But the Romanovs had their own problems. The war was not going well for them either. In March 1917 Marie wrote in her diary:

> A revolution has broken out in Petersburg... I hope Ducky [her sister] is not in danger, I hope the fire will not spread, it would be dreadful for our cause, and, oh, what a disaster in every way![106]

It was not just a family disaster for Marie of Romania but also a political disaster. Despite their poor performance, the Russians were the Romanians' closest allies; if they dropped out of the war, Romania could no longer survive. To the Romanian Queen it seemed evident who was responsible for the outbreak of the revolution. As usual she saw politics in dynastic terms: for her the Tsarina, her cousin Alix, was the main culprit.

In her memoirs, Marie of Romania wrote that many, including her sister Ducky, had tried to warn the Tsarina:

> Ducky, who had a difficult position, being her [Tsarina Alexandra's] ex-sister-in-law, had the courage to go to her and warn her about the smouldering discontent,

showing her how she was taking the wrong turning, how she was gradually losing the love of high and low. Courageously Ducky told her the whole dreadful truth, but in vain.[107]

Now that the revolution had broken out Marie was convinced of Alix's guilt:

What an hour for that woman, who because of her fanaticism has brought about this crisis; she who would listen to no one except Rasputin, and separated herself little by little from all the members of the family, then from the whole of society, never showing herself anywhere any more . . . surrounding herself with quite unknown people who had a disastrous influence upon her, and whom she imposed on the Emperor. Into the bargain, she was passionately ambitious, absolutely convinced that her judgement was infallible, that she alone understood Russia, and the need of the country and people . . . Blinded by her faith in herself and advised by Rasputin, she believed she alone was rightly informed, that she alone understood the situation. She was worse than blind, she was a fanatic, and her husband was as clay in her hands! And this is what she has brought upon him and her children and her country.[108]

To blame the Tsarina for the outbreak of the revolution was something that only Marie of Romania dared to do in print by the 1930s. After the murder of the Tsar's family, such criticism became a taboo subject in monarchical and aristocratic circles.

Behind closed doors, however, the majority of Marie's relatives had always agreed that Alix was a social disaster.[109] From the start she had been highly unpopular amongst her international relatives, who thought that she 'did not pull her weight'. Already the German Empress 'Vicky', after all an aunt of the Tsarina Alexandra, was scathing: '[Alexandra] is a beautiful woman . . . but with a cold heart. Everything washes over her without leaving any trace. She is very egotistical, does not make the slightest effort and has nothing of the sensitivity of her husband and the warmheartedness of her mother Alice.'[110]

It was mainly the Tsarina's brother, the Grand Duke of Hesse, who made sure after 1918 that her reputation was defended. Hesse claimed in his memoirs that she had been a victim of circumstances. The Russian court had always vilified her, calling her 'cette raide anglaise', and made her life impossible.[111] Hesse was also very critical of Kaiser Wilhelm II's reaction to the Russian Revolution. In Hesse's opinion the Kaiser seemed to take a sadistic pleasure in the downfall of the Tsarina. Indeed Wilhelm II had phoned the Grand Duke of Hesse on 13 March 1917, the Grand Duke's jubilee day. Matter of factly he told him that a revolution had broken out in

Russia and that the Tsar and his family had been taken prisoner. Without a word of sympathy he added, 'happy anniversary,' and put down the phone. The Grand Duke was outraged about the way the news had been broken to him. He had always despised Wilhelm II, but thought this to be the height of cruelty. Two months later, in May 1917, a telegram from the Kaiser's headquarters arrived for Hesse, bluntly stating that the Tsar's family had now been murdered. In fact this was a false rumour, the family was killed later, in July 1918.[112]

That Germany was not much interested in the fate of the Tsar, and had actually encouraged the revolution by permitting Lenin's passage to Petrograd, was not surprising from a strategic point of view. However, feelings should have been different among the Entente powers. Russia was after all Romania's and Britain's ally and one would have expected at least some sympathy from these royal houses. That solidarity had become a rare commodity among Victoria's grandchildren became blatantly clear in 1917: Marie of Romania cared little for her cousin Alexandra while George V famously turned down the idea of giving the Tsar asylum in Britain. His failure to render assistance was not that unusual, though, if one puts it into a longer historical context. Traditionally the monarchical system had seldom treated its exiled cousins well. Whether a dynasty survived or not had more to do with international relations than with family ties or the concept of legitimacy. Giving asylum to a dethroned monarch was always a political and often a financial burden reigning monarchs dreaded.[113] Particularly after the press attacks on them as 'hybrids' in 1914 monarchs had to do their utmost to make sure that their image was a purely national one.

One effort to help the Tsar was made by the Spanish King, Alfonso XIII. He saw the Russian Revolution as a chance to end the war. As has been shown earlier, Alfonso offered himself for peace talks repeatedly. He also approached his German contacts as well as Buckingham Palace to rescue the Tsar. In the end his efforts came too late; the Tsar had been killed.[114]

While the members of the Tsar's family were about to lose their lives, Marie of Romania barely managed to stay alive herself. Her decision to side with the Entente had turned into a disaster. In March 1918 peace was dictated to the Romanians by Germany and Austria-Hungary. The Austrian Foreign Secretary, Marie's old acquaintance Count Czernin, arrived together with his German opposite number Kühlmann. Marie recorded in her diary: 'they demand everything with smiles and politeness and the iron hand.' She was against her husband signing the peace agreement: 'I prefer war à outrance.'[115] She did not have to wait long for her revenge. Eight months later, with the victory of the Entente, Romania turned the tables on Germany. In 1919 it would become one of the great beneficiaries of the Paris Peace Conference.

Of course the reasons why Romania had given up its neutrality in 1916 had been complex and mainly driven by the hope of making territorial gains—gains that Germany could not offer because they concerned the territory of its ally Austria-Hungary. Yet strangely enough one of the conclusions the German Foreign Ministry came to after the Romanian debacle was that it had not worked hard enough on a personal level.

There had always existed hope in the German Foreign Ministry that another neutral country could be won over: Sweden. The country was important because it protected the German army from the north, and because it offered access to world markets. Thanks to Sweden Germany still received iron ore supplies.

To win over Sweden, aristocratic go-betweens were employed again. At the outset their mission seemed not as difficult as the Romanian one: Germany and Sweden had a close relationship. After German unification in 1871 Sweden had turned increasingly to its southern neighbour. There existed a feeling of cultural kinship. The Swedish upper classes in particular were known to be traditionally pro-German. This was also due to close business contacts that had been established (a fact that Göring would exploit for his go-between missions during the Second World War).

In 1914 vocal conservative and military circles in Stockholm wanted to side with Germany. To lure Sweden out of its neutrality therefore seemed feasible. To achieve this, every avenue had to be explored, including the dynastic one. This looked particularly promising since Queen Victoria of Sweden was German. Though she was 'only' a Queen consort, her husband was, thanks to the Swedish political system, quite influential. Until the 1917 elections the Swedish monarch's powers were substantial.

Victoria was the daughter of Luise von Baden and therefore a granddaughter of Emperor Wilhelm I. Her close relationship with her cousin Kaiser Wilhelm II formed part of her political influence in Sweden. She was known to visit the Kaiser often and to support his politics. This also included a friendship with Wilhelm's 'favourite' Count Eulenburg. How close they were is shown by a letter Victoria wrote to Eulenburg in 1894: 'Please believe me I am doing everything to feel at home. I am doing my best to feel Swedish and Norwegian.'[116] (Sweden and Norway were in a personal union until 1905.)

Victoria's critics in Sweden did not believe in such assurances. They saw her as a little 'Prussian soldier', strongly conservative and a disciplinarian. This was certainly true and it had its effects on her husband the Swedish King. Though their marriage was not considered a success (King Gustav was homosexual), when it came to German affairs Victoria seems to have had influence over her husband. Her private papers are still embargoed by the Swedish royal family, but it is obvious that Gustav became very pro-German. He continued this stance long after his wife's death in 1930. His enthusiastic letters to Hitler will play a part later on.

The couple certainly shared a fear of 'radical elements' on the left. Since the great strike of 1909, they were worried that revolutionaries would take over Sweden. They therefore supported the conservative party and tried everything in their power to prevent the rise of the Swedish socialists. Sweden was not only divided in its domestic politics, but also in its foreign policy. When war broke out, the Swedish felt torn between the Entente and the Central Powers. On the one hand they saw themselves as part of the 'Nordic race' and had close ties to Germany. On the other hand Britain was important for Swedish business.

Victoria made it clear that she wanted Sweden to join the Central Powers. She showed her commitment by giving every man in Sweden who volunteered to fight for Germany a special present. During the war she continued to visit her German relatives, Wilhelm II and her mother Luise von Baden. To her mother she complained about her difficult position in Sweden: 'where the brutal pressure of England weighed heavily on the neutrals.'[117] She also talked to her cousin Prince Max von Baden. He immediately realized that there was an opening here that could also further his career. He wanted to become a go-between to Sweden (Figure 5).

Until 2004 Max von Baden was portrayed as a positive figure in German history—he was the 'liberal' Chancellor who in 1918 turned Germany into a republic. Newly discovered records have changed this view entirely. The Max von Baden who emerged in an article in the *Vierteljahrshefte für Zeitgeschichte* was anti-Semitic and an admirer of Russian autocracy. His aim during the war was to fight against England 'à outrance'.[118] Privately he had expressed the view that the 'western' model of parliamentarism would not work in Germany. In a correspondence with the reactionary Houston

Figure 5. Failed go-between Prince Max von Baden with his cousin Queen Victoria of Sweden and her husband Gustav V King of Sweden before the Great War.

Stewart Chamberlain, who was at the heart of the anti-Semitic Wagner circle in Bayreuth, Max wrote in 1917 that he was 'burning' to resist the 'democratic infiltration which has been spread by England and America with its tricks, hypocrisy and defamation'. His letters to Chamberlain show that Max von Baden was far from being a German 'Whig', but a much more complex, torn personality—or, to choose an uncharitable interpretation, an opportunist.[119] During the war he was playing the autocratic and democratic cards simultaneously to get ahead in politics. His young adviser and ghost writer Kurt Hahn would later create an idealized image of him as a liberal modernizer. Contemporaries like the diplomat von Rosen had however realized that all these 'modern ideas' were Hahn's alone: 'Nihil est in Max quod non antea fuerit in Kurt.'[120]

In his memoirs, which were published in the 1920s, Baden did not mention his negotiations with Sweden. There were two reasons for this: first of all, they failed and, second, mentioning them would have caused his cousin Queen Victoria great embarrassment. After the abdication of Kaiser Wilhelm II she had lost most of her influence in Sweden and had to tread carefully.

Max von Baden was not the first go-between the German Foreign Ministry used in Sweden. Before him, Count Ludvig Douglas (1849–1916) had been involved in negotiations. Douglas worked for Victoria of Sweden and was a true *sujet mixte*. He had once served as Swedish Foreign Minister but was at the same time an aristocratic landowner in southern Germany. Apart from him, German bankers had been drawn into negotiations as well. The Hamburg banker Max Warburg had contacted his Swedish opposite number Marcus Wallenberg, who was a brother of the Swedish Foreign Minister Knut Wallenberg (the influential Wallenberg family would again play a major part in the Second World War). These back channels were of high quality but had not achieved much yet.

Now Max von Baden got involved. He was 'encouraged' by the German Chancellor Bethmann-Hollweg to write a personal letter to his friend King Gustav V of Sweden. Max felt close to Gustav because they were both homosexuals and suffered from the various problems arising from this. Max certainly thought that he had over the years developed a special relationship with the King. In his letter to Gustav, he now argued that Germany and Sweden had common interests against Russia. The King replied immediately in a 'warm tone', but did not refer to the Russia argument. Max von Baden did not give up. He wrote to the German Chancellor, Bethmann-Hollweg, that Germany should continue to make Sweden cooperate. 'The King is the decisive factor...and he was pleased about my recent letter.'[121]

So was his cousin Queen Victoria of Sweden. To keep in contact with her, he offered to travel to Sweden. Max von Baden was so persistent in urging that this royal channel should be used that he even moved into the Hotel Adlon in Berlin in August 1915 to stay in close contact with the German Foreign Minister. He finally received his instructions to go to Sweden in November 1915. As a camouflage he used his official role as a welfare officer for prisoners of war (*Kriegsgefangenenfürsorge*). This was ironic, because the trip was far from being of a peaceful nature. For two weeks Max stayed at the royal castle Drottningholm, talking to the royal couple. Victoria had instructed him that these 'German/Swedish political and military talks should be motivated by negotiations regarding the German-Russian war'.[122]

While at Drottningholm, Max did not just talk to the King but also to the Swedish Prime Minister and the Foreign Minister. The King was leaning towards war, but the Swedish government decided in the end that the advantages of neutrality were greater for the country. The talks had failed, Max von Baden's mission was over.

Though Max later tried to erase this whole go-between episode, the Swedish diplomatic historian W. N. Carlgren resurrected parts of it. Carlgren thinks that Max von Baden got involved in the whole mission because he 'wanted to make his name as a great political negotiator'.[123] Since the House of Baden has closed its archive, Max's motives are not entirely clear. That he was highly ambitious was certainly true. His aim must have been to move from successful clandestine missions to an official position of power. He would indeed achieve this in the end by becoming German Chancellor in October 1918.

The Swedish failure upset Max von Baden. He later claimed it was a mission he was forced to carry out: 'my military instructions in Stockholm were against my inner convictions in regard to what was useful for Germany.'[124]

Unlike the Queen of Romania, the Swedish Queen did not manage to get her country into war. But the communication channels to Germany continued. To her delight, Queen Victoria's second cousin Victor of Wied became a member of the German embassy in 1919. The closeness between members of the German and Swedish aristocratic families remained strong during the inter-war period and was used by the Nazis.[125] Wied in particular became a great asset and a personal friend of Göring. As we will see later, King Gustav would help the Nazis as much as possible.

Though Max von Baden 'forgot' to mention his Swedish go-between work in his memoirs, he did mention that he made contact with his Russian relatives during the war. This was relatively easy for him due to his mother's family tree. Maria von Baden (1841–1914) was a granddaughter of Tsar Nicolas I and in her widowhood had moved back to St Petersburg. Because of these family connections, Max had visited Russia frequently before the war and had conversations with Tsar Nicholas II.[126] Furthermore Max's wife Maria Louise (1879–1948) was a niece of Maria Fyodorovna (1847–1928), the Tsar's mother. Max therefore felt close to the 'female Russian network'. He now dreamt of a peace deal with Russia. In his memoirs he writes cryptically: 'Originally it was my intention to find out via the Russian ladies whether the situation at the Tsar's court was ripe for the decisive step.'[127] He was more explicit in private, when he claimed a peace with Russia was paramount 'so that we can get even with England, France and Italy'.

Still it is unclear what Max von Baden was exactly up to. There existed two aristocratic factions in Russia at the time: one was close to the Tsarist court and ultraconservative, the other was critical of the Tsar and played with ideas of reform.[128]

Max must have been aware of the split within the Russian elite. Whether he tried to gain from it will not be possible to verify. That a critical group within the Russian aristocracy provided an opening for the German Foreign Ministry is, however, evident. Supporting revolutionary developments of any kind in Russia was an important goal for Germany. To offer Lenin safe passage was not the only method they had in mind. Whether Max von Baden was thinking along similar lines is unclear.[129]

The only 'Russian lady' he mentions by name is Marie Alexandrovna, the dowager Duchess of Coburg. She had already been involved in the Romanian case and was therefore seen as a useful link by the German Foreign Ministry. In March 1917 Max visited her in Coburg to discuss a letter to the Tsar and to ask her 'for advice and mediation'.[130] However, the timing was extremely bad—that very day he heard of Nicholas II's abdication. From then on, Max stated, 'the thread was broken'.[131]

When he wrote his selective memoirs in the 1920s, the Tsar had been murdered and it had become a social taboo to mention any anti-Tsarist support. Max von Baden would not have dared to write whether he had had contacts with the anti-Tsarist faction of the aristocracy.

In the end, he was not forgiven by his peer group for a completely different deed: In 1918 he become the 'traitor' who made Kaiser Wilhelm II abdicate. Wilhelm II never got over this betrayal. In one of his rants the ex-Kaiser indirectly referred to Max's go-between work. In 1922, he stated that one reason why Max von Baden had been made Chancellor was his 'valuable connections abroad'. The Kaiser added that when he returned to power in Germany one day, Max would have to leave the country within 24 hours otherwise he would be hanged. A bullet was 'too good for that man'.[132]

Operating from London

Max von Baden could not have carried out his missions without the help of women. Women therefore played an important part in enabling back channel work. But were they also *active* go-betweens or had Princess Sarsina and Lady Barton been exceptions?

Officially aristocratic women were mentioned in newspapers only three times during their lifetime—when they were born, when they got married, and when they died: 'Hatch, match, and dispatch.' Though women's influence was not acknowledged in public, in many families it existed behind the scenes. To this day, the parts aristocratic women actually played in Protestant and Catholic networks have not been properly researched. Officially men dominated aristocratic families, yet the gender roles were less polarized than in other classes. Compared to their bourgeois or working-class counterparts, aristocratic women—once married—could have an unusual amount of freedom. One reason for this was that they had greater financial security guaranteed by marriage contracts.[133] Marrying into another aristocratic family meant that this family was now responsible for a woman's upkeep. Since a bride had to be from an equal background it was also part of the aristocratic social code that she should be treated respectfully by the family she married into. Of course this was an ideal and there were many cases of maltreated wives, yet the aristocratic community tried to minimize this by socially ostracizing the male culprits. It was important that a wife was well integrated and cooperated with her husband and his family because she could not be replaced so easily. Separation and divorce were becoming more common in the late nineteenth century, but they were seen as a social disgrace that could easily damage a house's reputation. The ideal was therefore that the wife felt included. Her status and power within the house rose when she produced male children. Once heirs had been born, more options opened up.

Aristocratic women were certainly not 'Noras' who stayed in their doll's house. The German historian Monika Kubrova has recently analysed autobiographies by German aristocratic women from a variety of backgrounds—from the lowest rank (e.g. women who were gentry level) to the highest (crown princesses). The memoirs were published after 1900 and therefore looked back on their lives in the second half of the nineteenth century.[134] The surprising result was that these autobiographies were written like a career report. Even though the first aim of an aristocratic woman was to bring up a family, she did not see herself solely as a wife and mother (a description bourgeois women used for themselves). Aristocratic women thought of themselves as wife, mother, manager of a larger household, *and* society lady. The last of these gave them a role outside the house, and this could mean influence if they wanted to use it. These women often described themselves as active co-workers when it came to their husbands' careers. In general they were a team that had to work closely together to enlarge their house's success and therefore the chances for their children. These wives ran the estate when their husbands were absent or helped socially to enhance their careers in the military or diplomatic service. In fact they completely identified with these services. An example of this is a diplomat's wife, Mary Isabella von Bunsen, writing in her memoirs in the first person plural, meaning not just her husband but the whole Prussian diplomatic corps. She talks about: 'our new colleagues' and 'our chief' and 'our embassy'. These women did not live segregated lives. They were included in their husband's world: at court, at their country seat, in the radius of the military or civil service worlds. They therefore were what one would call today 'incorporated wives', playing a public role and at the same time increasing the social relations of their family.

As important 'news agencies' they made sure that a variety of contacts with other aristocratic houses were maintained, which in the long run was useful for the marriage and career advancements of their children. It was these female news agencies which became important for go-between missions.

That aristocratic women could play a part as go-betweens in the First World War is surprising because nowadays women are unlikely to have such opportunities. In fact female negotiators in war situations are extremely rare. Within the UN there is a 'glaring deficit': 'in 2005, of the United Nations Secretary General's 61 special and personal representatives and envoys and their deputies engaged on specifically peace-related work, there are four women.... Research and anecdote suggest that women have been considerably and powerfully more active at the grassroots.'[135]

Though grassroots work is certainly very honourable, it is seldom as effective as high-level contacts. In this respect aristocratic women were more privileged than women working for the UN today.

An important requirement for a go-between mission is instant access to decision makers. During the war it was naturally much more difficult to get such access than in peacetime. Aristocratic women had, however, several advantages. Many had built the aforementioned wide-ranging network of female friends in reigning houses. They were either distantly related to a consort or had served as ladies-in-waiting. Furthermore, by 1914 another network opened up: female aristocrats took on ornamental positions in hospitals or prisoners of war work. These positions brought them closer to high ranking civil servants, members of the military, and politicians. Since these ladies were now doing 'important war work', they had to be listened to.

To make sure that they were indeed listened to, they also took advantage of the courtesy rules of the aristocracy. These rules made access to decision makers easier: a high born lady had to be received whatever the time pressure, turning her away was seen as ungallant and amounted to a social taboo. Her request had to be taken seriously otherwise she would spread her displeasure across her wide communication network. Aristocratic men had also been brought up to avoid disagreement with women of their own class. The only tolerated mode was icy politeness but even that could become risky. In general one had at least to pretend to make an effort.

Furthermore, aristocratic women usually did not suffer from a lack of self-confidence. The pre-war generation seems to have been particularly confident and did not let anyone get away with excuses. Lady [Walburga] Paget, who became a go-between, thought of herself as a political asset:

> I know that nowadays [1917] it is not the fashion for women to interest themselves in politics but I still belong to the old school of Cavour, Dizzy [Disraeli, Lord Beaconsfield] who did make use of women's brains. Lord Beaconsfield told me himself how much he relied on women's help and in my long life I have done many bits nobody knows anything about.[136]

Lady Paget's generation of women, who had run their own salons, clearly considered themselves as part of the political scene.

It is interesting, however, that Lady Paget thought such an involvement was on the decline. At a time when suffragettes were actually fighting for women to play a part in politics this seems a contradiction. One explanation for Lady Paget's argument is the professionalization of the political parties in Britain. Until the 1890s parties had been dominated by a small group of Tory and Whig grandees with wives who were discreetly involved in politics. But with the emergence of a broader, more professionally organized party system this intimate club had lost power. Politics were no longer run from a lady's drawing room. The same was true of the diplomatic service. In Lady Paget's time embassies had still been run as a family embassy, with a thin line between the private and public worlds. An intelligent 'ambassadoress' could play much more than a social role. In the nineteenth century Count Alvensleben's political successes in St Petersburg were helped along by his wife's charm, and Prince Radolin had in Paris a mother-in-law who was a Talleyrand—an obvious asset.

The professionalization of the diplomatic service slowly changed this. The irony therefore was that in a parallel development women at the top lost their *unofficial* influence and shrank more and more into the background, at the same time that suffragettes fought for official, legal rights.

Still, some aristocratic women continued to be influential well into the inter-war years. To persuade them to carry out go-between missions was not difficult. An appeal to their aristocratic code of honour was often sufficient. Apart from that, women had lots of other reasons to get involved. Their children had often married abroad, and the war now threatened to break up the family unity (and endanger the family fortune as well). International connections also made some aristocratic women more immune to war propaganda. Because they had lived in several countries, they tried to see the political situation from multiple angles.

One of these women was the aforementioned Lady Paget. She wanted nothing more than to become a go-between for peace.

Lady Paget was not the only member of the Paget clan who worked as a go-between. As has been shown earlier, General Paget was highly successful in Romania, helping the Romanian Queen to strike a deal with the British. The General was related to Lady Paget's husband but more importantly his daughter had married Lady Paget's son Ralph. Since they were cousins, this was rather incestuous, but in a way mirrors well the mental maps of go-betweens. Everyone was somehow related to everyone else. Lady Paget might not have known about General Paget's mission, but as an intelligent woman she probably guessed that his journeys to Romania in wartime were not holiday trips.

Today Lady Paget's mission has been forgotten because it was unsuccessful and people associated with it eventually distanced themselves, trying to leave no traces behind. What remained was the picture of Lady Paget as a well-meaning yet eccentric loner. It did not help that she was known for an interest in spiritualism. Her go-between mission, however, had been a very serious effort. She had official support and was taken seriously by the country she approached—Austria-Hungary.

Walburga Paget's international background certainly predestined her for the mission. She was born Countess Hohenthal-Püchau in 1839 in Saxony, the daughter of a rich landowner. Her maternal grandfather was the famous Field Marshal August Neidhardt von Gneisenau, a hero of Waterloo. Thanks to this pedigree Paget became in 1858 lady-in-waiting to the young Princess Victoria 'Vicky' (the eldest daughter of Queen Victoria). She identified with the English born Princess, and over the years Paget would become, like Vicky, a critic of Bismarck. It was the connection with Princess Victoria and her mother Queen Victoria that introduced Paget to work as a go-between.

In 1917 Lady Paget informed the mother of the King of Spain about her longstanding credentials for such work:

> I may say that Queen Victoria several times entrusted me with secret and difficult missions and always honoured me with her confidence.[137]

Apart from dealing in this grey area, Paget also knew the official side of diplomacy well. Her marriage in 1860 to the diplomat Sir Augustus Paget had shown her the inner workings of embassies: her husband was posted to Copenhagen, Lisbon, Florence, Rome, and Vienna.[138] Her time in Vienna had left a particular impression on Paget. She became an admirer of everything Viennese and this had turned her into a passionate go-between for the Austrian cause. The main reason why she loved Austria seems to have been that it was the opposite of Prussia. Her aversion to Prussia had hardened during the war of 1866 when her native Saxony fought the Prussians. It increased when one of her brothers was fatally wounded in the war of 1870/1.

To prefer Catholic Austria-Hungary to Protestant Prussia was surprisingly common in Foreign Office circles, as Lady Paget's son Ralph acknowledged during the First World War: 'the feeling in England towards Austria was not the same as towards Germany and [Austria's] advances would meet with a sympathetic hearing.'[139]

This atmosphere was the starting point for Lady Paget's special kind of war work. In 1914 she was already 75 years old but completely lucid and very much part of the diplomatic scene. After her husband had died, her son Ralph had introduced her to a new generation of Foreign Office officials. Sir Ralph Paget had been Envoy Extraordinary and Minister Plenipotentiary to Serbia from 1910 to 1913 and maintained a lifelong interest in the Balkans. During the First World War he had been posted to Copenhagen. Lady Paget did not just take a motherly interest in her son's work. She also used his information for her go-between mission. Though she would later protect her sources and in particular defend her son it was obvious that he had helped her. Sir Edward Grey was another of her backers. He had a reputation for using conspiratorial methods: 'secretiveness and a preference for discreet, behind-the-scenes dealing remained a hallmark of his style.'[140] Lady Paget's role reflected that style.

Grey had been Foreign Secretary until December 1916. During his time in office he had tried to recruit neutral countries to support the Entente—a method that worked well in regard to Italy and Romania. Separating Austria-Hungary from its German ally would of course have been the ultimate coup and Grey realized Lady Paget's usefulness for such an endeavour. Apart from Grey, Lady Paget also mentioned a mystery adviser who 'suggested several ways and means',[141] and who was particularly knowledgeable about the Habsburg dynasty: 'Help and information flowed to me tho' I cannot tell you from whom, but it was from several sources.'[142]

Whoever were Lady Paget's 'employers', they also 'encouraged' several people to write pro-Austrian articles in magazines 'like the Fortnightly, the 19th century and other Reviews'.[143] That governmental circles 'inspired' the press was of course not a new method. Lady Paget was one of several people 'inspired' and she wrote two pro-Austrian articles in the magazine *Nineteenth Century*: 'Austria's Doom' in March 1917 and 'Austria and Prussia' two months later.

Despite the fact that she knew the Prussian court so well (or perhaps because of this), she blamed Germany for the outbreak of war. She argued that the Habsburg monarchy had become just another Prussian vassal, serving German war aims. The new Austro-Hungarian Emperor Karl should save his crown by making a separate peace with the Entente.

Her articles filtered into Austria and were quoted in a Viennese newspaper. She knew they had had an effect and this spurred her on: 'I kept on hearing things from Austria through all sorts of channels which showed how desirous they were of making peace with us.' This could be vital for Britain: 'unless we separate Austria from Prussia, we cannot and never will crush the latter.'[144] In her opinion a strong, independent Austria-Hungary was the only balance against Germany dominating the Continent.

Following her arguments, the next natural step would have been to actually approach the Austro-Hungarian Emperor Karl. Since Paget knew of the power of female go-betweens from past experience, the idea seemed not unusual to her. To set up such a meeting, she counted on the support of two influential women. On the Austrian side she hoped that Maria Josepha, the mother of the Emperor Karl, could influence her son in the matter. Maria Josepha was, like Paget, originally from Saxony and very critical of Prussia. Paget saw a bond here. In her articles she had not only praised the Austrians, but also the Saxons. To her they were the embodiment of true German culture—having produced Bach and Wagner (while the Prussians had nothing to offer but 'iron').

The other lady she targeted was the Queen dowager of Spain, Maria Christine. She was an Austrian Archduchess by birth and Paget had already known her mother.[145]

Paget's idea was that it would be best to approach the Austrian Emperor via neutral Spain. In her first letter to the Queen dowager of Spain on 24 March 1917 she proposed that a high ranking British politician (she did not name him) should come to Switzerland for peace talks and meet a delegate of the Austro-Hungarian Emperor. She asked Maria Christine to support this idea and pass on the letter to the right people.

It is very likely that Paget did not write the letter herself. Though she might have had the original idea, others 'channelled' it and used her as the go-between. This is substantiated by the circumstances in which the letter was delivered. Paget handed 'her' letter to Sir Eric Barrington, formerly private secretary of Lord Salisbury and Lord Lansdowne. Barrington was already retired (which meant that, if the mission became public, it could not damage his career). He made it possible for the letter to be handed over to the Queen dowager of Spain by a member of the British embassy in Madrid, therefore giving it respectability. It was also accompanied by a note from the British ambassador in Madrid, Sir Arthur Hardinge. This made the communication semi-official and for this reason the Queen dowager and the King himself took Lady Paget seriously from the start.

However, the Queen dowager was dithering over what to do with Paget's letter, she feared that—if her involvement became public—Spain could be accused of supporting an anti-German peace deal. This might have serious implications for her country. Germany could argue that Spain had behaved in an aggressive way and consequently was no longer entitled to its neutral status.

The Queen therefore chose to reinterpret the letter, arguing that it was meant as an indirect way of getting in contact with Germany as well. This was not the intention of the letter at all, but it helped the Spanish to keep face. On 30 July 1917 the Queen finally invited the Austro-Hungarian ambassador to Spain for a private conversation. His name was Karl Fürstenberg, brother of Emperor Wilhelm's closest friend Max Egon Fürstenberg. Because of this closeness the Queen thought she had to tread particularly carefully. She did not want to be seen as anti-German. This caution was not necessary. Karl Fürstenberg was not as loyal to Germany as one might expect. After the meeting with the Queen, he sent a telegram about their conversation. To be on the safe side, he used a courier to deliver Lady Paget's original letter separately. The addressee was a private individual, his brother Max, who then handed the letter over to the Austrian Foreign Minister Czernin. This complicated route ensured that the letter stayed outside the usual diplomatic channels.

As we saw earlier, Czernin was involved in several back channels and hoped to create the *status quo ante bellum*.[146] It is very likely that Lady Paget had heard from her many Austrian contacts of Vienna's interest in talks.

Czernin had used Spain before and the Paget signals were therefore convenient for him. Before he replied, however, he contacted his ambassador in Berlin. The ambassador was instructed to inform the German Chancellor about the offer and make clear to him how easily the British could use it as a propaganda coup. If this offer became public many Austrians would hope for a quick peace. If the offer was, however, not even seriously discussed it would turn the Austrian public against Germany. The German Chancellor understood this argument and encouraged the Austrians to give a positive reply. They should stress that they were not interested in a separate peace agreement but that England should comment on a general one.[147] Czernin therefore replied to Spain that Vienna was aiming for 'an honourable peace' that would not exclude Germany.

Lady Paget never received this version. The message was changed again by King Alfonso XIII. In the final reply that reached Paget six months after her initial letter, the Spanish King now asked her for more details of the British peace proposals. This new version was due to the fact that the situation had changed again. In the meantime the French had approached Alfonso XIII and confirmed that the Entente was indeed interested in a separate peace treaty with Austria-Hungary. Alfonso thought that one should take advantage of this keenness and bargain.

Lady Paget did not know about these parallel negotiations, of course. She was surprised and relieved to receive an encouraging reply from Spain. After so many months she had almost given up hope. She now asked her son Sir Ralph and Lord Milner for advice. They encouraged her to continue the conversation and she replied to the Queen dowager in October. Her suggestion was that Emperor Karl should agree to an informal meeting.[148]

She also praised the Queen dowager for her help and made it clear that it was not safe to leave go-between work to men since they had handled good opportunities badly in the past. In her letter Lady Paget mentioned that one incident in particular had triggered her determination to play a role. From her Foreign Office contacts she had heard that in February 1917 the Austro-Hungarian ambassador Count Mensdorff had met Sir Francis Hopwood for secret negotiations. The meeting was a disaster, in Lady Paget's eyes:

> Austria has in the past year taken a step for a separate peace, which was met by us by sending somebody to meet [the Austrian envoy] on neutral ground. So badly chosen were these persons, *so ungeschickt* [clumsy], that neither would speak first and they separated without a word! It seems impossible to believe. Such a thing as this could never happen if Your Majesty and Your august son would take Austria's cause and that of peace in hand and the meeting could take place under Your Majesties' influence.... I must now implore Your Majesty to trust your intuition, as I trust in your greatness of heart.[149]

Lady Paget was appealing here not only to a former member of the Habsburg dynasty, but also to a woman and mother. In her opinion it was women who had to keep families together in times of war. The idea that they should work together to end wars dated back to Aristophanes' play *Lysistrata*. Of course Lady Paget could hardly mention to a devout Catholic like the Queen dowager of Spain a risqué Greek play in which women withheld sexual privileges to force their men to end war. Yet she could appeal to 'sentiments'. She also wanted to emphasize how important it was to save Austria-Hungary before the Central Powers collapsed: 'England is now in a far stronger position than she ever was and feels sure of victory, and with the American millions to help and their thousands of aeroplanes which will be ruthlessly used, few doubt that a peace will be signed in Berlin.'[150]

For this letter, however, Lady Paget had to use the postal route. It was obvious that her work was no longer supported by people inside the Foreign Office.[151]

The reason why she was dropped seems to have been that other channels had become available and one did not want wires crossed. What was more decisive was the hope of getting an even better peace settlement, including Germany.

Lady Paget was now dropped in a highly hypocritical way. The permanent undersecretary of foreign affairs Lord Charles Hardinge of Penshurst got involved. He claimed that Lady Paget's second letter to the Queen dowager of Spain had been stopped by censors and landed on his desk. He pretended to be shocked by it. This seems odd because the Paget mission could not have been a surprise to him. Hardinge's cousin was the ambassador to Spain Sir Arthur Hardinge. Sir Arthur had helped Lady Paget from the beginning and he was rumoured to be well informed about intelligence networks in and around Spain. It would have been very odd if he had not informed his cousin and superior about such an important overture. Whatever his reasons the permanent undersecretary claimed to be outraged about the whole affair. He now reprimanded Lady Paget's son for supporting her work and ordered her to write to the Queen dowager of Spain that the 'present moment is not opportune'.[152]

He also claimed that the Foreign Office had no desire to talk to the enemy. This of course was not true and shows that Hardinge just wanted to shut down this channel while other talks were in full swing.

Everyone now deserted Lady Paget, and her son feared for his career. It was known that on her instructions he had visited Lord Milner asking for advice. In fact it is very likely that Paget had supported his mother's work from the start. If she had been successful it would also have given him a career boost. Instead it had almost ended his career and Sir Ralph even offered his resignation. Hardinge did not accept it. That he knew of go-between missions in general became obvious, however:

> we have had considerable experience of unofficial action in these matters and it generally contains an element of danger, however sound the motive.[153]

Lady Paget's mission had not been misguided, though. She had been a good choice and had done well. The ease with which she had made contact with Czernin and the Emperor remains impressive. Furthermore her mission triggered other missions.

What the Paget case also illustrates is that she had read the signs correctly. The Austrian side was yearning for peace and hoped the Pope's peace plan in August 1917 might be successful. On 9 October 1917 *The Times* published a speech that Prince Liechtenstein, a member of the Austro-Hungarian upper house, had given:

> A Vienna telegram says that an impressive peace demonstration by the Christian Social party took place yesterday in Vienna, at which many thousands of people were present. Prince Liechtenstein said 'we have come together to express our heartfelt thanks to the Pope and the Emperor. We want a peace by agreement, general disarmament, and arbitration.'[154]

The year 1917 was a decisive one in world history and it was also a decisive year for go-betweens. Never before had so many of them been so busy. For the chess players amongst the politicians the board seemed suddenly to offer new combinations. With Russia imploding and America getting involved in the war, every nation reconsidered its next moves. It seemed an ideal time for peace missions and from the Pope downwards many illustrious players got involved. Yet in the end their efforts came to nothing.

All Austro-Hungarian peace feelers were hindered by their German ally. A similar picture emerges from the Anglo-French relationship—allies blocked each other. As Winston Churchill so aptly put it: 'there is only one thing worse than fighting with allies, and that is fighting without them.'

The work for a peace agreement was also blocked by emotions. After making enormous sacrifices, governments were simply scared of offering their people a peace without victory. Good money was thrown after bad. Rather than writing off the losses and coming to a quick peace deal, more senseless deaths were accepted.

The First World War had been a frustrating experience for go-betweens. Apart from General Paget's mission to Romania, all other go-betweens had failed. Worse, the very method had been discredited by the Sixtus mission. Go-betweens were now seen as traitors.

Ghost missions

The angry reactions to the Sixtus affair illustrate that by the spring of 1918 deference to the ruling classes was in steep decline. The longer the war and the higher the death toll, the more intense the search for culprits had become. Somebody had to be made responsible. Apart from the enemy, hatred was also directed towards the 'corrupt' ruling classes.

Since 1914 the suspicion about 'aristocratic hybrids' had never gone away. The upper classes with their 'international friends' and 'loose morals' remained a target. Even in Britain where deference towards the establishment had been fairly strong, the Sixtus affair triggered rumours about dangerous go-between missions. That people thought such missions were undertaken against the national interest illustrates the level of distrust. Secret diplomacy and its methods were now discussed and seen as one factor responsible for the war going wrong. In this climate of suspicion, even an imagined mission could become political dynamite.

An example for such a ghost mission in Britain involved Alice Keppel, the former mistress of Edward VII. It is interesting to look at this case, because it illustrates the fact that as a reaction to years of war propaganda and censorship, conspiracy theories had sprung up everywhere. At a time when there was no proper information available, it was simply made up.

Shortly after the Sixtus letter had become public, in May and June 1918 a bizarre court case took place in London.[155] Ostensibly it was about the lost honour of an erotic dancer, but the real targets were prime ministers, peers, and London society.[156] The case was initiated by a man who had the charisma of a 'great' leader. Noel Pemberton Billing was in some ways a forerunner of Oswald Mosley and could, if he had handled his case better, have developed into a leading member of the radical right. He was an eloquent speaker, good looking, energetic, and equipped with an intuitive understanding of the prejudices of the average Englishman. He had been an actor, journalist, and inventor before he turned to politics in 1916.

As an independent MP for East Hertfordshire, he fought for a stronger air force (he built aeroplanes himself). Other items on his agenda included the fight against 'a German-Jewish infiltration' and 'sodomites', i.e. homosexuals, who were in his opinion soiling British society. Billing was an ardent opponent of Prime Minister David Lloyd George. Like many others on the radical right, he feared that Lloyd George could make a compromise peace with the Germans. Billing therefore fought in Parliament against a 'Peace without victory'—demanding the total surrender of the Central Powers. In Pemberton Billing's eyes, even thinking of negotiations with the enemy bordered on treason.

According to his theory, such treason had already been committed by many members of the British upper classes. He believed there existed a secret society, the Unseen Hand, run from Berlin with the sole aim of undermining British institutions. High ranking members of these institutions had been recruited secretly by the Germans and Billing had identified two reasons for their treachery—first of all their 'mixed blood' and secondly their 'perverse' love life for which they were being blackmailed.

In 1918 Pemberton Billing found a chance to give publicity to his theory.

Apart from building aeroplanes and being an MP, Billing also published a little newspaper called the *Imperialist*—a mixture of anti-German, anti-Semitic, and anti-Catholic ideas. In January 1918 he ran an article in which he claimed that a German prince was in the possession of a secret black book with the names of 47,000 British men and women. Among them were cabinet ministers, diplomats, newspaper proprietors, authors, and courtiers. All these people had been blackmailed because of their sexual preferences. Since 1914 they had been working as German agents. Billing's source for this story was a Captain Harold Sherwood Spencer, an American who claimed that he had seen the black book himself. Sherwood Spencer had become a friend of Billing and shared his politics wholeheartedly.

Nobody read the *Imperialist* and the article therefore had no effect. Naturally Pemberton Billing was disappointed, yet he did not give up. At the time he was also running a small, radical right wing group called the Vigilantes and he now changed the name of his newspaper into *Vigilante*. In it he published an even more sensational piece, which finally got attention. Under the headline 'The Cult of the Clitoris' he announced that a deeply amoral dance spectacle was about to be performed in London, based on Oscar Wilde's play *Salome*. The title role would be played by the dancer Maud Allen, a woman with a dark secret.

Maud Allen had performed her version of *Salome* in Britain before the war and Edward VII had attended one of her performances. She was famous for her voluptuous body and lack of costume. It was also rumoured that she had had an affair with Margot Asquith, the wife of the former Prime Minister. (Billing would later publish a poem written by Lord Alfred Douglas which referred to Lady Asquith as 'merry Margot, bound With Lesbian fillets'.[157] The *Vigilante* also accused wives of Cabinet ministers of lesbianism.[158])

For Pemberton Billing, Allen was the ideal target. He could not call her a lesbian in print, though. Instead he chose what was, in his eyes, a medical description by calling her sexual orientation the 'cult of the clitoris'. His sensational article went on to say that if Scotland Yard wanted to find out the names of the British traitors listed in the black book, they should simply attend one of the private performances of Maud Allen and take a close look at the audience.

It took Allen and her producer Jack Grein some time to find out what the 'black book' was actually referring to. Once they had realized it, they decided to sue Pemberton Billing for libel.

To this day libel laws in Britain are extremely strict. Pemberton Billing therefore had to prove (a) that Maud Allen was a lesbian and (b) that a black book listing British traitors actually existed. He decided against hiring a lawyer and represented himself—though behind the scenes his anonymous supporters probably paid for legal advice. Apart from being a self-publicist, his main aim was to use the court case to attack the establishment. Over the following weeks this was allowed up to a point, but stopped abruptly when Billing claimed he could uncover a British go-between mission.

First of all Billing did his best to ruin the reputation of Maud Allen and her director Jack Grein. Grein was a Dutch Jew, a naturalized alien, who before 1914 had received a German decoration for his cultural work. People who had had connections with enemy countries before the war were natural suspects and Billing succeeded in insinuating that Grein was in the pay of the Germans. He was also highly successful in 'exposing' Maud Allen's past. This wasn't so difficult since she had a rather unusual family background. Originally a Canadian, her family had moved to America, where her mad brother had been executed for murder. Despite the scandal, Maud Allen had managed to reinvent herself and become celebrated for her unusual dances all over Europe and America. Her close friendships with society ladies, however, seemed to be of an 'improper nature'. This insinuation was shocking enough for the audience at the Old Bailey. But Pemberton Billing also managed to persuade his listeners that Grein and Allen had chosen to perform *Salome* for one particular reason—to corrupt the British public. The play, he argued, was highly subversive and immoral, written by the infamous sodomite Wilde. To prove this point Pemberton Billing even managed to call Oscar Wilde's former lover Lord Alfred Douglas (Bosie) into the witness box.

Bosie had been a literature groupie when he first met Wilde in 1891. Within four years the fan had thoroughly ruined the author's life in an *amour fatale*. Wilde died in 1900 in poverty. In the meantime Bosie had conveniently broken with his homosexual past. As Billing's star witness he enthusiastically confirmed that *Salome* had been written by Wilde to corrupt his audience and was littered with 'sodomite' references.

Thanks to Bosie, Billing had succeeded in giving the impression that a Sodom and Gomorrah gang of artists was trying to undermine the war effort. Bosie also confirmed that Wilde's work had been influenced by German literature on sodomites. The German link was useful for Pemberton Billing's general argument. He himself had a wife of German descent, something he successfully tried to hide during the court case. He was on firmer ground, though, when it came to his sexual orientation. Being an ardent heterosexual, Billing was naturally immune to blackmail by the enemies of Britain—or so his admirers thought. But this was not entirely true. One of

Billing's next star witnesses was Eileen Villiers-Stuart, a lady with whom he was having an extramarital affair. Villiers-Stuart was a *femme savante* with an impressive network of male friends. Though from a humble background she had become a 'companion' of politicians and high ranking members of the military. How much she was paid for her companionship was unknown. It was also unknown whether she had been sent to Billing as an agent provocatrice as she later claimed. According to her story she was so impressed by the rectitude of his crusade that she switched sides. Whether lapsed agent provocatrice or not, one thing was for sure, though: she started an affair with Billing and lied for him in court.

Her acting qualities were certainly impressive. Cross-examined by Billing she stated that her friend Neil Primrose had shown her and another friend, Major Evelyn Rothschild, the black book. Unfortunately both men had been later killed in action and could not verify this story. According to Villiers-Stuart, Primrose had not fallen in battle, but had been murdered because he knew too much. Billing now wanted to know the names listed in the black book. That day the judge had already called him to order several times and an angry Billing now demanded to hear all the names. It was an impressive show, and Villiers-Stuart, played her part brilliantly. She dramatically 'revealed' the shocking truth—that apart from the Asquiths, Lord Haldane, and Jack Grein, the judge's name was also listed in the book. This stunned the judge into silence.

It was now left to Maud Allen's lawyer Ellis Hume-Williams to try to undermine this bizarre story. If Primrose, who was a politician after all, had been in possession of this book why had he not done something about it? Villiers-Stuart said that he had planned to reveal all after the war. However, she had been more courageous and told several high ranking people about it. Among these people had been Hume-Williams himself. She reminded him that they had met at a 'tea party' and he had listened to her 'intently'. This was another unexpected twist. It turned out that Villiers-Stuart and Hume-Williams knew each other. It was quite an embarrassing moment for the lawyer and he handled it badly. They were probably more than superficial acquaintances from a 'tea party' and Hume-Williams rightly recognized that she was making a subtle threat. From then on he gave up questioning her story.

Other people had less to lose. At first members of the upper classes had made jokes about the trial. The Earl of Albermarle had quipped: 'Who is that Greek Clitoris? I haven't been introduced.' Not everyone thought Billing and his witnesses funny though. The former Prime Minister Lord

Rosebery was outraged about the case. He was the father of the deceased Neil Primrose and feared his family's reputation had been damaged. That his son should have been in possession of such a book was an insult to his memory. After Lord Rosebery exerted political pressure, the War Cabinet discussed the trial on 4 June. It was debated whether the press articles on the case should be censored. Also the idea of establishing an inquiry was discussed and dropped. The Home Secretary argued that they should not interfere while the case was ongoing. He was in the possession of reports from plain clothes policemen who had attended meetings of Billing's Vigilante group as early as March 1918. The upshot seemed to be that this was an anti-Semitic group whose members suffered from paranoid tendencies. In fact one group member who was suffering from paranoia was Captain Spencer.

He was Billing's next star witness. Spencer stated he had definitely seen the black book. At the beginning of 1914 he had been adjutant to the King of Albania, the German Prince Wilhelm zu Wied. Among many secret papers he had come across the black book and had reported it to the British authorities. However, they had not taken any interest in the case.

Like Villiers-Stuart, Spencer also 'remembered' the names of several German agents: Lord Haldane, the Asquiths, and Alice Keppel, the former mistress of King Edward VII. The last name was a new revelation. According to Spencer, Keppel had been involved in secret negotiations with the Germans. Her contact was none other than the German Foreign Secretary Kühlmann whom she had met in the Netherlands.

The mentioning of Alice Keppel's name had the desired effect. Especially to well-informed circles this story must have sounded highly plausible. Keppel had the experience and the opportunity to carry out such a mission.

Up to Edward VII's death in 1911 Alice Keppel had been one of the best-connected ladies in London. She had accumulated ample experience of behind the scenes work, sorting out 'misunderstandings' between the Foreign Office and the King. Lord Hardinge of Penhurst, though he had terminated Lady Paget's aforementioned go-between mission, had been an admirer of Mrs Keppel's work:

> I was able, through her, to advise the king with a view to the policy of Government being accepted... It would have been difficult to have found any other lady who would have filled the part of friend to King Edward with the same loyalty and discretion.[159]

Discretion was vital to her position and she was upset when people made her influence public. When Margot Asquith mentioned in her memoirs that Alice Keppel had been a political adviser to the King, Mrs Keppel was far from pleased.

Keppel was also well known for having German friends, including the German born financier Sir Ernest Cassel. He had been helpful in increasing her personal portfolio and made her wealthy. It is also true that Alice Keppel knew Germany well. She had sent her daughters to Munich before the war to learn German and she often visited the Netherlands, where her friend Daisy, Baroness de Brienen, had a castle.[160] Whether she had travelled there during the war cannot be verified. In the spring of 1916 she had been to Paris for a rather frivolous reason—to buy clothes for her daughter's birthday party. This was an odd journey to make in wartime, but whether there was more to this trip than shopping cannot be proven either.[161]

It was also true that Keppel knew the German diplomat Kühlmann, who had been posted to London from 1908 onwards. Though Kühlmann had only been the number two at the German embassy at the time, he had been highly popular in society circles and was known for his tireless work for a better Anglo-German understanding. In 1914 he had been devastated by the outbreak of war. When he was made German Foreign Secretary in August 1917, he did try to approach Britain with peace feelers. In German circles Kühlmann was seen as extremely pro-British. Wilhelm von Hohenzollern-Sigmaringen noted after a conversation with him in October 1918, 'this man is highly intelligent, but I am convinced that he is a great friend of England which might have a negative effect on our foreign policy'.[162]

Since Kühlmann had many old contacts in London and consequently many discreet channels available, it is not known whether he actually activated Alice Keppel. Kühlmann's private papers were partly destroyed in the Second World War and in his memoirs he is cautious about naming names. Therefore we do not know whether he met Alice Keppel again. In the inter-war years she continued to cultivate her German contacts, though. The celebrated novelist Virginia Woolf met her in 1932 and gave a scathing portrayal: '[she has] the extensive, jolly, brazen surface of the old courtesan... immense superficial knowledge, going off to Berlin to hear Hitler speak.'[163] By then Keppel lived in Italy and was interested in dictators.

In 1918, however, she denied any contact with Germany. Still, that Spencer and Billing knew of Kühlmann's communication with the British is surprising. It can't have been simple guesswork because they were also informed that the contacts took place via the Netherlands. Like Spain and Sweden, the neutral Netherlands were used repeatedly for secret peace feelers. The last one took place after Billing's trial, in the summer of 1918. Kühlmann then met Sir William Tyrrell (head of the Political Intelligence Department). Yet, like so many other Anglo-German peace feelers before, this came to nothing.

The explanation must therefore be that Spencer and Billing had been given insider information about secret negotiations. These insiders were probably critics of Lloyd George. By May 1918 Lloyd George was close to being ousted. The situation in France had deteriorated and the Prime Minister was made responsible for it. He expected the war to last at least until 1919 or 1920 and had therefore indeed played with the idea of peace negotiations. As a consequence he faced an intrigue by the military, under the leadership of General Maurice. It was probably Maurice's circle that fed Pemberton Billing with information. And Billing and his star witness Spencer could immediately demonstrate how the public would react to such a 'peace without victory'. There was outrage at the Old Bailey when Spencer claimed that the upper classes were making secret deals with the enemy and that one of the go-betweens for such a deal was Alice Keppel.[164]

But was she really a go-between? Conspiracy theories can only work when they include a certain degree of plausibility. And Alice Keppel was a very plausible go-between. She was close to members of the Foreign Office and could offer them private channels abroad. She had experience in sorting out 'misunderstandings'. She had the opportunity and legitimate reasons to travel to France (where she 'helped' run a hospital) and the Netherlands at a time when travelling was difficult. But since Pemberton Billing could not actually prove that she had done anything like that, she remained a ghost go-between.

In fact it would have been very risky for Mrs Keppel to be involved in such a go-between mission. Hatred of Germany was strong in Britain and to be seen as pro-German could make one a complete social outcast.

Mrs Keppel therefore reacted forcefully. Her lawyer contacted the judge in the Billing trial. Mrs Keppel was willing to swear under oath that she had not been to Holland since the outbreak of war. The judge dismissed this by stating that she and other people who had been mentioned during the trial had to endure similar allegations; after all he himself was also supposed to be in the black book.

In his completely irrelevant closing statement, Billing won over the jury. He stressed again that mysterious influences were undermining the war effort. If his allegations were wrong, why had nobody brought in witnesses to prove him wrong? The truth was that German Jews were protected while honest Englishmen lost everything. The judge completely failed to give the jury useful instructions. He was either intimidated about being seen as biased or he had made a deal with the authorities to let Billing walk free. To the public's great satisfaction that was exactly what happened. Maud Allen lost her case. Noel Pemberton Billing triumphantly left the court room with his wife and Mrs Villiers-Stuart. The cheers of his supporters were deafening.

Not everyone felt jubilant. Cynthia Asquith, daughter-in-law of former Prime Minister Asquith, who had been vilified by Billing, wrote in her diary: 'Papa came in and announced that the monster maniac Billing had won his case. Damn him! It is such an awful triumph for the unreasonable, such a tonic to the microbe of suspicion which is spreading through the country.'[165]

The British establishment was well aware of the potential dangers this court case exposed. The novelist Hugh Walpole, who had had first hand experience of the Russian Revolution as head of the Anglo-Russian Propaganda Bureau, saw Billing's aquittal as the beginning of 'an English revolution'.

It might have been, if the war had been lost. Yet Billing's popularity subsided once the news from the front improved. Furthermore his demands that foreigners should wear signs on their clothes so they could be identified seemed 'slightly' over the top. Also his subsequent idea that people with a German parent should be imprisoned seemed not to go down well either. After all, members of the royal family would have ended up behind bars.

It was in the aftermath of the trial that the government took its revenge on Billing. The authorities now revealed a few facts about him (e.g. that his wife was of German descent). They also exposed his star witness and mistress. It turned out that Eileen Villiers-Stuart's first husband had not died at the front (as she had hoped and claimed) but was still alive driving an ambulance, which made her a bigamist. Faced with a long prison sentence she admitted that she had lied during the trial. It was also revealed that the other star witness, Captain Spencer, had been kicked out of the army for his repeated attacks of paranoia. As a result Billing did not become a leader of the radical right and was not the new Oswald Mosley. Instead he concentrated once more on his aeroplanes.

Today it seems obvious that Billing used two classical ingredients of conspiracy theories: he identified first the 'enemy within' the nation, the sodomites who had wormed their way to the top. He then merged this with the idea of an 'enemy above', the upper classes.[166] Together this mixture was irresistible.

Detecting potential go-betweens, he certainly had come close to the truth. His court case and the scandal of the Sixtus letter had made the method of go-between missions public. People on both sides of the trenches were outraged that such figures existed at all and that they belonged to the upper echelons of society.

Now a different age had dawned. President Wilson promised a new diplomacy and new transparency in international relations. It would become a pious wish. The appearance of a common enemy changed everything again. Communism would give go-betweens a new lease of life.

3

Bolshevism

The Fear that Binds

In October 1941, four months after the German invasion of Russia, King Gustav V of Sweden wrote a letter to Hitler congratulating him for 'getting rid of the Bolshevik pest'.[1] Gustav V's feelings were common among his peer group. They would be one reason why aristocratic go-betweens became active again in the inter-war years.

The new enemy appeared on the European stage in 1917. Prince Ernst von Hohenlohe-Langenburg was one of the first German aristocrats who encountered real life Bolsheviks. In January 1918 he attended the German–Russian ceasefire talks at Brest Litovsk as an unofficial observer. Since Hohenlohe was not part of the negotiating team he had time to study his Russian counterparts. What he saw scared him. In a letter to his aunt the Grand Duchess Luise von Baden he reflected:

> the composition of this delegation made a shattering impression, if one considers that these anarchists are the official representatives of the formerly powerful Russian Empire: their leader is a Jewish doctor who has abandoned his profession to became a politician, then there is a journalist, brother in law of the so often mentioned Trotsky, then a factory worker, a peasant, common soldiers and sailors, and then a woman who had been in prison in Siberia for political murder. Working as military advisers for this bunch and without a voting voice are officers. Their bleak mood was obvious.

One of them, General Skalon, set next to Hohenlohe during dinner one night and shot himself two hours later. This was not due to Hohenlohe's lack of conversational skills. At least Hohenlohe believed the reason was something very different. The general felt deep shame about the new Russia: '[Skalon] could not bear this situation and shot himself out of despair. We had a very dignified funeral which was attended by all the German officers in Brest Litovsk and which seemed to impress the Russian delegation. Between us and the Russian officers a friendly cameraderie developed.'[2]

One can imagine what the rest of the Russian delegation thought about such fraternization between officers.

Despite the German diplomatic successes at Brest Litovsk, Hohenlohe was well aware that he had been given a glimpse of Russia's future and what he saw alarmed him. He also realized that this revolutionary spirit could easily spread. While he was at Brest Litovsk, strikes had broken out in Germany. The knock on effect seemed to have started:

> At the negotiations here it is obvious that the Russians have great hopes for a revolution in Germany. . . . Trotsky is only peripherally interested in the peace, what he really cares about is giving speeches with revolutionary propaganda. With great skill he has managed to drag out the negotiations.[3]

Trotsky had every reason to do so. He was determined that world revolution would wipe away capitalist states. A year later he made an announcement that confirmed Hohenlohe's worst fears:

> From provincial Moscow, from half-Asiatic Russia, we will embark on the expansive route of European revolution. It will lead us to a world revolution. Remember the millions of the German petite bourgeoisie, awaiting the moment for revenge. In them we will find a reserve army and bring up our cavalry with this army to the Rhine to advance further in the form of a revolutionary proletarian war.[4]

The aim of bringing about such a revolution was maintained by the Soviet Union until 1923.

Hohenlohe had sensed the infectious potential of the Bolshevik movement. But he had always been one of the more perceptive members of the aristocracy. Others would take longer to realize what was happening. Shortly after the revolution had broken out, even Russian aristocrats were not as alarmed as one might assume. When the Tsar abdicated on 2 March 1917, genuine relief was felt among large sections of the Russian nobility. The Tsar and his wife had been unpopular and according to Princess Cantacuzene the news was greeted with 'a thankfulness that was almost religious'. The Russian Baroness Meiendorff agreed: 'the old system was rotten, everyone knew that.'[5] The majority of the German aristocrats shared this naive reaction. Margarete von Hessen-Kassel, who was related to the Tsarina, wrote on 24 March 1917: 'The situation in Russia is confusing. Perhaps something good will come of it and bring peace quicker. I am sorry for the Tsar and Tsarina, and it is horrible that nobody intervenes and they are left to their own fate.

I hope they will be spared. They are such kind, lovely people, however, too weak and completely unsuited to their position.'[6]

Since imperial Russia was Germany's enemy, from a patriotic point of view German aristocrats had every reason to hope for the country's descent into chaos. From a monarchical point of view the arrest of the Tsar was, however, a disaster. Prince Löwenstein summed up the dilemma when he wrote in the early stages of the revolution, in May 1917:

> what one hears from Russia is encouraging—as regards our foreign policy. Regarding our domestic policy I cannot think of anything more dangerous than this harmless revolution which has occurred so far. To depose a monarchy, redistribute property and put oneself at the top, is very tempting. But if during this game a great nation goes to pieces, order and security is drenched in blood, this example must lose its advertising appeal.[7]

The monarchical principle in which Löwenstein believed seemed fragile enough. For this reason he warned that Germany should not take revenge on another country that was in disarray at the time—Romania. To oust the Romanian royal family would be a disaster: 'Today, more than ever, monarchs should not topple other monarchs, even if they truly deserve it.'[8]

By early 1918 Romania was indeed sandwiched between German and Russian Bolshevik propaganda. Marie of Romania was well aware of this: 'The great danger is that Bolshevism, which surrounds us on every side, might also gain our country. The Germans, on the occupied side, are doing all they can to spread it. It is the chief danger.'[9] The situation did not improve after the war: 'Under the leadership of Bela Kun, Hungary had turned Bolshevik, voting for Russia and communism. A wave of revolution was sweeping the country: Towns and properties had been ramsacked, and intentions towards Romania were anything but peaceful. As Hungary was our next-door neighbour this could mean great trouble and danger for us.'[10]

Aristocratic women in particular informed each other via their networks about the imminent danger of Bolshevism. After the peace treaty between Soviet Russia and Germany was signed in March 1918, both countries were officially on friendly terms. Yet when the German ambassador Count Mirbach was killed by the revolutionaries in Moscow in the summer of 1918, Princess Löwenstein lost all restraint:

> I have known him [Mirbach] all my life and he was always so nice and family oriented.... These beasts in Russia, it is not possible for civilised people to live in this cave of bandits. That's what one gets when one works with the canaille.[11]

A few days later the Tsar and his family were murdered. Princess Löwenstein found it beyond belief that even the German conservative press seemed to: 'play this down, since our intimate new friends the Bolsheviks have killed him. How disgusting I find the friendship with these pigs! One day this will exact vengeance.'[12]

Many German aristocrats were now becoming very uncomfortable with the fact that a monarchy like Germany had to be on friendly terms with Bolshevik Russia. This seemed to go against the grain. Princess Oettingen-Spielberg hated the idea: 'I find the Russian envoys very dangerous. Lots of anarchists who spread their Bolshevik ideas all over Germany.'[13]

To Löwenstein and Oettingen it now seemed highly dangerous that Germany's policy had been to encourage Bolshevism in Russia and other enemy countries in order to win the war. Rather like the sorcerer's apprentice in Goethe's famous poem, they feared that the 'Spirits that I've cited || My commands ignore.'

That the Löwensteins and Oettingen-Spielbergs had spotted revolutionary dangers earlier than the rest of the German population also had something to do with their close links to Austrian aristocrats. In Vienna strikes had started much earlier. Austrian aristocrats had already given their German relatives graphic descriptions of what was going on in the Habsburg Empire. The go-between Prince Fürstenberg was the best informed and the most concerned one. He wrote in early 1918 from Vienna:

> We are in the middle of a serious strike which was triggered by a revolutionary appeal from the workers' council. Everyone thinks that agents of the Bolsheviks are behind it. Of course our government is weak. One could despair.... It feels as if one is at the beginning of a revolution. At least we can see all the symptoms which usually appear in uprisings of this kind. Added to that is the lack of food.... I would like to write more, but I dare not.[14]

It was also the Austrian network that brought news about the collapse of Germany's ally Bulgaria. The Bulgarian King Ferdinand, a member of the House of Coburg, had abdicated a month before the war ended and fled to Coburg. In the German press Ferdinand was portrayed as a man bound by honour but Princess Löwenstein, a member of the Austrian and German network, knew the true circumstances. To her husband she wrote:

> The newspaper is in tears about the 'nobleness' of Ferdinand of Bulgaria who sacrificed his throne rather than be disloyal to Germany. Yet in fact...Franzi Auersperg said the whole Austrian embassy had to flee Sofia, not because of the Entente Powers,

but because of the Bulgarian Bolsheviks who rule the whole city, pillaging and plundering. I therefore think the 'magnanimous' Ferdinand just wanted to save his skin![15]

When the revolution finally reached Germany in November 1918, aristocrats had had plenty of warning. Still, the extent of the attack surprised them. Lower nobles only had to cope with unruly tenants in the German countryside, but the grander families had a wider experience. They encountered Bolshevism on three different fronts: on their country estates, in cities, and on their widespread properties in Hungary, Poland, and Czechoslovakia: 'the landowning aristocracy became the second prominent target (after the Habsburgs themselves) of the revolution. Land reform would be the first major step in a thirty year upheaval that would utterly change the social and national landscape of Czechoslovakia.'[16]

Max Egon Fürstenberg was one of its victims:

The Czechs have put me as a German leader and German friend of the Kaiser at the top of the black list, my property has been sequestered and I am forbidden to set foot on it.[17]

However, his former employees continued to inform him what was going on in his castle Lany and Fürstenberg passed this on to his exiled friend Kaiser Wilhelm:

President Masaryk has moved into my old castle as his summer residence. Since the Castle wasn't *elegant* enough for him [Masaryk's mother had been a cook], it had to be renovated for 10 million Krona. Three electric lifts were put in,...wooden floors and marble, since the daughter of the President declared she could only walk on marble and wood. President Hainisch of Austria is going to come and visit Masaryk there to hunt in my old hunting grounds. Nice! I am not taking these things to heart but look at them the way one would look at a play by Sudermann. The more upset one gets the more it affects one's health and it doesn't help anyway. And if this bunch knew it they would only get more pleasure out of it.... I just hope that one day a deluge of acid rain will pour on them and kill the whole gang off.[18]

Hitler would eventually offer Fürstenberg a gift of such acid rain.

Aristocratic property in Poland also caused a problem. Again Max Egon Fürstenberg wrote to Kaiser Wilhelm about this:

My cousin [Prince] Ratibor is here to recover from his ordeal, after he and his wife were almost completely robbed [in their Silesian castle] and then humilated by Poles and the French. He told me outrageous stories. Today a letter arrived saying that his castle is now occupied by the French and all officers are accompanied by 'ladies' who are giving endless parties.[19]

Though after the Versailles Treaty the threat of disposession was actually made by republics, the aristocracy believed all this had been triggered by the Bolshevik revolution in the first place.

A direct threat certainly existed in 1918/19 in the cities, especially in Munich and Berlin where many aristocrats had their town houses. Here they were a visible target for revolutionaries. Prince Fürstenberg's half-sister Amelia, for example, experienced the revolution with her second husband Gustav Scanzoni von Lichtenfels in Munich. In 1919 Fürstenberg heard that his sister had almost been executed:

> She was taken hostage and was until the last moment, unaware what would happen. She had to spend the night in a station and was told that if this building was targeted [by the reactionary forces], she would be shot immediately.[20]

Amelia's husband seems to have taken this ordeal particularly badly and contemplated divorce. Scanzoni von Lichtenfels was a member of the lower nobility and up to 1918 it had been of great social prestige for him to be married to a lady of the higher aristocracy. Now it had become a dangerous predicament. He wrote to his brother-in-law Fürstenberg that he was not enjoying his wife's company any more: 'because of the aversion of the new rulers towards the higher aristocracy, capitalism and landowners.'[21]

Thanks to 'financial support', Scanzoni von Lichtenfels was persuaded to stay a little bit longer with Amelia.[22] The fear of a hostile environment also worried stronger characters than him. Prince Emich Leiningen stated in April 1919: 'We are facing the dictatorship of the proletariat.'[23] In his diary he wrote: 'Civil war is unavoidable.'[24] Princess Pless was of a similar opinion: 'A wave of communism had insidiously spread like poison gas over the whole country.'[25]

Ever since the right wing historian Ernst Nolte argued that the rise of communism encouraged the spread of fascism, it has been taboo to use this 'cold war' argument. When it comes to the aristocracy, however, this taboo has to be broken.

Of course, it is true that the old elites used the fear of Bolshevism as a political tool to manipulate public opinion. Kaiser Wilhelm II even hoped for a 'deluge' of Bolshevism in order to gain power again. From his Dutch exile he wrote in 1920: 'I think that soon our people will be faced with the question of whether to fight. Bolsheviks will soon overrun Poland and together with the Spartakists suppress our country. They will carry Bolshevism across the Rhine and via the channel into England. Then the Entente will have to unite with Germany. Then our time will have come!'[26]

Wilhelm both made use of and feared Bolshevism. In this he was no different from many aristocrats. The idea of a European infection of Bolshevism was a very real one to them. Understanding this fear is vital if one wants to understand why originally conservative aristocrats were radicalized and used by Hitler. Aristocrats as well as dynasties had feared socialism before 1917, but Bolshevism significantly increased the threat level. Now it became the new danger to their way of life.

Of course, focusing on the danger of Bolshevism was also convenient. Aristocrats were not eager to reflect much on their own failures during the war. Shortly after 1918 there had been a few honest moments. Prince Castell-Castell wrote to his wife: 'we have disgraced ourselves. And why? Whose fault is it? These questions are difficult to answer.'[27]

He never found the time to answer them. In the end Bolshevism was blamed and overshadowed everything. Hohenlohe thought of it as a disease. To Grand Duchess Luise von Baden he wrote that Germany was now 'infected by a serious illness, experiencing feverish phantasies and one wonders whether the heart of the patient is strong enough to survive the fever'.[28]

Hohenlohe felt particularly knowledgeable because he was close to the victims of the revolution, Russian émigrés. He spent a lot of time in Coburg which after 1918 had filled up with aristocratic asylum seekers. The most prominent one was Ferdinand, the former Tsar of Bulgaria. There were also many surviving members of the Romanov family. One of them was Grand Duke Kirill, married to Marie of Romania's sister Victoria (Ducky). Both women had been resolutely anti-German, but by 1918 'Ducky' had become so desperate that she turned to Germany for help. Her sister the Queen of Romania was disgusted:

> [Ducky's] spirit is so broken that even the Germans begin to be looked upon as saviours, so ghastly is their situation in the land of the Bolsheviks. Poor, poor Ducky, when I think of how she felt about our mutual enemy the last time she was here! And never shall I know all the details of their suffering, their fear, their horror.[29]

'Ducky' had fled with her family to Finland first, where Ernst Hohenlohe visited her in 1918. He was shocked by how much she had aged and tried to persuade her to come to Germany. Ducky refused. She wanted to stay in Finland as long as possible in the hope that her husband Kirill would be called back to Russia as the new Czar. Prince H. Reuss XXXIII thought this was quite feasible. He wrote in June 1918 to Ernst Hohenlohe that:

> Kirill should be the future Tsar since he has always been the head of the moderate, the blonde party named after your sister-in-law's hair colour [Ducky's] and in contrast to the black party of Nicholas and his Montenegrin wife who have always agitated.[30]

The blonde faction naturally agreed, but eventually had to give up on a quick return to Russia. In 1920 'Ducky' and Kirill moved to Coburg and continued to fight for their 'rights'. Despite all assurances to the contrary Ducky was the driving force, ambitiously working for her husband's return. To her sister Alexandra Hohenlohe she wrote:

> Of course you have seen in the papers that Kirill issued a manifesto to our people that he is henceforth adopting his title of Emperor giving his full reasons for this step. You know that it was being forced upon him and all he went through. He was being pressed from all sides, whilst his heart and soul revolted against the definite step which would rob us once and for all of our quiet and peace of mind. Well, now it is done and in many ways he has already been amply rewarded by the worldwide approval he has received. Especially in Germany except for Parliament which sent an official [a Regierungspräsident] to ask Kirill to sign no more manifestos on German soil, which is quite comprehensible. Curiously enough we are receiving endless congratulations from the lower classes, workers, middle class people etc. and from foreign countries. Our own imperial family seems at last to be uniting around Kirill...The English papers were decidedly favourable.[31]

With this step Victoria made her family a prime target for the Soviet intelligence services. In fact the Bolsheviks took the threat of Russian monarchists and White Russians extremely seriously. They had every reason to. Two million Russian emigrants fled between 1918 and 1922, telling stories of persecution. They went first to Czechoslovakia and Poland and later to Germany, France, and Britain. Among the aristocratic White Russians were many with famous German-Russian names, like Baron Pytor Nikolaevich Wrangel, who celebrated the death of every murdered Bolshevik, or Roman Fyodorovich von Ungern-Sternberg (pet name the 'Red Baron'), who embarked on a revenge campaign after his wife was raped and killed by Bolsheviks.[32]

The Russian nobles who got out, though poor, were listened to and not ostracized socially. Marriages with them continued after 1918. The 6th Prince Leiningen, for example, married in 1925 Maria Grand Duchess of Russia, and their son was christened—following the German and Russian family tradition—Emich Kirill.

In fact the power of the powerless should not be underestimated: 'White Russians were fashionable, Eastern European princesses were fashionable.'[33] Russian emigrants appeared as a portent to their worried hosts. They told stories about the revolution ad nauseam which had their effect: 'Romanovs did feel that they possessed a certain expertise on revolutions, an expertise that they were all too ready to share with royalty in Copenhagen, Windsor, and Madrid.' Whenever there was a postwar strike, White Russians seemed to say: 'Ah yes, I've seen this before. Your turn, affectionate cousins, is only a matter of time.'[34]

They certainly did not forgive or forget. Many saw it as their aim in life to overthrow the Soviet regime. As Jonathan Haslam has shown, the Soviet Intelligence services spent considerable time and effort in fooling White Russian groups.[35] The Cheka (later OGPU) turned out to be especially creative. They were well aware of the fact that aristocratic networks were held together by family ties and mutual *trust*. It was therefore with some irony that they invented an organization called 'The Trust', which pretended to be a monarchist group. It was so cleverly organized that many White Russians invested money in The Trust, not knowing that they were financing their own enemies.[36]

Ducky and her husband fell for this and eventually also came into close contact with fascist groups. Ducky became interested in the NSDAP and the attraction was mutual. She was invited to attend a Nazi Rally in 1922 and met Hitler in October 1923, shortly before his failed coup.

As will be shown later, in the houses related to Russian aristocrats, the tendency to support fascism was more common than anywhere else. The Anglo-German houses of Coburg, Hesse, Leiningen, and Hohenlohe were all related to the Russian pretender to the throne—all four supported Nazism. Hitler's strongest supporter would be the Duke of Coburg.

It was of course logical for former ruling houses and aristocrats on the Continent to be scared of Bolshevism since they had first hand experience. But they were also good in passing this experience on. This was made possible because the communication channels had only been interrupted, not broken off, by the war.

At the top end, dynastic communication channels were up and running almost immediately (albeit clandestinely). In November 1918, two days after the armistice, a British officer visited the Grand Duke of Hesse in Darmstadt. He told the Duke that he had been sent by George V and Queen Mary who wanted to say how glad they were to be in contact again, and that their feelings for Hesse had not suffered because of the war. According to Hesse, George V always remained the same towards him, the most 'verwandtschaftliche' (family oriented) human being.

The Grand Duke also claimed that George had been genuinely upset when Hesse had lost the Garter during the war: 'He wanted me to keep it, but it was impossible, because at the beginning of the war, the Duke of Coburg gave it up first and then the Kaiser.'[37] It was surprising how accepting Hesse was of such transparent assurances. He probably did not know at the time that 'family oriented George' had been responsible for denying the Tsar refuge in England (instead the decision was blamed on Prime Minister Lloyd George). It might indeed have upset Hesse to know the truth—the murdered Tsarina Alexandra was after all his sister.

Another person who could have had grievances about the British royal family also put them aside to make contact again. The mother of the Queen of Romania, Marie Alexandrovna, dowager Duchess of Coburg, had spent the war in Germany. Many of her Russian relatives had been killed and her considerable income from Russia terminated. She now feared that Germany would be the next country to fall into Bolshevik hands. After the Versailles Treaty of 1919 she appealed to her British in-laws. Together with her son-in-law Prince Ernst Hohenlohe she wrote a long letter to King George V:

> Having lived in Germany during the time of war and subsequent revolution, I think it my duty to send you a few words, showing my personal impressions about the really desperate state of affairs.
>
> As to Germany's military strength, anybody who has been here in the last months, cannot understand how the German army can be considered as still representing a danger to any other country. The troops, on their return from the front, immediately became infected by bolshevik ideas and lost all discipline. If you had seen the men as I saw them, you would be convinced that the formerly formidable German army has ceased to exist. The volunteer regiments formed by the new government last winter are barely sufficient to suppress the serious riots in many large towns. From what I see in extracts from English and French papers, I think that you cannot be aware of the state of famine prevailing in most parts of Germany, principally in the large towns, in consequence of the blockade, of the number of persons, especially women and children, who have died and are dying from want of food.... The utter ruin of finance, trade and manufactuary with which Germany is threatened by the clauses of the treaty, would inevitably reduce innumerable families to a state of poverty... Whoever may be guilty of this terrible war, it is certain, that these unfortunate people had nothing to do with it... I cannot conceive that England or any other country could profit by the starvation of innocent women and children. I have

spent so many years of my life in England and well remember the widespread respect for principles of religion and humanity. I cannot believe the English character having changed so completely, that measures should find approval, which now that Germany is defenceless, seem to represent mere unnecessary cruelty. What pursues me like a nightmare is the probability that the great mass of the German population, losing all hope for their future existence, might be driven by despair into extreme bolshevism. You probably know, that very serious disorders, under the influence of Russian bolcheviks, have occurred during the last months in many German towns. Acquaintances of mine who were in Munich during the riots in April, described to me the terrible excess committed there under the reign of the anarchists. Until now the government-troops have succeeded in gaining the upper hand. But the severe fighting which was necessary to break the resistance of the anarchists shows the desperate determination of these people and I shudder at the thought of what might happen, if in consequence of starvation and misery by which the country is threatened through the proposed terms of peace, bolshevism should spread all over Germany. Nobody can feel more intensely than I do, what that would mean. As you know Russian bolshevism has not only deprived me of what fortune I had, it has also caused the murder of my nearest and dearest relatives, the death and ruin of friends and the hopeless breakdown of my native country. The undermining of authority and order in Germany by the agency of Russian Bolsheviks proves the infectious nature of this frightful disease. If I warn you of what might become a danger to the rest of Europe, you may be sure that I am not prompted by any anti-English or pro-German feeling, but by the intense pain I have suffered through the horrible fate of my family....The suffering of innocent people, which I see, the pain I have gone through myself and the fear of what the future may bring, induced me to write these lines. They are not meant to contain uncalled for advice. I merely wish to beg you to use your influence, if possible, so that the Germans may be given a fair chance...that a whole nation, including women and children whatever you may think of the guilt of its former rulers, may not be driven into the last extremities of ruin and misery.[38]

Apart from emotionally blackmailing George V (she might or might not have known via her network that he had refused to help the Tsar), Marie Alexandrovna was also appealing indirectly in her letter to the higher aristocracy's long memory, their common European roots—the 'international chain of the aristocracy'. Marie Alexandrovna was not the only woman who put pressure on George V. He also had his mother, Queen Alexandra, as a constant reminder of the Bolshevik threat. In 1919 Queen Marie of Romania described Alexandra's fears: 'Alix was suffering intensely because of the long and painful separation from her favourite sister, Empress Maria (the Tsar's mother), still in a dangerously precarious situation in the Crimea, cut off from everything and surrounded by Bolshevik danger.'[39]

These anxieties had their sobering impact on the British royal family and for some of its members became one factor in their support of Germany in the 1930s. That the murders of 1917 were never forgotten can be illustrated by an episode in 1936. When Edward VIII received the Soviet foreign Commissar Litvinov on 29 January 1936 for his first audience, he kept coming back to the subject of the Tsar. Litvinov was surprised about the pace of the interview. The new King jumped from one subject to the next during the fifty minute conversation and Litvinov felt that: 'some questions were extremely delicate. Edward VIII asked why and under what circumstances Nicholas II was killed. Wasn't he killed because the revolutionaries feared his reinstatement to the throne?'

Litvinov explained that the murder occurred because the local authorities feared that Ekaterinburg would be taken by Czech forces. They also talked about foreign policy issues and the King was interested in Soviet relations with Germany and Poland. Litvinov stated that the USSR was trying to have good relations and follow a policy of peace. Edward retorted: 'Everybody wants peace, no-one wants war.' He then added that 'Germany and Italy have nothing, they are dissatisfied something has to be done to improve their lot in relation to raw materials, trade etc.'

Litvinov pointed out that Germany, Italy, and Japan were preparing for war. They were aggressor countries.[40] Edward VIII could hardly have been satisfied with this explanation. His admiration for Hitler's Germany was driven by his strong anti-Bolshevik sentiments.

The fear of Bolshevism would not leave the royal family. After the Second World War, the Duke of Edinburgh's uncle, Lord Mountbatten, developed with the Foreign Office the top secret plan 'Blue Thread'.[41] It provided that in the event of a Soviet invasion of West Germany, German relatives of the royal family would be evacuated first.[42] This plan was kept well hidden from the British public, which might not have appreciated the fact these German relatives—of whom many had been members of the Nazi party—would have received precedence over British citizens.

That the British royals were—via their vast network of relatives and friends—infected by the fear of Bolshevism made sense. Yet this fear was by no means confined only to the royal family. It also played a part further down the hierarchy, amongst the British upper classes.

The dowager Duchess of Coburg was wrong in assuming that the danger of Bolshevism had not been taken into consideration by the British at the Paris Peace Conference. In fact the British delegation had tried to use this point to make the French adopt a more conciliatory line towards Germany. For many British politicians, the Bolshevik threat was severe. As Churchill agreed in the early 1920s: 'from the days of Spartacus-Weishaupt to those of Karl Marx, and down to Trotsky (Russia), Bela Kun (Hungary), Rosa Luxemburg (Germany), and Emma Goldman (United States), this world-wide revolutionary conspiracy for the overthrow of civilization and for the reconstruction of society on the basis of arrested development, of envious malevolence, and impossible equality, has been steadily growing.'[43] For Churchill Bolshevism was closely connected with Jews:

> And the prominent, if not indeed the principal, part in the system of terrorism applied by the Extraordinary Commissions for Combating Counter-Revolution [the Cheka] has been taken by Jews, and in some notable cases by Jewesses. The same evil prominence was obtained by Jews in the brief period of terror during which Bela Kun ruled in Hungary. The same phenomenon has been presented in Germany (especially in Bavaria), so far as this madness has been allowed to prey upon the temporary prostration of the German people. Although in all these countries there are many non-Jews every whit as bad as the worst of the Jewish revolutionaries, the part played by the latter in proportion to their numbers in the population is astonishing.[44]

Britain had fought against Soviet Russia well into 1919 and would continue to see it as a threat. This threat was particularly strong in the Empire, and especially in China. Even though China was not technically part of the British Empire, it was next to India, Britain's second most important trade territory. Here from 1920 onwards the Comintern built a network aimed at the West.[45]

The Times and the right wing *Morning Post* reported in depth about the undermining of the Empire and came to the conclusion: 'Moscow...is making war on England.'[46] This opinion was shared by influential politicians. In 1920 the British Foreign Secretary Lord Curzon complained:

> [The Foreign Office] sees itself expected to enter relations with a State [the Soviet Union] which makes no secret of its intention to overthrow our institutions everywhere and to destroy our prestige and authority particularly in Asia.[47]

Even though trade relations were established, criticism grew on the right towards the weak British government which did not defend the Empire enough.[48] In the 1920s Lord Sydenham of Combe and Alan Ian Percy, the eighth Duke of Northumberland, used the House of Lords as a platform for anti-Bolshevik speeches.[49] Northumberland published *The Patriot*, a newspaper which was also anti-Semitic. The ennobled Press tycoon Lord Rothermere, who would later play an important role in a go-between mission, founded his 'United Empire' party out of similar motives.[50] His fears were directly related to his friendship with White Russians: 'Rothermere's watering-holes were filled with White Russian aristocrats who had had to flee their native land, to live out their lives as idle and discontented vagabonds in foreign climes.'[51]

Their fate seemed to Rothermere and his supporters a warning. The General Strike of 1926 increased this fear even more. To the British upper classes it seemed now evident that the working classes were being infiltrated by Moscow. The British communist party itself seemed too weak to have much impact (in the 1920s there were only two communist MPs sitting in the House of Commons). But Moscow had indirectly supported the strike, even though they denied it:

> The aid to the British miners came entirely from Soviet Trade Unions from voluntary collections by the workers, and the Government had sent no money to Great Britain from the Treasury. The Soviet Government could not be blamed for the sympathies which the toilers of the Soviet Union had manifested towards the British miners during the strike.[52]

That 'spontaneous' collections did not exist in the Soviet Union was known, and the *Manchester Guardian* quoted Churchill's attack on Moscow: 'On one thing I have not even a doubt, namely that in the struggle with communism we shall succeed in strangling it.'[53]

In 1933 Churchill changed his opinion and came to regard Hitler as the greater threat. He was in a minority. Hitler hoped to manipulate British fear of communism for his own ends. Who was better placed to help him in this endeavour than the Anglo-German Duke of Coburg—a man who hated nothing more than Bolshevism?

Battling the Bolsheviks

On 9 November 1918, Carl Eduard faced an abyss. Red flags were hoisted and the last German monarchs and reigning dukes were confronted with revolutionaries who insisted on immediate abdication. To everyone's astonishment the conservative parties did not lift a finger to rescue them. As a Bavarian politician rightly put it years later: 'those conservative politicians who now claim to be royalist, did not even offer their Munich flats as a refuge for their King and his ill wife. He had to escape in a car at night.'[54]

There was certainly nothing dignified about the last days of the German royal families.

On 1 November 1918, Carl Eduard Duke of Coburg had been, like other heads of German reigning houses, confronted with the question whether he would support the abdication of the Kaiser. Though his respect for Wilhelm II had long gone, he rejected the idea. The institution had to be propped up against all the odds—if Wilhelm II abdicated this could trigger an avalanche. Not all heads of reigning houses agreed with this interpretation. Some hoped to save their positions by sacrificing the Kaiser. However, on one thing everybody agreed: they were not willing to play the role of Brutus and break the news to Wilhelm II. It was therefore left to Chancellor Max von Baden to solve the problem. He finally decided to announce the abdication and in return would be vilified by his peer group for the rest of his life.

Once Wilhelm II had gone, he became an embarrassment, the elephant in the room. He and his eldest son, in fact the entire Hohenzollern family, were highly unpopular. Already in October 1918 the diplomat von Stumm had told Prince Hohenzollern-Sigmaringen that the Kaiser's abdication would be a 'well deserved calamity' ('ein gerechtes Unglück'). This did not seem to shock Hohenzollern-Sigmaringen much. He was related to the Prussian Hohenzollern and the Catholic Bavarian royal family and was convinced that the royal with the greatest potential was Rupprecht, the Crown Prince of Bavaria: 'he is admired as a human being and as a military leader. Everybody says that among the three Crown Princes he is the only true commander.'[55]

Despite fearing a Bolshevik future, most aristocrats therefore did not mourn the Kaiser's fall or even want a restoration. At least not a restoration of the Hohenzollern family. Yet which monarchies, if any, should be restored was never resolved (for the Catholic aristocracy the Bavarian monarchy was the strongest contender).

The Grand Duke of Hesse had especially hated the Kaiser and also condemned all the other German dynasties, arguing that his colleagues had never understood the 'pressing questions of the time'. Now, the revolution had erased their last power bases and Hesse came to the conclusion that they had left no legacy because they had been 'such zeros'.[56] Among the very few people who had some sympathy for Wilhelm II was bizarrely an old enemy of his. Marie of Romania wrote in November 1918:

Kaiser Wilhelm and the Crown Prince have abdicated! It seems impossible. Proud cousin Bill! I cannot say that I like it! No doubt it is a logical end, but I, for one, like a country to stand and fall with its ruler, its King, a father with his family. Kaiser Wilhelm tried to destroy us, but I did not want to see him destroyed. I wanted to see him beaten: yes, that I passionately desired because he wished to have this country wiped off the face of the earth.... But honestly I do not like to hear of his abdication. It hurts me somehow. Perhaps it is solidarity of the caste, because certainly there was no special love lost between us.[57]

Carl Eduard Coburg did not show any such emotions. For a long time he had been extremely close to Wilhelm II—a surrogate son in many ways. The Kaiser had dominated his life since his 15th birthday. He was brought up by him, indoctrinated by him, and even married off by him. Now Carl Eduard got rid of him. After almost twenty years of dependency it must have been a liberating experience. The Duke of Coburg discarded his former mentor like an embarrassing lover. From now on he only sent the ex-Kaiser the obligatory birthday wishes, a duty he was expected to perform as head of the House of Sachsen-Coburg und Gotha. Though he soon took up his restless travelling again, Carl Eduard visited the Kaiser only once in exile. He was too busy with the fallout from the war.

The socialist press had started to call the Duke of Coburg 'Mr. Albany' by November 1918, a reminder that he was an unwanted foreigner. The plain 'Mr' also seemed reminiscent of the King of France Louis XVI, who in 1792 had been transformed into Citoyen Louis Capet. But the people of Coburg were far from being as radical as the French. In the end the demonstration that took place on 11 November 1918 was peaceful. A thousand people marched through the city calling for the Duke's abdication. The Duke's Prime Minister Hermann Quarck handled the situation brilliantly. He won over the local Social Democratic Party (SPD) which contained a significant middle-class component and easily persuaded them that an uprising would endanger the city's beautiful cultural heritage. They agreed and the dukedom of Coburg therefore experienced a bloodless handover.

The twin duchy of Gotha was, however, in a much worse condition: here people were starving and cadaverous faces could be seen everywhere. During the war this had already led to social unrest. Gotha had always been a centre of the German Social Democratic Party (SPD) but by April 1917, a radical splinter group had been formed there: the USPD (U standing for *unabhängig*, i.e. independent). It called for strikes which had started in May 1917. Unlike the bourgeois town of Coburg, Gotha was ruled by the Workers' and Soldiers' Council (WSC). On 9 November pamphlets had been distributed all over Thuringia calling for a revolution. The new WSC in Gotha declared itself to be in charge and Carl Eduard was informed that he had ceased to be Duke. He hardly agreed, but the developments in Gotha scared him. By then, one of his next door 'neighbours', the King of Bavaria, had already fled in a terrified state, while another neighbour of Carl Eduard, the King of Saxony, had reacted with more nonchalance, and told the revolutionaries: 'go ahead and do your own crap now.'

Carl Eduard was forced to realize that resistance had become pointless. On 13 November he finally relented and signed his abdication. He was 34 years old and officially unemployed for the first time in his life. It was a fate shared by many. Yet like his future friend Adolf Hitler, the Duke of Coburg discovered in November 1918 a new passion—politics.

The irony of Carl Eduard's life was that, once deposed, he became much more involved with his surroundings than ever before. The events of 1918 seemed to have shaken him out of his coma—he suddenly 'awakened'. Until then he had been a fairly unpopular Bundesfürst (reigning prince) and now, while the others vanished into the dustbin of history, he became one of the most political of the ex-rulers. He also began bankrolling political murders. That this fact was hidden for decades is due to the impressive whitewashing techniques of his devious sister Alice. According to her selective memoirs, Carl Eduard's life after 1918 was devoted to good works:

> He continued to support all the social enterprises and led quite an interesting and pleasant life as a large landowner. He became President of the Red Cross which post he held at the beginning of the Second World War. It became quite a sinecure as the Red Cross became a Nazi institution serving only the German army and was never allowed inside a concentration camp.[58]

In fact the Red Cross did visit a concentration camp. Alice also knew that her brother had been one of Hitler's greatest supporters. After all Carl Eduard had proudly informed her over the years of the real 'enterprises' he was involved in. And it would be Alice who helped him to carry out his go-between missions in Britain.

It is understandable that after the Second World War Alice and the Coburg family had no interest in sharing this information. The current Duke of Coburg and his heir have so far allowed only selective access to key papers.[59] One therefore has to reconstruct Carl Eduard's life from many different sources. When in 2007 Channel 4 commissioned a documentary on the Duke entitled 'Hitler's Favourite Royal'—they had to cope with many gaps. Though the programme incorporated some new material, its thesis became slightly muddled. This could perhaps be attributed to the producer's wish to portray Carl Eduard as a victim of circumstances—a tragic figure in the wrong country at the wrong time. The director felt differently and resigned. Parts of the programme therefore drew a positive portrayal of a man lost in time, while in other parts Carl Eduard's work is connected with the extermination of mentally ill children. Whether he was simply an Englishman lost abroad or a criminal remained unresolved.[60]

New revelations suggest that he was in the criminal camp. Though Carl Eduard did not himself murder, he financed murderers. This became clearer when in 2011 a biography of the Duke of Coburg appeared in German. The author, Harald Sandner, a historian of Coburg, had access to one new source—Carl Eduard's appointment books. In some ways the appointment books were a disappointment because they simply listed meetings without giving any clue of what had been discussed. But at least they revealed how many Nazi organizations the Duke was actually involved in and the number of illustrious contacts he had within the Nazi party. The main problem with Sandner's biography is that he did not include footnotes. His work has to be treated with care. But combined with new findings from private archives it helps to give Carl Eduard the limelight he undoubtedly deserves. The Duke of Coburg was obviously not a naive victim of circumstances but a very active supporter of Hitler. His defence team would after the war successfully portray the Duke as a harmless, slightly potty aristocrat. They were helped by Alice who argued that Carl Eduard worked for peace in the 1930s.[61] She knew better.

In fact, previously unearthed sources suggest that Carl Eduard's moral responsibility for the rise of anti-Semitic and radical right wing groups in Bavaria was considerable. He was a generous donor to these parties and he networked behind the scenes, bringing the 'right' people together. As a go-between for Hitler he also interested members of the British royal family in Nazi Germany. During the decisive crises of the 1930s it was Carl Eduard who was sent to Britain to calm everyone's nerves.

To finance his political passion, the Duke needed money. When he had taken over the duchies in 1905 he had become a multi-millionaire over night, but his financial situation seemed highly insecure after 1918. Like so many of his contemporaries he had bought war bonds, which were worthless. He also had to negotiate with the new government the difficult division of state and family property. In the Duchy of Coburg the negotiations ran relatively smoothly and ended with Carl Eduard receiving a generous financial compensation for museums, art collections, and the theatre. He was allowed to reside at the Veste (the main castle in Coburg) during his lifetime and he kept two other castles, Callenberg and Rosenau, as his private property, as well as a considerable amount of farmland. Carl Eduard would later use these palaces for hiding the weapons of radical right wing organizations which were fighting the Republic.

As we have seen, aristocratic landowners found the revolutionary months of 1918/19 traumatic. The degree of trauma could, however, depend on how popular the family had been locally. Ideally this popularity would go back generations. Families which had been perceived as 'alien' (like the British Carl Eduard and his predecessor Duke Alfred) naturally faced more criticism than families that had long been integrated in the region. Religion also played a part. For example the Leiningens (relatives of Queen Victoria) were suddenly accused by the locals of having enriched themselves by 'stealing' Catholic church property over 100 years before. Old political divides were resurrected. In regions that had been heavily involved in the 1848 revolution, the opposition to the local landowning family could be stronger than in quieter parts of the country.

In Coburg the memory of 1848 had been positive. Even though Carl Eduard was not popular (an 'Englishman' in some people's eyes), he could still live peacefully in Coburg.

Whereas the town of Coburg behaved like the good twin, its other half, the former duchy of Gotha, was the evil twin. The negotiations with 'Red Gotha' about state and private property had been much more difficult than with Coburg. Gotha did offer to pay the Duke one million Marks in February 1919 (which would have meant his losing 96 per cent of the actual worth of his assets) but he insisted on 10 million Marks (an equivalent of 37 million Euros today) instead. As a result of the stalemate the Gotha government simply decided to turn the Duke's assets into state property. He was now dispossessed and this radicalized him considerably. He would never forgive what Gotha had done to him. In October 1919 he wrote to his sister Alice:

> Gotha still continues to behave disgracefully, but they are driving it to such a point now, that the Bauern [peasants] have at last woken up and are preparing to fight the government there. It is too disappointing after all the trouble one had had to bring Gotha on. The word 'thanks' is at present unknown in Germany. I never thought that German civilisation was so near the surface.... I get on quite well with the

present blighters in power here in Coburg, which is a great help. One even asked my advice the other day, what he was to do, what do you say to that?[62]

Two months later, however, his old fears were back: 'The last fortnight here was the scene of sharp election fights... our dear little Duchy was to be swallowed by the Bolshewiki [Bolsheviks] of North Thuringia... or by Bavaria.'[63]

He would continue to fear a communist take over until 1928. Ten years after the revolution, Carl Eduard wrote to his sister Alice:

I only hope our winter will remain quiet but the Russians seem to be getting our communists on the move... In different parts of Germany they have begun attacking our nationalists, but have luckily been beaten off with cracked crowns. If only the leaders would leave the workmen in peace. They are so sensible, 'wenn sie nicht verhetzt werden' (when they are not poisoned).[64]

In May 1919 Gotha had officially become part of the state of Thuringia and encouraged its former twin Coburg to follow this path. For the Coburgers this was not a serious option. Instead they discussed whether to join the newly formed 'Free States' of Prussia or Bavaria. The latter option seemed to offer more security and the merger was sealed by a state treaty in February 1920.

In hindsight it turned out to be a wise decision because it would keep Coburg on the western side of the Iron Curtain in 1945. Short-term, however, it backfired for the supporters of the Weimar Republic. After having experienced a Soviet republic in 1919, the state of Bavaria turned sharply to the opposite extreme and became a safe haven for radical right wing groups. The newly 'Bavarian' Coburg supported this development in every possible way. Many radical nationalist groups became highly popular in Coburg over the years: the Wiking Bund, the Deutschvölkischer Schutz- und Trutzbund, and the Jungdeutscher Orden.

Apart from support for Bavarian right wing politics, for the average Coburger it seemed at first rather unreal to be part of the Bavarian state. They had grown up in a dukedom and for many people therefore the first family simply remained that of the Duke of Sachsen-Coburg und Gotha. Also for Carl Eduard it must have seemed somehow ironic that he was now a Bavarian citizen. Because of his Protestant Prussian upbringing his relationship with Catholic Bavaria had always been distant. He had naturally never been part of the Catholic aristocratic network and this religious divide within reigning houses continued to run deep. Though Carl Eduard attended the funeral of King Ludwig III of Bavaria in November 1921 this was simply a gesture of courtesy. In fact he was very unwilling to support the restoration of the Bavarian Crown Prince Rupprecht. Though Carl Eduard still thought of himself as a monarchist, he certainly had no interest in the restoration of the *Bavarian* royal family. From 1917 to 1922 he supported the Bund der Kaisertreuen (League of Kaiser-Loyalists) but after that he remained rather uncommitted about any notions of restoration—a general feeling among his Protestant peer group.

Yet even though Carl Eduard had removed the Kaiser from his life, he could not get him entirely out of his system. He was used to the parades, the pre-war glamour, and the military life Wilhelm had represented and he was used to the idea of strong leadership. Since the Kaiser had turned out to be weak in a crisis, a stronger alternative was needed.

This was *one* of the reasons why Carl Eduard moved to the radical right. But of course there were many others. First of all the 'new' radical parties *looked* familiar. Carl Eduard had already known right wing circles before the First World War. Their martial language had appealed to him and he recognized many of their old slogans after 1918. This gave him a feeling of continuity at a time when continuity had become scarce.

Another important factor persuading him to support these parties was of course sheer fear. The experiences with 'Red Gotha' had been traumatic for him. Furthermore as has been shown the fallout from the Russian Revolution affected Carl Eduard's family more. First of all there was the loss of his Russian relatives. It strengthened his belief that a revolution could break out at any time and that his family was a prime target. He fully identified with the experiences of the Russian fugitives. Though the Workers' and Soldiers' Council in Gotha never achieved the power of its Soviet counterpart, to Carl Eduard the parallels were obvious.

His political fears were compounded by anxiety about status. His British title and property were lost. The Duke had been declared a traitor peer by Parliament and it was made clear to him that he was not welcome in Britain. He had been able to travel to London in 1921 to visit his mother and sister unofficially, yet when his mother died a year later he lost his English home, Claremont. The British government disallowed the inheritance and Claremont was sold by the Public Trustee. When his sister Alice sent him some mementos from the house, Carl Eduard replied:

> It was so nice to have the old furniture and pictures about one, although it makes one very sad to know one will never see dear old Claremont again as it was. I can only always repeat this damned war.[65]

His British property was gone, but he did not give up on his German estates.

One of his main lines of defence during his trial in 1947 would be that he had joined the Nazi party to protect his 'private property from left circles'.[66] One has to assume that he did not mean the British government. But he could not have meant the German one either. For in 1925 a Leipzig court overruled Gotha's dispossession of Carl Eduard as unconstitutional. Altogether real estate and art treasures worth 37.2 million Reichsmarks (today's equivalent of 139 million Euros) were returned to him. This was fortunate timing indeed. After the years of hyper-inflation, the newly established Reichsmark was now a stable currency. The Weimar Republic had turned Carl Eduard into a multi-millionaire again. In return, he would methodically use the money to plot the Republic's downfall.

But though he had nothing to fear from the democratic Weimar Republic, Carl Eduard strongly believed that the communists would in the end get the upper hand. He wanted to pre-empt this by supporting several radical right wing groups. As we will see, many aristocrats shared Carl Eduard's fears.

Another reason for supporting radical right wing groups was the international aspect of fascism. Carl Eduard was, like many of his peers, fascinated by Mussolini. Italian Fascists seemed to have succeeded in merging the old elites (the monarchy and the aristocracy) with a new Fascist elite. This was a blueprint for Carl Eduard's own hopes. In 1931 he founded, with Waldemar Pabst, the 'Society for Studying Fascism'. The aim was to study the methods of Italian Fascism and adapt them as a 'solution' to Germany's problems. The Society helped Carl Eduard to bring together influential conservatives with members of radical right wing parties. Many of them would later join the NSDAP, including the steel magnate Fritz Thyssen, the banker Hjalmar Schacht, and the industrialist Günther Quandt.

Another reason to join the radical right was Carl Eduard's obsession with homoerotic role models. Being physically weak himself, he admired virile dare devils. From 1919 onwards he was therefore attracted to leading men in the counter-revolutionary Freikorps scene. Joining a Freikorps had become de rigueur for many aristocrats. The son of the British born Princess Daisy described how after the war he simply continued being an officer by joining the Freikorps.[67]

The Freikorps, bands of young volunteers, had originally been formed to maintain internal order against left wing revolutionaries but they had quickly developed a life of their own. Since the Social Democratic government under Friedrich Ebert had given them too much power, they learnt to abuse it. In the end radical members of the Freikorps developed into terrorists. Captain Ehrhardt was one of them. He ran a naval brigade which was involved in brutal clashes with the equally brutal Workers' and Soldiers' Council. Carl Eduard was attracted to Ehrhardt's brutality from the start. He must have seen in him everything he did not have: enormous physical energy and overwhelming charisma. As a consequence the Duke took great political and financial risks for his new leader. He underwrote many of Ehrhardt's operations and would later hide him from the authorities in his Austrian castle Hinterriss. Ehrhardt was also highly useful for Carl Eduard's private agenda. In the spring of 1919 the Brigade Ehrhardt had been transferred to Thuringia. Carl Eduard hoped that Ehrhardt would eliminate the Gotha Bolsheviks as quickly as possible, so he could get his property back. Ehrhardt did not mind doing the dirty work for the Duke but he was involved in several other 'projects'. In April 1919—against instructions—he and his men rushed to Munich to overthrow the Soviet Republic. The ensuing street skirmishes turned out to be extremely vicious. Both sides were equally brutal, but the Brigade got totally out of hand, executing people at whim. The Weimar government could hardly tolerate this anarchy much longer. By spring 1920 it became obvious that the Freikorps had served their purpose and now posed a threat to the newly founded democracy. The Weimar government therefore decided to dissolve them. Though General Lüttwitz—a founding member of a Freikorps—tried to prevent this, Reichspresident Friedrich Ebert and the government remained firm.

Carl Eduard had just been made the district representative of the Brigade Ehrhardt when the Minister of Defence dissolved the Brigade on 29 February 1920. The Freikorps did not take this decision well. On 13 March they marched to Berlin and tried to overthrow the government. One of the aims of this so-called Kapp-Putsch was to restore the monarchy—an idea that did not appeal to the public. Ehrhardt was one of the leaders of the putsch and employed his trademark brutality. Carl Eduard's involvement, however, is difficult to reconstruct. He had learnt to be careful in his correspondence, fearing—quite rightly—that his letters were being intercepted. Though no letters on the coup have surfaced so far, Carl Eduard supported Ehrhardt financially at the time and therefore was indirectly involved.

The Kapp-Putsch was incompetently planned and badly carried out. President Ebert and the government fled Berlin, yet the revolutionaries did not manage to take key government positions. A general strike ended the whole affair after four days. The Brigade Ehrhardt was dissolved in May and the captain was now on the run. Carl Eduard offered him refuge in Callenberg castle and on the Veste. Here Ehrhardt lived under the name 'Neumann' (to give him the pseudonym 'new man' was probably an accurate description in Carl Eduard's eyes). Along with Ehrhardt, the weapons of his Brigade were hidden in the castles.[68] All of this was of course illegal and Carl Eduard could have faced prison for it.

That his support for Ehrhardt turned out to be far from transient is shown by the events of the following years. Only parts of the Brigade Ehrhardt were incorporated into the reduced German army, some of the hardcore extremists joined a secret underground society, Organisation Consul (OC), also run by Ehrhardt. The aim of its approximately 5,000 members was to overthrow the Republic with terror acts against its representatives. Carl Eduard became the district chief of this organization in Coburg and later for the whole of Thuringia.[69]

Members of the OC were indirectly and directly involved in several political murders in the 1920s. One of its hitmen was Ernst von Salomon who became Ehrhardt's adjutant and the Duke's new friend. Despite the age difference, they felt themselves kindred spirits. Like Coburg, Salomon had attended the military academy in Berlin Lichterfelde. He had only been 16 at the end of the war and since he had missed any combat, he was eager to make up for it. The Freikorps became his compensation. He fought first in Berlin, later in the Baltic and Upper Silesia. Salomon was always worried about his Jewish-sounding surname and made sure that his anti-Semitism was known. He later became a popular novelist writing rather distorted versions of the OC's actions in the 1920s. Carl Eduard was enthusiastic about young Salomon and entrusted him with parts of his precious medal collection. Salomon's assignment was to sell them secretly in Sweden. Such sales had become necessary to finance the growing operations of Organisation Consul.[70] Sweden was ideal since Carl Eduard could use his good contacts to Swedish elite circles (he would later marry off one of his daughters into the Swedish royal family). Yet Sweden was only one part of the OC jigsaw; Captain Ehrhardt and Ernst von Salomon were active on a wider international stage. From spring 1921 onwards they were also involved in weapons' deals with Hungary and Sinn Fein in Ireland.[71]

To finance the OC's 'political work', meant financing political murders. Though he did not pull the trigger himself, Carl Eduard was helping to load the gun. In 1921 Organisation Consul killed the USPD-leader Karl Gareis in Munich. Since the USPD had played the decisive part in dispossessing Carl Eduard's Gotha property, he must have seen this murder as a 'fair' retribution. A second 'retribution' came on 26 August 1921 when Finance Minister Matthias Erzberger was killed by OC members. The Organisation Consul was also responsible for the failed attack on the former SPD Chancellor, Philipp Scheidemann, in June 1922 and shortly afterwards the assassination of Foreign Minister Walther Rathenau. Hermann Fischer and Erwin Kern had carried out this assignment by throwing a grenade into Rathenau's car that killed him instantly. Salomon and another accomplice had been their lookout men. Hermann Fischer's family had lived in Coburg.[72] Since Carl Eduard was the district chief of the Organisation Consul in Coburg, it is very likely that he knew Fischer. He certainly knew the lookout man Ernst von Salomon well. That Rathenau had been on a death list was common knowledge in radical right wing circles. A popular rhyme was: 'Shoot dead Walther Rathenau, the goddam Jew pig!' ('Rathenau' and 'Judensau' rhyme in German.) It would later be reported that General Ludendorff had even asked, 'why haven't you killed him yet?'[73]

Since Rathenau was from a wealthy Jewish family the murderers had hoped to gain public approval, but unlike their earlier killings, this one caused public outrage. Rathenau was highly respected across party lines as well as outside Germany. People were shocked and took to the streets to demonstrate against the murder, something that had not happened after the previous killings. This development took the killers by surprise, their escape had not been planned professionally, and they could not rely on public support. A chaotic race with the police began.

When Salomon heard that their escape route had been cut off he tried to get papers and money to them.[74] He failed. By then they were hiding in a castle, where the police eventually shot Kern. His accomplice, the Coburger Fischer, committed suicide.[75]

Hitler would later honour the Rathenau killers as his 'vanguard fighters'. In 1922, Germany was still a democracy, though, and the authorities tried to unravel the OC conspiracy. In the end they only convicted some of the murderers' accomplices. Salomon was one of them. He served five years' imprisonment for the Rathenau murder and after his release in 1927 was immediately involved in another killing for which he was eventually pardoned by the new President of Germany, Paul von Hindenburg.

The arrest and trial of his friend Salomon made Carl Eduard's life momentarily problematic. His connections with the Organisation Consul became public and he received death threats. From now on he employed his own security guards.[76] In May 1923 the OC changed its name to Bund Wiking (Viking League). Ehrhardt was in charge again and Carl Eduard a valued member.

That a grandson of Queen Victoria had become involved with a terrorist organization might seem bizarre.

Of course, not all of Queen Victoria's German relatives agreed with Coburg's killer instincts. When Erzberger was murdered, Ernst Hohenlohe was shocked: 'it is deeply to be regretted when people who believe in nationalist values use criminal means to effect the opposite of what they want to achieve. They play into the enemy's hands. Germany will not be resurrected through political murders.'[77] He was equally shocked by Rathenau's murder.[78]

But Carl Eduard's long-term plan was not to stay in the terrorist camp. He must have hoped to use the terrorists as a tool with which to bring 'respectable' politicians to power. However, his choice of 'respectable politicians' was muddled. He had contacts on the radical right that ranged from hardcore groups like the OC to more conservative parties. His ultimate aim was a merger of all right wing groups. To achieve this hosting a so-called 'German Day', a new form of nationalist rally, seemed ideal. Only three months after the unpopular Rathenau murder, radical right wing groups planned a show of solidarity. From 14 to 15 October 1922 Coburg became the host town for the third 'German Day'. A still fairly unknown Adolf Hitler and his NSDAP were among the guests. For Hitler this was an excellent opportunity to extend his Munich-based party to the region of Franconia. The prospects for making an impact were good. In response to Coburg's 'German Day', groups in Thuringia had mobilized and sent over their own demonstrators—Socialists and communists. The ensuing street fights turned out to be particularly vicious with about 600 fighters on each side. Reportedly even Hitler got physically involved—something he was not known for, and would certainly not repeat again. After a day's 'work out', in the evening the Führer metamorphosed from street fighter into politician and celebrated with Carl Eduard and other local dignitaries in a pub. While the Duke listened to Hitler's speech in the Coburger Hofbräuhaus, fights continued throughout the night and a local Jewish businessman was attacked. This German day was later branded as the 'Train to Coburg'[79] and became one of the foundation myths of the NSDAP. It was also the foundation of the friendship between Hitler and the Duke, who would—once the Nazis were in power—claim poetically that from this moment onwards he had felt 'the happiness of having a personal relationship with the Führer'.[80] Hitler demonstrated his friendship over the years by showering Carl Eduard with medals, among them in 1935 the 'Coburger Ehrenzeichen der NSDAP', an honour awarded to Nazi party participants in the Coburg 'German Day'.

It has been argued that the two might have known each other before these events drove them together. They both regularly stayed at the same hotel in Berlin—the Hotel Sanssouci. Though this hotel was down-market, the Duke became a frequent guest. The reason was simple: the hotel was a meeting place for radical right wing parties and frequented by members of the Ehrhardt Naval Brigade.[81] (Later, when these groups moved up in the world they preferred the more elegant Hotel Kaiserhof.) Whether Ehrhardt was the matchmaker who introduced Carl Eduard and Hitler in the lobby of Hotel Sanssouci, cannot be verified though. What is obvious is that Hitler and the Duke got on extremely well at the Coburg 'German Day' in 1922. Despite their rather different social backgrounds they had a lot in common: their ideologies and of course their narcissistic personalities (the only creatures they both declared a fondness for were their dogs). Yet even if the two men had already clicked a few months earlier in Berlin, the events of October 1922 were much more decisive for their relationship. They now shared a 'war story' and like old veterans they would retell this story many times over the next decade. The impact of the early experiences in Coburg is evident from a diary entry by Goebbels in 1937: 'Führer talked about memories of Koburg and the early years.'[82] At such moments the Führer seemed at his happiest.

The 'Train to Coburg' was not just another random stop on a wobbly trip to power for Hitler but actually speeded full steam ahead into NSDAP-propaganda. In 1937, on its fifteenth anniversary, Hitler visited Coburg in triumph, showing a rare sense of humour when he joked on arrival: 'the criminal is returning to the scene of his crime.'[83] It was a crime he was particularly proud of. Unlike his ranting speech in 1922 he now acted in a more statesmanlike manner, solemnly declaring that: 'The fight for this town became the foundation stone of our movement.'[84]

In 1922 Carl Eduard's support for this 'great Coburg event' had only been reported in the local papers and Hitler did not mention the Duke's name in *Mein Kampf*. The reasons why he kept Carl Eduard's cover are manifold. When *Mein Kampf* was published Carl Eduard was still closer to Ehrhardt than Hitler. Hitler of course wanted to win over the Duke and avoid causing him embarrassment (being associated with a prisoner was not helpful at the time). There were many reasons why Hitler needed to be on good terms with the Duke. He needed Carl Eduard's social contacts, of course, but also the Duke's money. The NSDAP was constantly out of funds. Apart from fund raising, Hitler also understood that the old dynasties still had glamour appeal in certain German circles. Though he told his cronies privately that the German aristocracy was degenerate, he knew only too well how useful they could be.

The worse the political situation got, the more the NSDAP benefited. And it was getting much worse. In 1923 Carl Eduard wrote to his sister Alice:

> We are tumbling and rolling down hill faster than ever. At the cheapest pub a plate of soup costs. 1,000,000 Mark. For 1 Pound one gets 50,000,000 Marks. Work is getting scarce, the smaller factories closing one after another, the big ones only working two days a week.... The Berlin government is a disgrace. Just when [Chancellor] Cuno was beginning to get on a bit better, they change the government.[85]

At this point, the radical right and the radical left came to the same conclusion. The Weimar government was about to collapse and it was time for a revolution. In Saxony and Thuringia the communists tried to trigger a 'German October'—based on the Russian October Revolution. The radical right was more than ready for this and planning its own coup. Captain Ehrhardt was in Coburg at the time with 5,000 followers ready to march into Thuringia. With him was Carl Eduard's eldest son Johann Leopold (Leo). The proud father reported back to Britain that his son was involved in the fight:

> Leo is now back after playing at being a soldier at the Thuringian frontier. He was enrolled as volunteer in the Ehrhardt Brigade and his section had a brush with Thuringian constabulary, killing one and wounding two severely, our loss being only one badly wounded.... So you see we were quite warlike here. The life at the frontier and the drilling has done a lot of good to Leo and made him more manly, which was most necessary.[86]

Johann Leopold (Leo) was 17 at the time and a member of the Bund Wiking which was financed by his father.

The Weimar government now decided to intervene. On 29 October and 6 November respectively it ordered the army to be sent to Saxony and Thuringia to depose their left wing governments. This was done swiftly and made the Weimar government look 'effective' again. It was therefore bad timing that Hitler decided to carry out his putsch on 8–9 November. The Bavarian government failed to support Hitler as anticipated. It was later claimed that Carl Eduard had also been against the 1923 Hitler putsch. His chief administrator stated at the denazification trial: 'The Duke thought the coup was illegal.'[87] This sounded as if Carl Eduard had been a defender of the Weimar Republic. In fact he and Ehrhardt had planned their own coup and Hitler's doomed 'solo-trip' had upset their plans. Ehrhardt had met Gustav von Kahr, the new Bavarian state commissioner with dictatorial powers, on 6 November 1923. Kahr had told him that if there was not a parliamentary way of getting a right wing nationalist government into power in Berlin, they should think of 'other ways' to achieve this. He would give Ehrhardt a signal when the time was ripe. Ehrhardt had already been instructed by Kahr to organize his troops accordingly. When the Hitler putsch broke out three days later, Ehrhardt's troops sided with Kahr against Hitler. Later Ehrhardt admitted that he himself had hoped to become the leader of the radical right instead of Hitler. That Coburg was fully supporting Ehrhardt's plans of a putsch to achieve this becomes clear from a letter he wrote to his sister by the end of November:

> Dearest Tigs,
>
> What mad times we are going through. You cannot imagine what the last three weeks have been as a test for one's health and nerves. I am desperate at not being able to come to The Hague on the eighth. And then like a thunderstroke the cracker went off at the wrong end [Hitler's putsch] and the wrong moment and upset everything. Our mobilization that was just finished was put an end to. We have had to partially demobilise again. This awful strain on one's financial resources and nerves and time all for nothing. It is too disgusting. And to crown the whole thing I cannot cross the Bavarian frontier to the north of Germany at present without the risk of being arrested and sent to Leipzig; belonging as I do to the staff of the naval Brigade Ehrhardt a most illegal Freikorps, feared and pursued and persecuted in all Germany except in Bavaria.[88] We are working now like blazes to get all the vaterländische Kampfverbände [patriotic combat leagues] under the sole command of Captain E[hrhardt]. The Bavarian government allows us unofficially to work. Of course I can cross the frontier to Austria. It sounds ridiculous when I say I can't leave Bavaria. But I hope you will understand now, why I can't come. You will think I am mad mixing up in this business, but I had the feeling I was doing right and I have been able to help immensely, so that I do not mind being chained to Bavaria for only a few weeks as I hope.[89]

Carl Eduard did indeed help immensely. Though he wanted Ehrhardt as the new leader, he made sure that several Hitler supporters were hidden and looked after in his castle, Callenberg.[90] In many ways it was Carl Eduard's 'achievement' that in the days of confusion after the Hitler putsch the city of Coburg became the safe haven for radical right wing supporters. Coburg offered them protection and they could rely on everyone's discretion. The NSDAP was banned after the Hitler putsch, but in the meantime the Coburger Nazis joined other radical right organizations like the Deutschvölkischer Schutz- und Trutzbund and the Jungdeutsche Orden.[91]

Despite his support for Ehrhardt, Hitler did not forget Carl Eduard's post-putsch help and returned the compliment a few years later during the Princes' Referendum. The Princes' Referendum was hotly debated at the time. The enormous compensation the Duke of Coburg had received from Gotha in 1925 triggered a wave of criticism of former ruling houses. One consequence of this was a national referendum about the dispossession of the princes. While the communists (KPD) wanted to dispossess them, Hitler of course took the opposite stance. In a speech he gave in Bamberg (a Franconian town close to Coburg) he advocated a united and classless society—a true *Volksgemeinschaft* (national community): 'There are no Princes, there are only Germans!'—was the slogan he had borrowed from Wilhelm II's famous August 1914 declaration, 'I no longer recognize parties, I know only Germans!'[92] Though Hitler's sentence could also have been interpreted differently, it endeared him to the aristocracy. His stance in the Princes' Referendum in no way incurred a political risk; the majority of Germans agreed with Hindenburg's argument that dispossession was unconstitutional. In the end the referendum decided in favour of the princes. For Carl Eduard and his peer group this came as an immense relief.

Whether Hitler would in the end become the leader of the radical right was not at all clear to Coburg in the mid-1920s, but he did his best to help the radical right in general. Their anti-Semitism particularly appealed to him. In his eyes the Jews had been at the forefront of the 1918 revolution in Germany; consequently all Jews were Bolsheviks. His anti-Semitism was, however, not 'simply' politically and religiously motivated; it was also racial. When he visited America in 1934 he noted that Jews played an 'unrestricted' role in society and 'abused' it, as much as they had done in Germany before 1933. He got particularly impatient with Americans asking him about the 'Jewish question' in Germany. These Americans, Carl Eduard argued, did not understand that the German opposition to Jews was not based on religious differences but on racial ones.

To Carl Eduard's delight, in 1929 it was the issue of anti-Semitism that finally helped the Nazis to win an election in Coburg. Instrumental in this was Franz Schwede, who eventually had a big career in the Nazi party and changed his name to Schwede-Coburg. Schwede was a Nazi who had been sacked from his job as an inspector at Coburg's municipal power station in 1929. He had attacked a Jewish customer, who made a complaint. After his dismissal Schwede started an impressive revenge campaign. With slogans like 'Coburg for Coburgers! And Palestine for those who belong there!' he encouraged hundreds of Coburgers to demonstrate against his dismissal. In the end the democratically elected town council was ousted and a new election called. In June 1929 Hitler arrived in person to support the election campaign. He was welcomed enthusiastically. The NSDAP won 13 of the 25 council seats. Coburg was now officially the first Nazi town in Germany—a symbolic step forward that would be used ad nauseam by Nazi propaganda. Carl Eduard's moral support had helped to deliver this victory. Court circulars did not exist any more, but the local newspapers did make mention whenever he attended functions. The Duke's attendance at Nazi meetings gave them perfect publicity and enormous social prestige. That the Duchess was joining her husband in these male-dominated gatherings made an even bigger impact. Ever since the couple's arrival in 1905, the Duchess had been popular amongst the Coburgers—a woman who seemed approachable. After the Second World War it was claimed that for religious reasons she had not approved of his political work, but this was a family myth. Though the marriage was considered to be far from emotionally successful, politically they had no differences. Neither changed their views after the war. In his postwar interview with Stefan Heym, Carl Eduard stressed that Jews had dominated German affairs before Hitler came to power. Carl Eduard also claimed he had no knowledge of the extermination of the Jews. This is very unlikely since he was very close to his cousin Prince Josias Waldeck-Pyrmont—a man who had Buchenwald under his jurisdiction. Neither Carl Eduard nor his sister Alice mentioned Josias after the war. But he was their first cousin and they had been very close to him indeed.

Waldeck was born in 1896 as heir to the sovereign principality of Waldeck and Pyrmont. His family was well connected on a national and international level. Josias was a cousin of the Queen of the Netherlands and a nephew of Helene, Duchess of Albany. Helene's children, Carl Eduard Coburg and Alice, were among his closest relatives. Since Helene kept visiting her Waldeck family on a regular basis, Josias and Carl Eduard knew each other from an early age. Carl Eduard was twelve years older than Josias, but despite this age difference they became firm friends. For Carl Eduard, Josias was not just a relative, he also became the kind of man he admired. From an early age onwards Josias's character had shown great 'promise' for future brutalities. As a 16-year-old he had thrown one of his teachers, a small man, into a bin and set him on fire.[93] This incident had no disciplinary consequences and Waldeck's sadistic streak was able to 'blossom' during the First World War. Being gassed and receiving a head wound made Josias only more determined than ever. He won the Iron Cross and was eager to continue to fight to the bitter end. Instead, he had to accept his father's abdication in November 1918—an insult he never forgot. Like his cousin Coburg, Josias was determined not to give up playing a political role and fought in a Freikorps. In the 1920s he did not settle down into civilian life, though he half-heartedly pretended to study agriculture at Munich University. During his time in Munich he became acquainted with radical right wing groups and cousin Carl Eduard made sure to introduce him to the 'right' people. Waldeck joined the 'Jungdeutsche Orden' and, together with Carl Eduard, in the autumn of 1923 was involved in the above-mentioned military operations against the governments in Saxony and Thuringia.[94] He continued to follow his cousin Carl Eduard's lead, even outshining him by joining Himmler's SS as early as November 1929. A year later he became Himmler's adjutant and one of the few people allowed to call him by his first name. It was also a great honour when Hitler and Himmler both became godfathers to Waldeck's eldest son in 1936.[95] Himmler had a soft spot for the aristocracy. His father had been a tutor to the Bavarian royal family and Himmler based his SS on aristocratic ideas of blood and honour. Waldeck was also close to Göring who helped him in April 1933 to get into the diplomatic service. Waldeck had never passed the relevant exams and was rumoured to have no languages, yet the ever obliging Foreign Minister Konstantin von Neurath did not dare to object since he had been told it was at Hitler's request. However, Waldeck soon got bored in this low-level position and started seeking power elsewhere.[96]

He preferred physical to verbal combat. His 'hands-on approach' would become useful when some of his old SA friends were executed during the Röhm 'Putsch' of 1934. At first Coburg and Waldeck were slightly taken aback that their old comrades were about to be killed, but they soon rationalized it as a necessary operation. They were after all used to political murders. Waldeck only felt uncomfortable for a brief moment, when he realized that Count Spreti, a fellow aristocrat whom he had known for years, was among the SA people to be shot. But in the end Waldeck 'did his duty' and scouted for an appropriate place for the execution of Spreti and other SA men. Cousin Coburg was understanding about the whole affair too, but did complain when he was forced to give up his SA uniform. Eighteen months after the assassination of Röhm, Coburg was still writing letters insisting on his being allowed to wear this particular uniform. The murders seem to have been of secondary importance for him. He insisted that he had been made an SA group leader in July 1933 by Adolf Hitler and therefore would not give up his SA uniform.[97] It was indeed an important point for him. Like every royal Carl Eduard had collected uniforms since his youth and it had been difficult for him to live without them after 1918. He had reverted to using hunting outfits for a while, but they did not look as flattering and hardly demonstrated his importance. In 1927 he had acquired a uniform of the right wing veterans' organization Der Stahlhelm, which had given him enormous pleasure—until Hitler offered him better outfits. The SA uniform was therefore very valuable to him. In the end a compromise was found. Carl Eduard was compensated. Hitler honoured him with the uniform of a Wehrmacht general.

Waldeck was also fond of uniforms but he had never worn a SA one and therefore did not make a fuss. After showing loyalty to the Nazi party by murdering his former friends, his career progressed even faster. He became a 'people's judge' at the *Volksgerichtshof* (People's Court), was made an SS-Obergruppenführer (the highest SS rank) in 1936, and with the outbreak of war put in charge of military district IX. This gave him police and judicial powers which he used to the fullest extent. Among the many things Waldeck was responsible for during the war was ordering the execution of Polish slave workers for 'Rassenschande', i.e. sleeping with German women. When in doubt, Waldeck always favoured the death penalty. He also had supervisory authority over Buchenwald concentration camp and was very well informed about what was going on at the camp. In fact it was his micromanagement of Buchenwald that resulted in a bizarre incident. One of the inmates, Walter Krämer, had treated Waldeck successfully when he had been taken ill. The Prince appreciated this and was not pleased when one day he found his helper's name on the Buchenwald death lists. Krämer had been shot. Though shooting prisoners was hardly unusual, the reason for this particular murder turned out to be that Krämer had also had another high ranking patient, the commandant of Buchenwald, Karl-Otto Koch.

Koch was known to be outstandingly corrupt. In a corrupt system this was not necessarily a problem. Yet what he actually wanted to hide was something else. Krämer had treated him for syphilis and this was not something Koch wanted to be known. It seems rather ironic that Koch was so greatly concerned about his reputation, since he was well known within the NSDAP to be a psychopath. Perhaps Koch did not want his wife Ilse to find out about the problem. But Ilse Koch, an overseer at Buchenwald herself, was far from moralistic. She certainly must have had an inkling, because, a habitual sadist herself, she specialized in torturing female inmates. Whatever the Kochs' marital arrangements, Waldeck continued to be displeased about the killing of a favourite. He started a personal feud against Koch which ended with Koch's execution in April 1945.

It is very unlikely that Waldeck did not discuss his 'work problems' at Buchenwald with his cousin Carl Eduard Coburg. The two men shared a villa together in Berlin—the Villa Coburg. Furthermore, Austria's biggest concentration camp Mauthausen, was 23 km from Carl Eduard's hunting lodge and he could hardly have missed what went on there. Still, after 1945 Carl Eduard claimed he had had no knowledge of concentration camps. There were many others things he would hide.

PART II

Hitler's Go-Betweens

4

Approaching the Appeasers

The Duke of Coburg

By 1918 go-betweens seemed obsolete. President Wilson's idea of a new diplomacy, disposing once and for all of secret alliances and backroom talks, was applauded by the public. Transparency was yearned for.[1] Even though most go-between missions had never become public, the well-documented Sixtus scandal was seen as a case in point. Clandestine manoeuvres appeared doomed. Yet the inter-war years became far too complicated to follow through with such well-meaning ideals. Go-betweens were soon employed again—by democratic and undemocratic regimes. One of these go-betweens was the Duke of Coburg. His employer was Hitler.

To this day Hitler's system of using go-betweens has been ignored by historians. There is a certain snobbishness involved in this. Since it was run by 'amateurs', i.e. non-professionals, it was simply written off by diplomatic historians. This is a very narrow way of looking at the issue.[2] When it comes to Hitler's foreign policy, focusing on official routes has never been enough. We already know of three separate organizations which covered foreign affairs for him. There was the *Außenpolitisches Amt* der NSDAP (foreign policy department of the NSDAP, or APA for short) which resided in the Hotel Adlon and was headed by the Nazi party's chief ideologue Alfred Rosenberg. Then there was the less important *Auslandsorganisation* (Foreign Organization branch of the NSDAP or NSDAP/AO) run by Ernst Wilhelm Bohle responsible for Germans living abroad, and at last Joachim von Ribbentrop's office, the increasingly important *Büro (office) Ribbentrop* (later renamed the *Dienststelle Ribbentrop*). These organizations alone show that Hitler obviously had no trust in the German Foreign Ministry (referred to in the note below by its acronym, the AA). Rosenberg wrote after a conversation with his Führer in 1934: 'he still believes in the good will of Neurath [the Foreign

Minister], the AA is, however, a group of conspirators. He regrets that he is still bound by the promises he made when the Cabinet was formed, according to which the President [Hindenburg] makes decisions about the army and the AA. The [army] was fine because of Blomberg, the other one [the AA] is not.'[3]

When Hitler came to power in 1933, diplomats were in his eyes the old guard, who had not yet accepted the revolutionary ideas of his movement. Though he had nothing to worry about and most diplomats soon fell into line, the relationship Hitler had with his first Foreign Minister, von Neurath, remained distant, as Rosenberg rightly guessed. The historian Zara Steiner has noted: 'Neurath's role in Berlin was extremely circumscribed; he rarely saw the Führer.'[4] Steiner, however, does not ask the obvious question. Who carried out foreign policy then? In fact Hitler kept the obedient Neurath on for image reasons, knowing how important it was to make a show of continuity to the outside world. In the meantime he developed an alternative system of diplomacy.

Hitler did not think or act like a nineteenth-century statesmen who coordinated his policies with the Foreign Ministry. If one wants to understand his peculiar way of conducting foreign policy, one has to look at his go-betweens. His contemporaries were aware of the importance of these go-betweens. Hitler was, as his adjutant Fritz Wiedemann stressed, 'a revolutionary who did not think much of the old ways of diplomacy'. The Rothermere journalist Ward Price wrote in his enthusiastic book on the 'Great Dictators' that Hitler preferred to bypass bureacracy and 'rank' and instead used 'confidantes' to implement policy. A person of rank, such as the German ambassador to Britain, von Dirksen, had to take this into account as well. After the war he complained that Hitler's method was indeed highly unconventional: 'its versatility, avoidance of the appropriate offices.'[5] One reason why Hitler liked to use go-betweens was because he distrusted professional diplomats like Dirksen (even though Dirksen was a member of the NSDAP). Apart from distrusting his own diplomats, there were many other reasons why Hitler used back channels. One can be found in his own past. As mentioned above, his adjutant Fritz Wiedemann described Hitler as a 'revolutionary' and, like so many revolutionaries, Hitler had indeed, in the early phase of his political life, learnt to work illegally. After his failed putsch, the NSDAP had been dissolved on 23 November 1923. It continued to work illegally after Hitler was released from prison in 1924. The party was officially refounded on 27 February 1925. This means that Hitler had plenty of experience outside formal structures. He had learnt the value of clandestine channels; it came naturally to him. In some ways he had been a kind of go-between himself once, a military one. During the First World War he was a 'Meldegänger', a dispatch runner between different sections of the front. Since he romanticized military life, he most likely romanticized this way of communication as well—man to man.

There is only one monograph that tells the story of an Italian intermediary for Hitler. It follows the links the Hesse family established for Hitler in Italy.[6] Yet the Hesse family was no exception but only one of many aristocratic families Hitler used.

During the inter-war period the aristocracies of Britain, France, Belgium, the Netherlands, Spain, Italy, Romania, and Germany were very active in trying to play a political role again. Yet for a long time research on these aristocracies has been neglected.[7] This was due not merely to the fact that private archives were closed to historians, but also because the study of the aristocracy was simply seen as unfashionable.[8] Since nobody assumed that the old networks continued to exist, nobody followed E. M. Forster's sage advice: 'only connect'.

But why would a revolutionary like Hitler use aristocrats as go-betweens? At first sight the relationship between Hitler and the aristocracy seems asymmetric. Instead of aristocrats Hitler could have employed many other people he had become close to—e.g. internationally connected businessmen like Thyssen or the Krupp family. That he chose aristocrats instead had several reasons—rational as well as irrational.

Rationally he had had good experiences with aristocrats. They were allies. As Stephan Malinowski has shown, the German nobility had helped Hitler to get ahead socially *within* Germany. Lesser German nobles had been proportionally among the strongest supporters of the Nazi movement. In his study Malinowski did not include the international help for Hitler, though. As will be shown this was in many ways even more valuable.

Seating plans can give a first indication of how aristocrats were used. Whenever high ranking foreign guests came to Berlin, noble names were employed to entertain them. At state dinners for the Hungarian Prime Minister, the Bulgarian Prime Minister, or Italian dignatories, the Hohenzollerns, Richthofens, Bismarcks, Alvenslebens, Arnims, Jagows, and many others were providing traditional glamour. They were particularly useful during the Olympics. A list of the people who attended the Olympics on 11 August 1936, for example, reads like an extract from *Burke's Peerage* combined with the *Almanach de Gotha*: Lord and Lady Aberdare, Lord Barnby, Lord Camrose, Lord Douglas Hamilton, Lord Hollenden, Lord Rennell Rodd, the Duke of Coburg, the Prince of Wied, the Hesse Princes, the Duke of Braunschweig, 'Auwi', the Hohenzollern-Sigmaringens.[9]

Despite making fun of the degenerate aristocracy Hitler was not entirely immune to the glamour of old names. This was the irrational side of his decision to take them on. He had grown up under a monarchy. Though he had hardly approved of the Habsburgs, since his school days in Austria-Hungary he had been surrounded by their stories. In his history class, he was taught how the Habsburgs built their empire and used dynastic marriages to form political alliances in the early modern period. Even though such alliances were anachronistic, Hitler seriously toyed with the idea of resurrecting them. In 1934/5 he had Princess Victoria Luise approached, the only daughter of ex-Kaiser Wilhelm II. She was married to the Duke of Braunschweig, a sympathetic follower of Hitler. In her memoirs Victoria Luise wrote:

> we received an astounding demand from Hitler, conveyed to us by Ribbentrop. It was no more nor less than that we should arrange a marriage between [our daughter] Friedericke and the Prince of Wales. My husband and I were shattered. Something like this had never entered our minds, not even for a reconciliation with England. Before the First World War it had been suggested that I should marry my cousin [the Prince of Wales], who was two years younger, and it was now being indicated that my daughter should marry him. We told Hitler that in our opinion the great difference in age between the Prince of Wales and Friedericke alone precluded such a project, and that we were not prepared to put any such pressure on our daughter.[10]

Victoria Luise protested too much. Her family was thoroughly pro-Nazi and would have wished to please Hitler. Furthermore the Prince of Wales was the son-in-law every ambitious mother dreamt of. But after 1945 such feelings were naturally no longer admitted. Even though this marriage could not be engineered, using German relatives of the British royal family as go-betweens was another logical route for Hitler. He understood that elites prefer to mingle with other elites. Since aristocrats in particular trusted one another and enjoyed each other's company exclusively, it made sense to use German aristocrats to get into contact with their British counterparts. That the British royal family and the aristocracy were still important was obvious to Hitler. Seen through the eyes of a National Socialist, Britain had a strict class system where bearers of illustrious names could play a decisive role. Britain seemed to be a meritocracy only in name—family background combined with the right public schools and universities decided career chances. It was also assumed that upper-class networks were extremely tight and hard to penetrate. For the Nazis such penetration was at the top of their agenda and German aristocrats were therefore extremely useful.

Hitler was not carrying out this plan on his own. He had a trusted ally—a man who was ideal for contacts with the international elites: Hermann Göring. In some ways Göring could be called the master of the go-between method. He spotted the potential of this method and acquired great expertise.

His background seemed to predestine him to mingle with aristocrats. He had been interested in the nobility and its customs since childhood. His godfather was Hermann von Epenstein, a rather dubious figure whose wealth and snobbery dominated the whole Göring family. Epenstein was the lover of Göring's mother and little Hermann grew up in Epenstein's castle, while his father was banished to an annexe (Epenstein would later bequeath his castle to Göring, which led to rumours that he had been his biological father). Despite, or because of, this strange upbringing Hermann Göring fled into a fantasy world of knights, castles, and shining armour. His godfather was obsessed with noble pedigrees and he passed this obsession on to little Hermann. Hermann wanted to fulfil Epenstein's ideal and become a Renaissance man. He eventually achieved this with the—looted—paintings to go with it. Being indoctrinated about aristocratic concepts of honour and royal marriages made Hermann Göring realize the potential of illustrious names. He targeted and cultivated aristocrats with great success. Though he had no noble background to flaunt, his reputation as a flying ace during the First World War helped him socially after 1918. So did his time in Sweden. He married Carin, a Swedish noble. She opened up contacts for him within the Swedish elite that he would use until 1945.[11]

Göring did not surround himself with aristocrats simply out of snobbery but also because he rightly guessed that they could give him an entrée to other countries. He had never forgotten his difficult time in Italy when after the failed Hitler Putsch in 1923 he was received by no one in Italian society, let alone his main target Mussolini.

This changed completely when he courted the Princes of Hesse. As Jonathan Petropoulos has shown, they opened the doors to Mussolini for the Nazi leadership. In fact they soon became part of Göring's growing menagerie of go-betweens—each having different countries to look after. As we will see, Prince Max zu Hohenlohe would work for the regime in Czechoslovakia and Spain; several people did so in Britain and Göring's friend Prince Viktor zu Wied in Sweden.[12] Another good channel was Duke Adolf Friedrich von Mecklenburg-Schwerin (1873–1969), cousin of the Queen of the Netherlands, who used his international contacts for Nazi propaganda. In Berlin society he was called the 'grand ducal Nazi agent'.[13]

Carin Göring proudly wrote to her mother in 1930 about how well connected her husband was by now:

> The (Princes of) Wied and August Wilhelm [a son of Kaiser Wilhelm II] have introduced us to some very interesting people. Yesterday we had breakfast with Prince Henckel-Donnersmarck . . . he attends all the gatherings at which Hermann talks.[14]

Carin died shortly afterwards, but now Göring's sister-in-law tried to support him. Her name was Fanny Countess von Wilamowitz-Moellendorff (1882–1956) and she had been married to a German noble. Fanny was a Swedish novelist and ardent Nazi. Like Carin she would do anything for Hitler and Göring. In 1934 she visited the German Foreign Ministry and discussed her possible work in Britain with the diplomat von Plessen. Plessen in turn informed his colleague at the German embassy in London, Otto II von Bismarck. He reported that the Countess was about to travel to Britain and wanted to use the opportunity to solicit support 'for Germany through private conversations'. This seemed useful since she was a friend of two pro-German voices in Britain at the time—Lord Noel-Buxton and Lady Snowden.[15] The offer of the Swedish-German countess was welcomed by Otto II von Bismarck. He knew her well himself. She had been a guest at his wedding and he shared her beliefs. Bismarck and his wife had become enchanted with the Nazi movement in February 1933, shortly after Hitler's appointment as Chancellor. Joseph Goebbels happily acknowledged: 'Afterwards [saw] Prince and Princess Bismarck. They are enthusiastic. The Princess is a beautiful woman.' Goebbels developed a crush on the Princess ('she is wonderful') and enjoyed his conversations with her and Winifred Wagner.[16]

The Bismarcks knew what a good impression noble names made in British society. Wilamowitz was not the only female noble who helped them with propaganda work. On 4 March 1935 the German embassy reported that Baronesse von der Goltz had given a series of lectures 'on the new Germany in England'.[17] The unpopular Hohenzollern would not have been able to draw crowds in Britain but they were helping in other countries instead. On 11 March 1939, for example, Prince Auwi gave a talk to the *Auslandsorganisation* of the NSDAP (Germans abroad) in Brussels and was received by King Leopold. Auwi spent several hours of conversation with the Belgian King and reported the details to the German Ministry of Propaganda.[18]

So why were aristocrats so willing to work for Hitler in the first place? The aforementioned fear of Bolshevism was one reason. As usual the Queen of Romania put it simply: 'Fascism, although also a tyranny, leaves scope for progress, beauty, art, literature, home, and social life, manners, cleanliness, whilst Bolshevism is the levelling of everything.'[19]

She saw herself as a seeker of beauty. Her stance was quite common among her peer group. As the National Socialist Prince Rohan explained, dynasties and the aristocracy had twice been faced with great political challenges. In the nineteenth century they had had to cope with the emergence of democracy and nationalism. They chose the less threatening one—nationalism. After 1918 another political challenge appeared, the choice between Fascism and Bolshevism. Again it was obvious to Prince Rohan which one would be more appealing for his peer group. The third option, supporting democracy, did not occur to him. The reason was obvious, particularly in Germany. As Prince Hohenzollern-Sigmaringen put it: 'the constitution of Weimar has to be revised. Parliamentarism has proved itself incapable. But most of all Marxism has to be broken.'[20]

Of course, not all aristocrats took the straight route from anti-Bolshevism to Hitler. The Duke of Coburg was one of the earliest converts. Others hoped for a while that an arrangement could be found with the Weimar Republic. During the golden years of Weimar, before the crash of 1929, they seemed to be slowly coming to terms with the new system. This had something to do with the election of Field Marshal von Hindenburg as Reichspresident of Germany in 1925. Since Hindenburg was a lesser noble and a war hero, aristocrats felt politically represented again for the first time. The contemporary journalist Bella Fromm noted: 'With the coming of Hindenburg, some of the former nobility began to return to Berlin during the season. They had not done this for some time, having retired to their estates in a huff after the revolution and taken up residence in smaller towns like Darmstadt, Dresden, Meiningen or Hanover where there was still the flavour of a miniature court and some sort of princely household to give them a whiff of the royal atmosphere they had always enjoyed so much. Now, during the social season, they are returning to Berlin and flocking in tremendous numbers to shows, theatres and restaurants, and social events.'[21]

That Hindenburg would tolerate and make National Socialism eventually acceptable was also encouraging for the German aristocracy. The synergy worked.

Naturally in order to be able to support Hitler many aristocrats had to pretend a lot of things were not happening. They had to ignore the parts in *Mein Kampf* where Hitler made fun of the limited intelligence and general indolence of the old ruling houses. Though *Mein Kampf* was full of mixed signals to them, the majority of the aristocracy lived in denial about the more troubling ones. The attractions were so much greater.

Via their international networks, aristocrats had first come across authoritarian and fascist regimes in Hungary and Italy. What a great number of aristocrats found attractive about them was that these regimes included the old elite and seemed to give them new relevance. They were also anti-parliamentarian and anti-Bolshevik.

Though fascism has an ultra-nationalist core, it also has a transnational side. This appealed to the higher aristocracy who thought of themselves as a transnational group. They were certainly influenced by what their peers in Italy experienced. The Duke of Coburg was an ardent admirer of Mussolini. His study of Mussolini's Fascism required several field trips and in 1933 he took along seventy German soul mates on an outing to Italy.[22] In Rome they visited an exhibition on the achievements of Fascism and were received by Mussolini. The Duce gave Carl Eduard a special present as the journalist Bella Fromm recorded: 'After dinner the unprepossessing Duke strutted around with his Fascist dagger, an honour bestowed upon him by Mussolini.'[23]

Coburg was not the only one who admired the Italian model. One aspect that appealed to the British and the German aristocracies was that Mussolini integrated the Italian royal family into his regime. Though Jens Petersen argued that 'In essence, the regime used the aristocracy as a symbol for the hierarchical model but did not regard it as a strategic factor,' this was far from obvious to contemporary observers.[24] In their eyes Mussolini had brought the postwar chaos in Italy under control and created a bulwark against Bolshevism. Many members of the British upper classes also travelled to Italy in the 1920s including Winston Churchill, Harold Nicolson, the Duke of Westminster, the Duke of Buccleuch, and Oswald Mosley. Churchill was impressed at the time:

> I will... say a word on an international aspect of Fascism. Externally your [Mussolini's] movement has rendered service to the whole world.... Italy has shown that there is a way of fighting the subversive forces.... She has provided the necessary antidote to the Russian poison. Hereafter no great nation will be unprovided with an ultimate means against the cancerous growth of Bolshevism.[25]

Wilhelm II also thought that Mussolini integrated traditional ideas. When the ex-Kaiser was interviewed by the *Evening Standard* and asked: 'What do you think of Mussolini?' Wilhelm replied: 'Mussolini has brought order into his country—a real, disciplined order. Italy today has become a land of peace and of work under the united concentration of all the forces of the nation. That is Mussolini's achievement. A real man!!'[26]

The Italian King had supported Mussolini and was amply rewarded—an example Wilhelm wanted to repeat. This would also become the dream of ex-King Alfonso of Spain. In 1938 Alfonso told the representative of the Berlin International News Service, Mr Pierre Huss, that he welcomed the Rome–Berlin axis. His daughter, the Infanta, was even more outspoken and informed Huss that her family was hoping to return to the Spanish throne. So far Mussolini had been blocking this, but she believed he would change his mind, thanks to the influence of the Italian royal family. She certainly believed that their connection with the Duce was important and profitable. Though the Infanta made negative comments about Mussolini, she stressed the fact that her father had great sympathy for the new Germany.[27]

That Mussolini continued to do well for the monarchy was also praised by Prince Otto II von Bismarck. In 1936 he was impressed by Mussolini's 'beautiful voice' and what he had achieved for the Italian monarchy. When Mussolini made the Italian King Emperor of Ethiopia, aristocrats thought they had been proved right to set their hopes on the Duce: 'The little king would not have thought in his wildest dreams that he could become Emperor.'[28] If Mussolini could make the (diminutive) King Victor Emmanuel III Emperor of Ethiopia, anything seemed possible.

The Italian model was therefore a tempting reason to align oneself with fascist regimes. Another reason for German aristocrats was Hitler's foreign policy. As we will see in Chapter 6 on Max Hohenlohe, Austro-German aristocrats felt attracted to Hitler's policy towards Austria and Czechoslovakia. They hated the Czechoslovak republic and hoped to get their property in Bohemia back courtesy of Hitler. This was one reason why the old go-between Max Egon Fürstenberg was able to switch effortlessly from the Kaiser to the Führer. He had always worked for an Austrian–German alliance and Hitler offered a modern version of it. After 1918 several pressure groups had sprung up in Austria, lobbying for unification with the German Reich. Organizations like the Austro-Bavarian Oberland League argued that postwar Austria was too small to survive.[29] In 1920 Baernreither wrote to Fürstenberg: 'Slowly the Entente—at least the English and the Americans—seems to grasp that Austria cannot stand on its own feet, but is still far away from envisaging annexation to Germany as a possible solution.'[30]

Fürstenberg agreed and waited for the right opportunity. He continued to visit his old friend Kaiser Wilhelm in exile, regularly promising things he could not deliver (the Kaiser's adjutant noted: 'F. promised to do everything necessary for the Kaiser's return. He wants to start a sort of central office').[31] By 1933 Fürstenberg's true loyalty was with Hitler. In the same enthusiastic tone he had once used for Wilhelm II, he had started to praise the Führer: 'it was overwhelming to face this great man.' To support 'the great man' made sense to Fürstenberg and many other German aristocrats. Unlike the Bolsheviks, Hitler did not threaten to dispossess property. This was a very important point for German landowners.[32] Among Fürstenberg's papers is a memorandum that circulated in many German aristocratic families at the time. It is an interview Hitler gave to a man called Friedrich Svend. Svend tackled the key question big aristocratic landowners in Germany cared about. Did Hitler's agrarian programme mean expropriation? Hitler assured Svend that this would never happen. He also assured him that his party wanted to win the support of the landowners, and the 'educated classes' (the *Intelligenz*). 'From the son of the Kaiser down to the last proletarian' they all had to work together 'to fight Bolshevism'.

Fürstenberg reacted to such uplifting talk by becoming a member of the NSDAP on 1 May 1933. He also joined the SA.[33] Despite his age he now tried his best to help the new movement. He wanted it to be successful across the generations and he therefore wrote to a young Hitler supporter, Prince zu Bentheim-Tecklenburg: 'You are for me the role model of a young aristocrat who understands the new times. . . . I am convinced that you will succeed in leading the aristocracy in the right direction!'[34]

Bentheim-Tecklenburg did his best and won over the young and the old. One of the reasons why aristocratic houses joined the NSDAP en masse was the avalanche-effect in these large, close-knit families. If the head of house joined, the wife, children, and cousins often followed.[35]

That the Nazi ideology included anti-Semitism was not a hindrance. Like Carl Eduard Coburg, German aristocrats in general had identified Jews with two movements they deeply resented—liberalism and socialism. By 1917 a third movement had been added to the list. Jews were now seen as the carriers of Bolshevism. This made them part of the aristocracy's greatest threat.

Recovering status and power were other great driving forces for German aristocrats to join the NSDAP. Carl Eduard also stressed how important it was to feel 'useful' again. He wrote to his sister Alice in 1939: 'What pleases me most is that they still need our help. In spite of their saying nowadays that the young must rule.'[36]

While they had felt 'useless' and discarded during the Weimar Republic, the Third Reich needed them. Princess Wied wrote in her memoirs that she had appreciated the idea of the Nazi movement that 'Gemeinnutz geht vor Eigennutz'—the common good was more important than individual self-interest.[37] By the 1930s Carl Eduard von Coburg could therefore proudly state that 'apart from a few exceptions the aristocracy was an opponent of the parliamentary regime. It now supports Hitler.'[38]

It is interesting that, despite his great commitment to the NSDAP, the Duke of Coburg did not become a party member until 1933. He would later state that he had from the beginning fought 'for the nationalist forces and for Adolf Hitler to become leader... despite my environment not understanding it and even personally defaming me'.[39] This was a version of the truth. One reason why he did not join the NSDAP before 1933 might have been his old loyalty to Ehrhardt, his preferred right wing leader. Another reason seems to have been that Coburg was more useful to Hitler not being a party member. He could still pretend to his conservative friends that he was an honest broker while at the same time subtly proselytizing for Hitler. Once Hitler was in power, Coburg became an official, highly honoured, party member. He now proudly sent off signed photos of himself in uniform and had himself photographed at Nazi functions always in the front row, next to other Nazi dignitaries. He had worked hard for this front row seat and enjoyed his place in the spotlight. He gave up his hotel life in Berlin and purchased his own headquarters in the capital—a place where he could network. It was called Villa Coburg and run like a second court, away from his 'regional court' in Coburg—and of course away from his wife.

To understand what an important asset Carl Eduard became for Hitler, one has to look at the Duke's regional, national, and international contacts—ranging from local Coburg businessmen to members of the British royal family.

Regionally Carl Eduard still dominated the social circles of Franconia. Franconia also included the world of Bayreuth which offered more than Wagner operas. By the 1920s Bayreuth represented a combination of music and the ideology of the Wagner family. Hitler made his first pilgrimage to Haus Wahnfried, the Wagners' villa, in 1921 to meet one of his heroes—the anti-Semitic writer Houston Stewart Chamberlain, son-in-law of Richard Wagner. During this trip Hitler caught a glimpse of the excellent network system of the Wagner family. Richard Wagner's widow Cosima was still alive at the time, forever busy cultivating an international elite. Thanks to her, Bayreuth had remained a place that attracted the rich and famous. Cosima was supported in this by her son-in-law Houston Stewart Chamberlain and later by another obedient in-law Winifred Wagner. The bizarre world view of Houston Stewart-Chamberlain was attractive to Hitler and Carl Eduard because of its racial concepts but also because of his firm belief that the war between Great Britain and Germany, those two 'racially connected countries', had been a mistake. They agreed that this mistake should not be repeated. When Houston Stewart Chamberlain died in January 1927, among the prominent mourners were Hitler, the former Tsar of Bulgaria, Ernst II Hohenlohe-Langenburg, and Prince August Wilhelm of Prussia. Carl Eduard was out of town and sent an expensive wreath. He would continue to attend the thoroughly Nazified Bayreuth Festival. Shortly before the outbreak of war in August 1939 Carl Eduard and Hitler listened to *Tannhäuser* together.

Apart from these Franconian connections, Carl Eduard offered good contacts for Hitler at the national level. The Duke was close to many members of the—Protestant—German aristocracy through friendships and marriage. His sister-in-law had been married to August Wilhelm, nicknamed Auwi (one of Kaiser Wilhelm II's younger sons), and though she divorced him in 1920 for his homosexuality, Carl Eduard stuck by him. He had after all almost grown up with 'Auwi' and his brother the Prussian Crown Prince Wilhelm. The Crown Prince had already been close to radical right wing movements, such as the Pan Germans, before 1914 and therefore showed an early interest in Hitler. So did Auwi, who became an ardent Nazi.

These contacts were useful for Hitler. Before he gained power, he therefore employed Carl Eduard's aristocratic network *within* Germany. When in 1930 aristocrats discussed the future of the monarchy at Pommersfelden, the Duke of Mecklenburg was named as a likely successor to President Hindenburg. Hitler was naturally keen on meeting Mecklenburg. The person who arranged the meeting for him was none other than Carl Eduard.[40] It gave Hitler the opportunity to find out how much of a rival Mecklenburg actually was. He need not have worried—Mecklenburg was no serious threat to him.

But the question remained which of the radical right wing parties would in the end win the upper hand. The idea that they should all pull together was something Carl Eduard had been working on for years. In October 1931 it seemed to be within his reach. Together with the DNVP leader and media tycoon Alfred Hugenberg (the DNVP, Deutschnationale Volkspartei, was the main conservative party, with anti-Semitic sympathies), Carl Eduard organized a meeting of anti-democratic right wing groups in the little spa town of Bad Harzburg. The DNVP, NSDAP, Stahhelm, Alldeutscher Verband, Bund der Frontsoldaten, and many others declared a united front against the Weimar Republic calling themselves the Harzburg Front. It was a rather unfortunate name. The left wing press ridiculed Carl Eduard as the 'Duke of the Harzburg Front'. The word 'Harzburg' sounded odious to Germans, since a particularly smelly cheese, Harzer Käse, is produced in Bad Harzburg. It was not only the left wing press that created a stink about the meeting. Despite Coburg's best efforts the right wing groups within the Harzburg Front continued their infighting behind the scenes. Hitler himself was at the centre of this, playing everyone off against each other and never seriously contemplating a merger with anyone. His aim remained absolute power.

Carl Eduard was still slow at comprehending this. His eagerness to unite conservative and radical right wing elements was again tested in the election of the German President in 1932. Against all the odds the Duke tried to get the DNVP and the NSDAP to agree on a single candidate—without success.[41] The DNVP put forward their own candidate. In the first round of the election Hindenburg received 49.3 per cent, and Hitler 30.1 per cent of the votes. The DNVP came third. Not surprisingly the NSDAP achieved its best result in the town of Coburg—48.1 per cent. Carl Eduard publicly endorsed Hitler in the second round and the people of Coburg followed his advice. This was a very public gesture by a man who so far had preferred to play the whole right wing field. Hitler received 57.1 per cent of the votes in the town of Coburg, and in the rest of Germany 36.8 per cent.[42]

In the end Hindenburg won the election against Hitler, but Carl Eduard continued to be an excellent propagandist for the NSDAP. Coburg also used his daughter's wedding a few months later to demonstrate his support for the Nazis. The nuptials offered a wonderful opportunity to combine two points on his agenda: his behind the scenes networking for the Nazi party and improving his own family's fortunes. The war had damaged them considerably but an advantageous marriage was a way forward. By marrying off his oldest daughter Sibylla to Gustav Adolf (the son of the Swedish Crown Prince) Carl Eduard brought prestige back to the tarnished house of Coburg. Sibylla conformed dutifully to her father's expectations, yet her depressed look on the wedding photos may have been an indication of what was to come. Her life in Sweden was not a success and she never became queen.[43] Such personal feelings hardly mattered at the time. Many high ranking party members were invited and amply used the opportunity to mingle with the old elite. The whole town was decked out with Nazi flags and a torch parade took place in honour of the happy couple. Hitler and Göring sent congratulatory telegrams.

The wedding also gave the ducal family—fourteen years after the war—an excellent chance to be at the centre of international society again. Although the guest list was dominated by German and Swedish aristocrats it also included English cousins: HRH Prince Arthur of Connaught, his sister Lady Patricia Ramsay, and of course Princess Alice.[44] Their presence established that relations between the German branch and the royal family were back to normal.

After the successful wedding of his daughter Sibylla, Carl Eduard hoped to repeat the coup. One of his cousins was Queen Wilhelmina of the Netherlands and another advantageous match would have been to marry Wilhelmina's daughter Crown Princess Juliana to his oldest son Johann Leopold Coburg. In the end this did not happen and Carl Eduard—always bad at losing—blamed his 'useless' son. When Johann Leopold finally did get married, though morganatically, he was disinherited. Carl Eduard's other children also turned out to disappoint him—a second son was secretly homosexual, and a younger daughter kept marrying inappropriate men (she would later accuse her father of sexual abuse, backed up by one of her brothers). Whether this abuse actually took place could never be verified, but looking at family photos, it is clear that the Coburgs were a far from happy family. Carl Eduard seemed to run his children like a military unit and they obviously lived in fear of him.

He was not just hardheaded when it came to running his family. Hitler knew that he could rely on Coburg's ruthlessness. The Duke's national contacts had been of great use, but they were no longer needed once Hitler had seized power. Decisive from now on was what Carl Eduard could deliver on an international level, i.e. his foreign contacts. Not all members of the higher aristocracy could offer them. The Hohenzollern princes, for example, had helped the Nazis at national level, but were useless abroad. Their reputation was ruined after the war, particularly in Britain. They would forever be identified with the 'war criminal' Wilhelm II. Carl Eduard on the other hand would be rehabilitated with the help of his influential sister Alice and was soon being received again in British circles. He was therefore ideal for missions in the English speaking world.

His general capability was first tested on a world tour in 1934—via Britain and America to Japan. The Duke summarized the whole trip meticulously in a memorandum for Hitler. (It is not recorded whether his Führer, who was not known for reading reports attentively, actually studied it though.) The Duke reported on Roosevelt's New Deal, expressed the opinion that the black population was under control, and stated his fear that German-Americans were losing their connection to the fatherland.[45] On this trip Carl Eduard acted as if he were still the head of a reigning house. Like Emperor Wilhelm II, he continued to distribute signed photographs of himself to his various hosts. The process followed a hierarchical order—depending on the recipient's status the photo frames were either of cheap wood or elegant leather.[46] Though the Americans seemed fairly flattered by the visit, they were just a sideshow. The second leg of the trip was Carl Eduard's visit to Japan. After the war his lawyers claimed that the Duke had not been involved in any of the negotiations for the German–Japanese anti-Comintern pact. This is not entirely true, his role was certainly part of a larger propaganda tour. To send a high ranking Nazi with a long pedigree to a monarchy like Japan demonstrated to the status conscious Japanese how much the German government valued rank and traditions. Coburg was president of the German Red Cross and in this capacity he now attended a conference in Japan. Using him as a Red Cross figurehead was also a highly sophisticated move by the Nazis. First of all to appoint a member of the old elite to such a position signalled continuity and stability. Aristocrats had traditionally been associated with medical and charity work and Carl Eduard's distinguished name would help to camouflage the fact that the German Red Cross had been turned into a Nazi organization. Secondly the position gave Carl Eduard a convenient cover. While cultivating his contacts abroad he could travel without arousing suspicion. In Japan Coburg gave the obligatory speeches in which he talked about 'his personal relationship with the Führer'.[47] He also attended many glittering social events with the German ambassador Willy Noebel.

This world tour was a highly visible trip, yet Carl Eduard was also used for the more 'shady' ones. His brief was to establish contact—behind the scenes—with the highest social echelons in Europe.

In 1934 the Nazis had prohibited monarchical organizations in Germany, but though Hitler got rid of indigenous monarchists he still courted British ones. It is surprising how much time and energy he invested in cultivating the British establishment. One of his contemporaries called him an 'anglophile romantic'.[48] His hope of winning over Britain—via its upper classes—has often been belittled as a case of 'wilful blindness'. There was—according to this argument—no realistic chance that he could succeed. So was he really just an irrational romantic? Or was it a sensible move to start courting the higher echelons of British society?

The British aristocracy has sometimes been portrayed as a political role model for its European cousins. According to this argument it helped to prevent the rise of a Mussolini, Horthy, or Hitler in Britain. Peregrine Worsthorne puts forward this thesis in his book *In Defence of Aristocracy*, namely that aristocrats guaranteed 'for three centuries ... the rights and liberties of all the British people so effectively as to make a written constitution unnecessary.'[49] Even David Cannadine, a historian at the opposite end of the political spectrum, argues that the British aristocracy in the inter-war years retreated into an 'aristocratic equilibrium', suffering its loss of power stoically. The general verdict is therefore that apart from a few eccentric exceptions—the Cliveden Set and other characters portrayed in novels like Kazuo Ishiguro's *The Remains of the Day*—everything remained quiet on the western front of European aristocracies. This ignores the fact that, long before the war, many British aristocrats felt attracted to radical right wing ideas and that this attraction grew after the First World War. While before 1914 diehards advocated a national and military awakening, fought the House of Lords reform, and tried to prevent Home Rule for Ireland,[50] after the war, the fear of social unrest haunted the British aristocracy. To them British society was in a deep crisis. Indeed one could argue that, despite winning the war, Britain had problems coping with the peace. The economic and political challenges seemed huge and the Empire had overextended itself after the Versailles Treaty. The Liberal party had fallen apart, the Labour party had produced the weak Prime Minister Ramsay

MacDonald. The conservatives showed no sign of reforming and the monarchy seemed to be frozen in aspic. British elites reacted to this in an extreme way. Much of the intellectual elite turned to the left, while many members of the upper classes (including members of the royal family) went the other way.

There was certainly admiration for Mussolini among the higher echelons of British society. The same was true for Horthy. The relationship to Hitler's Germany was more complex, but it became of greater interest to many after the outbreak of the Spanish Civil War. According to the British historian Maurice Cowling,

> the Franco-Soviet pact was disliked and was a source of sympathy for German action in the Rhineland. Disillusionment about the League, the Russian intervention in Spain and Labour hysteria against Franco then turned the coin over.[51]

That Spain became a republic in 1931 had come as a shock to continental as well as British aristocrats. Princess Löwenstein wrote about the abdication of King Alfonso XIII:

> We are shattered by the news from Spain. It has happened so fast, without a whimper. As with all our Princes' abdications. Was it really necessary? One cannot assume that the King lost his nerve, that would not be like him at all... What thankless beasts these peoples are!... The moment the Socialist government is in power they will start passing dispossession laws.... The German press will probably be very happy that another Republic has been founded.[52]

It was not just the Austro-German Princess Löwenstein who feared the consequences of another abdication. The news from Spain also travelled to Britain via dynastic networks. King Alfonso had a British consort, a cousin of George V who brought her accounts of the Spanish situation to London. Even without her stories, it was obvious to the British establishment that Spain was now becoming a centre in the war of ideologies. British politicians felt that they had to take sides. According to Cowling, Franco was perceived among British conservatives as a 'Christian gentleman' and 'one did not expect British interests to suffer if he won'.[53] One great propagandist for Franco in London was the right-winger and staunch monarchist, the Duke of Alba (by 1939 officially Spanish ambassador to London), who was related to the Duke of Marlborough. A famous Marlborough offspring, Winston Churchill, was particularly close to Alba.[54]

Cries for help by Spanish aristocrats certainly had an effect on their British counterparts. In June 1937 the Duke of Windsor's close friend

Don Javier Bermejillo (nickname Tiger) had become a refugee in the Romanian embassy in Madrid. He wrote to Windsor:

> The moral and physical suffering we are going through is indescribable, over two stones of weight have I lost, but my real agony is not the fear of being shot, like over 70.000 in Madrid alone, but not to be able to be on the side that fights and dies for one's ideals.

Bermejillo then went on to ask the Duke of Windsor to get him out of Spain. This was arranged by the Duke.[55]

Thanks to Ernest Hemingway and countless books on the subject we know a lot about the prominent supporters of the Republican forces, but we do not know how many aristocrats actually fought on the other side, in Franco's army. It was not only British circles who supported Franco. Princess Löwenstein saw herself as one of many aristocrats who supported Generalissimo Franco. But she was not entirely happy that her friends' children fought in Spain. To her husband she wrote in 1936 that the 'young Metternich—who is 19—has gone to Spain to fight in Franco's army! It is incomprehensible that one has allowed this. He is the sole heir and not Spanish. I do not understand why his mother allowed it. I don't know who would be next in line, if he died. The fear that he might be massacred by those beasts.'[56] (This did not happen. Metternich became, after the Second World War, president of the German automobile Club ADAC.)

When Franco's troops won in 1939, there was a sigh of relief in many families.

Coburg tried his best to use the Spanish situation for his work in Britain. He knew that one way to impress the British upper classes was to stress Hitler's record in the fight against Bolshevism. Hitler was perceived as a man who had crushed the trade unions and helped against Russian interference in Spain. As Cowling indicated, anti-Bolshevism in the British establishment was an unspoken assumption. An anonymous member of the Cambridge Apostles rebelled against this in the 1930s: 'we were all of obvious military age, and the war we saw coming was clearly not going to be one that we wanted to fight. It was already clear to anyone with any sense that the main aim of British policy was to send a re-armed Germany eastwards.'[57]

Hitler would have certainly welcomed this. Since he and Coburg both dreamt of an understanding with Britain, it seemed natural that Carl Eduard went there on endless reconnaissance trips in the 1930s. From being a social outcast after the war, Carl Eduard turned within a few years into a welcome visitor to Britain. He owed this to three factors: to Hitler, to members of the royal family, and to the changing opinion of Germany in British society.

That he was welcomed again was made possible by his sister Alice. She fought for his acceptance and how well she succeeded is illustrated by Carl Eduard's appointment book. He was received again in British salons and most importantly by the royal family. These visits did not appear in the court circular; they took place in private. Carl Eduard was at first invited in January 1932 and 1933 to Sandringham to see George V and Queen Mary during their Christmas holiday.[58] From then on he came to England several times a year and, as will be shown, always at crucial political moments. He also brought high ranking Nazis with him. This was an embarrassment that Alice had to play down after the war. In her memoirs she wrote:

One day Granpa [her husband 'Algy' Athlone, the brother of Queen Mary], Charlie and I lunched with Ribbentrop whose continuous talk about the 'New Deutschland' we found most objectionable.[59]

Alice was portraying herself here as a sceptic of Nazi Germany. Like so many of her peer group she made fun of Ribbentrop—after 1945. Ten years earlier she welcomed him as a guest because her brother worked closely with him. Her husband Athlone's aversion to Ribbentrop cannot have been so intense either. Athlone was Chancellor of the University of London and Ribbentrop donated to this very university volumes of the *Monumenta Germaniae Historica* in 1937. A few students protested when Ribbentrop turned up for the handing over ceremony, but nobody really cared. It had been organized extremely well.

That Coburg managed to play a special role in Britain was confirmed by the Nazi diplomat Carl August Clodius. Clodius was captured by the Russians and interrogated in 1946:

The Duke of Coburg as a close relative of the English royal family, had spent his youth at the English court. In pursuit of an Anglo-German rapprochement he offered his social connections and as president of the [Deutsch-Englische Gesellschaft] tried to invite to Germany many prominent Englishmen and put them in touch with important people in Germany. In England at that time not only Lord [*sic!*] Mosley... but many representatives of English society close to the Duke of Coburg were ready to act in the same spirit. Also in Germany among leaders of the National Socialists party, there were supporters of a rapprochement with England. Above all was Hess who grew up in Egypt and knew the English frame of mind well and as a consequence sustained influential ties in London. In addition there was Rosenberg who in the course of many years was considered as a replacement for Neurath as Foreign Minister. He was also a supporter of the English orientation in Germany's foreign policy.[60]

MI5 was aware of Ribbentrop's modus operandi in Britain. In a report that the Russian spy Anthony Blunt passed on to Moscow, MI5 had noted that the senior staff of Ribbentrop's Dienststelle commuted between Berlin and London: 'Their job, in essence, was to influence the broadest possible range of British public opinion in a pro-German direction. The Dienststelle [Ribbentrop's office] thus included individuals with connections in royal as well as diplomatic, political and industrial circles.'[61]

Ribbentrop was an excellent networker. His aide, Wilhelm Rodde, later explained to Russian interrogators:

> Ribbentrop began working by making a series of trips to England and France where he met up with his foreign friends with the aim of drawing them in and making use of them in the interest of his work. In France there lived a famous Count Polignac [Melchior de Polignac, whose firm would do extremely well out of the German occupation] the owner of a famous champagne firm and in England Sir Alexander Walker, from the Whiskey firm Walker. They were old friends of Ribbentrop, and eased his way accomplishing his political goals.[62]

Coburg helped Ribbentrop as well. German aristocrats who supported the NSDAP used their country seats for secret get togethers and Coburg was no exception. To keep meetings discreet he organized them in his various castles. Horthy, for example, was usually invited by Carl Eduard to hunts at his Castle Hinterriss in Austria (Coburg himself travelled to Hungary often and was a board member of the German-Hungarian Society). At such hunting weekends he could successfully deploy all the old pre-war charm.

The problem was, however, that in Britain Carl Eduard did not own a country house any more and therefore had no hunt to offer. Alice had to help him out. Her country house Brantridge Park had royal approval, being visited frequently by Alice's sister-in-law Queen Mary.[63] This made it attractive for other prestigious visitors and useful for Coburg's missions. In her memoirs Alice just wrote that 'my brother Charlie visited us several times and was so happy amongst so many relics of Claremont'.[64] But it was not just the furniture that gave him comfort. At Brantridge, far away from prying journalists, he could create a relaxed atmosphere for meetings. The beautiful surroundings (and illustrious hosts) impressed the participants. How many visits took place is difficult to verify; only thank you letters give an inkling. For example, after the Rhineland Crisis had been resolved to Hitler's satisfaction in 1936 Carl Eduard wrote to his sister:

> Dearest Tigs,
>
> I do not know how I can thank you enough for all the hospitality you extended to me and my gentlemen at Brantridge. At any rate I want to thank you once more with all my heart for all the help you gave me and for all the love you showed me. You and Alge are really two dears. You both made Brantridge a true second Claremont for me. I felt so at home this time staying with you, that when I left Croydon, I felt quite as if I was leaving home.[65]

As usual Carl Eduard was careful in this letter. But it is clear that he tried to mix in 'his gentlemen' with British politicians at Brantridge. The Secretary of State for War Duff Cooper, however, was not impressed. In January 1936 he was on the guest list and as usual Alice acted as hostess. Cooper resented having been lured by her:

> The point of it was to meet the Duke of Coburg, her brother. It was a gloomy little party—so like a German bourgeois household. It reminded me of the days when I was learning German in Hanover. I was tactfully left alone with the Duke of Coburg after luncheon in order that he might explain to me the present situation in Germany and assure me of Hitler's pacific intentions. In the middle of our conversation his Duchess reappeared carrying some hideous samples of ribbon in order to consult him as to how the wreath that they were sending to the funeral [of George V's] should be tied. He dismissed her with a volley of muttered German curses and was afterwards unable to pick up the thread of his argument.[66]

Even had Carl Eduard been able to concentrate more, it would have been pointless. Although Duff Cooper was a great friend of the pro-German Prince of Wales, he was suspicious of Germany and resigned the day after the Munich agreement.[67]

Coburg had to face a variety of opinions in British parliamentary circles, and he was fully aware of the uphill struggle. His title, however, did help. Great names could still impress in London, as the example of Otto II von Bismarck shows. In a Chatham House discussion in April 1933, he had explained to his British audience the policy of the NSDAP and was praised by another discussant, Colonel Christie:

> The fact that a man of Count Bismarck's breeding and tradition has given his wholehearted support to the Nazi Movement should persuade us to examine without prejudice the underlying principles of this somewhat feverish nationalism which has been accepted by millions of well educated Germans.[68]

Today we know that Christie worked in the intelligence world and needed to act as a pro-German. But he expressed something that others thought. If Hitler's regime was supported by the upper echelons of German society—a Bismarck, a Coburg—it could surely not be *that* revolutionary. Of course Otto II Bismarck advertised his country as an *official* diplomat, but when even a 'private individual' like the Duke of Coburg, a grandson of Queen Victoria, admired Hitler, it made an impact.

Ironically, behind the scenes, the official and the private Nazi diplomats—Coburg and Bismarck—indulged in rivalry. Though both were committed NSDAP members, the *official* diplomat Bismarck felt threatened by the *unofficial* diplomat Coburg. When in the summer of 1934 Coburg appeared in London, Bismarck reported back to the German Foreign Office in Berlin:

> I told the Duke of Coburg at a reception this morning that the Foreign Editor of the Daily Mail visited me yesterday and asked me whether Lord Rothermere should receive the Duke and Ribbentrop. The Duke was very affronted by this and avoided my question whether there really was a meeting taking place with Lord Rothermere. In an embarrassed tone he said 'that it seemed to be impossible to carry out private trips these days.' I would like to add that I had a feeling the Duke's circle had strict instructions not to inform the embassy about the fact that von Ribbentrop was here. In my opinion this case is further proof of the distrust towards our diplomatic representatives abroad. It also shows that even the best kept secrets usually come out.[69]

This summed up Hitler's method of using back channels quite well. But it naturally caused resentment. Bismarck in particular felt that such distrust of diplomats was unnecessary; after all he and his wife had lobbied for Germany relentlessly. Indeed, his Swedish wife Ann Mari was doing her best in British society circles for the Nazi cause. It was of course a question of honour for the German embassy to collect the few glittering prizes available and not be outshone by 'amateurs' like Coburg and Ribbentrop. One of the advantages the German embassy had in England was the fact that some British royals still saw it as a point of contact. This dated back to Queen Victoria's time and, despite the war, old habits seemed to have died hard. In 1928, for example, Princess Alice simply employed the embassy as her postal service. She instructed them to send 'two small accompanying parcels in the [diplomatic] bag to Germany... leather cigarette lighters for her two nephews, the sons of the Duke of Saxe-Coburg-Gotha'.[70] Her uncle, Arthur Duke of Connaught, felt the same. Arthur had been Queen Victoria's favourite son and was married to a Prussian princess. Despite his advanced age (he had been born in 1850) he was lucid and still very much interested in Germany. The German embassy was a useful communication channel for him. An overjoyed Otto II Bismarck reported in March 1934 that he had caught a big English fish: 'a close acquaintance of mine, the adjutant of the Duke of Connaught, Captain Fitzroy Fyers, has told me that he would like to travel to Germany to meet prominent representatives of the new Germany.' A few weeks later Bismarck was more precise:

> Fyers wants to be brought into contact with several members of the [German] government and the NSDAP to inform the Duke of Connaught about Germany from the best sources. The Duke is very interested in Germany and because of his influence within the royal family it is important to inform him correctly. Fyers wants to know about:
>
> 1. Our fight against unemployment. If possible he would like to visit an *Arbeitslager* [forced labour camp] near Berlin [the Duke of Connaught had probably heard about Oranienburg Concentration Camp. In March 1934 it consisted of communists, social democrats and homosexual prisoners]
> 2. The current situation regarding the Jewish question
> 3. The conflict within the evangelische Kirche [protestant church].[71]

Fyers was a member of the English Mistery (a reactionary political group that was ultra-royalist) and eagerly provided his Nazi friends 'Dr Diekhoff and Dr. Hanfstaengl' with information material about this dubious organization.

The Duke of Connaught was by no means the only well-connected person who was interested in German labour camps. The Marquess of Graham and his brother Lord Ronald Graham had a similar interest and also wrote to the German embassy. They wanted to visit Germany to find out what the Nazis did 'to bring race purity and fitness... We would also like to see if possible a Labour Service Camp and a concentration camp—in fact anything which might help to throw a true light on the situation as opposed to what we read in the Press.'[72]

Like Connaught's adjutant, the Graham brothers' enquiries were welcomed by German diplomats.[73] Counsellor Rüter came to the conclusion that the Grahams were useful for German interests. They could help to spread Nazi ideology in South Africa (where the Marquess lived most of the time). However, Rüter was hesitant about them visiting a concentration camp and told them that such wishes were fulfilled rarely because not everyone who showed interest 'wanted to achieve a better understanding between Germany and Britain'. It was, however, arranged that the brothers could meet Goebbels. The Marquess of Graham later continued his racial obsessions in South Africa. In 1954 he succeeded to the title of Duke of Montrose and eventually became Minister of Agriculture in Rhodesia. Graham and the Duke of Connaught were a good catch. But one of the greatest trophies the German embassy gunned for was the then Prince of Wales (by 1936 Edward VIII). His interest in Germany was constantly monitored by German diplomats. In September 1935, for example, Diekhoff, Otto II von Bismarck's superior in Berlin, wrote happily that he had received a distinguished visitor from Britain: Ralph Wigram, head of the German desk at the Foreign Office. Wigram was considered to be anti-German and his trip to Germany seemed completely out of character. Diekhoff therefore thought it might have been due to the influence of the Prince of Wales:

> Perhaps this visit was triggered by the Prince of Wales who has been reported to have told (Wigram) some time ago that it was scandalous that the German expert in the British Foreign Office did not know Germany.[74]

Though the trip did not change Wigram's opinion of Germany, it confirmed to the Germans that the Prince of Wales was trying to play a role when it came to Anglo-German relations. It would turn out to be a completely unconstitutional role.

Indeed the Prince of Wales enjoyed visiting the German embassy. On such occasions Ann Mari von Bismarck helped the unmarried ambassador Hoesch to entertain Edward and Wallis Simpson. The pretty Ann Mari was an ideal hostess, who talked with Edward in German. The friendship between the Bismarcks and the Duke and Duchess of Windsor would continue after the war, when they all holidayed together at the Bismarcks' villa in Marbella.[75]

Even though the Bismarcks got close to the Prince of Wales in the 1930s, the Duke of Coburg got closer. As a relative he had the advantage of seeing 'David' (as everyone within the family called the Prince of Wales) more often and was able to talk openly. He had two motives to charm his nephew—personal as well as political ones. Personally he hoped for the return of his English property (in the same manner that he had been compensated for his Gotha property after the war). Politically his aim was nothing less than an Anglo-German alliance. That the Prince of Wales listened to his German cousin once removed had several reasons: like many men of his generation he was committed to the idea of preventing another war. He was involved in veterans' organizations and this commitment combined with his interest in welfare policies made him susceptible to Nazi propaganda.

That Carl Eduard managed over the years to gain influence over 'David' has been shown by the press officer at the German embassy Fritz Hesse. In his memoirs, Hesse describes meeting Carl Eduard in June 1935 in London and telling him how difficult negotiations with the British were in the run-up to the Anglo-German Naval Agreement.

The Naval Agreement was meant by Hitler as the first step in building an Anglo-German alliance against the Soviet Union. It was also intended to undermine the Versailles Treaty and alienate Britain from France. Indeed it turned out to be a slap in the face for the French.

Ribbentrop was sent over to London for the negotiations on 2 June 1935. With him came the Duke of Coburg. Both men stayed at the same hotel. From the beginning Ribbentrop alienated the British Foreign Secretary, Sir Samuel Hoare. Hoare was outraged about the demands the German side made and the negotiations were about to collapse.

According to Hesse, the Duke of Coburg was very agitated about the situation. He claimed that there existed an anti-German circle in Britain that was trying its best to ruin relations with Berlin. He also criticized King George V who 'indulged in his private hobbies and ignored politics'. In his conversation with Hesse, Coburg said that it was the royal family's 'historic duty' to stand up for Germany:

> Has the House of Windsor forgotten that it has German roots and that Great Britain and my grandmother owe their Empire to Bismarck's help? Are we in Germany not allowed to have the same rights that Great Britain would give to any negro tribe?[76]

Carl Eduard then declared that he would give the Prince of Wales a piece of his mind about 'the pitiful part the monarchy was playing' in this affair.[77] It obviously worked.[78] On 11 June, while the naval negotiations were still in full swing, the Prince of Wales gave a speech to the British Legion. He was patron of the Legion and very involved with their work.[79] *The Times* reported on it with the headline 'Suggested Visit to Germany'. In the speech the Prince of Wales encouraged 'his fellow comrades' to visit Germany and to stretch out their hand. In fact it was not such a spectacular statement, but Ribbentrop used it in a follow up comment for *The Times* portraying it as a great pro-German gesture. It certainly seemed to be sufficient to upset the

French and also the Foreign Office.[80] 'David' was reportedly reprimanded by King George V.

To everyone's surprise Hoare suddenly gave in to all the German demands. It seemed obvious that the successful conclusion of the Naval Agreement had something to do with behind the scenes work.

The Duke of Coburg certainly saw it as a great success. The British Legion eventually visited Germany and Carl Eduard, who was in charge of its German equivalent, made sure that a return visit was arranged.

A more personal reason for the Prince of Wales listening to his cousin Coburg seems to have been the influence of his mother. In many ways, Queen Mary is the main link to the network her sons Edward VIII, the Duke of Kent, and George VI had with Germany. This aspect has never been analysed, though. Letters from German relatives to Queen Mary or copies of her letters to them for the period after 1918 are not made available by the Royal Archives. According to the royal archivist, Queen Mary only received one postcard from the Duke of Coburg in the 1930s. Since Queen Mary invited him regularly, it seems rather impolite that he never wrote a thank you note. Mary's correspondence with the Duke of Braunschweig, another dedicated Nazi, is also currently unobtainable.[81] We will see later that Queen Mary's son George VI was concerned about this correspondence after 1945. It is clear that Queen Mary stayed in touch with her German relatives in the inter-war years. It was part of her concept of family that she passed on to her sons. She strongly believed in an idealized aristocratic code of conduct which meant loyalty to one's roots, i.e. one's ancestors and all current members of the wider family. Marie of Romania has probably given the best analysis of her 'cousin May'. She saw the Queen as a person who was interested in family, pedigrees, and order: '[May] told it to me herself: she does not like uncomfortable things. She likes prosperity, ease, politeness, everything running on well-greased wheels.... She is fundamentally tidy, orderly, disciplined. She likes possessing, collecting, putting things in order. She likes wealth and position, jewels, dresses. She has little imagination, but she likes reading, history interests her, and family trees.... A placid, undisturbed woman who keeps all that is unpleasant at arm's length.'[82]

The war had been a disaster for her and all she wanted after 1918 was to unite the wider family again. No more unpleasantness.

That her own husband had obviously broken the ideal of royal solidarity in the First World War had to be glossed over. The murder of their Russian relatives was something Carl Eduard could certainly capitalize on in his conversations with 'David'. Ever since Carl Eduard had been surrounded by royal Russian refugees in Coburg, he considered himself an expert on the subject of Bolshevism and its consequences. It has already been mentioned how interested Edward VIII had been in the murder of the Tsar, interviewing the Russian ambassador at great length. His biographer Ziegler has shown that in the year of the General Strike, 1926, Edward sat up until 2 a.m. to talk about Russia with Robert Bruce Lockhart: 'By the end of the 1920s his thinking was dominated by sharp fear of the communist threat from Russia... It was his fear of the communists and doubts about the French that combined to make him view the future of Germany first with apprehension than with hope.'[83]

Indeed, to Count Mensdorff he stated in 1933 apropos the Nazi party: 'of course it is the only thing to do. We will have to come to it, as we are in great danger from the Communists too.'[84]

That the Prince of Wales was known to be pro-German did affect the rest of the establishment. It made it respectable, even fashionable. That the Nazis were anti-Semitic did not seem to hinder the Prince's admiration. His benevolent biographer Philip Ziegler thinks that Edward was only 'mildly anti-Semitic, in the manner of so many of his class and generation'.[85] This is a very generous interpretation. As the papers of General Franco show, Edward was *deeply* anti-Semitic.

The Spanish government had a good contact with the Duke of Windsor, Don Javier Bermejillo. He reported in June 1940 that the Duke was upset about the war: 'He throws all the blame on the Jews and the Reds and Eden with his people in the Foreign Office and other politicians all of whom he would have liked to put up against a wall.' To Bermejillo this was nothing new; he stated that Edward had already made remarks about the Reds and the Jews to him long before he became King.[86]

In fact Edward would keep up this 'tradition' well into old age, after the concentration camps had been filmed.

It was therefore relatively easy for Coburg to remind Edward of family values, his duty to his German roots, and to encourage his anti-Bolshevism at the same time.

To this day there are numerous conspiracy theories circulating as to how far Edward VIII was willing to go in his support for Germany. This has not made it easier to reconstruct the actual facts. That there was a cover up of Edward's activities has been suggested since the 1950s, when American historians insisted on publishing parts of the Windsor file (the captured

German Foreign Ministry documents concerning the Duke of Windsor and his closeness to the Nazis).[87] They were outraged about the way that documents had been suppressed. As the Churchill papers indicate, the Prime Minister was genuinely shocked about the Duke of Windsor's behaviour, but as a convinced monarchist did everything to keep the institution intact.[88] This policy is continued by the Royal Archives, which also embargo papers of the Duke of Kent, brother of the Duke of Windsor. We know from other sources how involved Kent was in establishing contacts between Britain and Germany up to 1939. His cousins, the Princes of Hesse, saw him as a useful ally. Prince Ludwig von Hesse wrote in 1938 about Kent: 'Duke of Kent. Very German-friendly. Clearly against France. Not especially clever, but well-informed. Entirely for strengthening German–English ties. His wife is equally anti-French.'[89]

In 1939, Kent met Prince Philipp Hesse, who was part of Göring's menagerie, in Italy with the intention of preventing the war. Kent was eager to act as a go-between and wanted to arrange a face-to-face meeting with Hitler. At the time he was acting on the instructions of his brother King George VI. The King had suggested to Chamberlain that Philipp von Hesse be utilized to approach Hitler. Petropoulos therefore comes to the conclusion that the Hesse Princes and the royal family cooperated 'to avert a war'. Several members of the royal family were involved in this cooperation: 'on the British side alone one has the Duke of Windsor, the Duke of Kent, and King George VI.'[90]

The Duke of Kent/Prince of Hesse channel has therefore been established. Yet the channel between Edward VIII and the Duke of Coburg is still played down. This is surprising, given the role Coburg played during the Anglo-German naval negotiations. Furthermore some of the rather damaging conversations Coburg had with Edward VIII surfaced soon after the war. The official biographer of Edward VIII, Philip Ziegler, quoted them (only to dismiss them). He comes to the highly disputable conclusion that the Duke of Coburg was deluding himself when he believed that his royal nephew was an avid supporter of the 'new' Germany. Instead Ziegler describes Coburg as the embarrassing uncle who everybody endured but nobody took seriously. He thinks Carl Eduard must have been hallucinating when he sent Berlin a telegram stating:

> British King sees an alliance with Germany as a necessity. It has to become a *Leitmotiv* of British Foreign Policy. The alliance should not be directed against France but should include it.

Coburg had reported to Berlin that he also asked the King whether Hitler and Baldwin should meet. Edward VIII answered according to this report: 'Who is King here? Baldwin or I? I myself wish to talk to Hitler, and will do so here or in Germany. Tell him that please.'

Ziegler concludes that 'it is inconceivable that Edward VIII would have expressed himself with quite such freedom or such folly'.[91] This is a very benevolent, if not illogical interpretation. As we know, Edward did get his meeting with Hitler eventually (albeit when no longer king) and Coburg was one of his German hosts in 1937.

Ziegler, who could not know about the Duke of Coburg's special role in Britain and his frequent invitations to Buckingham Palace, just dismisses him as the 'absurd Duke of Saxe-Coburg'.[92] This is bemusing to say the least, since in many other instances Ziegler has to admit that Edward VIII did show interest.

Edward was certainly indiscreet to many more people than his cousin, Coburg. In January 1936 a report arrived from the German embassy in Washington, which Hitler read two days later. It must have cheered him up. The American diplomat James Clement Dunn had said at a meeting with State Department officials that he expected the British position to become more pro-German now that Edward was king. Dunn's comments had been leaked to German diplomats, who reported the gist of it to Berlin. Dunn had talked to Edward when he was still Prince of Wales in spring 1935. During this conversation the Prince had been quite 'open' about his political views.[93] He had said that he disapproved of France's efforts to revive the *entente cordiale* and force England onto the French bandwagon. He was convinced that France was thinking only of its own interests and would drop England, if it got into difficulties. He also disapproved of the French line of forcing Germany onto its knees and showed a lot of understanding for Germany's difficult situation. He had stressed that he was not adopting his father's stance, who blindly followed the Cabinet's decisions. On the contrary he, as Prince of Wales, felt obliged to interfere when the Cabinet was planning something which was contrary to British interests. Dunn had been impressed by these straightforward comments. He had come to the conclusion that the new King Edward VIII would not openly and directly intervene in politics, but would try to use his influence as much as possible behind the scenes. Dunn was of the opinion that King George V had been passionately in favour of peace and therefore supported the Hoare–Laval Pact, but that Edward VIII was cold towards France.[94]

It is obvious from this statement that Edward VIII saw himself as a political actor. In 1940 he would tell a Spanish diplomat that he had retired 'from politics four years ago.' This meant that he had tried to *be* a political player up to his abdication in 1936. Edward VIII was indiscreet not just when talking to an American. More significantly he was also candid with the German ambassador von Hoesch. Hoesch's dinner parties accompanied by Hungarian dance music had obviously paid off. He reported home repeatedly about the Prince of Wales and summed up in January 1936 that the feelings of the new King towards Germany were 'so deep and strong that he would resist contrary influences'.[95] His report praised the easy manner of the new King, and his strong temperament (which differed so markedly from his father George V). He described him as a man of the world who was also interested in social problems including the living conditions in mining communities and housing problems in general. German diplomats with a good knowledge of history must have been reminded of Queen Victoria's husband Prince Albert by these descriptions. Like his Coburg great-grandfather Edward VIII seemed to care about social problems. The question was therefore: would he also want to realize his great-grandfather's dream of an Anglo-German alliance?[96]

Hoesch saw some potential here. He went on to say that Edward

> was not a pacifist but wanted a strong, honourable Britain which was ready to defend its honour and possessions if necessary...But he was of the opinion that a new European war would mean the end of Europe and a descent into Bolshevism and therefore the end of all culture. Despite being rooted in the parliamentary tradition, [Edward VIII] does understand the development of other states, and, in particular, Germany....E. has the firm intention of attending the Olympic Games in Berlin. He (also) asked me to tell the members of the German Frontkämpfer [veterans' association], whose visit is expected, that they should put aside two hours because he wants to talk to them all. And he also wants to join the dinner afterwards at the German embassy. King Edward will, of course, from the start have to show restraint regarding tricky questions of foreign policy. But I am convinced that his friendly disposition towards Germany will have some influence on the formation of British foreign policy. There will be a king on the throne who understands Germany and is willing to have good relations between England and Germany.

The King's wish to visit the Olympic Games in Germany in 1936 was never fulfilled and never became public.

Edward VIII may have listened to father figures like Hoesch and his cousin Coburg for personal reasons too—as a rebellion against his own father. The aversion towards his father was already obvious to contemporaries. Hoesch had indicated in his report that Edward wanted to be different from George V, and so had Dunn. It was also the opinion of Edward's cousin Queen Marie of Romania. She had spent a lot of time partying with 'David' in Paris after the war and was famously shrewd in her analysis of people. In 1935 she wrote about the Prince of Wales: 'For the moment he is inclined to be a revolutionary, that is to say, one in opposition, especially to his father's steadiness. David (as we call him in the family) kicks against traditions and restrictions, without realising that tradition made him, is his raison d'etre; he will have to find the right balance between today, yesterday, and tomorrow. Not easy.'[97] An astute observation.

After the death of George V in January 1936, Carl Eduard's social standing in England had taken another leap forward. The former traitor peer was invited to attend the King's funeral. On film Carl Eduard cuts a pitiful picture, stooping and limping in row six of the funeral parade, looking much older than his 52 years. He was wearing an unflattering German army uniform and corresponding helmet which did not enhance his looks either. Yet the pitiful nature of the picture was deceptive. Though his health problems haunted him again, he was at the height of his networking game. It was, after all, Carl Eduard who had been chosen by Hitler as the official representative of Germany (together with the German ambassador) to offer his condolences to the new King. At the funeral dinner Carl Eduard was seated at Edward VIII's table. They both seemed to have before them a promising future. In Berlin Hitler was also eager to show his sympathy with Britain and attended a special church service at the Anglican church of St George on 25 January 1936. Quite a sacrifice for a man who was not known as a church-goer.

Such symbolic gestures were certainly understood in Britain. After the success of the Naval Agreement in 1935, the first test for Anglo-German relations came during the Rhineland crisis.

The remilitarization of the Rhineland was expected by the British government, but the timing was not. Zara Steiner has shown that from February 1936 onwards the Foreign Office had considered 'the dangerous question of the demilitarized zone', but had not expected the Germans to act so quickly.[98] Foreign Secretary Anthony Eden never seriously contemplated fighting over the Rhineland. But, since remilitarization would violate the

Locarno treaty, he developed the idea of using this as a bargaining chip, e.g. negotiating an Air Pact in return for giving up the demilitarized zone.[99] As Steiner puts it so succinctly: 'In other words, Britain would abandon its commitments with regard to the Rhineland, in an agreement negotiated behind France's back.'[100]

However, Hitler could not be sure how the Baldwin government would react. He had no informant inside the British government and was rightly concerned lest the British, under pressure from the French, might stop German troops from marching into the Rhineland. Consequently he used all available channels to London—official and unofficial ones—to make sure the British government did not act against Germany. The unofficial channel was the Duke of Coburg whose brief was to influence Edward VIII as a conduit to the Prime Minister. The official channel was the German ambassador von Hoesch.

In March 1936 the world—including the British Foreign Secretary—was distracted by the atrocities Mussolini had committed in Ethiopia. Hitler, via his ambassador von Hassell in Rome, had already made sure that Italy would not side with France and Britain in case they were considering steps against the Rhineland remilitarization. Once he had this assurance he had his troops march into the Rhineland on 7 March. Confronted with a fait accompli Eden was taken aback. To calm French nerves, the British government asked Hitler to withdraw the troops—naturally he refused. Though the French were outraged, they had a weak hand. First of all they were under the impression that Germany had a much greater military capability than was actually the case. Secondly they were well aware of their own lack of military preparedness. They could not risk a serious conflict.

In his ghosted recollections Edward VIII portrays himself during the crisis as the confidant of several European statesmen:

> some of my visitors advocated a policy of standing up to Germany; others wanted my Government to pursue the opposite course. While I saw the pros and cons of both courses of action, I must confess that I was not convinced that either would lead to a peaceful solution. Intuitively I felt that another great war in Europe was all too probable; and I saw but too clearly that it could only bring needless human suffering and a resurgent Bolshevism pouring into the vacuum of a ravaged and exhausted continent.[101]

The argument in Edward's favour has been that since he was only King for eleven months and wasted most of the time on his personal problems, he played no part in this at all. Yet his cousin Coburg certainly hoped he would.

It has been argued that the few people Hitler consulted before 7 March could not have gone beyond Ribbentrop, Göring, and Goebbels. Coburg worked closely with Ribbentrop and had been making unusually frequent trips to London in January and February 1936. On 7 March, the day of the remilitarization, he was sent immediately to London and stayed there until 16 March. His mission was obviously to calm British nerves. And they needed calming. Though the British never seriously contemplated fighting for the Rhineland, they now looked extremely weak. Since Hitler could not be entirely sure during the first 48 hours after his 'coup' how the Locarno powers would react, he accompanied the move with his usual peace rhetoric, including the offer of a twenty-five-year non-aggression pact and even the idea that Germany might resume its place at the League of Nations.

The German ambassador, Hoesch, was decisive in selling this offer.[102] Hoesch definitely played his part in the whole drama with great aplomb. It helped that he was not considered to be a Nazi, but a respected diplomat—a gentleman who would honour his word. He could therefore sell Hitler's peace rhetoric convincingly to the Foreign Office (admittedly a Foreign Office which had not much choice but to pretend to believe it).

It is not uncommon for 'successes'—and the unhindered remilitarization of the Rhineland was a great success for Hitler—to be claimed by several people. Whether Carl Eduard's efforts to influence the King were really important remains debatable. But since Hitler had an overblown idea of the King's influence, it was a logical step for him to send his most illustrious go-between. Thanks to Coburg's and Hoesch's reports it must soon have became clear that 'the congress was dancing, but never moving'. Once it was obvious that Hitler would get away with it, the Duke of Coburg left London. Back in Germany he wrote to his sister:

> What an awful lot has happened in the world since I left Brantridge [Alice's country house]. I do so hope we should pull through this strong weather and bring our ships into a good well-built harbour. The possibility is there I feel. If only the neighbours quieten down and contemplate everything peacefully.... Did Alge see D. after I left and what did he say? Alge was going to let me know.[103]

Alge was of course Alice's husband and Queen Mary's brother. The opinion of D. that was so important for Carl Eduard to know was the opinion of David, Edward VIII. The 'neighbours' were the French and they had had no choice but to quieten down.

Relations between Carl Eduard and the German embassy had improved considerably after this crisis and they were about to get even more friendly. This was due to the arrival of Ribbentrop as the new ambassador. His predecessor Hoesch had never been completely trusted by Hitler. When Hoesch died unexpectedly, the Duke of Coburg wrote to Alice: 'Is that not too sad, poor old Hoesch going off like that at this critical moment. I never knew he was not up to the mark. Really a loss.'[104]

It turned out to be his gain, though. Ribbentrop and Carl Eduard had worked well together since 1934. The closeness between the new ambassador and Carl Eduard was also noticed by the British press. According to the *Morning Post* of 25 October 1936 it was Ribbentrop who had arranged for Carl Eduard to become head of the Ex-servicemen's Association—a great honour for a man who had never actually fought in a war. This honour was further proof that since the King's funeral Carl Eduard had become increasingly visible in Britain. He now dined regularly with conservative politicians (including Neville Chamberlain). But then in December 1936 Edward VIII suddenly abdicated because—as his lover Wallis Simpson herself succinctly put it—'he could not have his crown and eat it'. Not everyone appreciated the humorous side of it. Edward VIII's close relative Marie of Romania was outraged: 'Personally I am too royal not to look upon David as a deserter... The whole world was open to him.... it seemed so unnecessary to stand the whole British Empire on its head, to compromise the throne, and shake the foundations of monarchy... Perhaps I am full of royal prejudice.'[105]

We do not know of the Duke of Coburg's reaction to the abdication. He was in bed with flu at the time and the news must have raised his temperature. Edward VIII's downfall was certainly seen as a tragedy by the Nazi leadership while it raised spirits at the Soviet embassy. The Russians had been nervous after the Naval Agreement and Britain's apparent indifference to the remilitarisation of the Rhineland. Now Maisky, the Soviet ambassador, sent a telegram to Moscow stating what a blow Edward's abdication was to Germany—a common analysis at the time.

It was certainly a blow to the Nazi leadership, but it did not mean the end of go-between work in Britain. The Nazis wanted good relations with Britain and consequently the German press did not attack the British royal family. After the abdication scandal this was appreciated in London. In a confidential report the German Foreign Ministry stressed that it was seen in Britain as a 'noble gesture' that the German press had been very helpful during the abdication crisis. 'The King [George VI] was very angry about the American scandal press. He will not forget the attitude of the German press. If he remains on the throne the German attitude will be useful since he has great sympathies for the Third Reich [Nazi Germany].'[106] George VI's sympathy for Nazi Germany made it possible for Carl Eduard to stay in contact with both kings—the former and the new one. He now cultivated George VI and at the same time helped organize the Duke of Windsor's visit to Germany. He probably discussed the details with Hitler during the celebrations for the fifteenth anniversary of the 'Train to Coburg'. For the occasion Hitler had arrived in Coburg and spent an hour with Carl Eduard.[107] Both men were determined to make the Duke of Windsor's visit a great social and political success. Carl Eduard's first step was to prepare the international press.

It was, of course, not unusual for the German government to organize information trips for foreign journalists.[108] This tradition had started long before the First World War with Baron Würtzburg, who in 1907 had been the host of a British press delegation. He was chosen because he was related to the Duke of Norfolk and could explain in perfect English how much Germany had learnt from British institutions. Thirty years later, British journalists still preferred an aristocratic tour guide. Now the Duke of Coburg was doing the guiding. As a duke he offered even more glamour than a baron. The difference with 1907 was, however, that Carl Eduard was not a politically moderate *grand seigneur* like his predecessor Baron Würtzburg, but a committed National Socialist. With German press policy now run by Goebbels, Carl Eduard subjected the international gathering of journalists to a perfect propaganda offensive.

On 21 October, one day before the Duke of Windsor and his wife arrived, Carl Eduard opened his charm offensive. The group he entertained included journalists from the USA, Italy, Sweden, Denmark, the Netherlands, and Belgium. The British contingent included correspondents from the *Manchester Guardian*, *The Times*, the *Daily Mail*, and the *Daily Express*. The Duke himself was supported by minders from Goebbels's Ministry of Propaganda as well as people from the Dienststelle Ribbentrop. They duly reported back about the great success of the enterprise: Duke Carl Eduard had been a 'very friendly host' and 'established direct contact with the Anglo-Saxon race'.

Accompanied by their friendly host, the journalists had visited the sights that are still offered to tourists in Franconia today: a visit to the rococo

Figure 6. A front row seat again (left to right): Emmy Sonnemann (later Mrs Göring), Hermann Göring, the Polish ambassador Jozef Lipski, Carl Eduard Coburg and Joseph Goebbels, 26th February 1935.

Vierzehnheiligen church, a tour of Castle Veste in Coburg where Martin Luther lived for a while, and a visit to Banz monastery.

In Banz the young priests received their guests with the Hitler salute which 'impressed' the foreign visitors 'visibly'. According to the enthusiastic Nazi press report the priests then had animated conversations with the accompanying SS and SA members and got along with them extremely well. This was meant to prove to the foreign journalists that there were no problems between the government and the Catholic Church. In the report an unnamed foreign journalist was quoted as having been impressed that 'the nationalist-socialist revolution had not senselessly destroyed the values of the past'. The journalist claimed that he had now realized that a civilized and cultured life still existed in Germany: 'Values that the National Socialists respected while Bolshevism had destroyed them.'[109]

Whether this journalist worked for the pro-German Rothermere Press is not mentioned in the report. Also the comments of the (usually more critical) *Manchester Guardian* are not included. Whether any were made, however, is doubtful. Since expulsions of foreign correspondents were not uncommon, it can be assumed that all participants kept critical remarks to themselves. This little episode shows how useful it was for the NSDAP to employ a member of the old elite for representational events where the social capital of a former Duke had more influence than the power of a Nazi Gauleiter.

The actual visit of the Duke and Duchess of Windsor a few days later is well documented. They were received by Hitler in Berchtesgaden, by Göring at his country seat of Carinhall (playing with his train set), and Edward even gave the Hitler salute. His cousin Carl Eduard entertained him in Nuremberg. For the Nazis the whole trip (for which they had paid) had proved a great success.

The aftermath of this visit indicates that the Duke of Windsor continued to flirt with the regime. As will be shown later, the Nazi leadership never seems to have lost touch with him after 1937.

The royal family did not seem to disapprove of the Duke of Coburg hosting his nephew in Germany. One month after the Duke of Windsor's visit, Carl Eduard was invited by Queen Mary for tea.[110] One wonders whether she discussed her son's German visit. But she must have been aware of why Carl Eduard was in London again. He had arrived at the invitation of the British Legion and was also received by the new King, George VI. Later that year at the Anglo-German Fellowship (AGF) dinner he was the guest of honour, hobnobbing with the Earl of Glasgow and Viscountess Snowden. The Anglo-German Fellowship had been important to him ever since 1935. It was supported by people with business interests in Germany and was not intended to be a pro-Nazi organization from the outset. But the Nazis hoped to use it for their own ends. It turned out to be more difficult than they thought. First of all the Fellowship was full of businessmen and not, as the Germans had hoped, politicians. Second, some of them occasionally voiced criticism of the Nazi regime, which did not go down well in Berlin. As it turned out everybody tried to use the Anglo-German Fellowship for their own purposes: There were well-meaning members who wanted to avoid another war. There were businessmen who wanted to make deals with Germany. There were the British security services who hoped their moles would provide them with a fuller picture of private Anglo-German contacts. And there was the NKVD [Soviet Intelligence], which instructed their up and coming young spies Kim Philby and Guy Burgess to work for the AGF for the same reason (Kim

Philby was even made editor of the Fellowship's newsletter). Indeed Philby's analysis of the AGF raised fears in Moscow. The first information he passed on to his handler was 'a list, covering several pages, of the names of Nazi sympathizers in the upper echelons of government, in the political class, and among the aristocracy of Britain. Attached to the list was an analysis of the opinions of sundry aristocrats, business leaders, and politicians about National Socialism and about Hitler himself. This list seemed rather insignificant until the outbreak of war.'[111]

The Anglo-German Fellowship provided a good cover for the work of Carl Eduard. He used his visits to the AGF 'while he conducted negotiations with Edward VIII to try to engineer an Anglo-German pact'.[112] This was naturally going on without the knowledge of most AGF members. They would have been surprised that an unidentified Nazi agent reported to Hitler's Adjutant's office on 11 December 1935 from London that the AGF seemed to succeed in winning over members of the British elite for the Nazi cause. The informant first praised a football match between British and German players for which the Duke of Coburg had come over especially. According to the informant the game had had a great moral effect, because the British trade unions had tried to prevent it taking place. This had been perceived as an act of unfairness which the British public reacted against. When the game took place, the good behaviour of the German fans then made a very positive impression on the British. Afterwards the Anglo-German Fellowship continued the good work at a higher level, with a grand dinner. They entertained the German Sports Minister, Tschammer und Osten, on 5 December 1935—an event the Duke of Coburg attended as well. The informant was of the opinion that the dinner was a success, but that more had to be done. The big political names were still missing among the AGF. The reason for this was, according to the informant, that active politicians feared they could be criticized for supporting the suppression of Jews and Christians. Once the church question was solved in Germany, the membership of the Anglo-German Fellowship would grow. The informant summed up his report by saying:

> The organisation of the evening was outstanding and the German guests were chosen with great sensitivity to English psychology. The Duke of Coburg in particular is a personality who ought to be attractive to English society members.[113]

Hoesch also reported the meeting a success, apart from one unfortunate aspect: 'the Jewish problem is casting a dark shadow over German–English relations. Almost all English members talked about it with their German guests.' Mount Temple and Lord Eltisley had mentioned it in their speeches. Prince Otto II von Bismarck had then ended the discussion by saying that people should not believe the 'biased press reports but instead visit Germany and see what was going on for themselves'.[114]

Hoesch's report had immediate effect. Hitler exploded and ordered in December 1935 'that the German members of the Anglo-German Fellowship should be withdrawn immediately, since it was not acceptable for the German racial laws to be discussed in the way ambassador von Hoesch has reported'.[115]

Since there were no German members in the AGF, the instruction could be ignored. Ribbentrop wanted to play a long game. He had made Carl Eduard president of the sister organization, the Deutsch-Englische Gesellschaft (DEG).[116] The idea was to use the DEG to influence the AGF in an unofficial way. A recently published Russian source shows how Ribbentrop, as a first step, purged the German counterpart of the AGF of unwanted members. SS-Oberführer Wilhelm Rodde,[117] who had worked for Ribbentrop, told his Russian interrogators in 1947:

One has to remember that a great number of [British] industrialists and financiers and especially those who had long maintained friendly relations with Germany were members [of the Anglo-German Fellowship] the task of which was to strengthen the political and economic ties with Germany. Among them Ribbentrop was unable to find support. It was clear that friendly contacts by members of the English society with members of the same society in Germany were one of the reasons for the sceptical and partly hostile attitude of the English towards the Third Reich in so far as all the leading posts in the German-English Society in Berlin were taken by big financiers negatively disposed against the new Nazi regime. Extreme measures were necessary to reorganize this society so that it worked in the interest of the new regime, that is to say to replace all the leading figures by National Socialists who could be counted upon politically. Ribbentrop tasked me [Wilhelm Rodde] and Eugen Lehnkering with the difficult job. We should do whatever it would take to purge German-English Society people ill disposed towards National Socialism who had held up our work. We carried out this task speedily.

The Russian interrogator then asked how this was done and Rodde explained:

It was not difficult for us. As far as it was known that members of the Board were negatively disposed and uttered sceptical remarks directed at the leaders of the

National Socialist party we simply suggested to these gentlemen that they give up their powers and leave the Society in return for our promise not to take any repressive measures against them. Thus we got rid off people we did not like. In the positions they vacated, we put at Ribbentrop's suggestion, members of the NSDAP —namely as President the Duke of Saxon-Coburg-Gotha, Carl Eduard.[118]

At the first meeting of the 'sanitized' Deutsch-Englische Gesellschaft, Rudolf Hess and Joachim von Ribbentrop, along with the British ambassador to Berlin and the president of the AGF, Lord Mount Temple, were present. Between April 1937 and spring 1939 the membership of the Deutsch-Englische Gesellschaft rose from 176 to 700. The head office was in Berlin. There were branches in Bremen, Hamburg, Heidelberg, Essen, Stuttgart, and Wiesbaden. Ernest Tennant proudly wrote to a Cabinet Minister in February 1939 that 'in March further branches are to be opened in Frankfurt and Cologne and in April in Vienna and, given real support from the British side, there is almost no limit to the number of branches that the Germans propose to open throughout their country.'[119]

Wilhelm Rodde thought that the appointment of the Duke of Coburg as president of the DEG was decisive for the success of both organizations:

relations between England and Germany started to improve immeasurably. Being a member of the English royal family the Duke wielded great influence in commercial and industrial circles in England and met with complete support from influential English friends. As to Englishmen who took a pro-German position but weren't members of the [Anglo-German Fellowship] we persuaded them to join and undertake intensive propaganda for Germany. All the work in drawing the English in [the AGF] was undertaken by Count Dürckheim and Hewel [a diplomat] who had contacts in English society.[120]

Count Dürckheim was the desk officer for England at the Büro Ribbentrop (the office Ribbentrop ran before becoming a 'proper' diplomat). In postwar Germany Dürckheim would 'reinvent' himself as a psychologist and Zen teacher. Rodde was less lucky; he died as a Russian prisoner of war. But before that he named the following British contacts Ribbentrop 'counted on in his propaganda work in Britain':

Lord Rothermere [the newspaper proprietor], Ward Price [Rothermere's chief correspondent]; Jack Evans [owner of an insurance company]; Francis Cooper [President of Unilever]; Mr. Proctor, Industrialist; Lord Londonderry, a personal friend of Göring; Mr Ernest Tennant; Lord Mount Temple [President of the Anglo-German Fellowship]; Prof. Conwall-Evans; Sir Arnold Wilson MP; Captain Kennedy [political correspondent of the Times]; Captain Richardson [industrialist];

Lord Hamilton; Lord Duncan-Sandys [son-in-law of Winston Churchill]; Mr. Brant, an important banker; Samuel Hoare; Mr Oliver Hoare; Allan of Hurtwood; Mr Beamish; Lord Lothian.

The majority of the people named were members of the Anglo-German Fellowship and Rodde stressed that 'these people were used by us for propaganda and spreading the pro-German policy in England'. The interrogators then asked Rodde to give the names of Ribbentrop's agents in Britain. Rodde replied:

I know the following subjects who carried out intelligence work for us:

Sir Arnold Wilson. He was a private guest of Ribbentrop in 1935/36. He stayed at the Kaiserhof Hotel and for a short time spent large sums of money on alcohol, on Ribbentrop's instructions I paid for them myself.[121]

Arnold Wilson MP wrote his first pro-German article in the *English Review* in June 1934: 'Herr Hitler himself impressed me profoundly. After a conversation lasting three quarters of an hour I left with the feeling that I had been talking to a man who was national by temperament, socialist in method, but, like our best conservatives, desirous of change in particular directions.'[122]

The next person Rodde named as an agent was Thomas P. Conwell-Evans, who was probably playing both sides and will feature in Chapter 6. Conwell-Evans would later half admit that he was at first taken by the Nazis: 'I was sadly late in perceiving the real nature of the Nazi German menace'.[123]

Another more plausible candidate as agent Rodde identified was 'Captain Kennedy. He paid private visits to Ribbentrop and Count Dürckheim. As a correspondent of the Times he wrote pro-German articles.'

The fourth agent named was Henry Hamilton Beamish. Beamish had once been a supporter of Pemberton Billing and was now vice-president of the Imperial Fascist League and a supporter of the Madagascar Plan for Jewish deportation. According to Rodde he arrived in spring 1936 'in Germany without money and shabbily dressed. He was fully looked after by Count Dürckheim.'

Agent five was, according to Rodde, Ernest Tennant, a founding member of the Anglo-German Fellowship. According to Rodde,

one fact draws one's attention to him. On one occasion in the winter of 1935 I met Ribbentrop in his apartment and brought documents to sign. I opened the door and wanted to walk into his study and suddenly Ribbentrop grabbed me and literally

> pushed me out of the room, making excuses that he was in conference and asked me not to disturb him. Amongst those present I recognized Tennant and one employee of the Abwehr [the German military intelligence service]. From this I draw the conclusion that Tennant worked with Ribbentrop and was connected with the German intelligence services.[124]

Ernest Tennant does not mention such work in his autobiography *True Account*, which might more appropriately have been entitled 'Untrue Account'.[125]

The Deutsch-Englische Gesellschaft (DEG) and the Anglo-German Fellowship remained close to the Duke of Coburg's heart. He reported to Alice in March 1939 that his old friend Lord Brocket 'is now Chairman of the Anglo-German Fellowship. It was such fun talking about Brocket (Hall) and now he has also bought Bramshill.'[126]

Brocket spoke German fluently. He entertained leading Nazis at his houses and was a guest at Hitler's 50th birthday celebrations.[127] In 1940, as we shall see, he tried to persuade Chamberlain to reach a peace deal with Hitler.

Neville Chamberlain was a great hope for Coburg as well. When Chamberlain became Prime Minister in 1937 he initiated a new foreign policy towards Germany—appeasement. At the time two issues were in the foreground—Austria and Czechoslovakia. The Foreign Office had come to the conclusion that: 'the German establishment was united in its belief that Anschluss was inevitable and that an attack on Czechoslovakia was probable unless the Sudetenland was transferred to Germany.'[128]

Chamberlain had no serious intention of standing up to Hitler on these issues. He accepted the Anschluss and he would eventually accept Hitler's stance in the Sudeten question. Since the Sudeten question was handled by two other go-betweens, it will be discussed in more detail later. Coburg seems to have played a role though. According to his appointment book he arrived in London on 22 September 1938, the very moment Chamberlain was meeting Hitler in Munich. After his arrival Coburg was first briefed in the German embassy and, according to his appointment book, a day later saw 'Bertie and Elizabeth' (George VI and Queen Elizabeth). After meeting the King and Queen he reported immediately back to the embassy again. Altogether he went to the embassy five times within three days.[129] He also seems to have had several conversations with George VI, but there are no notes of these meetings (and there is no hope that if such notes exist the Royal Archives will make them available). But we know that George VI was a supporter of the Munich agreement. He later appeared on the balcony with Chamberlain to celebrate it. Originally he had planned to go a step further and welcome Chamberlain at the airport on his return. He was, however, advised against such a step. Queen Mary wholeheartedly agreed with her son's opinion: 'I am sure you feel as angry as I do at people croaking as they do at the Prime Minister's action. He brought home peace, why can't they be grateful?'[130] Her relative Coburg would have been pleased with such a statement.

While Britain remained his main target, Coburg was also busy using his other contacts. As head of the House of Sachsen-Coburg und Gotha, Carl Eduard had very uncomplicated access to many other royal houses. Only prominent members of the higher aristocracy could so easily have been granted audiences such as the following: 'At the end of January', Coburg wrote to his sister, 'I was 3 days in Rome during which I had a nice talk with the King and Emperor [Victor Emmanuel III] and a most interesting one with Mussolini.'[131]

It was therefore natural that after the annexation of Austria in March 1938, Carl Eduard was sent to Italy to deliver the Führer's special thanks to Mussolini.

Coburg continued to be sent on such charm offensives. Together with his 'adoptive son' Schwede-Coburg, Carl Eduard visited Poland in February 1939. It was a great success. Only six months later Hitler and Stalin would wipe out the Polish army, but before that Coburg solemnly laid a wreath on the grave of an unknown Polish soldier. He was received like a high ranking politician, having talks with the Minister of War and an audience with President Moscicki. After sightseeing visits in Warsaw and a trip to Krakov, he laid another wreath on Marshal Piłsudski's grave and then lunched with Polish officers.[132] This visit was typical of Coburg's work: the rather charmless charmer, making sure that the facade was kept up while war plans were finalized in Berlin.

But by 1939 the situation had certainly got more difficult for Coburg's work in Britain. After the invasion of Czechoslovakia in March, British appeasers were on the back foot. In the summer of 1939 political pressure forced Chamberlain to talk to the Soviet Union about an alliance. It was not just Labour or Liberal politicians but also Conservatives who had concluded that Germany was becoming too dangerous. Across party lines there was now support for an alliance with the Soviet Union. Chamberlain and Halifax still thought they could reach a deal with Hitler, but they had at least to pretend to be in negotiation with the Russians. While Chamberlain started this pretence in the foreground, in the background he signalled to Germany via a private channel that he was not serious about the Russian negotiations. Since Chamberlain did not trust his own diplomats, mirroring Hitler's methods, he used a go-between for the signalling—Lord Kemsley. He was the owner of the *Daily Telegraph* and on his way to Germany. As a 'fellow press magnate', Kemsley had been invited to Germany by Minister of Propaganda Joseph Goebbels in July 1939. The Nazi party's chief ideologue, Rosenberg was one of Kemsley's hosts. Rosenberg, like Coburg, considered himself an expert on Anglo-German relations. Together with von Weizsäcker from the German Foreign Ministry, he entertained Lord and Lady Kemsley for a leisurely lunch.[133]

Rosenberg told his guest that Germany had no intention of interfering with the British Empire. In return Lord Kemsley repeated several times that a war between England and Germany would be a disaster, since the only beneficiary would be the Soviet Union. He added 'that Chamberlain would negotiate in Moscow reluctantly and was ready to back out, but he had started the negotiations to take the wind out of the opposition'. He also stressed that 'Chamberlain was the leader of England and would remain it'. In other words at the end of the day, Chamberlain was deciding British foreign policy and not Parliament. This naturally pleased Weiszäcker and Rosenberg. Lady Kemsley's comments added to the cheerful atmosphere. She declared that 'only the Jews wanted to bring about a war between Germany and England' and then continued to explain that she had seven children, of whom five were sons of military age. For personal reasons alone she could therefore not support the madness of a war with Germany. Lady Kemsley's reproductive productivity naturally made an impression. So did her anti-Semitism. She also added that before they had left for Germany, they had received countless letters and telegrams from all over Britain, asking them to do everything possible to avoid a war. Rosenberg ended his report summarizing that Lord and Lady Kemsley had given the impression that they had been instructed by Chamberlain to speak for him and to stress that Chamberlain's position as Prime Minister was safe. This report was not simply wishful thinking. The German ambassador to Britain, Herbert von Dirksen, gained a similar impression of the Kemsleys shortly afterwards: 'Lord Kemsley spoke with pleasure of his conversation with Reichsleiter Rosenberg ("a charming personality"), to whom he had said that Chamberlain was in his way the Führer of England, similar to Hitler and Mussolini. This had visibly made an impression upon Rosenberg.'[134]

That the British negotiations with the Soviet Union were just a facade was therefore obvious to Hitler. The British appeasers were indeed 'guilty men' who had given him to understand that in Britain fear of communism was greater than fear of Nazism.

After the war Kemsley rejected the Dirksen report as fantasy. Like so many appeasers he suffered from amnesia. Not so his critic, the journalist Elizabeth Wiskemann, who challenged him. Despite her unusual name Wiskemann was British and had been arrested by the Nazis in 1936. She got out in time and later worked for the British intelligence services in Switzerland. She had quoted and read Kemsley correctly. So had another man who was in the intelligence services. Yet this man had a rather different biography from Wiskemann's and certainly did not make his knowledge public. His name was Guy Burgess. In his daytime job Burgess worked for the BBC (later for MI6 and the Foreign Office), yet his real passion lay somewhere else. Like Philby and Blunt he had been recruited as a Soviet agent. It was an inspired choice by the Russians. Burgess was from a wealthy and well-connected family and knew, since his time as a political journalist, all the key people in Whitehall. He was an expert on the Foreign Office mentality and understood Chamberlain well. In August 1939 when negotiations between the British, French, and Russians were going on regarding a possible pact, Burgess saw this as the facade it was:

> It is a basic aim of British policy to work with Germany whatever happens, and, in the end, against the USSR. But it is impossible to conduct this policy openly; one must manoeuvre every which way, without opposing German expansion to the East.[135]

Burgess was not the only one who believed this to be true. His contemporary Conwell-Evans, came to the same conclusion:

> It seems clear that the British government continued to believe that Hitler's affirmation of his anti-Bolshevism were wholly genuine, that he intended solely to crusade eastwards against Soviet Russia.[136]

Conwell-Evans noticed that Chamberlain was just pretending to negotiate with Russia when a senior Foreign Office clerk was sent to Moscow 'by boat instead of plane'.[137]

When the Russians learnt that Göring was planning to visit England, they realized it was time to commit.[138] The Hitler/Stalin Pact was signed on 23 August 1939. A week later Hitler attacked Poland and Britain declared war on Germany.

One would have thought that the outbreak of war with Britain might have been so traumatic that it would have ended Coburg's activities. Yet there does not seem to have been a single moment of reflection for him. The man who would later claim that he worked tirelessly for peace did not draw any conclusions from 3 September 1939. On the contrary. He now did his best to support the war effort. His presidency of the German Red Cross meant that Carl Eduard became responsible for the cover up of crimes against civilians in Poland. When he was informed that one of his cousins, the mentally ill Princess Maria of Sachsen-Coburg und Gotha, had been gassed, he dismissed this as gossip. He preferred to be in denial about concentration camps and the Nazis' 'euthanasia' programme.[139]

This was his 'domestic' record after the outbreak of war in 1939. His foreign record as a go-between continued as well. He was now used for trips to Germany's new friends—Japan and Russia. In January 1940, before Carl Eduard started on his second world tour he was first received by Hitler and then briefed in the German Foreign Ministry afterwards (Hitler and the Foreign Ministry were also his first port of call on his return in May). Officially Carl Eduard was travelling to Japan to congratulate the Emperor on his jubilee, yet his real mission was to 'explain' the situation (or better, calm Japanese nerves) five months after the Hitler–Stalin Pact. Since Russia and Japan had been enemies since 1904, this must have meant a lot of explaining. Carl Eduard seems to have been successful enough and included a trip to the United States to sound out the American commitment to neutrality. His last stop was Moscow, where he had the pleasure of meeting, together with the German ambassador v. Schulenburg, Molotov on 31 May 1940. He told Molotov his American trip had reassured him that Roosevelt was not going to join the war, even though he was surrounded by advisers who supported this. Molotov wanted to know more about these advisers and was told by the Duke that they were of course people who were warmongers.[140] After Carl Eduard had left, Molotov asked Schulenburg why the Duke 'looked so old'. Though Carl Eduard was only 56 at the time, he looked more like 80. His bent posture and leg problems were evident to everyone. Schulenburg tried to avoid an honest answer since Coburg's inherited family diseases were naturally an embarrassment to the Aryan ideals of the Nazi movement, and instead elaborated on Carl Eduard's long pedigree and that he had been a great supporter of the Nazi movement for a long time. He also made a joke about the Duke's connections with other royal houses. Three days before the meeting with

Molotov, Belgium had capitulated to Hitler. The King of the Belgians was Carl Eduard's cousin and Schulenburg had toyed with the idea of telling the Duke: 'your cousin has surrendered.' Molotov seemed fascinated by this connection and told Schulenburg 'that such old family relationships are a rather complex chain'.

They were indeed. It is not clear whether Coburg used his 'complex chain' for one last time in June 1940.

Much has been written about Hitler and Ribbentrop's plan to 'lure' the Duke of Windsor to Germany in the summer of 1940. Since Ribbentrop was working closely together with Coburg, it is likely that he asked him for advice on this endeavour. The mission was codenamed 'Operation Willi' and senior intelligence officer Walter Schellenberg was dispatched to Portugal. In his unreliable memoirs Schellenberg portrays the whole affair as doomed from the start. In fact the story was already circulating within the intelligence world at the time. According to the double agent Dusko Popov, Hitler wanted to offer the Duke a return to the British throne (and a crown for Wallis Simpson). In the meantime the idea arose of depositing

Figure 7. Celebrating their achievements in Coburg: Adolf Hitler and Carl Eduard 24th October 1935.

50 million Swiss francs in a Swiss bank account so that the Duke could 'live in the appropriate style'.[141] Whether the Duke was tempted could never be verified.

Several intelligence agencies were watching the Duke of Windsor in Spain and Portugal. One is of particular interest—the NKVD [Soviet Intelligence]. So far it has never revealed its reports. Yet it seems that it had good information on the Duke. In the summer of 1940 the head of the Fifth Department Pavel Fitin sent to the Kremlin a memo:

> The former king of England Edward together with his wife Simpson is at present in Madrid, where he is in touch with Hitler. Edward is conducting negotiations with Hitler on the question of the formation of a new English government and the conclusion of peace with Germany contingent on a military alliance against the USSR.[142]

This message fuelled Stalin's worst fears. By then the Nazi–Soviet pact was almost a year old. Would Hitler switch sides? Was this the beginning of a larger plan?

It would be interesting to know what else this source told the Russians, yet access to KGB files is even more difficult than access to files of the Royal Archives, Windsor. Still, in recent years the SVR (a successor to the KGB) has allowed trusted researchers to use material and publish it in Russian periodicals. Whether this new transparency has something to do with the current patchy Russian–British relations or is a way of advertising old espionage successes is irrelevant. Another source for insider material on the royal family was the Soviet spy Anthony Blunt, a relative of the Duchess of York (later Queen Elizabeth, mother of the current Queen). As children Blunt's mother and Queen Mary had been neighbours in Windsor Great Park and remained lifelong friends, sharing a passion for charity projects. Blunt picked up royal gossip easily and would later be promoted by Queen Mary's son George VI. It is therefore likely that he was one source for the Russians' information on the royal family. That he played a decisive role was insinuated in June 2014 by the intelligence analyst G. Sokolov who is close to the Russian intelligence services. He gave an interview a month after Prince Charles had compared Putin to Hitler, a comment which had caused outrage in Russia. In response, Sokolov hinted that Anthony Blunt's file would be released in the near future.[143] This would also include Blunt's clandestine work in Germany in 1945. This trip has fascinated historians for a long time. Officially Blunt was sent off in the summer of 1945 by George VI to retrieve the correspondence between Kaiser Wilhelm II's mother, Empress Frederick, and her own mother, Queen Victoria. Yet it is rumoured that he retrieved something very different, namely incriminating correspondence from members of the royal family to their Nazi relatives. Blunt travelled with the royal archivist Sir Owen Morshead, who later wrote an entertaining account of their 'archive trip'. Yet Blunt went to the Continent altogether three times that year retrieving 'artwork' for the royal family.[144] He also went to Holland to visit Kaiser Wilhelm II's former home. According to Sokolov, Blunt informed his handler in London about the details of his trip.

Blunt's work for the Russians was uncovered in 1963 but not made public until 1979. The MI5 counter-intelligence officer Peter Wright wrote a controversial book about his interrogation of Blunt. Asked about his trip to Germany in 1945, Blunt snapped at Wright: 'Now this isn't on. You know you're not supposed to ask me that.'[145] This exclamation may well suggest that Blunt struck a deal with the British intelligence services promising not to make public his knowledge about the royal family's German correspondence.

That this correspondence was collected is very likely. In his biography of Blunt the former ambassador to Britain Popov discusses the Morshead–Blunt mission to Germany. His research was inconclusive, but the Russian intelligence services informed him that Blunt was still working for them at the time and had instructions from Moscow 'to meet in Germany a person of interest to Soviet intelligence'.[146]

Apart from patchy Russian sources, there are also FBI files which were released in 2003. However they are full of unsubstantiated gossip, including the story that the Duchess of Windsor slept with Ribbentrop and that the Duke of Windsor was in close contact with Göring.[147] Still there exists a reliable source which so far has not been used: the Franco papers. They show that the Duke of Windsor was indeed making outrageous comments about his own country.[148] According to the Franco papers, the Duke of Windsor had a conversation with his old friend the Spanish diplomat Bermejillo on 25 June 1940 in which he said: 'if (the Germans) bombed England effectively this could bring peace. He [the Duke of Windsor] seemed very much to hope that this would occur. He wants peace at any price.' This report went to Franco and was then passed on to the Germans. The bombing of Britain started on 10 July.

On 15 July 1940, Bermejillo had another conversation with the Duke of Windsor who informed him that he had been offered the position of Governor of the Bahamas:

I had to laugh out loud and said it was impossible, absurd. It was only then I realised he had accepted the offer. He said the appointment was offensive but had several advantages: First, official recognition of *Her* [his wife Wallis]. (Second) not having to take part directly in the conflict, to which he had never been party. (Third) to have more freedom to exert his influence in favour of peace. Fourth, the proximity to Her native country (America). He also counted the reaction of public opinion in his favour. These are the reasons why he will accept what he called 'St. Helena 1940'.[149]

The Duke of Windsor was hardly in the same league as Napoleon I, but the British government spirited him away before he could cause any further damage. Damage limitation would be British policy for the next seventy years.

Coburg's work as a go-between probably ended after his world tour of 1940, but he continued to collect countless Nazi honours over the next five years. Even when one of his sons was killed at the front, he remained a fanatical supporter of Hitler. He was also not irritated when 'the Princes' decree' was issued in 1940. This was a decree excluding members of Germany's former royal houses from serving in the Wehrmacht. It had been triggered by a funeral. Reichsführer SS Heinrich Himmler had become increasingly suspicious of monarchical feelings among ordinary Germans after the death of two Hohenzollern princes. Their funerals had elicited an unforeseen degree of compassion amongst the German population. A monarchical renaissance threatened; the Nazis had every reason to intervene. The Princes' decree was followed in May 1943 by a secret sequel that took action against 'internationally connected men in the State, Party and Armed Forces'. This resulted in some princes having to leave the army. Coburg was not under suspicion, however, and he continued to wear his uniform and travel to occupied, neutral, and allied countries, a privilege not many had.

His trip to neutral Sweden is particularly intriguing. He visited Stockholm in February 1942, ostensibly to see his eldest daughter, who was married to the son of the Swedish Crown Prince. Coburg was a private guest of the royal family and it is therefore highly likely that politics were discussed. The relationship between the Swedish royal family and Nazi Germany was good. This is still a taboo subject in Sweden and has so far not been researched properly (papers in the Swedish royal archives relating to this period are closed). Intelligence material shows, however, that the Crown Prince of Sweden was certainly pro-German, while the Crown Princess, a Mountbatten, hated the Nazis. According to the couple's tennis coach Meller-Zakomel'skii this led to marital conflict, at least on the tennis court. The tennis coach moonlighted for Walter Schellenberg as a Nazi agent.[150] He was an impoverished White Russian aristocrat who hated Bolshevism and was therefore eager to help the Germans. According to him, the Crown Princess called National Socialism 'Barbarism', whereas her husband praised German institutions. In 1940 he had already expressed the hope that the British would 'come to their senses', i.e. make peace with Hitler, otherwise the whole of Europe would turn 'red'. The tennis coach fully agreed with such sentiments—if Germany did not win this war 'the red flag would soon be flying from Swedish castles'.[151]

Even more important than the view of the Crown Prince was King Gustav V's active support for the Germans. According to Churchill, the Swedish King was 'absolutely in the German grip.'[152] That Gustav was indeed pro-Nazi was confirmed by the reports of the German ambassador to Sweden, Prince Wied—a friend of Coburg's. Like Coburg, Prince Victor zu Wied was related to the Swedish royal family. He was a second cousin to Queen Victoria of Sweden (who during the First World War had tried hard to help Max von Baden to negotiate a Swedish–German alliance). Victoria had died in 1930 but her husband King Gustav V had stayed the pro-German course. He also seems to have been instrumental in Wied coming back to the German embassy in Stockholm. Since 1923 Wied had been on extended 'garden leave' from the German Foreign Ministry.[153] Yet after meeting Göring in 1930 his fortunes improved. He joined the Nazi party and introduced Göring to politicians and diplomats. Wied knew Foreign Minister Neurath well and in 1932 was used by Hitler as a channel to Neurath—promising him he could keep the Foreign Ministry in case of a Nazi election victory. As a reward for his good services Wied was 'reactivated' in 1933. For ten years, from 1933 to 1943, he acted as ambassador to Stockholm. The King invited him on summer retreats with Swedish politicians and treated him 'like family'.[154]

This closeness paid off. After the attack on the Soviet Union, Germany demanded a de facto end to Swedish neutrality. Prince Wied had a long conversation with Gustav V on 25 June 1941 and it was only thanks to the Swedish 'King, the Prime Minister and the Foreign Ministry' that a German division was able to use Sweden for transit.[155] Sweden eventually permitted access to its railways and allowed passage through its seas; it also gave access to its telecommunications as well as landing rights for German planes. The King seems to have played a decisive role in making all this possible. Though Swedish historians are still debating whether the King really threatened to abdicate if Germany did not get these rights, Gustav V and the Swedish Prime Minister Per Albin Hansson seem to have put enormous pressure on parliament to give in to German demands. That the King did his utmost to help Hitler was entirely in character. As we have seen in Chapter 3, when Hitler attacked the Soviet Union in June 1941, King Gustav V wrote him a congratulatory letter. His hatred of Bolshevism had made him a great supporter of Nazi Germany. This was an experience he shared with Coburg. Both men were united in their support for Hitler and it is very unlikely that they did not trade notes in 1942.

What Coburg did for Hitler during the rest of the war is unclear, but whatever it was it was well paid. Hitler had a special fund, the 'Dispositionsfonds', from which he paid selected members of his elite for their services. Until April 1945 Coburg was on this exclusive list and received 4,000 Reichsmark monthly.[156]

Looking back at his Nazi career, it is indeed impressive how long he survived at Hitler's court. Not everyone stayed in the Führer's favour for twelve turbulent years and Carl Eduard had, of course, many rivals. However, his previous experience with courts had taught him good survival techniques. After all he had been part of Kaiser Wilhelm II's court since his childhood. He knew that it was necessary to make alliances and that to be a lone fighter could be dangerous. He therefore worked together with Ribbentrop over the years and he also made sure that he stayed close to Hitler's adjutant, Fritz Wiedemann (who was in the opposing camp to Ribbentrop). Coburg often invited Wiedemann to his get-togethers in Berlin, his 'beer evenings' which were good networking opportunities. He even awarded the influential Wiedemann an order of his house, the 'Komturkreuz'.[157] Coburg had always loved to decorate people and old habits obviously died hard. Apart from distributing the Komturkreuz, he also used the opportunity to give out Red Cross medals. One of these honorary Red Cross medals (the Ehrenkreuz des Deutschen Roten Kreuzes) was received in 1937 by a very special friend of Wiedemann. She was an unusual recepient indeed—Princess Stephanie Hohenlohe.[158] This woman was no Florence Nightingale. But she was a colleague of Coburg's: Princess Stephanie Hohenlohe was another very effective go-between for Hitler.

5

Horthy, Hitler, and Lord Rothermere

Princess Stephanie Hohenlohe

In August 1939 a Mrs Stoffl approached MI5 to complain about her former employer Princess Stephanie Hohenlohe:

> The Princess was operating in England and elsewhere as a very active and dangerous agent for the Nazis. [Mrs Stoffl] declared that the Princess met many influential people in this country, that she regularly reported to Hitler's agents and that she had direct access to the highest German quarters.[1]

Since Stoffl had recently been dismissed by the Princess her report could have been merely an act of revenge. But she was by no means MI5's only source; people seemed to enjoy talking about the activities of Hohenlohe. Her file had grown steadily over the 1930s, coming to include interesting information from another intelligence service, the French Deuxième Bureau.

Stephanie Hohenlohe has been called many things over the years—a ruthless society hostess, a spy, and a high-class prostitute. She was a combination of all of these, but pre-eminently she was a go-between, working for Hungary's head of state Admiral Horthy, Hitler, Göring, and the press baron Lord Rothermere.

In November 1939, during her court case against Lord Rothermere, Goebbels wrote in his diary:

> There is a trial taking place in London, Rothermere versus Princess Hohenlohe about an annuity this 'lady' is demanding of the Lord. A lot of embarrassing things are coming out. Also about Wiedemann. But despite this I don't think that the Hohenlohe woman was a spy. After all she occasionally stood up for us.[2]

At some point even Goebbels had thought Hohenlohe worked for the other side. He certainly did not know that she was a go-between for his Führer.

Hohenlohe's private papers in the Archives of the Hoover Institution were donated and carefully sanitized by her son Franz. As the guardian of her reputation he was naturally protective. He also published his own version of events: *Stephanie: The Fabulous Princess*, a hagiography, in which he fought his mother's old battles one last time.[3] The book served its purpose. Many key events described by Franz Hohenlohe were copied verbatim by later biographers who supplemented their accounts with gossip.[4] Today new sources reveal a much clearer picture of the Princess and her clandestine work.

Princess Hohenlohe was born Stephanie Richter into Vienna's lower middle class. Her socially ambitious mother named her after the Austrian Crown Princess Stephanie. As it turned out the Crown Princess did not have a very successful life, while Stephanie Richter even exceeded all of her mother's hopes. Rising from her modest background she became a millionaire and an influential figure in American, British, and European society.

Stephanie Richter was small, with a voluptuous body that strangely contrasted with her sharp features. In 1938 the *Prager Monatsblatt* described it as a miracle that a woman without 'any noblesse in her features' had such an impact on men.[5] Since Viennese women followed the role model of Austrian Empress Sissy and were fabled for their chic and beauty, Stephanie's success seemed somehow inexplicable. She might not have lived up to the standards of her time, but she offered something much more beguiling. As Marcel Proust put it so succinctly, 'Let us leave pretty women to men with no imagination.'[6] Her strength of character and animalistic charm turned out to be irresistible to many imaginative men, including Goebbels. The highly sexed propaganda minister wrote about their first meeting in 1933: 'A strongly erotic woman. But has great influence on [Lord Rothermere]. I make an impression. Explain jewish question.'[7] This was rather ironic. Hohenlohe's mother was Jewish, something Stephanie denied vehemently to the end of her life. Since her 'official' father was in prison at the time of conception, Stephanie must have had a different biological father, according to rumours a Jewish businessman, whose identity was never fully established. In the 1930s Heinrich Himmler set his researchers on the case and concluded that Stephanie Hohenlohe was at least 'half-Jewish'.

Even though she failed the appropriate racial categories in one way or another, she would work enthusiastically for anti-Semitic men. Whether she suffered from an extreme form of Jewish self-hatred or, more likely, wanted to rise up the social ladder is hard to fathom, but she made her position clear. When her Jewish aunt Olga needed to leave Austria in 1938, Hohenlohe was not particularly helpful. Olga did not survive the war.

All her life Stephanie was economical with the truth, a quality that served her well. The first time this became useful was in connection with her impressive title. By 1914 she had accumulated a great variety of aristocratic male friends (or as Viennese gossip called them—'clients'). She was certainly not a 'tart with a heart' as her future husband Prince Franz Friedrich Hohenlohe-Waldenburg-Schillingsfürst was about to find out.

The house of Hohenlohe has many branches—Hohenlohe-Langenburg (closely related to Queen Victoria), Hohenlohe-Ingelfingen, -Öhringen, -Waldenburg, -Schillingsfürst, -Jagstberg, and -Bartenstein. Altogether it consisted of about 800 members who often did not know one another. Some branches had done better than others, but one rule united them all: marrying down, i.e. a morganatic marriage, was to be avoided at all costs. That Stephanie succeeded in becoming a member of the Hohenlohe dynasty, thereby breaking its sole dictum, is remarkable. It was made slightly easier by the fact that her fiancé, Franz Ferdinand, was not the eldest son of his, more impoverished, branch and could therefore not hope to inherit land or money. But he still carried a distinguished name. Before he descended into this marriage, he had had a successful pre-war career as military attaché in St Petersburg. His superiors in Vienna considered him to be a good officer who had even made an effort to learn some Russian. This might have been necessary since as a military attaché he was rumoured to be involved in intelligence work. MI5 certainly believed he worked as a spy during the First World War, which seemed to fit in with their suspicions about Stephanie's line of work. However, the security services' records on Franz Hohenlohe are not that reliable, occasionally mixing him up with his son Franz and also with another Hohenlohe, Alexander. MI5 was obviously confused by the many Franzes and the complexities of the Hohenlohe family tree in general.

Another confusion—shared by many—surrounded the motivations such a man would have to marry Stephanie Richter. After all a morganatic marriage was career suicide. Were the two of them by any chance working together? This could be one explanation, but so far no evidence has emerged for the theory of a husband and wife spy team. Over the years there circulated at least three other explanations for this strange union.

In the first version Stephanie Richter forced Franz Hohenlohe into marriage because she had fallen pregnant by him. This version is not especially convincing, since he could have simply denied his paternity without suffering any social consequences. His aristocratic peer group would have been quite understanding.

In the second version Stephanie was not entirely sure about the parentage and simply forced Hohenlohe into marrying her by paying his huge gambling debts.

The third version argues that Franz Hohenlohe was ordered to marry Stephanie because she was expecting a child by a member of the Habsburg family. According to this version the real father was Archduke Franz Salvator, son-in-law of Emperor Franz Joseph. Since Stephanie had carried on a well-recorded affair with Franz Salvator at the time, this story seems the most likely one. The Archduke continued to look out for her and the baby during the war and remained a family friend until his death. Stephanie Hohenlohe's son Franz, however, never acknowledged this version. He insisted he was named after his father Franz Hohenlohe, not after Franz Salvator.

Whatever the exact truth, society agreed that the bride was from an obscure background and had engineered a shotgun wedding. Rumours already circulated at the time that she was some sort of courtesan,[8] and consequently she had no chance of ever being received by Viennese society. But Stephanie Hohenlohe was patient and persistent. During the First World War she did what all society ladies did—she pretended to work as a nurse. The experiment was short-lived and she was sent home after a couple of months. She then reverted to entertaining Archduke Franz Salvator and other influential men, while her husband stayed away at the front and made sure he came home rarely.

In some ways Stephanie Hohenlohe was like a character out of Arthur Schnitzler's controversial drama *La Ronde* (*Der Reigen*). In this play Schnitzler clinically analysed the sexual hypocrisy of Viennese society before the war. As in a merry-go-round, everyone sleeps with everyone else across social boundaries: the tart with the soldier, the soldier with the chambermaid, the chambermaid with the young gentleman of the house, the young gentleman with a married lady, the married lady with her husband, her husband with a typical Viennese 'süßes Mädel' (sweet young girl), the sweet young girl with the poet, the poet with the actress, and the actress with the count. In the end the count goes back to the tart. Stephanie Hohenlohe probably saw the play after the war, but she certainly did not need any cues. She had always been capable of fulfilling various male fantasies including the *süße Mädel* and the tart. Her range would continue to impress. The irony was that she was far from being a sensual person. The alleged 'femme fatale' Stephanie was, according to her son, in fact a 'femme de tête'. This made sense, as to fulfil the fantasies of her 'admirers' required a certain degree of concentration. She could hardly afford being distracted by emotions in her line of work.

After the collapse of the Austro-Hungarian Empire, Stephanie Hohenlohe's chances of being socially accepted improved. The strict Habsburg court had dissolved and titles were abolished in Austria. Until 1918 the social network of the Viennese upper class had been impenetrable. Now members of the old Austro-German elite were ostracized. Stephanie Hohenlohe had always followed their work closely, picking up as much information as possible. She knew a great deal about Fürstenberg's German channel and would refer to it years later. She was well aware that Fürstenberg, her predecessor as go-between, had become an outcast after 1918. But Stephanie would still see him as an example. After all, his failure did not mean the end of the 'go-between profession' per se. Almost twenty years later, Hohenlohe would fill the gap expertly. She would use the same old techniques as Fürstenberg mixed with a few ideas of her own and with the advantage that she could always add a sexual component to her work.

Fürstenberg had not been the only aristocrat who had to leave Austria after the war. He decided to settle in Germany from 1918 onwards and many other aristocrats made similar decisions. Members of the House of Hohenlohe were in a rather difficult situation, as the collapse of the Austro-Hungarian Empire made it no longer possible to have dual Austrian-Hungarian nationality. The members of the Hohenlohe family were spread across Austria, Hungary, Germany, Poland, and Czechoslovakia and everyone had to determine which citizenship would now serve them best. Stephanie's husband chose Hungary. His reasoning was that his mother had been a member of the famous Hungarian Esterhazy family. He also must have hoped this would enhance his work chances. It is possible that Franz Hohenlohe did not discuss this step with Stephanie at all. According to the marriage law of the time his wife had to become Hungarian as well.[9] Since she did not speak a word of Magyar and would have probably preferred being a citizen of a more prosperous nation, it must have felt odd to be connected to Hungary—one of the greatest losers of the war. As usual in her life, Stephanie Hohenlohe managed to make the best out of a difficult situation. She turned her Hungarian passport into an asset, becoming a go-between for Hungarian politicians. It would become her first operation in this field and though her biographers think it was a coincidence, this was far from the truth. Things did not simply happen to Stephanie; she made them happen.

In 1920 her pro forma husband Franz Hohenlohe had divorced her. She kept his name and never married again, a decision that was more strategic than romantic. She had never had much use for the man, but needed the name. It would always remain her insurance policy and main meal ticket. With the name one invoked historical greatness, it triggered memories of past glories. 'Hohenlohe' was an exclusive brand name for Stephanie and, as will be shown later, she would do anything to keep it.

According to her son's unreliable memoirs Stephanie survived the politically turbulent postwar years in Vienna thanks to her friendship with Ignaz Seipel. The prelate Dr Ignaz Seipel, twice Chancellor of the Austrian Republic in the 1920s, was a member of the Christian Social party and, like the party's founder Karl Lueger, deeply anti-Semitic. Hohenlohe's son claimed that the friendship with Seipel went back a long way. Allegedly he had already given Stefanie theological instruction as a schoolgirl, but this seems very unlikely. Seipel was studying for a doctorate at the time and would not have had much interest in teaching a girl from the wrong side of town. Furthermore the teenager Stephanie Hohenlohe had already indulged in a rather unusual lifestyle (she was introduced to her first lover Count Gizycki at the age of 15 or 16). The story therefore sounds more like an insider joke. It is possible, though, that Seipel and Stephanie Hohenlohe had some other interest in common than theology, because Hohenlohe received police protection on several occasions along with other special favours including a box at the opera. Since amorous motives are unlikely in this case, another explanation could be that Stephanie worked in some unofficial capacity for the Austrian government.

What she had to offer was a rare commodity in the 1920s: press contacts with Britain. Before the war her aunt Clotilde had married Herbert Arthur White, *Daily Express* correspondent in Berlin. Though the marriage did not last, Clotilde continued to run an international salon in Berlin and introduced Stephanie to her British friends. By means of these contacts Stephanie befriended foreign journalists, connections that were important for the new

Austrian government, and in particular Seipel. Hohenlohe was interested not just in journalists, but also in international businessmen. To make contact with them she worked the way her targets lived—internationally. In the 1920s she spent much time in France befriending rich men in Cannes, Monte Carlo, and Deauville. Among her many admirers was Sir Henri Deterding, a Dutchman with a British knighthood. Deterding was the chairman of the Board of Royal Dutch Shell and a diehard anti-communist. He was an early financier of Hitler and was one of the first people to tell Hohenlohe about this 'promising' politician. But before she became interested in German politics, Hohenlohe focused on Hungary.

Whereas Germany felt humiliated by the Versailles Treaty, Hungary had been severely diminished by the Treaty of Trianon. It had to give up two-thirds of its pre-war territory which meant that one-third of the Hungarian speaking population was now living outside Hungary.[10] This trauma was connected to another one. In 1919 Bolsheviks took over the government and their leader Bela Kun proclaimed the Hungarian Soviet Republic. He started the Red Terror executed by his so-called 'Lenin Boys'. The backlash came swiftly and was equally vicious. The White Terror was a deadly revenge campaign that specialized in targeting the Jewish population.[11] Even after the fighting was over and Bela Kun exiled to Moscow, Hungary remained deeply anti-Semitic. It is therefore ironic that the closet Jewish woman Stephanie Hohenlohe would eventually be fêted by anti-Semitic Hungarian leaders. The first and most important was Admiral Horthy, who launched her career as a go-between. Though Hohenlohe did not speak Magyar, Hungary offered more than a difficult language.

Since 1920 Horthy was the all-powerful 'Regent' or 'Protector' of the Kingdom of Hungary. De facto he was the ruler of Hungary, which remained a kingdom without a king, since the Entente powers did not allow a return of the Habsburgs.

Horthy seemed an ideal substitute for a monarch, a military man, but with a grandfatherly manner that reminded people of Emperor Franz Joseph. Though his pedigree was not in the Habsburg league, Horthy descended from Calvinist Hungarian nobility. To be a Calvinist was slightly unusual. The majority of Hungarian nobles were Catholic and therefore tended to marry into Austrian or south German aristocratic families. Yet whether Catholic or Calvinist, all Hungarian nobles shared an admiration for Britain, and connections with the British aristocracy had always been highly valued in Hungary.

Since the nineteenth century the British aristocracy had been their social and cultural role model. An early example of the convergence of the Hungarian aristocracy with the value system of the British is Count Stephan Széchenyi (1791–1860).[12] Széchenyi travelled across Britain and was impressed by the industrial and social advances of the country. He was determined to copy the British model and over several generations the Széchenyi family formed close friendships with members of the British aristocracy.[13] Ironically a descendant of the famous Széchenyis joined the National Socialist party of Hungary in the 1930s.[14]

In 1920, however, it was obvious to everyone that after a lost war, Hungary had to renew any old bonds with the British. Horthy saw closer ties as a key solution for his country's economic problems and therefore relentlessly courted the British establishment. Among his guests were politicians like the Foreign Secretary Austen Chamberlain, but also aristocratic MPs like Viscount Lymington.[15] Lymington certainly became one of Horthy's most enthusiastic visitors. He later wrote: 'As a dictator [Horthy] was the nearest thing in my recollection to a larger English landlord... One felt instantly at home with a type of man one had always known.'[16]

To aristocrats like Lymington, Hungary seemed similar to Mussolini's Italy—a country where the nobility had profited from 'authoritarian' regimes. In a world of republican and communist chaos this proved that aristocrats could still play a key political role. The political return of the Hungarian aristocracy after 1918 was the more surprising since their influence had decreased before the First World War. But the 'red regime' of Bela Kun had sent shock waves through Hungary. The experience seems to have made many Hungarians look for old, familiar names to restore order. All of Horthy's prime ministers offered such reassuring names. They also shared a strong feeling of entitlement. Prime Minister Bethlen argued that the aristocracy was a 'natural elite' predestined to carry out a 'controlled democracy'. Count Pal Teleki (1879–1941), another Hungarian Prime Minister in the inter-war period, did not bother with euphemisms like 'controlled democracy' and favoured the idea of a corporate state based on the Portuguese model. Teleki was a friend of the Portuguese dictator António de Oliveira Salazar (1889–1970) and an ardent anti-Semite. In 1940 he explained why he also favoured Hitler: 'Communism we dread more than Nazism, because under the German system some of us might survive for better days, under Bolshevism all of us will be strung up on the lamp posts.'[17]

When the Germans did persuade Hungary to join the war in 1941, Teleki, however, preferred the lamp post and committed suicide. Horthy was more flexible and became Hitler's stooge, but as will be shown it was neither his first nor a lasting choice. Originally Horthy had hoped that the British would help to reverse Hungary's great national shame—the Treaty of Trianon. Even Hungarian primary school children knew one slogan by heart: 'Nem! Nem! Soha!' (No! no! never!) would they accept the shameful loss of Hungarian territory. Horthy wanted this feeling of injustice conveyed to the West. Not just via the official, diplomatic channels, but more importantly via go-betweens. Stephanie Hohenlohe seemed ideal. Though she was not British, her social network was a backdoor into London society, as Horthy was quick to realize. Over the years she would relentlessly work for Horthy and his changing prime ministers to get the 'injustice of 1920' reversed.

It is not quite clear how Hohenlohe was paid by the Hungarians for this work. Since she was not altruistic, some financial arrangement must have been made. She certainly received lavish 'gifts' whenever she stayed in Budapest. The Princess fought a lifelong battle with several tax authorities, therefore such 'gifts' were preferable to traceable paperwork. From a Hungarian point of view she certainly deserved every one of these 'gifts'. Her propaganda campaign for Hungary exceeded expectations.

According to her son's version of events the Hungary campaign was a 'coincidence'. Stephanie met the press baron Lord Rothermere 'quite by chance' in 1927. In other, less charitable accounts, she targeted him as a potential lover as early as 1925. This is unlikely since Hohenlohe researched her victims well and knew that Rothermere preferred the company of elf-like ballerinas. Stephanie's more voluptuous charms might therefore not have been appreciated. However, she probably used an elf creature to introduce her—Annabel Kruse. Kruse was a former girlfriend of Rothermere's and married to one of his employees.[18]

The Lord Rothermere whom Hohenlohe met in Monte Carlo was a restless multi-millionaire with an appetite for new projects. He and his brother Alfred Harmsworth (Lord Northcliffe) had built a press empire and as a consequence were rewarded with titles. Northcliffe had died in 1922 and Rothermere was now even more influential. To this day research on his life remains difficult as his private papers are not accessible.

Rothermere had lost his favourite son in the First World War and in the 1920s lived a nomadic life. He was not past his creative prime, though, and was still starting regional newspapers and running the *Daily Mail* and the *Daily Mirror*. According to his sympathetic biographer Rothermere was looking for a new mission: 'Curious and credulous, he was sifting through the trends of the age looking for clues about the future.'[19] Stephanie had been well briefed to offer such a clue, a PR crusade for Hungary. She was a persuasive storyteller and Rothermere listened attentively to how the Hungarian people hoped to be reunited with their fellow countrymen who were now living in Romania, Czechoslovakia, and Yugoslavia. Hohenlohe's son would later claim that at this first meeting Rothermere did not even know the difference between Budapest and Bucharest.[20] Since the Rothermere press had published propaganda articles about Romania during the war, this was pretty unlikely. But it was correct that until his meeting with Hohenlohe, Rothermere had not taken any interest in the postwar fate of the Hungarians. Hohenlohe changed this. Her timing was exquisite.

Inspired by her, Rothermere wrote two pro-Hungarian articles which had an enormous effect. In June 1927 'Hungary's Place in the Sun' was published, followed two months later by a second article. In both pieces Rothermere protested against the unfair treatment of Hungary after the war. He claimed that the land cessions to Czechoslovakia, Romania, and Yugoslavia had been the greatest 'frauds that have ever taken place in the public life of Europe'.[21] He assured his readers that Hungary was worth supporting since it was a natural ally of Britain and France and an important bulwark against Bolshevism. He also stressed the importance of Hungary becoming a monarchy again, though he carefully avoided suggesting a Habsburg for this role. This omission naturally led to speculation, and to many Rothermere's motives for the articles remained a mystery. Why did he support the former foe Hungary? And whom did he favour as king? Was he perhaps thinking of his son fulfilling this role?

The average Hungarian did not care about Rothermere's motives and was just thankful that the British public had noticed them. Once the campaign was rolling, Rothermere handed the day-to-day work over to a friend of Stephanie Hohenlohe: Viscountess Ethel Snowden. Snowden was a colourful figure who had campaigned for women's rights and pacifist causes in the First World War. She supported Labour and her husband had been Chancellor of the Exchequer in Ramsay MacDonald's government. Lady Snowden loved a crusade and wrote for several newspapers. For a while she became Hohenlohe's 'best friend' writing sensational articles about Hungarian suffering. Under Hohenlohe's guidance she would later fall for Hitler and submit enthusiastic articles about the Nuremberg rallies.

Thanks to the press campaign for Hungary Rothermere became a Hungarian national hero. Countless Hungarian streets were named after him and he continued to give advice. As a staunch anti-communist and monarchist he had come to the conclusion that Bolshevism could only be stopped by a resurrection of continental thrones. In 1928 he therefore wrote an article stating that a *foreigner* as Hungarian king would be the wisest choice, since the Entente would never accept a Habsburg on the Hungarian throne. This naturally offended the legitimist faction in Hungary, especially Prime Minister Bethlen. Other politicians like General Gömbös (1886–1936) did not share such positive feelings for the Habsburgs, and were attracted to Rothermere's argument. This was one reason why Hohenlohe was told by her employer to make contact with Gömbös. Rothermere and Gömbös soon started a 'conversation', which became useful when Gömbös was made Prime Minister in 1932. It was a very clandestine conversation and therefore run entirely by Hohenlohe. To avoid any traces, Gombös wrote to Lord Rothermere in 1932: 'I very much appreciate your messages Princess Hohenlohe has given me. Everything else I have to say, the Princess will tell you [herself].'[22]

Gömbös was thoroughly anti-Semitic. According to Hohenlohe, Horthy later claimed that he did not share Gömbös's views and had indeed tried to moderate his hatred of the Jews. This of course was a version of the truth. It had been Horthy himself who had dropped the 'milder' Bethlen and made Gömbös Prime Minister instead, fully aware of his racist and pro-German views. Thanks to Gömbös, Germany had become a vital trading partner for Hungary, making the country more dependent on Hitler. Horthy had tolerated this, and Rothermere was supporting Gömbös wholeheartedly.

In her dealings with Rothermere, Hohenlohe had to be highly flexible. His attention span was short and he changed his mind repeatedly. In 1932 he suddenly declared that he now favoured the 20-year-old Otto von Habsburg, eldest son of the deceased Emperor Karl, for the Hungarian throne. He made his support public in a *Daily Mail* article on 24 August 1932 and Hohenlohe was immediately dispatched to Budapest to inquire in which way Rothermere could 'help' to bring this idea about. Naturally the quasi-monarch Horthy was not interested in being usurped by a Habsburg, but he was experienced at pretending. So was Hohenlohe, who had to carry out a difficult balancing act, pleasing both men—Horthy and Rothermere. In her draft memoirs she wrote:

> It had been my principal duty to establish contact with the new rulers as well as with the heads of the deposed dynasties. As a man of fate behind the scenes, Lord Rothermere desired to meet the new supermen, to correspond with them, to

> influence them; as a romantic conservative his ultimate aim was the restoration of the Habsburgs and the Hohenzollerns. There was nothing in his scheme of things that was contrary to my own sentiments and dreams, and a liberal endowment of my function as His Lordship's Ambassadress made it possible to achieve what was expected of me.[23]

One of the heads of the deposed monarchies Rothermere wanted to contact was Zita, the ex-Empress of Austria-Hungary. Of course Rothermere took Stephanie at face value as a proper princess with a wide aristocratic network of relatives and friends. He had no idea that many members of the old elite knew about and hardly approved of her murky past. This was particularly the case with the deposed Habsburgs. For a devout Catholic, like the Austrian ex-Empress Zita, to receive a 'fallen woman' like Hohenlohe was completely out of the question. However, Stephanie pulled all her strings and in the end received a second-class audience at the exiled Habsburg court. There are various versions of the event. In Franz Hohenlohe's version the task of receiving Stephanie was delegated to one of Zita's brothers, a Bourbon-Parma. If true, this version is quite ironic. As has been shown earlier the Parma brothers, Sixtus and Xavier, had themselves once worked as go-betweens. The infamous Sixtus mission had played a part in the downfall of the Habsburg family and the failed go-between Sixtus would have therefore faced a 'successor go-between' in Stephanie. While he had lost all credibility in 1917, she belonged to a different generation of go-betweens backed by the new power player Rothermere.

In another version it was not a Parma brother who received Hohenlohe, but instead Zita's 'housekeeper and lady-in-waiting' Countess Mensdorff. Whether the Countess accepted a down payment for the 'monarchical cause' is also unclear. It was later claimed that Rothermere had offered to pay the Habsburgs $100,000 annually for ten years.

Zita's son Otto von Habsburg did not help to illuminate the affair either. In his memoirs he argued that he suspected Rothermere was supporting another Habsburg, Archduke Albrecht, for the Hungarian throne and therefore he and his mother Zita were highly suspicious of the whole overture.[24]

The mission shows that Rothermere's political instincts were extremely limited, as was his knowledge of Hungary. The majority of the Hungarians would not have tolerated another Habsburg ruler—Admiral Horthy made sure of that. However, despite her contact with the Habsburgs, Stephanie Hohenlohe was still supported by Horthy and their relationship continued to flourish. He gave her a photo of himself with the dedication 'to a great stateswoman', which she displayed prominently in her various drawing rooms (she must have travelled with the photo, so she could show it off wherever she stayed).

Stephanie Hohenlohe's 'statesman-like' work for Horthy lasted until 1938. According to her unpublished memoirs, the last mission she carried out for her Hungarian master was in October 1938, noting that when she arrived in Budapest, Horthy seemed, 'highly agitated':

> I knew Horthy could not tolerate Hitler. He realised that friendship with the Nazis meant death to his nation, but I also knew that popular pressure was slowly pushing him into an impossible situation, for he was but a single voice against a national sentiment.

Hohenlohe claimed Horthy confided to her at this meeting that Hitler had surrounded him with spies and that he therefore could no longer trust his own staff. Since his English was faulty and his translator untrustworthy, he asked Hohenlohe to draft a secret communication to Chamberlain:

> I want you to write me a letter, and I want you to take that letter to the British Prime Minister. I do not want to send it through official channels because the Germans have too many spies in too many places and I do not want my message to be relayed to the Reichstag. I am asking you this because your English is more fluent than mine. I want you to ask Mr. Chamberlain for help.[25]

Horthy explained that Hungary was under enormous pressure to join the German–Italian axis and Britain should help to prevent this. In this context Hohenlohe should mention the understanding Chamberlain's stepbrother, the one time Foreign Secretary Austen Chamberlain, had shown about Hungary's predicament. According to her notes, Stephanie drafted the following letter in Horthy's name:

> [Dear Prime Minister] Three years ago I had the pleasure to see your brother Sir Austen Chamberlain here as my guest. He showed great interest in all the questions concerning my country. He asked me to explain to him the case of my country—the wrongs and injustices done to her.

According to Horthy, Austen Chamberlain had assured him:

> that we would eventually find friends in the West, and particularly in England. He told me that the time was not yet ripe for action, but that when the day came, I would only have to appeal to the conscience of his country and aid would be sent.

Horthy then claimed he had waited patiently but now had to appeal to the British to help Hungary: 'German insistence is mounting. I am under constant pressure from without and within. I will be unable to justify my existence much longer without your help. I pledge my word that you will never have to regret it and assure you of the undying gratitude of the entire Hungarian nation.'

According to Hohenlohe Horthy then added: 'Tell Chamberlain that the Germans are too near. They must listen for if one country goes under, all nations are threatened.'

Hohenlohe said she did not see Horthy again after this meeting. She passed on his signed letter to Sir Thomas Moore, a conservative MP with good access to Chamberlain. Moore had met Hitler in 1933 and subsequently written the gushing article 'Give Hitler a chance'. Since Moore was an ardent appeaser, to choose him seems odd. In fact Hohenlohe's whole report about her last conversation with Horthy is contradictory. By 1938 she was known to be close to Hitler. Did the 'Regent' think she was still *his* go-between and not loyal to the 'Führer'? This would have been rather careless. A more likely explanation is that Hohenlohe exaggerated the conversation to portray herself as a patriotic Hungarian and critic of Hitler. After all she wrote these notes retrospectively in 1956, when she had every reason to rewrite her Nazi past and Soviet troops were invading 'her beloved Hungary'.[26]

While the mission to Empress Zita was a peculiar move, it was even more bizarre that in 1932 Rothermere of all people should have sent a go-between to ex-Kaiser Wilhelm II. After all it had been Rothermere and his brother, Lord Northcliffe, who had once supported Prime Minister Lloyd George's campaign to 'Hang the Kaiser'. Rothermere, the man who always claimed to be a monarchist, had actually advocated hanging a monarch. Now he had changed his mind. In his letter of July 1932, he instructed Stephanie to talk to Wilhelm II 'to find out whether his views are in accordance with mine'.[27]

Not many people were still interested in the Kaiser, who was even ignored by the deposed German reigning houses. Some, like the former Crown Prince of Bavaria or the former Grand Duke of Hesse, genuinely loathed him. After 1918 all of them had done their best to avoid being associated with him. Only a few members of the aristocracy had visited the ex-Kaiser in the Netherlands over the years and even Wilhelm's old friend Fürstenberg had started to dread these claustrophobic encounters. Staying with him for a 'monotonous' week, Prince Hohenzollern-Sigmaringen came to the conclusion that it reminded him of 'Napoleon I on St. Helena'.[28] Not many people were keen on such an experience. It was therefore rather surprising that a former foe, like Rothermere, asked for an audience for his go-between Hohenlohe. Though the Kaiser still had an overblown view of his importance, he was rightly suspicious of the approach. Stephanie Hohenlohe herself was well aware that she would have a credibility problem. She also felt unusually nervous because she had never met the Kaiser before. His son Crown Prince Wilhelm, nicknamed 'little Willy', was a close friend of hers and had helped to arrange and brief her for the audience. But little Willy was not the ideal adviser on handling the Kaiser. Father and son had never been on good terms, having had numerous rows over the years. Hohenlohe therefore had to rely on her characteristic mixture of shrewdness and intuition. Her first impression when she was finally introduced to the Emperor was how masculine he seemed despite his age: 'a masculine strong voice, a grey beard and blazing blue eyes.... His fundamental trait... was certainly masculinity.'

Hohenlohe felt as if she had stepped into Fürstenberg's shoes. In her unfinished memoirs she wrote: 'The surroundings and the atmosphere were decidedly pre-1914. It might have been a holiday gathering at Donaueschingen or at Liebenberg, in 1905, where it was difficult to say if Prince Fürstenberg was the host, the Kaiser, or Prince Eulenburg.'[29]

Handling the ex-Kaiser's entourage was not easy, though. Hohenlohe had always been an expert at room reading and she quickly took in the six men surrounding the Kaiser. All of them seemed courteous in a hostile way. As she rightly guessed from this moment onwards, the interview did not go well. Her rehearsed 'Vorspiel' was to start off with British insider stories, but nobody seemed to be interested in any news from London. All the entourage wanted to discuss were the German elections that had taken place a couple of days earlier and which Hohenlohe had not read up on. Even worse, her proposal—the whole reason for her visit—failed miserably:

> I stated Lord Rothermere's views on the political situation in Europe and on the inevitability of the immediate return of a Hohenzollern to the throne of his fathers, as best I could.... With all the emphasis at my disposal I submitted to His Majesty the unconditional and unqualified support of Lord Rothermere and his powerful papers. It was a peer of England on whose behalf I was speaking, and probably the most influential peer of England. It was not only a Press Lord whom I represented, but a statesman of singular standing. His unsolicited offer was not the first move in

a political deal, but an emergency step in a European calamity. If I had expected an outburst of enthusiasm, an uproar of excitement, as indeed I had, I was to be sadly disappointed. Calm and courteous and clear as ever the Kaiser began by asking me to thank Lord Rothermere for his kindness, and by thanking me for the trouble I had taken in transmitting Lord Rothermere's offer. As to the general political situation His Majesty did not agree with Lord Rothermere; it did not seem more alarming than it had been for years. Desirable as a revival of the monarchistic principle in the heart of Europe might be, the psychological conditions for its re-assertion seemed most unfavourable at the time. As for himself, the Ex-Kaiser accentuated that he was *not* a pretender for the throne of Germany, and if he were, he could not possibly be sent back to his throne by an outside power; he would have to be called back by the only proper authority, the German people. Monarchy or Republic—it was a German question, that could be decided only by the Germans. Any interference by foreign elements would be resented, and would certainly be resisted. As for any other member of his house, he was certain that they all shared his views and sentiments.

Hohenlohe realized there was no hope: 'Somehow I had bungled my mission. My first diplomatic mission....!'

She exaggerated: it had not been her first and it would not be her last 'diplomatic mission'.

Hohenlohe was never depressed for long. At first she felt humiliated, then she decided to blame Wilhelm II:

The Kaiser and his entourage ... were ghosts of a dead age, and what is more, they were ghosts who did not have the guts to become revenants.[30]

She came to the conclusion that her timing had been off. If she had approached the Kaiser a few days earlier, before Hitler's impressive results in the elections (the NSDAP had emerged as the largest party in the Reichstag on 31 July 1932), Wilhelm II might have been more interested in Rothermere's offer: 'I remembered that I had heard some years ago that the Ex-Kaiser was one of the heaviest financial backers of Adolf Hitler.'

The Kaiser was, indeed, not averse to the rise of the Nazis (hoping for a while that Hitler would bring him back to power). His interest in Hitler was also a family affair. As mentioned before, Wilhelm's younger son August Wilhelm (Auwi) had joined the NSDAP early on. Sefton Delmer describes how the eager Auwi, 'a chinless wonder', would bring chocolates with him on election tours (to have sweets ready always ingratiated one with the Führer).[31] The Kaiser was also encouraged in the Nazi direction by his second wife, Hermine. She had organized Hermann Göring's visits to Doorn in 1931 and 1932. On top of that Wilhelm's close friend Fürstenberg encouraged him to listen to the 'marvellous Hitler'. One aspect all of them found attractive was the anti-Semitism of the Nazis. The Kaiser had already in the 1920s ranted that Jews should be 'erased'. His wife Hermine did not even find pogroms newsworthy. The day after Kristallnacht in 1938 she wrote to her friend Fürstenberg how outraged she was. The reason for her outrage was that her youngest son Ferdinand had committed 'a deed of true madness'. She was naturally not referring to her son's dedicated work in the SS, but to his choice of wife. Ferdinand had announced his marriage to 'musical star' Rose Rauch—utter 'madness' that had to be kept from his stepfather, ex-Kaiser Wilhelm. While Kristallnacht terrified the German Jews, ex-Kaiser Wilhelm, self-obsessed as ever, was mourning the twentieth anniversary of his abdication. Fürstenberg did not mind Kristallnacht either. In his reply to Hermine he did not even mention it but instead lamented her son's 'disgraceful behaviour'.[32] Hermine would eventually suffer worse blows. She died under Soviet house arrest in 1947,[33] after her son Ferdinand made no effort to bring her to the West.

Though Stephanie Hohenlohe's mission to Wilhelm II had failed in 1932, Rothermere continued to employ her. A Hungarian lawyer later summed up the sequence of services she had rendered for Rothermere in Germany. According to this summary Rothermere

> conducted his own foreign policy. [Stephanie Hohenlohe] received instructions to cooperate with the reestablishment of the Hohenzollern Dynasty in Germany and to help put the Habsburg princes on the throne of Hungary. [Stephanie Hohenlohe] received instructions to see Empress Zita—His Majesty the Kaiser—then later with a sudden change General Gömbös as well as Hungarian and German politicians. At an even later date His Lordship found that the Anglo-German diplomatic service does not work well and acting on his own accord employed [Stephanie Hohenlohe] to act as substitute for the official agents until he came to the conclusion in early 1938 that 'the British and German diplomatic services are on excellent terms'.[34]

Indeed, in 1932 Rothermere and Hohenlohe did take a closer look at German politicians. Hohenlohe had had sound experiences with authoritarian leaders in the past and wanted to add Hitler to her impressive list. So did Rothermere. For some time his newspapers had covered the Nazis' rise to power sympathetically and he was now interested in direct contact with Hitler. Rothermere's biographer seems to have missed this development and has a more positive take on the lord's Nazi contacts. To her they were not based on genuine interest in the Nazi ideology but simply to win time to strengthen Britain's air force. In other words, Rothermere was a good appeaser.[35] This is a rather generous interpretation. In 1932 Rothermere may indeed have believed that Hitler would reinstate the monarchy and help Kaiser Wilhelm's son, Crown Prince Wilhelm ('little Willy'), to ascend the throne. 'Little Willy' and Stephanie certainly believed this for a while. Willy had already been close to the radical right before the First World War. During the war he had become one of its greatest supporters. Prince Hohenzollern-Sigmaringen, though a conservative, had been shocked by Willy's political views. In 1917 he wrote:'Despite the war, the Crown Prince was no more mature than before. He is badly informed and under the influence of the Pan Germans (the radical right).The impression he made on me was very unsettling.'[36]

Willy had not matured since that conversation and was now completely in the camp of the radical right. As already demonstrated he had been successful in getting Stephanie an interview with his father and was now getting her one with his new friend Hitler.

Though 'Little Willy' was an important link in Hohenlohe's aristocratic network, she never relied on one contact alone. Her most important channel to Hitler would become Fritz Wiedemann, adjutant to the Führer. Together with Wiedemann she would organize several go-between missions over the next years.

Wiedemann had been Hitler's commanding officer in the First World War. After 1918 he had married well but his postwar career as a farmer had frustrated him. When he heard by chance that one of his former soldiers had become a successful politician, he joined the NSDAP. Eventually he rose to run Hitler's Adjutant's office, a highly influential position. It made him a gate keeper determining who had access to the Führer and who was blocked. Martha Dodd, daughter of the American ambassador to Berlin, describes Wiedemann 'as tall, dark, muscular . . . with the shrewdness and cunning of an animal'.[37] Character-wise Wiedemann had therefore a great deal in common with Stephanie Hohenlohe. He was ideal for her purposes and because of his good looks she combined the working relationship with a private one. Apart from Wiedemann and the Crown Prince vouching for her, another reason why Hohenlohe secured access to Hitler so quickly was Rothermere's 'good' track record. His chief correspondent at the *Daily Mail*, Ward Price, had been supportive of the Nazi movement since the late 1920s.

He reported enthusiastically on Hitler and Mussolini and acted as a tourist guide for interested English dignitaries on their trips to Germany. In 1936 he brought Lady Maureen Stanley, wife of the president of the Board of Education and daughter of Lord Londonderry, to 'experience' the commemoration ceremony of 9 November 1923 (the failed Munich putsch) and to meet the Führer.[38]

Apart from Ward Price's coverage, Rothermere's pro-Nazi-article 'Youth Triumphant' was enthusiastically received at party headquarters. On 7 December 1933 Rothermere's and Hitler's long-time correspondence therefore began with the warm words: 'Dear Lord Rothermere, You have been good enough to communicate to me through Princess Hohenlohe a number of suggestions for which I wish to express to you my most sincere thanks.'[39]

A magic dwells in every beginning and Hohenlohe and Hitler's first encounter was indeed magical. They were smitten by each other, though neither wished to be reminded of it years later. Once war broke out Hitler would call Hohenlohe 'das Scheusal' (the beast) and she reciprocated. In 1942 Walter C. Langer interviewed Hohenlohe for an OSS intelligence report on Adolf Hitler. Together with other former Hitler friends, like Putzi Hanfstaengl and a renegade granddaughter of Richard Wagner, Stephanie became one of the key sources for Langer's *The Mind of Adolf Hitler.*[40] The information she gave for this report had the aim of ingratiating herself with the American authorities. It naturally left out parts that were embarrassing for her (including the fact that she received the Nazi party gold badge in 1938). Apart from the Langer report, another useful source on the Hohenlohe–Hitler relationship is her draft memoirs. Despite obvious bias, Hohenlohe remains a shrewd observer, who noticed many little details. Meeting Hitler for the first time she wrote:

> The general impression, but one which you only get on seeing him at close range, is that of a very keen and simple man.... A suburban teacher, or better some small employee, that is exactly what he looked like. I challenge anyone to say the contrary.[41]

This was not such an unusual observation in itself. The journalist Dorothy Thompson, who interviewed Hitler in 1932, thought it laughable that he could be the future 'dictator of Germany: he is formless, almost faceless, a man whose countenance is a caricature, a man whose framework seems cartilaginous, without bones... He is the very prototype of the Little Man.'[42]

Thompson's British colleague Sefton Delmer agreed. He accompanied Hitler on an election campaign in 1932 and was struck by the contrast between the mesmeric, public Hitler and the dull, private man. Away from the crowds Hitler resembled a down on his luck 'salesman',[43] grey and worn out by endless road trips. But it was exactly this grey salesman that Hohenlohe was so good at understanding. She had grown up in a neighbourhood full of struggling salesmen, shopkeepers, and insurance agents—'the little people' of her time.

To this day, Vienna is like so many capitals divided into socially different boroughs. The borough Hohenlohe grew up in was the *fünfte Bezirk*, 5th borough, a lower middle-class district. During her colourful life the Princess lived in London, Monte Carlo, Paris, and Palm Springs. Yet the longest she had to travel was from Vienna's 5th borough to an elegant flat in the 1st borough overlooking the opera house. Geographically a short distance, it took enormous determination to cross those boundaries. The 5th was certainly not something Hohenlohe ever wanted to go back to, but occasionally it became useful to remember its mindset—the narrowness, anti-Semitism, and chauvinism of its inhabitants. Especially when talking to Hitler memories of the 5th were useful. That Hohenlohe, a 'Princess', was capable of talking this 'familiar language' was one reason why Hitler took to her immediately. Hohenlohe was Viennese and Hitler, who had grown up in Linz, was known to resent the Viennese. But Hohenlohe could also 'do Linz', i.e. the provinces. She later stressed that Hitler was 'lower than middle class and his language the lowest'. She quite rightly pointed out that when he spoke German it often sounded stilted, like a man speaking a foreign language. Because Hohenlohe was so gifted at languages and intonations herself (her voice was described as melodious and one of her greatest assets) she detected fake accents easily. Hitler's intonation was revealing to her:

> He spoke, particularly back in 1933, like a low class Austrian. By low class I mean not even middle class. One who tried to speak a language better than the one he was born to, or used to.... Although the difference between him now [1942] and back in 1933 is enormous: his language still sounds to me terribly stilted and artificial, phonetically as well as grammatically. This is all the more astonishing as no one seems to notice it. Everyone has always acclaimed him as an outstanding orator and no one seems to have noticed this striking deficiency. Least of all he himself. He once told me when I expressed my astonishment at his not learning English that the reason he would never be able to learn any other language

outside of German was his complete mastery of the latter, which was a full time job . . . I have never found that Adolf Hitler speaks or writes German as well as he claims or thinks. I have had many occasions to read letters of his, where all he did was revel in heavy, involved teutonic sentences. A single sentence often attains as much as eight or ten lines. . . . I have always admired his interpreter, Legationsrat Schmidt . . . for his prodigious memory. He retains these endless sentences, where I have forgotten the beginning by the time he reaches the end.[44]

Lathering the froth herself, Hohenlohe was good at detecting it in others. A further thing she noticed was that despite the fact that Hitler wanted to appeal to all classes, the Habsburg Empire with its strict social strata had left its mark. He was socially insecure and at the same time a snob. He made fun of the 'degenerate aristocracy', but eagerly surrounded himself with members of it. It had certainly paid off for him to associate with them. After he gave up his early revolutionary gangster look (always in a trenchcoat and carrying a whip), he went through a phase of 'domestication', keen on displaying the best manners to his many upper-class benefactors, male and female, eagerly kissing hands whenever appropriate (only those of married women). The journalist Dorothy Thompson noted in 1932 that Hitler 'was going very high hat and frock coat . . . He associates with industrialists. He goes to tea with princesses.'[45] Anything for the party. One of these princesses was Hohenlohe who noted: 'his manners are exceedingly courteous especially to women.' In this he acted like the perfect opportunist politician, dressing chameleon-like and winning over people with all the old politician's tricks: 'often taking [your hand] into both of his and shaking it for a time to emphasize the sense of pleasure it gave him to see one. At the same time looking one in the eyes.'

Naturally, Hohenlohe later claimed that she was not taken in, though she never showed this in her enthusiastic letters to Hitler. Admittedly in her dealings with him business was uppermost and therefore she had to concentrate on her brief. Although she was genuinely attracted to the adjutant Wiedemann, she certainly did not find his boss, Hitler, *physically* attractive. Looks were always important to her, and in Hitler's case she listed in great detail her objections. She started with his hair that

is so thin like that of a child. . . . His ugliest features are: nose, moustache, feet and mouth. When talking his teeth hardly ever show. But when they do, you can see that they are not nice in colour or shape . . . The mouth itself is small, much too small for a man, and opens in an unbecoming way.

She liked, however, the 'sensitive hands of an artist', and 'his eyes, which are of a very nice, light blue (and) could be called beautiful, with a rather far away expression, were they not slightly bulging. This, together with the extremely delicate texture of his skin, always gave me the impression that he is not a healthy man. He is always either very pale, or he has little pink spots on his cheeks. I have always heard that both are characteristic signs of heart or lung trouble.' It was these details about Hitler's possible health problems that made Hohenlohe's report useful for the American Office for Strategic Services (OSS).

According to Hohenlohe's analysis, a minor, yet interesting reason for his appeal was the simplicity of his clothes. The Germans seemed to interpret this as true modesty: 'Usually he wears a not very well fitting beige uniform coat with black trousers. With that a white shirt and beige tie, with a swastika emblem as a tie pin. The iron cross, first class, nothing else.' This minimalism seemed to produce maximum effect, as did his seriousness: 'he is always either dead serious or cross; I never could understand why. He hardly ever smiles, except when making a sarcastic remark. He can be, no, he often is, very bitter.'

She also noted, as did many others, that he was incapable of having a proper conversation. He was either giving a monologue or sulking. Hohenlohe, however, proudly stated that she had managed to engage him in dialogue:

> I am one of the few persons with whom he held normal conversations. By that I mean one where both parties speak in turn. A conversation of two human beings. Usually though, this is not the case: either he makes a speech and one has to listen, or else he sits there with a dead serious face, never opening his mouth.[46]

While Hohenlohe was lamenting the texture of his hair, Hitler was seriously taken by her. There were several reasons for this, starting with their closeness in age. Hohenlohe was never honest about her real age, but Hitler was only two years older than her and they had gone through similar generational experiences. Second, he liked her type. She must have reminded him of another forceful woman who had been useful to him in the past—Winifred Wagner, the matriarch of the Wagner-clan. The British born Winifred, like so many other 'motherly' types of the German upper classes, had been instrumental in furthering Hitler's career. Hohenlohe, therefore, seemed to be another motherly figure who would devote her energy and network to him. It would take Hitler years to realize that, behind all the fussing over him, Hohenlohe was not exactly altruistic.

This was certainly not news to Hitler's entourage. For almost seven years they had to cope with the interloper Hohenlohe and they were far from pleased. Like the MI5 watchers, who were puzzled about Hohenlohe's social and sexual successes, their German counterparts were confused too. After all, 'the Princess' looked anything but Aryan.

Two men felt especially threatened by Hohenlohe, Hitler's 'experts' on Britain and America—Ribbentrop and Ernst (Putzi) Hanfstaengl. 'Putzi's' case is interesting because it mirrored Hohenlohe's: he was a star at Hitler's court, fell from grace, and ended up in an American prison.

Hanfstaengl was the son of an American mother and a German father. The Hanfstaengls were a well-connected Munich family. They had been privy councillors to the dukes of Sachsen-Coburg und Gotha for two generations and Ernst 'Putzi', born in 1888, had been named after Duke Ernst II of Sachsen-Coburg und Gotha, the brother-in-law of Queen Victoria. Putzi therefore knew the man who took over the dukedoms in 1905: Queen Victoria's grandson Carl Eduard, Duke of Coburg. Both Coburg and Putzi shared the same political outlook and became interested in Hitler in the 1920s. Both fulfilled the role of upper-class assets for the Nazis. Putzi's wide social network helped Hitler to meet many key benefactors. In his memoirs Putzi would later describe how in the early 1920s they travelled constantly together to raise funds for the party: 'Hitler seemed to think that I would give an air of respectability to his begging expeditions and we went on several trips round Munich and its environs visiting prominent citizens.'[47]

Hanfstaengl liked to play the clown but he also occasionally flaunted his upper-class background to his fellow Nazis—an unwise thing to do in an environment full of socially insecure people. That this could backfire is illustrated by an incident from April 1923. Hitler's car was stopped at a communist roadblock in Saxony. Putzi saved the situation by telling the suspicious guards in a heavy American accent that he was a US citizen on the way to a trade fair. Pointing at Hitler, he said, 'this is my man, Johann. I hired him and the chauffeur in Hamburg.'[48]

Hitler was grateful for the ruse, but years later Sefton Delmer had the impression that it had harmed Hanfstaengl in the long run. A socially insecure person like Hitler could not forgive the fact that he had once been described as a manservant.[49] Still, Putzi was useful for a while. He had studied at Harvard and thanks to his many international contacts was made the head of the NSDAP's Foreign Press Department in September 1930. Hitler had told him: 'You know England and America. Watch what they say about us. Also, make sure that they hear what we are doing; perhaps they will wake up to the importance of what we are trying to accomplish.'[50] Hanfstaengl had done his best to fulfil this brief. He had brought in a deal with the American newspaper baron William Randolph Hearst, who had been a friend of his mother's. Hitler agreed to write an occasional article for Hearst and Putzi received 30 per cent of the fee.[51] Other newspapers made similar offers and Hanfstaengl and Hitler received good commissions. But Hanfstaengl's eagerness to earn more started to annoy Hitler. When Stephanie Hohenlohe and Rothermere came along, he wanted to demonstrate to his press chief that he had alternatives. 'Princess Hohenlohe' offered an opportunity to teach snobbish Hanfstaengl a lesson. Hitler's interest in her was therefore threefold: political, financial, and personal.

Hanfstaengl did not grasp this dimension but simply despised his new rival from the bottom of his heart. It was now Hohenlohe who posed as the expert on the English speaking world and, to Hanfstaengl's annoyance, was taken seriously. Putzi would later claim that he had warned Hitler of the Princess who was a 'blackmailer and Jewish'. According to Hanfstaengl Hitler retorted that her pedigree had been checked and was 'pure'.[52] By awarding her the golden party badge in June 1938 he silenced her critics. Making her an honoured party member naturally meant she was Aryan.

Hohenlohe soon realized that Hanfstaengl was not her only problem. With Ribbentrop, the rivalry was even fiercer, and much more dangerous. Ribbentrop and Hohenlohe had too much in common. Both had engineered a title for themselves and relentlessly cultivated up and coming politicians. Ribbentrop had married money and invested it, like Hohenlohe, in lavish entertainment. The most decisive reason for their mutual hatred was the issue of Britain. Both saw it as their patch and both would eventually take a very different line over Anglo-German relations. As a consequence Ribbentrop did his best to block Hohenlohe in every possible way. Once he became ambassador to Britain he banned her from the German embassy. He was also adamant in not inviting her to the big coronation party 'his' embassy gave in 1937. On the list were 1,200 people including Wiedemann who had been sent to the coronation as part of the German delegation. Wiedemann did his best to get his lover Hohenlohe invited, but in the end Hitler himself had to intervene, ordering Ribbentrop to host her. Triumphantly Stephanie sailed into the embassy on Wiedemann's arm. Ribbentrop never forgave her.

The rest of Hitler's entourage were also increasingly enraged by Hohenlohe. They were men used to obedient housewives and Hohenlohe was therefore a rather alien creature. Yet apart from Captain Wiedemann, there was one other person who showed interest in her—Göring. He saw her potential and, as will be shown, used her for his own purposes.

Survival at Hitler's court was a severe test and Hohenlohe had early on realized that one had to demonstrate loyalty continuously. Even wearing the right clothes mattered:

> The one who is seen [in the brown shirt] most is the Führer's 'Stellvertreter' [deputy] Rudolf Hess and Mr. von Ribbentrop who wears a brown shirt even with his civil clothes, to give proof of how good a Parteigenosse that is party member, he is. Almost, everybody, including his own staff, comment on it, because it looks out of place and very ugly.

Since Hitler disapproved of cosmetics, Hohenlohe made sure not to wear lipstick in Germany.

She was now almost commuting between Berlin and London. According to FBI reports 'she conferred with Hitler on Rothermere's behalf on at least 50 different occasions'.[53]

The many letters and messages Hohenlohe carried between Rothermere and Hitler showed that the press tycoon wanted to do everything he could to help Hitler to reverse the Treaty of Versailles. In April 1935 he wrote:

> The recent correspondence in the Daily Mail in regard to the claims of your government for changes in the Treaty of Versailles show that seven out of every 10 of the persons writing letters were in favour of Germany's claims being entirely acceded to.[54]

And a few months later:

> No one is more whole-heartedly in favour of an Anglo-German understanding than myself, and if there is any information which your Excellency can impart which might further this cause I can assure your Excellency that such information would only be used as you might desire and determine. I esteem it a great honour and privilege to be in correspondence with your Excellency. It is not often that anyone has the opportunity of learning the views of one who may occupy the first place in European History.[55]

Rothermere saw Hitler as a 'bulwark against bolshevism', exactly the type of leader Britain lacked. He even contemplated building up a copy of Hitler: Oswald Mosley.[56] In 1934 the *Daily Mail* had actively supported Mosley and his British Union of Fascists with the infamous 'Hurrah for the Blackshirts' article. The Rothermere newspaper *Evening News* bought 500 seats for the Blackshirts rally in the Royal Albert Hall and the *Sunday Dispatch* financed a raffle for female Blackshirts (an idea that did not take off). The FBI later informed President Roosevelt that 'it was reported [Stephanie Hohenlohe] has in her possession a longhand notation believed to be in Rothermere's handwriting, reading: "I believe the blackshirts will rule Britain within three years."'[57] When the movement lost its dynamic, Rothermere dropped Mosley. According to his biographer the press tycoon resented the Blackshirts anti-Semitism and did not like the expression 'Fascist'. This does not sit comfortably with the facts. Rothermere's anti-Semitism was so strong that it impressed even Goebbels. Yet when Jewish firms like Lyons or Carreras threatened to withdraw advertisements from his papers after the Blackshirt rally, Rothermere had to make a business decision. His break with Mosley did not mean that the press tycoon had lost interest in Hitler though. In any event, the Führer had never been enthusiastic about Mosley.

Hitler had been informed about him by several people, and while Unity Mitford naturally praised her brother-in-law, other reports had not always been flattering. In October 1933 Günther Schmidt-Lorenz explained in detail to the German Chancellery the split amongst the fascists in Britain. One of his sources was Viscount [Richard] Downe and his wife.[58] Lady Downe was an active fascist opposed to Mosley. She explained to Schmidt-Lorenz that, after the war fascism was not embraced by the British because they were at heart conservative and the revolutionary side of fascism scared them. But another reason had been the lack of a proper leader. According to Lady Downe, Oswald Mosley could never play this part for two reasons: first because he was a turncoat who had changed his political affiliation several times. And second because he was too liberal towards Jews, accepting large sums of money from them and mixing socially with people like Baron Rothschild and the Sassoons.

The Nazis were obsessed with researching the 'racial background' of all their British discussion partners, including Mosley. Their probing caused a lot of confusion over the years. In 1935, the German ambassador Hoesch for example wrote to Berlin that Sir Samuel Hoare, despite the name Samuel, was not Jewish. On the contrary, he 'was not anti-German and open to dialogue'.[59] Suspicion remained. In 1937 the infamous Gestapo chief Müller demanded a list from the German embassy of everyone Jewish who had been recently knighted. He also demanded to know exactly which members of the British aristocracy were Jewish. In reply to this enquiry the German embassy sent a copy of the book 'Our Jewish Aristocracy' which had been published by the Imperial Fascist League in 1936.[60] The authors had divided their 'study' into several sections including one on 'mixed blood' and 'half-breeds in the making'. The latter included people who might soon reproduce, including the daughter of the Marquess of Londonderry who had married a Jew. Hitler was particularly obsessed with the idea that his main critics in Britain had to have a Jewish connection. The German embassy therefore received a direct enquiry from the Führer whether the wives of Anthony Eden, Winston Churchill, and Duff Cooper were Jewish or half-Jewish. They were not. Yet this paranoia explains why the report about Mosley's Jewish connections had a long-term effect. Schmidt-Lorenz completely agreed with Lady Downe's analysis, even though he had had a long conversation with Mosley in 1933. Mosley told him that he was also of the opinion that the British were scared of the revolutionary side of fascism, but that the world economic crisis would be helpful for his movement. He vehemently dismissed rumours that he was financed by Jews and stressed that nobody should doubt his anti-Semitism. Hitler was never convinced by Mosley despite the fact that (or perhaps because) he liked Mosley's wife Diana. She was almost as keen on the Führer as her sister Unity. Like Unity, she looked for every opportunity to meet Hitler. His adjutant Wiedemann was one route into the inner circle. In 1937 she wrote to the 'gatekeeper' Wiedemann in good German:

> I looked for you all over Germany, Berlin, Würzburg, München, but you had vanished. I am now travelling back home to England.

She was hoping to see Wiedemann at the upcoming party rally in Nuremberg—she was '*so* excited about it'.[61] Unity also tried to help her find Wiedemann, admonishing him in a letter that because Diana made her drive around 'chasing him' she had had a serious car accident in Nuremberg: 'This was all your fault.' Wiedemann wrote a rather cool reply to Diana asking her to be patient.[62] He was a bit more sympathetic when her husband Oswald Mosely was attacked by 'Reds' and had to be hospitalized in October 1937. Reading these letters it becomes obvious that Wiedemann deliberately gave Diana the run-around. He knew that she wanted two things from him—more access to Hitler and a go-ahead for what she called her 'Angelegenheit' (preoccupation)—a propaganda station in Heligoland. Of course Diana could not know the reasons for Wiedemann's inexplicable resistance to her charms—he was working and sleeping with Stephanie Hohenlohe, a fierce rival of both Mitford sisters.

In the end, Mosley's banishment from Rothermere's orbit was Stephanie Hohenlohe's gain. It ensured that she remained his main channel to Hitler. Working for Rothermere had also helped to extend her British circle of friends considerably. She had managed to create a surprisingly impressive number of them. Her two assets were the Rothermere connection and her illustrious name. She was not a 'princess of the blood', but in the inter-war years, this was not taken so seriously. With several royal courts gone and an influx of White Russians, Baltic, and other displaced members of the former upper classes floating around the Continent, it was easier to pretend to have an aristocratic background. Certainly the chances to get away with a white lie were higher, since not so many people could check up on the details. That Hohenlohe had married to gain her title was also not so relevant in Britain where a long pedigree counted less than in Europe. The name itself was sufficient, preferably with money attached to it. Hohenlohe's British success was therefore due to her name and her message. The name opened the doors, the message ensured that they stayed open. There was a genuine curiosity about Hitler among the British upper classes that Hohenlohe could satisfy.

She was a classic 'fisherman', trying to cultivate everyone of importance. To study her social success in London helps to untangle the complicated net of Hitler admirers. Among them were many members of the far right, like Lord Sempill, the Duke of Westminster, Franco's envoy to London the Duke of Alba, but also conservative British MPs. MI5 viewed this with the greatest concern:

> In 1933/34 [Stephanie Hohenlohe] seems to have become acquainted with Lady Margot Oxford [Margot Asquith, Countess of Oxford] and Lady Cunard and through introductions from them to have wormed her way into society circles in London. Among her friends at the time were Lady Austen Chamberlain, Sir Horace Rumbold, Sir Barry Domville, Lord and Lady Londonderry.... Princess Hohenlohe has acted as a link between Nazi leaders in Germany and Society circles in this country.[63]

This shows that she did not just specialize in men. She capitalized on the fact that a powerful group of society ladies existed in Britain—most of them upper class but also some who had, like Hohenlohe, worked their way up. The historian Ross McKibbin described them as 'formidable' ladies. They had 'unusual drive and native intelligence determined to "prove" themselves in the most difficult way they could imagine—by the social acquisition of people who would otherwise have cut them dead.'[64] Hohenlohe had had her own experiences with overcoming such hindrances. She had been cut dead many times in her life: at school when classmates made fun of her father being an ex-prisoner and later as a courtesan barred from the salons of Vienna. Traditionally women had not been her close allies, but in Britain nobody knew of Hohenlohe's past and she won over many influential hostesses. She offered them exciting and rather 'exotic' new causes—Hungary and Germany.

That society ladies fell for her puzzled the intelligence services. In the case of Lady Asquith it must have been relatively easy. The wife of the former Prime Minister collected unusual female friends and was rumoured to be in love with some of them. During the First World War she had been close to the dancer Maud Allen, who played a part in Chapter 2. Lady Asquith's taste for women had always been a subject for gossip and in some ways Hohenlohe fitted the pattern well. Of course not all women were so taken with her. A new generation of younger society ladies like Unity and Diana Mitford became her greatest social rivals. But Hohenlohe was luckier with women of her own generation, women who still liked to play a part. 'The Princess' capitalized on their vanity. She was an expert in figuring out peoples' weaknesses and insecurities. Through contacts in female society she accumulated insider information that was highly valuable for her Hungarian and German friends. In her own words she was well informed about 'the City, Westminster, Downing Street, [the gentlemen's clubs] in St. James's, Buckingham Palace or Mayfair'. And she reported her research in whatever form was necessary: 'I was ready to be serious, matter-of-fact, exact, light, superficial, flippant, or, as I hoped, even interesting and amusing.'[65] It simply depended on the recipient.

Her main recipient remained Rothermere. He wanted an Anglo-German alliance against the Bolshevik threat and did everything to please the Germans. Over the years he sent many valuable presents to his new Nazi friends and continued to pay Hohenlohe well. Again it is unclear how much she actually received because of her tax evasion, but it was certainly an astronomical sum for the time. When they met in court in 1939, the Princess claimed Rothermere had promised to pay her $20,000 a year for the rest of her life. According to *Time* magazine Rothermere had 'boomed "Preposterous!"'

He admitted paying her '$250,000 in six years to handle his relations with Adolf Hitler and other European bigwigs, naively explaining: "I expected her to live like a queen." '[66]

According to her son, Hohenlohe invested most of the money in the London property market. She did not wish to live in these houses but preferred to reside at the newly founded Dorchester Hotel. The manager had made her a special offer, thereby hoping to attract 'the right clientele'. Until 1939 Hohenlohe was the right clientele. The same was true for German hotels. On visiting Berlin she stayed at the most expensive, the Adlon. Here she regularly received Wiedemann's bouquets of roses and it was here that they planned the next steps for 'improving' Anglo-German relations.

One coup was to have Rothermere invited to Hitler's mountain retreat. The two men had met before but to be asked to the Berghof on the Obersalzberg was a special honour. It turned out to be a great success. Hitler entertained the British media tycoon from 5 to 8 January 1937. Stephanie and Magda Goebbels were the only women present (Eva Braun was hidden away) and enjoyed the occasion tremendously (Figure 8). Goebbels was especially keen on Rothermere. Their friendship had started in 1934. In his diary Goebbels noted:

> At Ribbentrop's. Lord Rothermere, a real Englishman. John Bull. Very generous views. If all Englishmen thought like him! Against Versailles, for our rearmament, for colonies, friendship between Berlin and London. Against the diplomats. Phipps [Sir Eric Phipps was British ambassador to Germany at the time] almost fainting. I talk with him non-stop. At the end he calls me the 'greatest propagandist in the world. If you don't want to work in Germany anymore, I will hire you for a salary ten times the amount you are earning.' We both laugh. I think I have won his heart. It is worthwhile to talk with such people.[67]

The 'Führer' shared this opinion. Afterwards Goebbels had put great effort into the next Rothermere visit: 'Watched films with Führer for Rothermere. Can't use any of them. In the evening, reception for Rothermere at the Führer's. Spectacular. Führer is excellent to Magda who looks beautiful.... Rothermere totally won over by us. This is a great success. He tells me a lot of flattering things. The Führer in great form. A wonderful evening.'

This new friendship must have been ironic for Hitler though. In an early speech in 1923 he had claimed that Rothermere's brother Lord Northcliffe was 'Jewish'. (This was not just an *idée fixe* of Hitler's. Wilhelm II was of a similar opinion. He and his cousin Prince Wilhelm Hohenzollern-

Figure 8. Go-between for many masters: Princess Stephanie von Hohenlohe-Waldenburg-Schillingsfürst (front left, next to Magda Goebbels). Standing from left to right behind her: Lord Rothermere, Ward Price, Hitler, Fritz Wiedeman, and Joseph Goebbels. Photo taken at the Berghof, January 1937.

Sigmaringen agreed that these 'dreadful' English press tycoons were originally from a 'Jewish family called Stern'.)[68]

But by 1937 Hitler had ascertained the truth. He was hosting a man who was anything but pro-Jewish, who hated communism, and wanted nothing more than an Anglo-German alliance. Goebbels was particularly eager to impress, noting in his diary that Rothermere had seven million readers and would therefore be highly 'useful'. The conversations opened with Stephanie giving them the latest gossip about the Duke of Windsor. Then they all watched the war film *Stoßtrupp 1917* which touched Rothermere visibly and made Stephanie cry charmingly. When it finally came to political discussions, Rothermere told his German hosts that in his opinion the British government was pro-Franco but could not openly say so for domestic reasons.[69] He stressed that he shared completely Hitler's anti-Bolshevism and admired Mussolini as much as the Führer. His great aim was to bring Baldwin and Hitler together. Goebbels was satisfied and wrote that 'we won him over completely'.[70] Rothermere was equally satisfied, lauding Goebbels once more as the 'greatest propagandist in the world', and asked him again to come over to England to 'reform his newspapers'.[71]

Indeed, the visit at the Berghof had a great impact on Rothermere. Afterwards he wrote a strong article advocating an Anglo-German alliance and stressing his support for the Führer. It pleased Goebbels particularly that Rothermere referred in his article to the time spent at the Berghof: 'so those days were useful after all!'[72]

Afterwards, Rothermere also helped the German cause in Spain; something that delighted Goebbels: 'Franco is making good progress. Rothermere firmly stands up for him. He is a decent boy.'[73] As we will see, he was also very useful in the Sudeten German question.

Everyone was satisfied with the Berghof visit and Rothermere bestowed generous presents afterwards. Hohenlohe received a special financial bonus and Wiedemann a cigarette case with a personal inscription.[74]

Stephanie Hohenlohe became a regular at the Berghof from then on. Some of her enthusiastic 'thank you' letters to Hitler have survived. She praised his hospitality and 'well run house', sending presents afterwards. Among them were books about American bridges, an interest of the 'architect' Hitler. Hohenlohe described his interest in bridges as appropriate since he was a 'political bridge builder'. In return Hitler thanked her for the presents and the fact that: 'in the past year you have sincerely and warmheartedly supported Germany and its vital interests (*Lebensnotwendigkeiten*) in your circles.'[75]

On one occasion in 1937 he also sent her a very special present—a dog. Hohenlohe claimed to be overwhelmed by this dog who would be her 'wolf' (wolf being an insider name for Hitler). It was an ideal present because she pretended to 'adore dogs and everything they stood for—loyalty and friendship'. 'Unfortunately,' she wrote, she had to go off on one of her many trips and would have to collect the dog later.[76] Doubtless she never did.

Hitler had every reason for giving her special presents. Hohenlohe was an excellent saleswoman for the new Germany. Only once did she get stuck and need back up. One of her friends, Margot Asquith, had grown concerned about the fate of the German Nobel Peace Prize winner, Carl von Ossietzky. To placate Lady Asquith, Wiedemann and Hohenlohe drafted a letter in 1937 in which Wiedemann assured her that 'Mr Ossietzky was in a sanatorium near Berlin. He was currently planning to use his Nobel prize money to purchase a nice house near Berlin.'[77] This was a cynical lie. In fact Ossietzky had been imprisoned by the Nazis since 1933. He became an inmate of several concentration camps, where he developed tuberculosis which was left untreated. He eventually died in 1938 in a hospital under police surveillance. Whether Stephanie Hohenlohe knew the real circumstances or not, she would not have cared about the truth. She needed to impress Lady Asquith and this letter was useful in placating the naive British woman.

Over the years Wiedemann wrote her any letter she required, including a sort of Nazi 'work permit'. It had an impressive *Adjutantur des Führers* letterhead, and was a laissez-passer instructing all German administrative bodies at home and abroad to help Hohenlohe in any way she desired. The letter stated that the Princess was known to the Führer personally and had worked for the 'new Germany' abroad in the 'most remarkable ways'.[78]

Though this was certainly true, not all her trips were successful. Her trip to America in early 1938 was in fact a disaster.

Since Hohenlohe was celebrated as the woman who had once pulled off an amazing press campaign for Hungary, the idea had materialized that she might be useful for other lost causes. A marketing campaign in America seemed to be just such a cause. Her fellow go-between, the Duke of Coburg, had already tried his best in 1934 and now, at the beginning of 1938, Hohenlohe was sent to New York. She knew the States well. According to the FBI report for President Roosevelt, she had been travelling to America since 1931.[79] Her mission was to persuade *Time* magazine to publish a positive article about Hitler. This time she brought a polished draft with her, which *Time* had no intention of publishing. Instead by the end of the year the magazine would crown Hitler as 'Man of the year 1938'. The designation was not meant as a compliment. After having annexed Austria and the Sudetenland, it was now obvious what a threat he posed.

The Nazi leadership was naturally infuriated by the insult, but strangely enough Hohenlohe was never considered responsible for the American failure. On the contrary. According to the FBI files, 1938 was a busy year for her. She travelled to Syria with Wilhelm Fluegge, an engineer who after the war worked at Stanford University, and she also travelled to Istanbul.[80] What she did there is still a mystery; none of it is mentioned in her draft memoirs.

She also managed to engineer a new lucrative job for herself. When Hitler took over Austria in March 1938 new sinecures came up for deserving Nazis. Stephanie Hohenlohe immediately grabbed one of them: Leopoldskron, a beautiful castle near Salzburg. Leopoldskron was not just any castle; it was a cultural jewel. Since 1919 its owner had been Max Reinhardt, the famous theatre and film director. Reinhardt had emigrated to America and left his beloved home with all its paintings and furniture behind. He would die in 1943 without ever seeing it again. It eventually became the film location for *The Sound of Music* and is today an expensive hotel.

Hohenlohe, a born profiteer, jumped at the opportunity to take the property over. She would later claim that she had done this to salvage Reinhardt's belongings (some were indeed forwarded to the United States on Hitler's—unusually generous—instructions). This was such a cynical excuse that nobody, and especially not the Reinhardt family, believed her. They were heartbroken about the loss. In some ways the castle had been Reinhardt's greatest production, an artwork and a piece of theatre in itself. His wife later remembered how they spent nights rearranging pictures, books, and furniture. It therefore showed real chutzpah that Stephanie Hohenlohe felt she had to 'redecorate the whole place'.

In 1941, when Hohenlohe was imprisoned by the Americans, she had some problems explaining her time in Leopoldskron. An old friend, who had once been Reinhardt's agent, tried to help her. His name was Rudolf Kommer and he claimed that Hohenlohe had altruistically 'saved' the castle. If she had not taken it over in 1938, some Nazi organization would have requested it and ruined the splendid interior. Since Hohenlohe was herself a sort of one-woman 'Nazi organization' at the time, this was a rather outlandish argument. During her interviews with the Americans she would also claim that she had helped several people in 1938 to escape Austria, including Max Reinhardt's wife (which was a blatant lie).

Decades later her son kept defending Stephanie's time at Leopoldskron. According to his memoirs, she paid rent for the castle. The accusations that she had received it as a present from Hitler were utterly wrong.[81] In fact Hitler's adjutant Wiedemann paid all the exorbitant bills for the refurbishment of the castle. Financially this experiment soon ran into difficulties, and neither was it a success socially. Its aim was to attract the international clientele who attended the Salzburg Festival and this failed. Some of Hohenlohe's aristocratic friends turned up in the summer of 1938, but not as many British ones as she had hoped. Her greatest 'catches' were a few Americans from the art world including the conductor Leopold Stokowski. She also entertained a friend of the Duke of

Windsor (who played golf with his wife Wallis nearby), the notorious Charles Bedaux. While Stephanie's guests admired the landscape, they were watched.[82]

This was certainly not a harmless holiday home for an apolitical princess. Gauleiter Friedrich Rainer reported that Hohenlohe ran a 'political salon'.[83] In fact Leopoldskron was intended to become a propaganda palace for the international upper classes. MI5 followed this attentively: 'In July [1938] she rented Castle Leopoldskroon near Salzburg, and was said to have entertained prominent Nazis there and to have introduced them to English friends.'

The idea of bringing right wing politicians together with international aristocrats had emerged in the 1920s in Germany. As we have already seen, aristocrats offered their castles as discreet meeting places for political get togethers. Later, they would use castle politics (similar to the British country house politics) for propaganda purposes.[84] Stephanie Hohenlohe's Leopoldskron therefore offered continuity. Even when she fell out of favour, the Nazis did not give up the concept. As the German Foreign Ministry files show, the NSDAP planned a similar 'country house' for Italy. Here it also thought of putting an aristocratic stooge in charge, Prince Rohan, an ardent National Socialist. A German Foreign Ministry official summed up the negotiations with him:

> Last February I talked to Prince Rohan about whether he could not move for a time or completely to Rome . . . to run a distinguished house in close contact with the leading circles of Roman society. I think it useful to have eyes and ears open in these circles, running a centre of exclusive entertainment, since these circles are connected with the Vatican and are open to English and French influence because of their relatives. It is of some interest that the ladies of Roman society are well informed about what is going on in the Foreign Ministry.[85]

The Berlin journalist Bella Fromm even suspected that there was a 'system of high society espionage' dominated by women.[86] As examples she mentions Edit von Coler (who worked in Romania and was as dangerous as Stephanie), Baroness of Heyden-Rynsch, and Walli von Richthofen. The latter was definitely in the pay of the Gestapo. The others also had connections to various intelligence services. Though Hohenlohe did not sign up with any of the intelligence services, Leopoldskron was probably bugged. It would explain why so much 'electrical work' had to be done when Stephanie took over.[87]

Apart from Leopoldskron, the Anschluss of Austria had brought other opportunities for profiteers like Hohenlohe. Austro-Jewish property could now be taken over and Stephanie had no qualms about benefiting from the situation. She did not just take over Max Reinhardt's castle, but also sought to make a profit out of Jewish art collections. As usual Wiedemann was ready to help. He wrote to the Prussian State Ministry in Berlin, suggesting the sale of Austrian 'objects of art' to a group of 'foreign investors'. Göring would support this and the Princess Hohenlohe could make the arrangements. It would, Wiedemann argued, be beneficial for Germany by bringing in a substantial amount of foreign currency.[88] The Ministry was not so sure. They had received a letter from Hungary earlier where Stephanie Hohenlohe had seemed to be involved in a similar racket. It had made them suspicious that the 'international art market' was trying to manipulate German art collections. They did not wish therefore to be involved in the Hohenlohe–Wiedemann scheme and did not think it 'necessary to involve Fieldmarshal Göring'. Wiedemann naturally disagreed.

From here the trail goes cold. No further correspondence exists showing whether Wiedemann, Hohenlohe, and Göring carried out their plan. Naturally no one involved had reason to leave any traces in writing. Göring and Hohenlohe probably came to some arrangement. The Princess was of course well aware of Göring's interest in stolen art as well as in accumulating as much foreign currency as possible. She was able to help with both. Whatever she provided for him, Göring showed himself grateful. In 1939 he helped with her last bills for Leopoldskron. By then Stephanie had moved out of the castle rather hurriedly. She had left it to Wiedemann to sort out the details and he dutifully wrote several letters to the Nazi chief in Salzburg, stating that Göring had decided to take the castle over as state property and that he had talked to the Führer about covering the remaining bills.[89] The Princess's possessions should now be sent on to London. All this was accepted, but Stephanie kept complaining that she had just received 'underwear from Leopoldskron', while her silver had not been forwarded.

Hohenlohe did not just profit from Leopoldskron and Austrian artwork. FBI files indicate that she also played a role in the negotiations regarding the capture of Baron Louis de Rothschild by the Nazis. Rothschild had been arrested in Vienna shortly after the 'Anschluss'. After fourteen months in prison, his family paid a ransom, the exact sum of which has never been revealed. According to an FBI report, Hohenlohe had offered her go-between services to the Rothschild family—naturally against payment.[90] She was rejected: an unusual experience for her.

After his success in annexing Austria in March 1938, Hitler turned to his next item on the agenda—Czechoslovakia. His aim was to use the grievances of the Sudeten Germans in Czechoslovakia as a vehicle to, in his own words, 'smash the country'. The question was how the French and more importantly the British would react to the smashing. Ribbentrop had claimed in 1937 that Britain would not accept a German attack on Czechoslovakia. Other experts on Britain begged to differ. Three of Hitler's go-betweens had come to the same conclusion: Coburg, Max Hohenlohe, and Stephanie Hohenlohe thought there was room for manoeuvre with Britain. And they were proved right. Their brief from May 1938 onwards was to make the British accept every step Hitler took.

The timing was auspicious. Former Chancellor of the Exchequer Neville Chamberlain had become Prime Minister in 1937. He thought of himself as an expert on foreign policy and this unfounded assumption would play a decisive part during the following years. Of course many valid arguments existed for appeasing Germany. Britain was behind in the arms race, its economy needed a stimulus, and the public did not want another war. Chamberlain therefore wanted to keep the German problem under control. His analysis in 1937 was that the Foreign Office had failed in its handling of Germany and needed to be restructured. First, he decided to get rid of Foreign Secretary Eden and the Permanent Under Secretary at the Foreign Office, Sir Robert Vansittart. In Chamberlain's eyes Vansittart did not understand Germany properly while Anthony Eden was not taking 'a consistent lead' either.[91] At the beginning of 1938 Vansittart was supplanted as Permanent Under Secretary by Sir Alexander Cadogan, who was pro-appeasement. So was the new Foreign Secretary, Lord Halifax, who took over from Eden in February 1938. Chamberlain had now put his new men in place. This was ideal for Hitler. Goebbels noted: 'Eden resigned. Lord Halifax is said to become his successor. That would be a good solution... Lord Rothermere has given an interview supporting the Führer. He is our most reliable press magnate.'[92] He was indeed. Rothermere and Stephanie would now work closely for the Nazis in the Sudeten crisis and Goebbels continued to be highly satisfied about Rothermere's supportive articles. In April 1938 he wrote: 'Lord Rothermere is once more delivering a sharp attack against Prague and in favour of us. He is really an upright and useful man.'[93] A month later Rothermere pleased Goebbels even more with a 'fantastic article about the Führer' and a volley against Czechoslovakia. 'He really is our friend.'[94]

The Sudeten crisis is particularly interesting in illustrating several go-between missions. As we have seen, the Duke of Coburg had successive talks in Britain during this period, but none of them has been documented (most of the relevant material is presumably in the Royal Archives). Fortunately the missions of Stephanie Hohenlohe and Max Hohenlohe are more readily substantiated. Both Hohenlohes acted separately in the Sudeten crisis but their missions had a shared aim. Both also shared the same employers—Göring and Hitler.

According to Stephanie Hohenlohe it all started in June 1938 when Göring invited her for a tête-à-tête to his country seat. She was intrigued. In her unpublished memoirs she recorded:

> Next to the Führer 'our Hermann' is the one Nazi leader, who continuously stimulates the imagination of the German people, who is the hero and the victim and the most ardent collector of innumerable stories and jokes, who is genuinely popular in the widest sense of the word. No matter what fate may have in store for him, this theatrical, bombastic, Falstaffian pour le merite flier will remain one of the great figures in German memory.[95]

For a long time Göring had played with the idea of visiting Britain. His former opposite number as Air Minister Lord Londonderry had visited Carinhall on one occasion; and Göring wanted to hear from Hohenlohe all the latest gossip about his new British friend. He had heard the rumour that Lady Londonderry had been the lover of the former Prime Minister Ramsay MacDonald. According to her notes, the suddenly prudish Stephanie was outraged at such a suggestion: 'With characteristic grossness of mind and judgement he chose to put a romantic complexion on [Lady Londonderry and MacDonald's relationship], and took it for granted that Lord Londonderry's air ministry had been the natural result of his wife's friendship with the head of the government. "Can you imagine me", he asked emphatically, "using my wife to gain personal advantages and positions?" I could not, but I did not say so. Yet, the genius loci of Carinhall compelled me to think of his first wife, Carin von Fock, who had sacrificed her whole fortune and health for his political advancement, and who had died, in battle, as it were.' On this point Hohenlohe was right, Göring's Swedish wife had helped him tirelessly in his career and it was thanks to her that Göring also had high ranking connections with Sweden which would be useful to him during the war.

Göring then went on to explain that he was a jealous man (a revelation that would hardly have surprised his rivals). He continued to be extremely interested in analysing the Londonderrys' love life and also wanted to know whether it was true that one of their daughters 'had married a Jew'. Hohenlohe confirmed that this was correct, and Göring, according to Hohenlohe's notes, barked: 'That's dreadful! It's ghastly! I made a terrible blunder! Imagine, I was arguing with Lord Londonderry about race and religion and I asked him what he would do, if his own daughter should want to marry a Jew.'

'And what did he answer?'

'He didn't! Imagine he never said a word! It wasn't fair! He let me go on, and never said a word! He should have stopped me! How tactless of him! Would you expect a Lord Londonderry to behave like that? It wasn't fair!' [In Hohenlohe's manuscript Göring talked in perpetual exclamation marks.]

After he calmed down, Göring seemed to remember the reason why he had asked Hohenlohe to Carinhall. He told her that Lord Londonderry had invited him to England or Ireland. 'Of course, I could not possibly accept this invitation. It is quite unthinkable that I should go to England on my first visit and stay in a private house. It would be different, if an invitation came from some official quarters...'

At this point, according to the Princess's manuscript, she finally realized why he had invited her. Naturally she did her best to encourage him—'in the hope' of stopping the deterioration in Anglo-German relations.

> My host chose to appear hesitant. He admitted that the political situation was getting worse with each crisis, and he agreed that a better understanding between England and Germany had to be reached soon, if a European war was to be averted. He had always favoured Anglo-German cooperation, and he had seen enough of warfare, not to be horrified by the mere prospect of another Armageddon.[96]

After such pious talk, he suddenly changed track and Hohenlohe was not quite sure what performance she was receiving next (since Göring was a habitual drug user, one could never know whether his mood swings were calculated or due to substances). He now started to rage against Czechoslovakia 'the bastard nation', actually quoting verbatim from Goebbels' propaganda articles. Hohenlohe sat through the tirade: 'It was as if a shrieking gramophone had suddenly interrupted a charmingly pleasant conversation. Fortunately, every mechanical piece ends as abruptly as it starts, and when the Goebbels record was through, I queried the indignant Field Marshal if he was willing to allow to plunge Europe into war.' He replied to the negative and they then agreed that a solution needed to be found. If Göring came to London to meet a member of the British government, 'a war might be averted'.

This was how Stephanie Hohenlohe wanted her mission to be portrayed: she had given Göring the idea of saving Anglo-German relations.

As usual Hohenlohe's version of events is faulty. First of all, Göring gave her a clear brief and not the other way round. Second, the chronology is wrong. She had already worked for the Sudeten cause earlier in the year. MI5 was busy covering the activities of the two Hohenlohes at the time—Max and Stephanie. On Rothermere's orders Stephanie had advocated the Sudeten cause in Britain for some time. Most importantly she entertained the leader of the Sudeten Germans Konrad Henlein in London in May 1938, making sure he was a success. Henlein explained the plight of the Sudeten Germans in Czechoslovakia to a Royal Institute of International Affairs [Chatham House] audience and appealed to British fears of communism. He claimed that the Soviet Union would turn Czechoslovakia into an air base, a scenario that was taken seriously by many of his listeners.

According to Hohenlohe, she approached Lord Halifax *after* the meeting with Göring in June. For this she used Lady Snowden and the younger brother of Samuel Hoare, Oliver Hoare. Oliver had met Hitler and the Hoare family remained useful for Anglo-German channels. The Hoares would also be an important contact point for another go-between, Max Hohenlohe (Sir Samuel Hoare eventually became ambassador to Spain and had several meetings with Max Hohenlohe during the war).

Halifax was interested in a secret channel to the Germans. Ever since his visit to Germany in 1937 he had wanted to stay in contact with Hitler unofficially. Now that he was Foreign Secretary he had no problem with leaving his own diplomats in the dark and he was aware of the fact that Hitler liked to use go-betweens. It is therefore highly likely that Halifax and Stephanie Hohenlohe had been in contact with each other before July 1938. Though Stephanie claims that the meeting she and Wiedemann had with Halifax on 18 July 1938 was just a 'one off', they seem to have been in touch since May. In a letter to Lord Rothermere Wiedemann mentions this as a fact: 'You surely know too that the Princess last May—without your assistance—started the negotiations with Lord Halifax.'[97]

Naturally there is nothing in the sanitized Halifax papers about these contacts. His diary for 1938 has for some puzzling reason been 'mislaid'. In fact Halifax and R. A. Butler 'weeded their correspondences and notes'.[98]

Halifax later tried to distance himself from Stephanie Hohenlohe and complained that she was 'not the go-between one would choose'.[99] His official route to Germany would indeed have been via Foreign Minister Ribbentrop. But everyone involved in this back channel was told that under no circumstances should Ribbentrop know about its existence. Göring did not run the Hohenlohe-channel on his own, he worked with Hitler. The 'Führer' supported it because he 'found it difficult to read the British situation' in the summer of 1938.[100] He believed in the system of go-betweens and was giving his instructions, something Stephanie Hohenlohe chose to forget. Instead she portrays it as her peace mission 'desperately' trying to avoid a war over Czechoslovakia. In her version Göring is a man who wants to visit Britain and talk about peaceful solutions, but also as one who needs concessions from Britain in the Sudetenland to calm an outraged Hitler.

In fact Hitler had been planning the attack on Czechoslovakia since May 1938. But it was a risky venture the German military had warned against and failure could have ended his reign. Göring thought that one might get a much better deal by postponing the attack and secure the Sudetenland for free. Halifax had already signalled that this would be possible. He had expressed understanding for Germany's 'grievances' regarding Czechoslovakia and Danzig in 1937—before he became Foreign Secretary. Though the aristocratic Halifax had not been impressed by Hitler's appearance when he met him in 1937, he certainly thought it wiser to work with rather than against him. Since a rapprochement with the Soviet Union was out of the question for the Chamberlain government; they had to use appeasement on a wider scale: in the East towards Japan and on the Continent towards Italy and Germany. They had therefore no intention of fighting over the Sudetenland—but they needed to keep face and calm French nerves.

Hitler, Göring, Wiedemann, and Stephanie Hohenlohe wanted to 'help' with this. Hohenlohe supported an aggressive German policy towards Czechoslovakia. As a product of the Austro-Hungarian Empire she had never accepted the creation of this country. She had actively supported Henlein's demands and understood that his movement could be used to break up Czechoslovakia.

On 18 July Wiedemann and Stephanie Hohenlohe arrived at Halifax's home in Eaton Square. Though we know that the meeting occurred, nobody took notes at the time and there exist many contradictory versions of what was actually said: by Halifax, Hohenlohe, Wiedemann, and by the then ambassador to London von Dirksen. Since everyone was suspicious of everyone else the reports differ considerably.

According to Halifax this was a preliminary meeting with the intention of planning a visit by Göring to Britain. He had informed Chamberlain about the meeting beforehand and made no commitments regarding the Göring visit. Instead he told his German guests that the Czech problem had to be solved peacefully first.

Von Dirksen claimed that he had been informed by Wiedemann about the meeting beforehand. He thought that Hitler and Göring were behind it. In his (postwar) verdict he described the mission as typical of Hitler's way of doing diplomacy: 'its versatility, evasion of the appropriate offices, its insincerity and lack of results as well as the inability to understand the mentality of the opposite side.'[101]

Stephanie Hohenlohe herself presented a distorted version of the affair. According to her, Wiedemann made two points at that July meeting: first he tried to wangle an invitation for Göring out of the British, but secondly he also wanted to push the fact that Hitler had decided to attack Czechoslovakia and that this could only be prevented by giving in to the Sudeten German demands. She did not of course mention that Wiedemann was following Hitler's instructions to the letter. Instead she claimed the whole meeting was a peace mission supported by Göring. However, we have several records by Wiedemann of this meeting, including a report he wrote for the outraged Ribbentrop. The Foreign Minister felt sidelined and he had a point. It was obvious that a channel had been run behind his back and he wanted to know by whom and why.

The report Wiedemann wrote is interesting for several reasons. First, it reveals something we do not have for many missions: the detailed instructions a go-between (Wiedemann) received from his employer (Hitler). Second, the report made it obvious that Wiedemann had been to London several times before to talk to his 'British friends' and that the Halifax meeting was not a one off. It is also interesting what Wiedemann hides in one of his reports: in his summary for Ribbentrop, he does not mention that Göring, an enemy of Ribbentrop, was running this back channel together with Hitler. He also does not mention Stephanie Hohenlohe (though among his other notes is the sentence: 'preparations done by Stephanie').

Under the headline 'My conversation with Lord Halifax on 18th July 1938' Wiedemann stated in his report to Ribbentrop:

> On my penultimate visit to London four weeks ago, British friends asked me to meet leading members of the Foreign Office. Shortly before [leaving for London] I received a message from my British friends, that Lord Halifax had asked to meet

me.... Before I left I therefore asked the Führer for permission to fulfil Lord Halifax's wish. The Führer agreed and gave me the following guidelines: I should tell Lord Halifax that I am the man who has known him the longest and the best. Threats, pressure and force would not work with him [Hitler], on the contrary it would result in the opposite and make him hard and unyielding.

To give Halifax a correct character analysis of Hitler was important for Wiedemann. On another piece of paper he had written: '[Hitler] is a revolutionary, who can't be handled with the methods of the old diplomacy.' This was a point which Halifax obviously understood, otherwise he would not have agreed to this clandestine meeting in the first place.

In his report to Ribbentrop, Wiedemann continued to list the instructions Hitler had given him:

Up to now England had always been on the side of our enemies, it had never had any understanding for German interests and has to understand Germany's '*Lebensnotwendigkeiten*' [vital interests]. An understanding with England would come eventually, but first central European problems had to be solved. Keeping Germany and Italy apart would never work. He [the Führer] was still bitter about the behaviour on 21st May.

This referred to the May 1938 crisis, an incident that Hitler had used for propaganda purposes. Two Sudeten Germans had been killed that day and Hitler had called this an 'unbearable provocation'. The Czech government had as a consequence ordered a partial mobilization and rumours circulated that war could break out any moment.

In his report for Ribbentrop, Wiedemann continued:

At the time he [Hitler] had told the British ambassador that no German soldier would get his marching orders. Despite this, [English] newspapers had portrayed the incident in a twisted way, writing that Germany had given in to English pressure. He [Hitler] was outraged about the behaviour of the English press.

In this context, Hitler also mentioned Rothermere as a supportive newspaper proprietor who 'had always done so much for Germany. That is why we have an especially close friendship.'

Regarding Czechoslovakia the Führer had said verbatim to Wiedemann:

Why do the Czechs not give the Sudeten Germans their autonomy? England has given it to Ireland, France had a vote on the Saar, why are the Czechs not doing this as well? The Sudeten question has to be solved anyway. If the Czechs don't give in, the question has to be solved one day by force, he [Hitler] was determined to do this. England has clearly declared itself to be on the side of the Czechs. The Czechs are sabotaging a sensible solution.

Wiedemann then mentioned the most difficult point, the potential visit of Ribbentrop's old rival Göring to England. According to Wiedemann's version he had been asked by English friends whether Göring could visit England. He had therefore told Hitler that Halifax might mention such an invitation at their meeting. This was of course a version of the truth since Göring himself wanted to be invited and Halifax's stance was unclear. In fact the visit was still a topic of conversation a year later and almost took place in August 1939.

According to the Wiedemann report, Hitler was not interested in the Göring visit and said that no results could be expected from something like this at the moment. The English press had to change its tone first. In any case he (Hitler) would have to be asked first.

More important, however, was another instruction Hitler had given Wiedemann: 'If you are asked about the Western fortifications, tell them, that on 21st May we saw what to expect from England and France. That is why we are building these fortifications. Tell them they will be finished in a year's time.'

These were the instructions Wiedemann listed in his report before he went into the actual description of the meeting. This part was much shorter than the preamble. The meeting had lasted two hours and 15 minutes (from 10 to 12.15). Wiedemann reported that only Halifax and Cadogan were present and that translations were not necessary because he spoke English well. It was only when it came to more complex explanations that he needed Sir Alexander Cadogan to translate for him. To cover his back, Wiedemann went on to assure Ribbentrop, he had always stressed that he was not an official emissary. Both sides had agreed on absolute secrecy and confidentiality about the discussions:

> I then told him [Halifax] exactly what the Führer had instructed me to say. Halifax asked me repeatedly whether it would be possible to get an assurance from Germany that force against Czechoslovakia was not planned. I told him outright: 'You will not get such an assurance.'

He then claimed that Halifax asked him whether Göring would visit England and he gave him the reply Hitler had instructed him to use. In his report Wiedemann was eager to stress that the whole conversation was held in a very cordial tone and that Hitler had asked him especially to keep it all 'very polite'.

The last sentences of the report are particularly intriguing. According to Wiedemann, Halifax said, 'I, as English Foreign Secretary, aim to get so far in my lifetime that one day the Führer will be seen entering Buckingham Palace at the side of the King of England (amid) the acclamations of the English people.'[102]

Was Wiedemann just making this up to annoy Ribbentrop, was his English faulty, or was Halifax really trying to ingratiate himself so much with Hitler? Since he was talking to a go-between and not a diplomat, it is possible that he may have made such a risky statement. That King George VI was willing to do his utmost to resolve the Sudeten question became obvious a few months later.

In his report to Ribbentrop, Wiedemann did not mention another point Hitler had made to him. He was instructed to remind the British that a meeting with Prime Minister Baldwin had been planned two years before. That it did not take place in the end had been a great disappointment. Wiedemann's other notes also show that he was instructed to tell Halifax that Hitler had always been an admirer of England and that he had always intended cooperation with England.

Wiedemann also made separate notes for Hitler. Here he emphasized how eager the British had been for Göring to visit London. Wiedemann had jotted down: 'would be a huge thing! If it works it could be a great success.' Regarding Czechoslovakia he added: 'very clear that they want to come to an understanding. Also obvious they fear that we could take measures that would make such an understanding impossible.'[103]

Nobody would have ever known about the Wiedemann/Hohenlohe visit to Eaton Square, had it not been detected by a journalist. Willi Frischauer, an Austrian, had recognized 'Steph' Hohenlohe. Frischauer had fled Austria and now worked for the *Daily Herald*. He had received a tip-off from Croydon Airport where Wiedemann had landed and been embraced by Hohenlohe on arrival. He had followed the pair to Hohenlohe's new home in Mayfair. The following day he saw them drive to Halifax's house. It was as easy as that. Frischauer had landed a scoop the world press picked up on immediately. They ran stories on Stephanie but also on Wiedemann with headlines like 'The most mysterious man in Europe'.[104] Journalists quickly pieced together his past as Hitler's commanding officer and how during the war 'Hitler clicked his heels [to Captain Wiedemann], ran across the desert of shellholes with the message, came back, reported, saluted and clicked his heels again.'[105] Now, the article went on, the roles had been reversed and Wiedemann was a messenger clicking his heels to Hitler: 'Wiedemann was to be promoted to be a listening post, a contact man, a negotiator, a checker-up, a man with a job without a name and without parallel. No one seems to emphasise how unheard-of it is for a kind of private secretary to negotiate with a Foreign Minister. To understand how it all came to pass you must try to follow the probable workings of Hitler's mind.' The article then went on to allege that Wiedemann was being used by Hitler for all kinds of foreign missions. This was not the press coverage Hitler wanted. Goebbels was not pleased either. In his diary he noted for 23 July 1938: 'Wiedemann's visit at Lord Halifax on Hitler's orders is dominating the foreign press. Wild rumours.'[106]

Halifax and Chamberlain had not intended the cabinet to know about this clandestine meeting either. But once the press made it public, the Prime Minister had to inform his ministers. The First Lord of the Admiralty Duff Cooper documented the sanitized version he received five days later:

> The Prime Minister informed us of Captain Wiedemann's visit [Hitler's aide], which it had been intended to keep dead secret but which had got out to the Press. He had come direct from Hitler; Ribbentrop had not been informed. The main motive of his mission was to suggest that Anglo-German conversations should be continued—that every possible subject of dissention should be discussed and settled and that Göring should come here to negotiate. The reply of Halifax had been non-committal. It was obviously no good sending an emissary until some approach to agreement had been reached.[107]

If one believes Wiedemann, Halifax was not telling the complete truth to the Cabinet. He had been much more proactive regarding the Göring visit.

Duff Cooper must have sensed this when he wrote: 'I pointed out to the Cabinet that it would be very dangerous to let Göring come here as owing to his being such a well-known personality his appearance would probably provoke a violent demonstration of hostility which would certainly do more harm than good.'

Duff Cooper thought there was something very odd going on. As the biographer of Talleyrand, he could detect Machiavellian politics:

> On the face of it Wiedemann's mission is a good sign. It seems to show that Hitler does not despair of an agreement with England and really wants peace. On the other hand all the information which reaches us from secret and other sources is most alarming. Rumours are rife of all leave being stopped in the German Army, of expert airmen being recalled from Spain, and of many other developments all pointing to the fact that Germany is contemplating war in September. At the same time the Czechoslovak situation shows no sign of improvement. The Czechs are being slow, obstinate and most unhelpful. It may well be that the Wiedemann

mission is designed to throw dust in our eyes or else to improve German propaganda at the outbreak of war as showing how Germany to the last moment was anxious for peace and how it was only the failure of any response from England to these well intended overtures that precipitated the catastrophe.[108]

As previously mentioned, Duff Cooper did not agree with the Chamberlain and Halifax policy on the Sudeten question. He would resign after the Munich agreement.

Once their mission had made headlines, go-between work was no longer possible for Wiedemann and Stephanie. Both had become too visible, the kiss of death for a go-between. Stephanie in particular was now on the radar of all British journalists. The *Daily Herald* reported that she was a leading personality in the London Nazi colony, an outpost of the Germany embassy.[109] Conservative papers agreed. Journalists were surprisingly well informed about Hohenlohe's position as one of the few women in Hitler's inner circle. They claimed that people in the know called her 'Europe's Number one secret diplomat, Hitler's mysterious messenger' or 'a modern Madame De Stael' who like her historic predecessor played a sinister role in 'political intrigue'. They also knew she was close to people at the German embassy: Prince Otto II von Bismarck and Dirksen as well as right wing journalists like Ward Price and aristocratic members of the Link such as Lord Elibank and Lord Sempill (the Link was a pro-Nazi, anti-Semitic organization). Her cover, as a harmless society lady, always thin, was now publicly blown.

In Berlin Ribbentrop was furious that Hohenlohe and Wiedemann were working behind his back. As usual when there was infighting amongst his circle, Hitler avoided taking sides. Wiedemann arrived at Berchtesgaden straight after the press had detected the Halifax meeting; Hitler saw him for a few minutes and then went for a long walk with Unity Mitford. If Wiedemann's mission had not been all over the press, his welcome might have turned out grander. Instead Hitler distanced himself from the whole affair.[110] But he continued to play all the available psychological tricks during the Sudeten crisis. After having employed Hohenlohe and Wiedemann, he even used Unity Mitford in September 1938 for psychological warfare. According to Stephanie Hohenlohe, Hitler sent for Unity and

when she arrived he told her that in view of the gravity of the situation, he wanted her to leave Germany. Though it would seem that such a gesture was prompted only by friendly concern towards one of his most ardent admirers and followers, his intention was of a different nature. His real purpose in sending for Unity Mitford and talking to her... was to make her return to England

and impress her people and all those she would naturally talk to with the gravity of the situation. This is an example of his cunning and supreme ability to make use of even the slightest incident. He is a master at the understanding of, and playing upon, the psychology of people, which I consider his greatest gift and asset.[111]

One master had clearly recognized another. The Unity Mitford story had a famous sequel a year later. This time it worked less well. When Unity realized that a war between Germany and Britain was inevitable she famously went to the English Garden in Munich and tried to shoot herself. Hitler even exploited this pathetic act. On his orders the injured Unity was sent on a special train back to England via Switzerland. Since Hitler was never known for his caring side, this calculated 'humanitarian' gesture was a subtle way of showing his British friends that relations had not broken down irrevocably.

By then Hitler could no longer 'play' Britain, but in 1938 he had done so extremely well. Göring's plan to bully the British into the Munich summit worked perfectly. Göring, Wiedemann, and Stephanie Hohenlohe were jubilant. In the Bundesarchiv in Koblenz is a gushing letter Stephanie Hohenlohe wrote to Hitler in October 1938:

There are moments in life which are so huge, I mean moments when one feels so deeply and so much, that one cannot find the right words to express one's feelings. Chancellor, please believe me that, I have lived and felt with you every phase of these past weeks. None of your subjects could have dreamed this in their wildest dreams and you have made it possible. This is the most beautiful thing a head of state can give to his people. I congratulate you from the bottom of my heart. In loyal friendship, Yours sincerely Stephanie Hohenlohe[112]

Rothermere felt the same. On 1 October 1938, he sent Hitler a telegram, congratulating him on marching into the Sudetenland and praising 'Adolf the Great'.

Stephanie Hohenlohe and Wiedemann had been useful go-betweens for Göring and Hitler in 1938, but shortly afterwards their stars were sinking. This was due to Rothermere. He had decided to drop Hohenlohe overnight. The reasons are unclear. He either thought she was becoming too greedy or simply did not need her any longer. Whatever the motive, she did not take it well. The letters of her Hungarian lawyer show that the moment Rothermere fired her, Hohenlohe started to build a court case against him. Her aim was to receive an annuity for life and her argument was that he had ruined her reputation. That she actually thought her reputation was worth defending seems in retrospect rather striking. But there was indeed one thing she could not afford to lose—her name. It was—literally—her meal ticket. Without the name Princess Hohenlohe, she would lose her social network and therefore potential income. The danger of losing that name was confirmed by her lawyer in May 1938:

> The Royal Court of Budapest by its decree granting the divorce [from her husband Prince Franz von Hohenlohe] reserved for you the right to use his title and the name of your husband. This is an extraordinary privilege granted to the woman who has not been found guilty. Consequently there exists the obligation of the wife even after the dissolution of marriage—if she continues in using her former husband's name—to safeguard the reputation of the same. If she vilifies it—if she becomes unworthy to use the privilege that the law exceptionally granted to her on account of her not having been found guilty in the divorce—then the former husband is entitled to request the court to prohibit his former wife from the use of his name.[113]

Her ex-husband could therefore use the negative press reports that kept coming up to strip her of the Hohenlohe name. Many of these articles repeated one libellous story that had appeared in French newspapers: Hohenlohe's alleged arrest in Biarritz in 1933. At the time Rothermere had advised her not to sue the French papers. Yet journalists now based the allegation that she was a spy on these French articles. Her Hungarian lawyer summarized in faulty English what—according to Hohenlohe—had happened in 1933:

> In the year 1933 certain French papers published that [a debt collector] has taken execution against you and found in your writing desk letters suggesting
>
> 1. Great intimacy between yourself and Lord Rothermere.
> 2. Acts amounting to espionage . . . and found further a cheque in blank signed by his Lordship. [They also claimed] that you were arrested in Biarritz as an international spy. These statements are entirely fictitious and have no foundation whatsoever. On the day of your arrest in Biarritz you were in America—Lord Rothermere was in Biarritz. Further the letters published and the cheque were forged. Lord Rothermere in a letter over his signature wrote you a statement saying—you had nothing whatever to do with all this and the blackmailers only introduced your name so as to extract easier money from him.

Her lawyer now argued that she had made a decisive mistake in not squashing this story back in 1933. Hohenlohe claimed that this had been Rothermere's fault. He had given her bad advice and used her as a go-between for years. But he had not protected her from the fallout. She was now in danger of losing her aristocratic name and Rothermere had ruined her chances of ever securing employment again. Her Hungarian lawyer argued that the press tycoon did not want her to sue the French papers in 1933 because 'his Lordship could not go into the witness box and give evidence about your mutual relations'. The activities he made her carry out for him were illegal: 'it would be therefore easy to argue and prove that His Lordship advised you to avoid French Court and French public opinion—in order to avoid publicity of quasi illegal actions.'

Hohenlohe also wanted her lawyer to make Rothermere's anti-Semitism public. She hoped this would harm him financially 'since Jews were advertising in the Daily Mail'. Her lawyer therefore summed up that Rothermere and Ward Price 'had influenced the Hungarian government in an anti-Semitic way'. This was a reference to his communications with Prime Minister Gömbös.

To gather even more ammunition Hohenlohe told Wiedemann to photograph all the letters Rothermere had written to Hitler. She still hoped to avoid going to court and wanted to blackmail her former employer instead. Wiedemann supported this strategy. In a letter to Rothermere, he argued that Hitler would be shocked about the way the Princess had been treated:

> You know my Lord, that the F. [Führer] greatly appreciates the work the Princess did to help improve the relations between our countries. The work was made [*sic*]—and this, the Princess never ceased to state and repeat—on your behalf and on your instructions. It was done by her with great ability, assiduity and tact.... Considering the chivalrous character and magnanimity of the F., leave in my mind no doubt that he will grant her help in her fight to re-establish her personal honour, which was attacked while in your service. He will grant her the permission to use the above-mentioned correspondence as evidence to prove that she was working for you, as he will feel it will be a great help for a woman in a fight against a powerful man, but no doubt it will be very unpleasant for him and he will have a strong aversion against the fact that any correspondence of his should be read in court.

In other words Wiedemann threatened to destroy the relationship between Hitler and Rothermere, if Rothermere would not come to some 'understanding'. After all nobody, he argued, wanted 'any publicity'. He therefore offered himself as a mediator: 'should you accept my offer and instruct me, then I will request also the Princess to grant me the same powers, and knowing her devotion to the F., I have no doubt that she will agree.'[114]

It is very likely that Stephanie Hohenlohe drafted this letter for Wiedemann. His English was simply not good enough and the phrase 'a woman in a fight against a powerful man' sounds very much like Hohenlohe.

Among her files is an undated, rather confused letter to Wiedemann, half-English half-German, telling him to send an enclosed letter to Rothermere under his own name. She gives the impression of being angry and upset: 'R is frightened he wants to discredit me.... Why should I stay quiet if everyone is throwing mud at me?' She then instructs Wiedemann to hand over the Rothermere letters to certain people (carefully not naming names) including the 'crown piece'. He should not meet her in London but come to Paris: 'please don't tell anyone where you are going.'[115]

The tarantella had begun. Both Wiedemann and Hohenlohe were highly nervous. They had 'played' Rothermere for so long that they had believed it would work one more time. However, Rothermere had called their bluff. They were confused. Did he really not mind that his gushing letters to Hitler were becoming public? Or did he think they would not dare to go ahead with this? Both parties in this little drama underestimated each other. Eventually it would bring down all three of them.

Stephanie and Wiedemann naturally never had the intention of telling the 'chivalrous Führer' what they were up to. In a second letter Wiedemann now tried a different track, reminding Rothermere in a coded way what 'great friends' he and Hohenlohe had been:

> Considering the terms of friendship on which you were with the Princess, and which I had occasion to observe about a year ago, travelling with you to and from the Obersalzberg, and at an even later date in your house in London, I was justified to conclude that it would only take a little help and goodwill to settle any misunderstanding between you and the Princess.[116]

Wiedemann was insinuating that Hohenlohe and Rothermere had carried on an affair after all. But the press baron did not seem to care and showed no intention of giving in. Time seemed to be on his side. In January 1939 Wiedemann lost his influential job in Hitler's Adjutant's office. In his recent biography of Hitler, Volker Ullrich gives Wiedemann's dismissal as a typical example of how badly the Führer treated his staff.[117] Hitler was indeed a far from exemplary employer (after all he encouraged members of his staff to commit suicide in 1945), but in the Wiedemann case he had every reason to be annoyed. Wiedemann had run a blackmail racket behind his back and photographed his private letters. Even a normal employer would have been outraged. Also Wiedemann had violated an unwritten rule. At Hitler's court, the courtiers were kept apart by jealousies and rivalries. That two of them had actually worked (and colluded) together undermined the system. This was another reason why Hitler dismissed Wiedemann and turned his back on Hohenlohe—they had become a couple behind his back, following their own agenda together. There had been endless rumours about Hohenlohe's Jewish parentage which Hitler had always ignored. But when he was informed about the details of her relationship with Wiedemann, he made 'angry scenes'. Putzi Hanfstaengl had been right, Hitler had been smitten with Hohenlohe.[118]

Naturally nobody at Hitler's court had reason to come to her rescue. Hohenlohe and Wiedemann had managed to add to their enemies by 1939. The most dangerous was Ribbentrop, who after the Halifax incident feared that Hohenlohe was trying to position Wiedemann as an alternative Foreign Minister. This was indeed a dream Hohenlohe entertained, a very implausible one. Another enemy seemed to be Göring. Though he had worked well with the couple in 1938, Wiedemann discovered shortly afterwards that Göring had been listening in on all his conversations. Göring's euphemistically entitled Forschungsamt (Research Office) busily bugged several party members. Wiedemann's complaints that he was on the list of the Forschungsamt were ignored. The Forschungsamt was probably not alone in listening in to his frantic telephone conversations with Hohenlohe. Admiral Wilhelm Canaris from the Abwehr, the German military intelligence service, was also fully informed about the Hohenlohe–Wiedemann enterprise.

It is ironic that shortly before Stephanie Hohenlohe's trial started, another former member of Hitler's inner circle was keeping the London courts busy. It was of all people Hohenlohe's old rival Putzi Hanfstaengl. His court case would have an indirect effect on Stephanie's. It showed that patience with Nazis was running out.

Like Hohenlohe, Hanfstaengl had also become the victim of court rivalry. He fled to Britain in 1937 seriously believing that he was about to be murdered by Goebbels. True or not, Goebbels immediately realized that Hanfstaengl was highly dangerous: 'if he reveals all he will put everything the other emigrants have said in the shade.'[119]

At first Putzi did not reveal anything. But he was stuck in London without any money. Like Stephanie he soon realized that it was time to cash in on his Nazi past. To make ends meet he also turned to blackmail and was threatening 'to expose everything' in a libel trial. He pretended to be concerned about his 'honour'. This was as implausible as Hohenlohe's claim that her reputation had been tarnished. While Hohenlohe argued Rothermere had ruined hers, Putzi was of the opinion that an American newspaper had violated his. In an article he had been called 'Hitler's boyfriend'—indicating that he was a homosexual. Putzi was in fact an ardent *heterosexual*, but in his private letter to Hitler of February 1939 he did sound like a jilted boyfriend:

My 52 birthday has passed.... I had hoped to receive a sign from you [Hitler], which would have shown me that I can finally receive justice. I have not received such a sign. In autumn 34 I was banned from the Chancellery for a mere trifle ... in 1937 on the eve of my 50th birthday, [you] feigned a mission to Salamanca which forced me to leave Germany. Two years have passed now in which I maintained, despite what has happened and in contrast to others, an embarrassingly loyal stance. Some time ago, as you well know, I was accused of homosexuality with you. Since I am not willing to endure this insult, I have sued. The date of the trial is set for mid-March. In this trial I will talk about three points:

1. About my former and current relations with you.
2. About the way I was banned from the Chancellery.
3. About the reasons for my departure from Germany.

Regarding this, I have to ask you Mr Hitler for the last time to clarify my case. For two years now several party members have given me vague assurances, but the rehabilitation by you Mr Hitler, has been denied to me. Now that I am defending my and your honour in the up and coming trial, I have to know whether I am doing this as the disowned exile or as a National Socialist rehabilitated in his honour. If I do not receive your clear instructions and rehabilitation by the end of March, I would have to conclude that you still do not want to give me justice. I would have to come to the conclusion that my long devotion and loyalty as well as my honour and future mean nothing to you. If this is the case I know what I have to do.[120]

Putzi's opponent in court was the department store Selfridges, which had sold the magazine with the libellous article. However, it became obvious during the trial that the whole case had been engineered by Hanfstaengl to extract damages from Selfridges (they had only sold one copy of the magazine to Hanfstaengl's secretary). It also became obvious that the court was tired of former Nazis bringing their feuds to Britain. Since the beginning of 1939 sympathy for them was in short supply. The court therefore ruled in favour of Selfridges.

Hanfstaengl was devastated. In an earlier libel case he had been awarded damages and he had hoped for another windfall. In a daring twist, he now sold the trial as a great success. In a letter to a German friend (who passed it on to Hitler), he wrote:

the honour of Nr. 1 [Hitler] has been completely restored by the trial. This was stressed in the verdict. However, the costs of the trial, my costs and the legal costs of the opponents have been unfairly dumped on me. This is because of the anti-German feeling in Britain. Judge and jury were against me as the former Hitler man.... If Nr. 1 had restored my honor by granting me an honourable return I would have been saved from all this.... If no miracle happens, if Nr. 1 does not immediately resolve this with me, the result will be an irreparable break with my home country. Have the doors to be closed on this senseless and cruel fate before the Fü. opens his eyes?... May God help that all will be resolved for the sake of the great cause, for which I have sacrificed my existence.[121]

Putzi waited in vain, Hitler did not send him a letter of reconciliation. He was busy planning his attack on Poland.

The fate of her old rival and fellow Londoner, Putzi, should have been a warning to Hohenlohe. But in the summer of 1939 she still lived in hope. So did MI5. They talked to one of their informants in June 1939 about the case:

(the informant) now thinks the case may not come for trial by reason of the fact that if it does it will cause such a sensation that prominent people will appear in a very unfavourable light.... information that Lord Rothermere sent a very indiscreet letter to the Führer, congratulating him on his walk into Prague, and a photo copy of this letter has been sent from Germany to the Princess. It is this letter (or letters) which will cause the sensation.[122]

Rothermere's reputation seemed beyond rescue:

Princess Hohenlohe will produce a series of letters to support her claim. These letters signed by Lord Rothermere, were sent to such persons as Admiral Horthy, Hitler, Göring, Goebbels and Ribbentrop. One, to Admiral Horthy, is concerned with the suggestion that Lord Rothermere's son, Esmond Harmsworth, should be made King of Hungary, and among those to the Germans are letters sent to Hitler favouring his marching into Romania, and congratulating him on the annexation of Czechoslovakia.[123]

Yet by the end of the summer of 1939 the climate in London was turning against Stephanie. It reached Arctic temperatures the day before Britain declared war on Germany. When Hohenlohe entered the Ritz that day, she was cut by the Duchess of Westminster and her aristocratic companions (one of them loudly complaining about the 'bad clientele'). In the case of the Duchess of Westminster, whose husband had been a member of the Link, this sudden change of heart seemed surprising. But many former admirers of Germany had abruptly shifted their positions, Rothermere included. He now tried to explain his infatuation with Hitler as a cunning strategy. He had started to inform the Foreign Office about his German contacts and claimed that he had appeased Germany solely to increase British air power. He quickly published a pamphlet 'My Fight to Rearm Britain' to back up his argument.

It did not help him as much as he had hoped. Guy Liddell, the MI5 Director of counter-espionage, noted in his diary in October 1939:

Princess Hohenlohe and her mother have applied for exit permits to proceed to the United States. The ostensible grounds are that her son is seriously ill. Actually she is probably going either to see Hans Wiedemann,[124] Hitler's envoy in San Francisco, whose mistress she has been, or else to consult an American crook lawyer in connection with her case against Lord Rothermere. There is also the possibility that Rothermere may be paying her to leave the country. She has been paid about 5.000 Pounds a year by Rothermere to work on appeasement. She is now suing Rothermere for breach of contract and in consequence his solicitors are trying to persuade the Home Office that the Princess is a dangerous Nazi agent and should be deported. Rothermere is considering whether he will now go to the Attorney-General and ask him to give his fiat that the case should be stopped in the national interest. Personally I think that it would be in the national interest that the case should be heard.[125]

And it was. In November 1939, despite a war being on, Hohenlohe's court case against Rothermere was covered by every British newspaper as well as *Time* magazine. In its trademark flippant style it had a field day:

In the high-vaulted, dark-paneled, Victorian-Gothic gloom of King's Bench Court No. 5 last week, heavily bewigged Honorable Mr. Justice Tucker opened in his kindly, dawdling fashion the most sensational trial London has seen since World War II broke: Her Serene Highness Princess Stephanie Hohenlohe-Waldenburg-Schillingsfürst versus Viscount Rothermere.... In recent years ardent anti-Semite Adolf Hitler and his then leading British admirer, potent London Daily Mail Press Tycoon Viscount Rothermere, conducted their somewhat confused and often ludicrous relations through Princess Steffi, the Mystery Woman of Europe (as tabloids tag her).[126]

Many of the letters were discussed in court and Rothermere came across as the worst kind of Hitlerite toady. So did Hohenlohe, who was seen as a greedy employee who had tried to get ludicrous sums of money out of a doting Rothermere.

In the end she lost. Like Putzi Hanfstaengl she saw herself as a victim of anti-German sentiment. At least she was not out of funds. Rothermere paid for the court costs and Hohenlohe could still afford a one way ticket to America for herself and her mother. She left in December 1939. It was good timing. If she had stayed longer she would have been arrested as an enemy alien. It would have been quite ironic if she had served time in prison with her old rival Diana Mosley. Two queen bees in Holloway prison would certainly have entertained the press for some time.

Though Hohenlohe had lost the court case, she would win the revenge campaign. Nobody in London society ever forgot the case and Rothermere's reputation was in tatters. While other appeasers recovered, Rothermere stood no chance. Stephanie Hohenlohe ensured that his embarrassing letters would always be remembered. He died a year after the trial, the deterioration in his health almost certainly brought on by stress. Never concede to blackmail was good advice Rothermere should not have taken. When it came to women like Hohenlohe it was much cheaper to pay than to endure the costs of public humiliation.

His sudden death in 1940, however, helped the Rothermere family and their press empire to recover fully from the episode. Even some of Rothermere's expensive gifts to Hitler were eventually returned. At the end of 1945 'twelve paintings from the Rothermere collection' were found in Munich and discreetly sent to the family.[127]

Though Hohenlohe had managed to ruin Rothermere's reputation, she was not entirely happy. She did not want to give up her lucrative life as a go-between. Once in America she planned a new mission. The chances for its success were, however, low. America was not welcoming to Hohenlohe when she arrived in December 1939. On her previous visits she had been a social novelty, handed around at glamorous parties. Now she was an embarrassment to her well-connected friends. This was understandable since Hohenlohe had been described during the Rothermere trial by the American press as a 'Nazi agent'. This had led to another problem. The FBI was following her from the moment she set foot on American soil. Worse, the possibility of deportation hung over her. As usual she tried to circumvent these problems. Her knowledge of the media proved useful. During the First World War, when the press had been censored, she had learnt a great deal about propaganda work: 'if one wants to sell a lie one has to get the press to sell it.' She therefore began telling credulous American journalists about her great wealth and that she was writing her memoirs explaining her tireless fight for peace in Europe. Her son Franz supported her doggedly, claiming in an interview with an American paper that his mother was far from being a dangerous woman involved in political 'games'. The only game she ever played was 'ping-pong'. This was a wonderful lie. In fact she tried to play an unusual ping-pong game at that very moment. It was her last effort as a go-between and every detail of it was recorded by the FBI.

Hohenlohe knew that the greatest go-between success of all times would be to broker a peace between Britain and Germany. She was not the only one trying this in 1940. She might not have known that several Germans, including Max Hohenlohe, were working on a similar line. But she knew that there was a peace party in Britain with which Göring wanted to establish contact. To manage this link would have been her ultimate triumph (and would have rid her of several personal problems). Wiedemann was as usual willing to help. After his dismissal as adjutant, Hitler had sent him as Consul General to San Francisco. Here he tried to develop a spy ring but also started to distance himself from Hitler. He knew that the British would not want to make peace with the Führer, but that they were interested in talking to the opposition. Wiedemann and Hohenlohe now contacted Sir William Wiseman to make suggestions. Wiseman had been a British intelligence officer in the First World War, working closely with President Wilson's adviser Colonel Edward House. Officially he had retired and was now a partner in a Wall Street firm. Unofficially he was still in contact with the British security services. He had been chosen by Hohenlohe because of his friendship with Lord Halifax.

The FBI missed the first meeting of Hohenlohe and Wiseman, but they recorded three conversations in November 1940. They took place in a hotel room in San Francisco. Hohenlohe, always the perfect hostess, had brought a bottle of Château Mouton Rothschild along (Figure 9). After opening the bottle, she told Wiseman that she had carried out missions for Hitler before and could now talk to him about a peace settlement with Britain. She was sure that Halifax (and other appeasers) would be interested in a quick peace. Wiseman replied that he could convey a peace plan to his friend Lord Halifax directly, by circumventing the British ambassador in Washington, Lord Lothian.[128]

Hohenlohe and Wiedemann responded that they had not forgotten their 'constructive' talks with Halifax in 1938. However, Wiseman first wanted to know from Hohenlohe and Wiedemann who 'one could talk to in Germany'. He naturally wanted to use the meetings to gather intelligence. Who in Germany wanted peace and would therefore be ready to overthrow Hitler?

Wiedemann now had to come up with names. He mentioned two men who would years later become involved with the German opposition: Count Wolf-Heinrich Helldorf, the Police President of Berlin, and Colonel-General Franz Halder (who in the end did not support the July plot of

1944). Wiedemann also argued that Hohenlohe's old friend, the Prussian Crown Prince Wilhelm, could be won over. Prince Wilhelm had become disenchanted with Hitler and had explained his disenchantment in a long letter to Rothermere.[129] In Stephanie's mind the Crown Prince could therefore become a useful member of the opposition to Hitler (he never met these expectations). Wiedemann also discussed Hitler with Wiseman, stressing that, despite the Stalin pact the Führer still hated Bolshevism. Hitler was also highly critical of America, though for the moment the German consulates had been advised not to provoke any anti-German feeling in the United States. Wiedemann, however, believed that eventually National Socialism would clash with the Americans (since his unofficial mission in the United States was after all to run a German spy ring, he should have known).

This was useful material for Wiseman as well as the FBI. Hoover took the discussions seriously and passed them on to President Roosevelt. That Lord Halifax might be interested in a peace deal with Germany was naturally of great interest to them. Yet this information was out of date. Halifax had already been sidelined by Churchill and would soon adapt his politics to the new tune. He became ambassador to Washington a few months after the Hohenlohe meeting, in January 1941.

Without any backing from the Halifax group, Wiseman was signalled by his British and American friends that they were severely displeased with his hotel meetings. Wiseman took the hint and immediately begged Stephanie Hohenlohe to forget their conversations. There might have been another reason for his sudden U turn. Stephanie had not been the only Hohenlohe who had approached Wiseman with peace feelers. He was also in contact with Prince Max Hohenlohe. This might have been a further reason why Stephanie's offer of go-between work had become superfluous. To run two channels at the same time would not only have caused confusion but also weakened any bargaining position. Furthermore, it is very likely that the British had had reservations about Stephanie Hohenlohe acting as a go-between. Since the Rothermere scandal she was damaged goods. A go-between who could not keep quiet and even went so far as suing her employer was hardly an ideal choice.

The MI5 director of counter-espionage, Guy Liddell, even thought of her as a 'loose cannon'. When the Foreign Office's clandestine sabotage and subversion department needed help in April 1941, he noted: 'SO2 have asked whether we can supply them with Princess Hohenlohe's letters for publication in America. They apparently want to help one of their contacts there. I have said that I think it is extremely undesirable since Hohenlohe might well retaliate by the publication of Lord Rothermere's letters which he wrote to Hitler, and also Hitler's replies.'[130]

As we will see in the following chapter, Max Hohenlohe was, in contrast, highly valued by British and American circles and therefore became the preferred channel. Stephanie Hohenlohe was closed down.

After the failure with Wiseman, she was in serious trouble. Her visa had run out and the Americans were threatening to deport her. Roosevelt himself had got involved after reading Hoover's summary of the FBI recordings. The President concluded that 'that Hohenlohe woman' should be put on a ship to 'Japan or Wladiwostok'.[131]

Stephanie was not used to failure and did not take it well. She started to throw tantrums and quarrel with Wiedemann who did not 'help her' to get out of this predicament. In fact Wiedemann had tried his best, giving her

Figure 9. On their last mission together: Princess Stephanie and Hitler's adjutant Fritz Wiedemann in the States.

money and inviting her to stay at the German consular residence in San Francisco. To accept this offer was, however, not exactly a wise move by Hohenlohe. The Americans quite rightly suspected Wiedemann of spying. By living with him Hohenlohe damaged her chances of staying in the United States. Once she had realized this she dropped him unceremoniously. Their fruitful collaboration ended in December 1940. Following her usual procedure, Stephanie did not want to leave without a parting gift and demanded money from Wiedemann. He refused to pay. On the contrary he sent her a detailed bill, asking for reimbursement himself. The cost of their relationship had obviously been high in more ways than one. According to Wiedemann's letter she owed him 3,003 dollars. However, this farewell bill was typical for a very confused lover—half threatening, half conciliatory:

> I cannot simply draw a line under the years, which thanks to you have been among the most wonderful and richest of my life. I know you will think it hypocritical if I say that whenever you call on me, I will be there for you as much as my resources permit.... You asked me for a sum of money, which I do not have. I can't just embezzle it.... I regret having given you a year ago my money set aside for emergencies.... Your shares and jewellery are worth several times what I have.[132]

He certainly had a point. Hohenlohe had earned large amounts of money over the years but she always seemed to be short of cash. It is unclear whether she had a gambling habit or whether she just stored away vast sums for emergencies. Wiedemann guessed the latter. However, after so many years with her, he should have known that she was not the type who paid her debts. He never received the $3,000. Once she had gone, it was not so much loneliness that Wiedemann had to fear. He still had a wife and also a new and very attractive mistress. His problem was that Stephanie knew too much about him and that he would therefore never be quite free of her.

In the meantime Hohenlohe had found a new female friend to look after her interests. She had always been good at befriending a certain type of dedicated woman. In Britain the role of her loyal female companion had been played by Lady Snowden. Hohenlohe's new lady friend was a similar type, a Mrs Owler-Smith. According to the FBI report Owler-Smith 'was an individual of pro-Nazi tendencies and a distributor of pro-Nazi literature, who was closely associated with Fritz Wiedemann'.[133]

Smith was wealthy enough to get Stephanie a good lawyer and would eventually also pay her bail (as with Snowden, the friendship with Stephanie would leave her considerably poorer). Despite this support, the American immigration services sent Hohenlohe to an Immigration and Naturalization

Service (INS) prison in San Francisco in March 1941. Her mother and son did everything to get her out of detention, but without much success. As usual, Hohenlohe took things into her own hands and managed to work her charm even from a prison cell. Though she was by now 50 years old and increasingly plump, she managed to charm the Commissioner of the Immigration and Naturalization Service, Major Lemuel B. Schofield. Schofield was a legend in his profession. He had handled the Al Capone case in the 1930s and was consequently not considered a pushover. But the Princess Hohenlohe was in a different league from Al Capone. She corrupted the law-abiding family man Schofield in every possible way. After long conversations with her Schofield made a 'deal' in May 1941 that she would be set free in return for helping with anti-Hitler propaganda. To the great amusement of the FBI agents who now followed Hohenlohe and Schofield everywhere, the pair immediately started a steamy relationship, which 'involved a great deal of drinking'.[134]

Hoover shared all the entertaining aspects with Roosevelt (who spent a surprisingly great amount of time on the case) and even claimed to have good photos of the unusual lovers.

Yet the juicy gossip came to a sudden end after the attack on Pearl Harbor. Now America was at war and not even Schofield could prevent Stephanie being interned again. The day after Pearl Harbor she was arrested on her way to the cinema. She was eventually transferred to a prison block full of Germans, who took an instant dislike to her. They saw her as a turncoat and suspected her of being Jewish. It must have been quite an ironic twist for Hohenlohe to be among German Nazis again, but she had by then lost her sense of humour. She tried everything to get out of prison. When Walter Langer came to interview her in the summer of 1942 for his OSS report on Hitler, she offered him 'top secret information' in return for her release. He did not give in and she eventually 'denounced' him to the FBI, causing him no end of trouble. She now claimed to have been anti-Nazi and started to describe Hitler as a 'salesman'. By this she was not referring to his expertise in selling an ideology but the fact that he was 'lower class'. Over the following years she had every reason to hope for the death of her salesman. The longer she had to stay in prison the more enraged she became that Schofield could not get her out. As a consequence she decided to offer Hoover material on her 'useless' lover. In an interview with one of Hoover's agents she made the allegation that Schofield's INS had worked against the FBI for years. Hoover did not fall for it. On the contrary he made sure that she stayed in prison until the very end. One day after the war in Europe had ended, on 9 May 1945, she was the last of the 'German' inmates to be released.

It was lucky for Hohenlohe that Schofield never found out about her overtures to Hoover. The couple reunited shortly after the prison gates opened and for the next ten years lived off Schofield's considerable income travelling the world and throwing glamorous parties. By the time he died of cardiac arrest in 1955, Schofield had made sure that Hohenlohe was well provided for. His wife and children inherited the debts.

It seems bizarre that a rather shady figure like Stephanie Hohenlohe could attain such an influence in the 1930s. But she and the Duke of Coburg were not alone. Another Hohenlohe also acted in the shadows as Hitler's go-between.

6

Munich to Marbella

Prince Max Egon zu Hohenlohe-Langenburg

Prince Max Hohenlohe usually receives a 'walk-on-part' in books on secret intelligence during the Second World War. Authors dedicate a few lines to him, mentioning that he was working in Czechoslovakia in 1938 and during the war was involved in talks with the Allies in Switzerland. It never seems to be quite clear though for 'whom' he actually worked: Göring, or Göring's rival Himmler or perhaps the German spy chief Canaris? The British journalist Sefton Delmer, who knew Hitler's entourage intimately in the 1930s, was adamant that Max Hohenlohe worked as an 'amateur agent' for Ribbentrop.[1] The Foreign Office did not share this interpretation, but saw him as a useful go-between nonetheless. The vagueness about his affiliation certainly helped Hohenlohe to survive turbulent times unscathed. As a result, some interpretations of him are to this day surprisingly friendly, culminating in his German Wikipedia entry which portrays him as a man who 'promoted peace'. Even the UK National Archives describe him rather generously as a 'Scarlet Pimpernel figure'.[2] Digging deeper into his work, it becomes clear that he certainly never rescued inocents from the guillotine.

There are several plausible reasons why Max Hohenlohe is seen in a positive light: first, the fact that his private papers have not been made available by the Hohenlohe family. Only selective parts were seen by the journalist Heinz Höhne in the 1960s.[3] Höhne worked for the German magazine *Der Spiegel* and was the first journalist to contact Prince Max Hohenlohe. Second, Hohenlohe had an interest in being interviewed. After the war he was naturally eager to set the record straight, portraying himself as an early critic of Hitler. His written replies to Höhne's questions are intriguing. He claimed he had never been connected with Himmler's SD (*Sicherheitsdienst*,

Security Service). He probably was not aware of the fact that Höhne had unearthed his SD number. Instead Max claimed that he acted as a private individual, who happened to know several leading people in Germany and 'the West', including Churchill and Alan Dulles. He conceded that he had talked to Hitler at the Olympics in 1936 and therefore got 'to know Ribbentrop, Göring, Himmler, ambassador Hewel [a Nazi diplomat] and others'. Whether some of the people he talked to had belonged to the SD he 'could really not say'.[4] He claimed to have cared about one thing only, persuading a member of the Nazi leadership to support his peace plans. For this end alone he stressed, he had worked before and after the outbreak of war with the Nazis. Max Hohenlohe's son Alfonso later continued this narrative, describing his father as 'an independent and trustworthy mediator... between the several fronts, a true European'.[5] At a time of European integration this was a politically correct line of argument.

Apart from his son, another man made sure that Max was seen in the most favourable light. His name was Reinhard Spitzy. Spitzy was a dedicated Nazi who fully identified himself with Hohenlohe. In his memoirs he portrayed him as a seeker for peace. Spitzy's books were popular in postwar Germany because he was a highly prominent talking head in TV documentaries. Witty, charming, and rotten to the core, his expertise was saucy stories about Hitler's private life. It was therefore due to Spitzy that Max Hohenlohe became 'a good Nazi'. He was certainly a very shrewd one. It was his shrewdness that turned him into a go-between.

Hohenlohe was the third of six children, born at the family seat Rothenhaus, in November 1897.[6] As a young man Hohenlohe would have described himself as a Bohemian German belonging to the Austro-Hungarian Empire. However, after the First World War his 'home' became part of Czechoslovakia and this placed Hohenlohe in a dilemma.

Unlike Stephanie Hohenlohe, who had married her name, Max was the genuine thing—a *grand seigneur* with a long pedigree. But even though they were not blood relations and did not even belong to the same branch of the House of Hohenlohe, in many ways they could have been identical twins. Both were larger than life characters, determined to succeed under whatever regime was in charge. Both had many reasons for becoming go-betweens. Neither of them was altruistic.

As we have seen in Chapter 5 on Stephanie, the House of Hohenlohe was divided into several different branches. Because of their connections with the British royal family the Protestant branch of the Hohenlohe-

Langenburgs had high status. They were, however, not a very rich family and Queen Victoria had more than once helped them out financially. She did not help the Catholic Hohenlohe-Langenburg line, though, of which Max was a member. Money was certainly a problem for a socially ambitious man like him. As a third son he had not much hope of an inheritance. His prospects of one day running at least a moderate estate collapsed completely in 1918. Until then he had been serving in the Austrian army and enjoyed the social status of his family. After the war he faced a social and financial abyss. His father's property was situated in the newly founded Czechoslovakia and threatened to be diminished by agrarian reforms.[7] It is therefore not surprising that Hohenlohe deeply resented the Czech government. But the Hohenlohe family motto was: 'Ex flammis orior' (I will rise out of flames) and Max would make sure of that.

Like Stephanie and so many other Austro-Hungarian aristocrats at the time, Max had to choose a new passport in 1918. He could have taken Czech citizenship but decided against it. Instead he chose the passport of a safe little place—Liechtenstein. This was possible because the Hohenlohes were related to the house of Liechtenstein. Once the passport was issued, Hohenlohe sorted out other pressing problems. To improve his dire financial situation he married well. This turned out to be easy since he was in his youth a good-looking man, described as 'tall, sporty, a good tennis and polo player' and therefore popular with women.[8] He chose them well. In 1921 he married Piedita Iturbe, Marquesa de Belvis. Her father had been the Mexican ambassador to St Petersburg and Madrid. Her mother, María de la Trinidad von Scholtz-Hersmendorff y Caravaca, came from a Spanish-Mexican family and ran an influential political salon in Madrid. Marrying Piedita therefore opened up the highest Spanish society contacts for Hohenlohe. He quickly made friends with King Alfonso XIII of Spain. The King became the godfather of Hohenlohe's first born son Alfonso, a great honour for the Hohenlohe family. The christening was held in the Spanish royal palace and little Alfonso Hohenlohe would later become as notorious a playboy as his royal godfather.

Max Hohenlohe's wife was not just well connected, she was also extremely rich. The Iturbes had in 1766 left the Basque country for a life in Mexico and accumulated a fortune in gold, jewels, and spices.[9] Piedita's wealth made it possible for Max by 1935 to buy the Hohenlohe family seat Rothenhaus in Bohemia from his older brother. In a subtle way he therefore made himself the most important member of this Hohenlohe branch, a development that must have confused his elder brother, who was after all the head of the family. While his brother sank into oblivion, Max rose to become a social star of inter-war society. His aim was to turn the Bohemian castle, together with his wife's Spanish palace El Quexigal, into centres of political influence. He was driven by the conviction that politics were his true calling. After all this was a vocation that had been in the family blood for generations. His friend Spitzy would later recall: 'Max Hohenlohe was made to think on a European scale, since his ancestors worked all over Europe, producing: 'a German Chancellor, a French Marshal, a Roman Catholic Cardinal, a number of Austro-Hungarian Field Marshals, Generals of Prussia and Baden, hereditary Marshals of Württemberg and ADCs General to the Russian Tsar. Hohenlohe got involved with foreign affairs, because this was what his family had done since the Middle Ages.'[10]

Indeed, in Max's eyes there seems to have been a natural continuity: generations of his family had served monarchs, he would now serve a new prince—Hitler.

The reasons why he chose Hitler were purely opportunistic. They were also quite common among his peer group. As we have seen, three points of Hitler's foreign policy were highly attractive to German and Austrian aristocrats who had been landowners in several countries: Hitler's anti-Czech policy, his plans for Austria, and his policy towards Poland. In 1934 no less a person than Goebbels fought for the property of the princely Pless family, confiscated by the Poles.[11] It was an act that made an impression on aristocrats. The Nazi party seemed supportive when it came to their grievances.

Max Hohenlohe-Langenburg was not particularly interested in Poland, but the other two foreign policy issues on Hitler's agenda were of great importance to him. First of all the Führer promised a new awakening of an old idea: a greater Germany. At long last Austria and Germany might become united. Reinhard Spitzy, himself an Austrian, wrote how much the ideal of a greater Germany meant to his friend Hohenlohe: '[Max] was a tough and clever grand seigneur with immense charm. He was a convincing patriot for the old and the new greater Germany.'[12]

Hitler offered something else that was irresistible: an aggressive policy towards Czechoslovakia. Hohenlohe was only one of many former Austro-Hungarian landowners who had developed a hatred towards the Czech government.

In the 1920s two aristocratic groups emerged in Czechoslovakia: the 'German' and the 'Czech' ones.[13] While the German group consisted of two-thirds of the whole aristocracy, the Czech one only covered one-third. They immersed themselves in Czech culture, they took Czech passports and made their arrangements with the Republic. These aristocrats naturally had a greater chance of being integrated into the new Czechoslovakia than aristocrats who made their pro-German leanings obvious.[14] However, in the 1920s both groups were sympathetic to fascist ideas. They saw them as an ideal counterweight to Bolshevism and liberalism.[15] Though they all favoured fascism per se, not everyone could agree with Nazism. The aristocratic Czech group had great problems supporting the Nazis, because Hitler seemed determined to break up Czechoslovakia. The gap between the German and Czech group of aristocrats consequently widened. It was a divide that is still playing out today in aristocratic circles, each faction accusing the other of their ancestors siding with the Nazis, the Czech Republic, or (later) the communists.[16]

For the German group Hitler represented in the 1930s a bulwark against their two greatest enemies—Czechoslovakia and the Soviet Union, allies from 1935. The fear of communism was an enormous driving force for Hohenlohe and his friends. During the Sudeten crisis in 1938 the British Foreign Office adviser Frank Ashton-Gwatkin pointed this out:

> They have a horror of Russia and 'Bolshevism', which they believe is a real danger to them, to what is left of their possessions, and to the tradition for which they still stand.[17]

To protect their possessions the German group of aristocrats sided with Konrad Henlein, the leader of the German minority in Czechoslovakia, the so-called Sudeten Germans.

What happened to Czechoslovakia in the summer and autumn of 1938 has already been discussed. We have seen how Stephanie Hohenlohe and Wiedemann tried to influence Halifax. Max Hohenlohe had an identical brief and he carried it out with the utmost finesse. Long after the war, his old friend Spitzy was still enjoying the coup they had pulled off in 1938: 'It was easy for our friend and benefactor Prince Max Hohenlohe-Langenburg to use his excellent contacts in the West to promote the case of the Sudeten Germans.'[18]

After the war, Hohenlohe always claimed that he had worked on his own and that his aim had been to prevent a war over Czechoslovakia. It was the same narrative Stephanie Hohenlohe used to describe her involvement. Both could hardly admit that Göring was 'running' them. It remained their closely kept secret. The Czechs as well as the British were under the misapprehension that Hohenlohe was their 'intermediary' to Henlein.[19]

Max Hohenlohe's role was to pose in Britain as the moderate, the voice of reason 'helping' the British to solve the thorny problem of the Sudetenland. It might seem surprising that he was listened to in London, but the Foreign Office had a history of being in contact with German-Czech nobles. Shortly after the First World War, the Czech socialist press had even suspected that the British were colluding with local aristocrats to install a King. The Czech newspaper *Ceske Slovo* wrote: '[Aristocrats] are conspiring to place a King on the throne of Bohemia, in which connection HRH Prince Arthur of Connaught is alluded to.' The paper went on to say that 'members of the British, French and Italian diplomatic and military missions are too often seen at the houses of the nobility and in particular at that of Prince Frederic Lobkowicz'.[20]

Though the idea of a king was far fetched, the visits to princely houses never stopped. British diplomats had forged good contacts within the local aristocracy and these contacts lasted well into the 1930s. Hohenlohe was eager to use them for his own purposes. He and Göring knew all too well that a go-between with an impressive pedigree would be appreciated in a class-conscious society like Britain. Indeed, Chamberlain and Halifax preferred to talk to someone with an impeccable background. Hohenlohe seemed to be a familiar type, a *grand seigneur* of the old school, whose country seat just happened to be in Bohemia and not in the Shires. As an international aristocrat he was obviously as much at home in Britain as in Paris, Vienna, or Madrid. He was independently wealthy and a jovial man—an ideal interlocutor. He knew Churchill, members of the Foreign Office, the Intelligence Services, and also many foreign diplomats in London—including Churchill's distant relative the Duke of Alba, and the number two at the German embassy Prince Otto II von Bismarck.

In retrospect the Foreign Office commented on his work in the Sudetenland: 'he was very active as an intermediary with Göring and other so-called moderate Germans before the Munich agreement.'[21]

By then it might have dawned on the Foreign Office that the 'moderate Germans' led by Göring never actually existed. But in 1938 Hohenlohe seemed an ideal 'intermediary', a man who would help to prevent trouble in Czechoslovakia.

The British government had not acted against the annexation of Austria in March 1938 and hoped for no more aggravation in regard to Czechoslovakia.

To his sister Chamberlain had written: 'If we can avoid another violent coup in Czechoslovakia, which ought to be feasible, it may be possible for Europe to settle down again, and some day for us to start peace talks again with the Germans.'[22]

Chamberlain thought this feasible because, among other things, he had back channels to the Germans. The Prime Minister had already made up his mind on Czechoslovakia. He had not much patience with the Czech President Beneš, whom he distrusted. In his opinion the Czechs should solve the Sudeten problem quickly and spare the French from having to fulfil their guarantee to Czechoslovakia in case of war. He was in denial of the fact that the Sudeten problem was just a pretext being used by Hitler to acquire the whole of Czechoslovakia. Chamberlain also did not realize that the Sudeten German leader Henlein was from the beginning Hitler's puppet. After a meeting with the Führer in March 1938, Henlein summed up the instructions he had been given: 'we must always demand so much that we cannot be satisfied.' As Zara Steiner rightly pointed out 'such instructions, unknown in London, Paris or Prague, made a mockery out of subsequent Czech efforts to find an acceptable solution to the Sudeten problem'.[23] In fact, what happened during the summer of 1938 was a long theatre performance with an excellent cast of German go-betweens. Max Hohenlohe had a good character role playing the well-meaning friend of the British who 'just wanted to help'. Apart from Max another excellent performance was given by Stephanie Hohenlohe. Like Max, she sold Henlein to the British as a man whose demands for autonomy were reasonable. As has been shown, Stephanie was Henlein's hostess in London in May 1938—a month after Henlein demanded political autonomy for his people in a major speech at Carlsbad. His demands more or less aimed at the disintegration of Czechoslovakia, but, despite this speech, he was well received in London. With the knowledge of Halifax and Chamberlain, Henlein talked to Vansittart and Churchill.

After selling Henlein as an upright politician on the London stage, Göring and Hitler had used a go-between in July to bring home to Chamberlain how serious the situation in the Sudetenland could become if Britain ignored Henlein's demands. As we know, Wiedemann had visited Halifax privately with Stephanie Hohenlohe and told him that if nothing was done about the problem, Hitler would start a war. While Wiedemann and Stephanie were busy in London, the other go-between, Max Hohenlohe, was busy in Czechoslovakia feeding the British with his own Sudeten

German 'spin'. His point of contact was Sir Robert Vansittart, until earlier in the year the Permanent Under Secretary of State at the Foreign Office. Vansittart, despite his anti-German stance was also interested in solving the Sudeten question peacefully. He trusted Max Hohenlohe and had sent one of his best men to liaise with him—Group Captain Malcolm Christie. Christie was an intelligence officer who had befriended lots of leading Nazis over the years.

In Vansittart and Christie's eyes Max Hohenlohe was a man one could do business with. To keep their conversations confidential, they chose code names for each other. Christie's code names were *Graham* and *Gordon* while Max Hohenlohe's was *Smiler* (which might have something to do with his sunny disposition). Henlein was called *chicken*, a translation of his German name. In July 1938 Christie reported on his conversation with *Smiler*: 'Prince Hohenlohe rang up, expressed anxiety about Czech tactics. Hohenlohe is absolutely convinced (and I am equally so) that nothing short of some reasonable measure of cultural autonomy (for the Sudeten Germans) would do. Hohenlohe feels that it will require at least such an offer to take the wind out of Germany's sails to undermine her pretext for intervention.'[24]

This sounded as if Hohenlohe genuinely wanted to help the British against a bellicose Hitler. In fact he knew that Hitler did not want autonomy for the Sudetenland, but to annexe it. This was the ultimate aim, but Hohenlohe rightly calculated that the British would not accept this outright. They had to be persuaded slowly and they needed help to save face with the French.

There were at least two reasons why Göring and his go-between Hohenlohe worked so hard on the British to achieve a 'peaceful' annexation of the Sudetenland. First of all Göring genuinely feared the reactions of the western powers if Hitler simply marched into the Sudetenland. But apart from the external threat, there was also an internal one. Göring knew all too well that the Führer's war plans for Czechoslovakia (codename Case Green) had been criticized by some of his own generals. They feared a political *and* military disaster. Indeed the Czech army was not weak; it had been increased over the years, and importantly most of the Czech fortifications were situated in the Sudetenland.

As we have seen in the chapter on Stephanie Hohenlohe, Göring hoped that if the Sudetenland could be handed over by peaceful means, Czechoslovakia would lose the majority of its border fortifications. German soldiers could simply take over the fortifications without a shot being fired. After that, occupying the rest of Czechoslovakia would be plain sailing.

Hitler knew about and had supported the Wiedemann/Stephanie Hohenlohe channel to Halifax and he probably also knew that Göring was running another back channel in Czechoslovakia. To this day his actions in the summer of 1938 puzzle historians. He seemed determined to carry out his 'Case Green' and attack Czechoslovakia. But he also had periods of doubt. He was not sure how the British would react and it was therefore important for him to get as much information via go-betweens as possible. Consequently people like Max Hohenlohe were extremely useful.

In July 1938 the 'moderate German' Hohenlohe therefore came to London and explained to his Foreign Office contacts that Hitler was bound to start a war over Czechoslovakia and that Henlein needed support so this could be avoided. Giving in to Henlein's demands for the autonomy of the Sudetenland would de-escalate the situation. Hohenlohe also portrayed Göring as the man in Hitler's entourage who was eager to find a peaceful solution.

The British listened carefully. By then they had come to the conclusion that a British arbiter should get involved. Chamberlain and Halifax had the right candidate for this endeavour, the 68-year-old Lord Runciman. Runciman was seen as a safe pair of hands: 'he could, be relied upon to put the results across. His background, political career and Establishment credentials left him naturally capable of knowing exactly how London would wish him to act.'[25] To the public Runciman was sold as 'independent'.

The Runciman mission to Czechoslovakia lasted from 3 August to 16 September. During this visit he talked to the Czech President Beneš, the Prime Minister Hodza, and the leader of the Sudeten party Henlein.[26] In his 'fact finding mission' Runciman was supported by Hohenlohe. Hohenlohe seemed a genuine mediator to him because he was trusted by Hodza and Henlein. It was Hohenlohe who brought Runciman and Henlein together at his castle for talks. He volunteered as a translator and after the meeting remained the link between the two men.

Runciman was not alone on his 'reconnaissance trip', but was accompanied by Ashton-Gwatkin from the Foreign Office. Ashton-Gwatkin came to the obvious conclusion that Hohenlohe and his fellow Sudeten German aristocrats were strong supporters of the SDP (Sudeten German party) and were personally very fond of 'the Chicken' (Henlein).[27] Ideally this 'revelation' should have led Ashton-Gwatkin and Runciman to find out more about the other side of the argument. Yet the Sudeten Germans tried their best to prevent this. Hohenlohe invited all his persuasive aristocratic friends to charm Runciman. The historian Eagle Glassheim has shown how well this succeeded: 'during his six week stay in Czechoslovakia, (Runciman) spent all but one weekend as a guest of Bohemian nobles. He ate lavish dinners with them, shot partridges on their estates, and toured the countryside in their motorcars.'[28] It was a country-house-style entertainment which Runciman felt thoroughly at home with. Hohenlohe introduced him to the best families in the region—the Kinskys, the Clary-Aldringens, and the Westphalens.[29] The agenda behind this was so obvious that it was already criticized at the time.

The *Daily Express* saw the closeness of Runciman to Hohenlohe and his friends as inappropriate, especially after the Sudeten Germans kept rejecting Czech offers:

> Until now Lord Runciman had dealt in his talks only with Henlein's lieutenants. This morning with all the Czech newpapers carrying attacks on the Sudetens for turning down the Government's offer yesterday of partial home rule, he and Lady Runciman sent for their car and set out for [Hohenlohe's] castle. Prince Max Hohenlohe, who is a Liechtenstein subject, and close Nazi sympathiser, was waiting for them.[30]

The Times claimed that Stephanie Hohenlohe had joined Max and Runciman in Czechoslovakia.[31] Stephanie always denied having been part of the Runciman entertainment group. For once she may have been honest; she was probably too exposed after the press had caught her and Wiedemann leaving Halifax's house in July.[32]

That Hohenlohe could work so well on the British was also to some extent the fault of the Czech government. They did not seize the chance to impress Runciman. This is the more surprising since the Czech President Beneš was offered help by Czech-minded aristocrats who wanted to entertain Runciman. Beneš did not take them up on the offer and lost the hospitality race. But he did try to solve the Sudeten question. On 4 September he declared he would fulfil all the demands Henlein had made. Hitler was not interested. Instead he ordered 'incidents' to be organized against the 'suppressed' Sudeten Germans to enable him to raise his demands.

In the meantime Hohenlohe continued to work on Runciman. To drum the point home that the Sudeten Germans were suffering under the Czech regime, Hohenlohe's friend Count Kinsky even gave Runciman a tour of some of the Sudetenland's more run-down areas. In a secret report to the

Foreign Office, an informant noted that Kinsky's tour utterly misrepresented the real conditions. Runciman had on purpose been shown 'the dirtiest smelters' and 'the worst houses' in the area.[33] He may have noticed that he was being manipulated, but his wife certainly did not. Hilda Runciman, herself a politician, accompanied her husband to Czechoslovakia and was 'worked on' by female Sudeten German aristocrats. One of her hostesses showed her a prized autograph picture of Hitler and marvelled about his achievements. Hilda Runciman noted in her journal: 'all this doesn't sound like a man who is eager to take over all of Europe, which so many people persistently believe.'[34]

Chamberlain would have agreed with her analysis, even though other messages were reaching him by now, urging him not to give in to Hitler. Anti-Nazi Germans begged the British to help the Czechs. They quite rightly pointed out that German generals were doubtful whether a war against Czechoslovakia could be won. This fear should be used to topple Hitler. But Chamberlain simply dismissed such arguments.[35] Instead he announced that he would negotiate with Hitler in Berchtesgaden. Runciman was ordered to leave Prague and come to London. But when he arrived in Downing Street he gave an ambivalent report. Chamberlain ignored this. He told the House of Commons on 28 September a different story:

> the Cabinet met and it was attended by Lord Runciman who, at my request, had also travelled from Prague on the same day. Lord Runciman informed us that although, in his view, the responsibility for the final breach in the negotiations at Prague rested with the Sudeten extremists, nevertheless in view of recent developments, the frontier districts between Czechoslovakia and Germany, where the Sudeten population was in an important majority, should be given the full right of self-determination at once. He considered the cession of territory to be inevitable and thought it should be done promptly.[36]

This was not what Runciman had said. Despite all the pressure of Hohenlohe and his associates, he still seems to have had his doubts. In the end Chamberlain manipulated Runciman into writing the report he wanted. The American journalist Dorothy Thompson was already describing it as a 'rigged report'. In fact Runciman's first draft seems to have been cut and adapted to suit Hitler and Chamberlain. The Runciman report should in fact have been called the Chamberlain report. Tapped Czech telephone conversations indicate that Runciman had been overruled by his Prime Minister.[37] Yet at the end of the day he bears the responsibility, because he did not stand up and air his doubts. His loyalty to Chamberlain and—in some ways—perhaps to his Sudeten German hosts was greater.

In the meantime Hohenlohe's pro-Sudeten German activities did not go unnoticed by the Czech government. He became the victim of reprisals. While Hitler and Chamberlain were working out the Munich agreement that would seal the fate of Czechoslovakia, Hohenlohe's castle was being pillaged. Hohenlohe's British protector, Sir Robert Vansittart, tried to help him:

> Prince Max Hohenlohe has just told me that he has news that his castle is being pillaged and its contents removed. In view of all that he has done recently by way of mediation in the Czech–Sudeten question, I feel that the least I can do is to ask you to make an appeal to the Czech authorities to stop this, and I shall be very grateful if you will put in a word on Hohenlohe's behalf as soon as possible.[38]

It turned out that Hohenlohe did not need their help regarding his castle, though. A day after Vansittart's note, on 30 September, the fear of Czech reprisals was over once and for all. The Sudetenland and Hohenlohe's castle now belonged—thanks to the Munich agreement—to Germany. The German army marched into the Sudetenland and took over all the Czech fortifications. From then on it was only a matter of time before they seized the whole of Czechoslovakia.

After the Munich agreement Runciman and Hohenlohe stayed friends. In 1939 they visited Göring together at his country seat Carinhall.[39] It probably never occurred to Runciman that his charming friends, Göring and Hohenlohe, had 'played' him during the Sudeten crisis.

The Munich agreement was not just a great victory for Göring and Hitler. It was also a great victory for go-betweens. We have seen that Stephanie Hohenlohe congratulated Hitler enthusiastically on its completion, thereby celebrating herself a little bit too. It was also a great victory for her fellow go-between Max Hohenlohe. He received recognition for his help in many different ways. One was financially.

According to the files of the British security services, '(Max Hohenlohe) was reported to have been rewarded for his undercover aid for the Nazis by membership of the board of Skoda Brün, the Czech munition works, which firm he subsequently represented in Spain.'[40]

The 'Waffen-Union Skoda Brün' was an armaments trust the Nazis set up in 1940. Hohenlohe later represented Skoda in Spain as well. According to Spitzy, Hohenlohe explained to him that Spain was useful for business and at the same time business was a good cover for his 'peacework with the West'.[41] It was also his wife's home and he could entertain there in style.

Hohenlohe had done well out of the Sudeten crisis. Czech aristocrats who had shown solidarity with the Czech government on the other hand were less lucky. They were outraged by the betrayal of Czechoslovakia. However, they would not be rewarded for their rectitude. After suffering reprisals under the Nazi regime, in 1948 the new communist rulers made sure that they lost all their remaining property.

With his Sudeten German mission over, Hohenlohe's next moves became even murkier. He continued to travel widely, so it is difficult to follow his tracks. He was in America but since his FBI files have not been released yet, we cannot verify what he was doing there, apart from sorting out his wife's business interests. He also appeared in London again in the summer of 1939 but his 'conversations' with politicians there must have become more and more difficult. Germany had invaded the rest of Czechoslovakia in March 1939 and consequently trust in Nazi representatives had become scarce. Chamberlain's appeasement policy was now increasingly under attack by the opposition and by Churchill.

Since Hohenlohe worked for Göring, it is highly probable that in the summer of 1939 he was involved with preparations for the proposed Göring visit to Britain. The visit was planned for August 1939 and of course never took place. Whether it was ever seriously contemplated by the Germans is unclear. Most probably it was an avenue Hitler left open for himself. Yet the visit was one of the many reasons why the British government did not see the Nazi–Soviet pact coming. The Foreign Office firmly believed that Hitler was deeply ideological, and would never negotiate seriously with the Soviet Union. When the pact was signed, it sent shock waves through Whitehall. They were not the only ones surprised. The pact must have irritated Hohenlohe as well. He had not been privy to such secret negotiations and must have been confused. Since the generally unprincipled Hohenlohe was a principled anti-Bolshevik he too must have found the pact hard to swallow. Worse was to come. After Germany invaded Poland and Britain declared war in September 1939, Hohenlohe appeared badly informed to his German employers (Figure 10). Up to the outbreak of war, he had always argued that an understanding with the British was possible.[42] In September 1939 he had

Figure 10. The shady go-between: Prince Max Egon zu Hohenlohe-Langenburg.

to adjust overnight. After the war he claimed that he went on the offensive and wrote a forceful memorandum to Göring:

In initiating World War II Germany has started from false premises and has miscalculated in every way. She did not calculate that England and France would fight for Poland, overlooking the fact that Poland is not the point—it is something quite different—the maintenance and assurance of peace in Europe.... Even at this late stage the possibility of an overall solution must be borne in mind. It must include: re-establishment of confidence, a guarantee for the respect of treaties, disarmament under mutual control and possibly withdrawal from Czechoslovakia and its reconstruction as a demilitarized state.[43]

The journalist Heinz Höhne believed this document to be genuine, but it could be backdated or a fake. Still, it points to something Hohenlohe did next. He wanted to work as a go-between again and bring about nothing less than a peace deal with Britain. He was not the only seasoned go-between who had such an idea. As we have seen Stephanie Hohenlohe hoped to pull off a similar coup from an American hotel room, using the intelligence officer Wiseman. Their ambition did not seem that misplaced. Both Hohenlohes had been successful before and they thought of themselves as much more effective than diplomats. After all, back channels had been useful all through the 1930s—why not now?

Indeed, with the outbreak of war, people like Max Hohenlohe became important again. What happened next was reminiscent of aristocratic peace feelers in the First World War. Since Britain and Germany could not talk to each other officially, they needed trusted go-betweens.

Another reason why go-betweens were listened to was the great insecurity within the British government. The hope that some kind of understanding with Germany (though not necessarily with Hitler) could still be found was not given up overnight. Hohenlohe understood this. He knew the psychology of the Chamberlain circle well. They wanted to talk to someone they could understand, a moderate, 'conservative' German, and he offered them such an option. His idea was to keep the conversation with the British going by creating the illusion of an alternative Germany. He therefore stressed in his first conversations after the outbreak of war that there was opposition to Hitler and that this opposition might be able to end the war. According to Hohenlohe Göring could be an alternative leader.

Today we know that an opposition to Hitler did exist and would form again later in the war. Yet Göring was a decoy. Though he had advised a more cautious route before the war, after Hitler's overwhelming successes he never seriously thought of challenging the Führer's position.

This does not mean though that Göring did not want to try peace feelers. But they were most probably with Hitler's approval and never intended to overthrow him. Göring just did for Hitler what he had always done. He made use of his go-betweens. The most famous go-between he used after the outbreak of war was his friend the Swedish businessman Dahlerus, who kept pestering the British. But Göring also used Max Hohenlohe, who was at this point still trusted by the British.[44]

That Göring thought he could be successful with peace feelers was not unrealistic. Though the Chamberlain government had failed with its appeasement policy, Britain was still in a state of 'phoney war' with Germany. Between the outbreak of war in September 1939 and the summer of 1940, there were several British appeasers who wanted to end the war. Hohenlohe and the Nazi leadership were informed about this group of people by the Duke of Alba.

Alba was the Spanish ambassador to Britain. He had supported Franco, was pro-German, and thoroughly anti-Semitic and anti-Bolshevik. He was connected to the British aristocracy through the Marlboroughs, i.e. the Churchill family. His diplomatic status gave him access to the British government but because of his perfect pedigree he also had easy access to the British establishment in general, including key peers of the House of Lords. What he was hearing from his friends in the House of Lords in February 1940 encouraged him. They were very much hoping to come to an understanding with Hitler and had agreed to put pressure on Chamberlain. Alba informed the Spanish Foreign Ministry in a secret report about this group. The report was passed on to the German embassy in Madrid. Reading it must have given considerable pleasure to the Germans.[45]

Because the Royal Archives are closed on this issue we do not know whether aristocrats tried to encourage King George VI to intervene as well. But we do know that Alba was right and many peers tried to put pressure on Halifax and Chamberlain to approach Germany. Among them were the Duke of Buccleuch, and the Lords Brocket, Buxton, Elibank, Darnley, and Holden.[46]

Their letters also show that the idea of using back channels had become an absolutely normal feature of political life. First of all the Earl of Darnley, on 10 November 1939, wanted to make sure this method was used. He advised Chamberlain to make a 'constructive forward step through the King of the Belgians', to get into peace negotiations. On 9 February 1940 the Duke of Buccleuch also urged such a method:

> [we should back up] our armed effort by active diplomacy behind the scenes....It would be natural for negotiations to take place with the official and accepted rulers of the German nation, but if ours refuse to have any dealings with Hitler are they prepared to discuss the future with anyone in Germany? If though, with whom? Individuals have a right to ask that there should not be an indefinite prosecution of the war if an opportunity for discussion of peace can be secured. I must assume that the Government is aware of the possibility of discussing this question with others than Hitler. May we not hope that they are willing to take active steps to arrange this? If not, will they accept or consider information from others?

Of course, the Duke had someone in mind:

> Would the Government negotiate with Göring...If not with Göring then with whom?...There has been strong evidence from knowledgeable forces that Göring and others were probably in a position and might still be able to discuss and arrange a peace provided proposals are fair towards Germany.... You assured Britain at the

beginning of the war that we were fighting Hitlerism and not the German nation. Now the belief is held both in Germany and in Britain that they and we are fighting for [our] very existence.

The Duke wanted a different war: 'If the British Government has any intention of saving Finland [which was at war with the Soviet Union] surely the only possible way is by ending war with Germany.'

Saving Finland would have meant attacking the Soviet Union. Lord Brocket also thought that the wrong war was being fought and Russia should be the target. He was a classic appeaser, who had supported the Munich agreement. Furthermore he was a friend of the Duke of Coburg and had taken over the Anglo-German Fellowship in 1939. He spoke German well and felt close to many members of the Nazi leadership. Now he tried to put pressure on Neville Chamberlain. On 27 January 1940 he wrote: 'a defeated Germany and a dictated peace may mean Bolshevism in that country, spreading to France and Britain.'

Brocket was also of the opinion that the British did not want this war. '[T]here is a great feeling of unrest and discontent and hopelessness.' He therefore urged Chamberlain 'to hold out a carrot' and give Germany some positive signal: 'has Germany any evidence that you would make peace?... from considerable experience from this country, its bluntness... I know for a fact that stiff speeches make them all the stiffer... in fact their reaction is "England has declared war on us and wants to destroy us"... Germany should be told by you [that there would be no] second Versailles and a reasonable peace can be made.'

Brocket even offered a go-between for Chamberlain:

I have reason to believe from a friend of mine who lately returned from Italy and whom I sent to see Halifax, that the Göring faction (which is in the document my friend brought home written by an Italian married to the daughter of a leading Nazi, estimated to be 70% of the Party) would be willing to agree to peace on the following terms (quoted from the document which Halifax has)

1. Austria remains in Germany
2. Czechoslovakia reconstructed except the Sudetenland.
3. Poland reconstructed, except Danzig, the corridor, Silesia and a few frontier villages.
4. Proposal of a disarmament conference
5. No demands for colonies.

Halifax could give you further details of this document and its source.... You may remember that I told you over a year ago and again just before the War, that Göring

> had said to me that in a War with the West he would not drop a single bomb on Britain or France until we did so on Germany. He has kept to that statement entirely and I believe he could be trusted to make a lasting peace.

Chamberlain's reply to Brocket on 6 February 1940 seems to have been cautious because Brocket told him indignantly: '[Peace at any price] is not my policy. A last attempt should be made to get an enduring and lasting peace. Germany should be informed that she would not be dismembered.'

Brocket believed that Germany had misunderstood British policy:

> I was told when I was there [in Germany] at the end of April [1939] that our pledge to Poland and the re-iteration of our determination to fight to fulfil it, were taken to mean that Britain had decided in any event to wage a preventive war to destroy Germany. From this assumption they argued, that as they would have to fight in any case, the conquest of Poland and the Russian agreement were necessary to them as a first instalment in the war they regarded as inevitable.

It seems that Brocket was lying here. In April 1939 the German–Soviet negotiations were top secret and it is highly unlikely that he knew about them.

But Brocket's claim that Halifax had been contacted was correct. It was known by several people that Halifax had not closed down channels to Germany. This was one reason why Stephanie and Max Hohenlohe hoped well into 1940 that a peace between Britain and Germany could be engineered via Halifax. Stephanie had no chance of brokering this one, though. Halifax made sure that he would not be associated with her again. He had many other options. As the diaries of Guy Liddell, the MI5 Director of Counter-Espionage, show:

> Stewart Menzies tells me that Halifax has been asked to see Lord Darnley and the Marquess of Tavistock regarding certain peace proposals. I gather that there have been six or seven approaches of this kind. It indicates that the Germans are feeling about but at present their terms are quite impossible. It seems also that these overtures may be a part of what the Germans call Zermürbungstaktik, the general purpose of which is to keep this country off the boil. Tavistock is, of course, connected with the British Council for Christian Settlement in Europe which is a mixture of the Link, Nordic League and BUF, and a most mischievous body.[47]

In fact Halifax's visitor Tavistock had worked for the Nazis for some time. In 1933 he had been singled out as 'useful' by the German embassy since 'he had always courageously stood up against the anti-German propaganda' [during the First World War]. He was keen on Nazi contacts and after the outbreak of the Second World War established them via Dublin. Halifax probably did not help Tavistock, but he helped Brocket. He made travel arrangements for Lord Brocket's go-between Jim Lonsdale Bryans. Lonsdale Bryans had first contacted members of the German opposition but then switched. He wanted to get directly in contact with Hitler. How far this went could never fully be verified. Halifax's role in this, however, came out in 2008.

Over the years Halifax has been portrayed either as the cunning fox who played a long game towards Germany, or as an unreformed appeaser who hoped to broker a peace deal with the Germans. For both versions there exists strong evidence. The truth is probably much more banal. By the beginning of 1940 he was out of his depth. He shared the opinion of many of his aristocratic friends that this war should be ended as quickly as possible and he therefore helped them unofficially.

That he had helped Lonsdale Bryans was known to the British intelligence services. They had come across an associate of Lonsdale Bryans named Anderson who was ready to talk: 'The main point which seemed to emerge from the interrogation was that according to Anderson, Lonsdale Bryans was a personal friend of Lord Brocket and also claimed to be something in the nature of an unofficial envoy of Lord Halifax. He wished to see Hitler and with this in view had asked Anderson to get in touch with a certain Stahmer.' For the rest of the war the Foreign Office (and in particular Halifax) must have feared that Lonsdale Bryans and Anderson would sell their stories to the press.[48] Instead Göring would cause Halifax a final uncomfortable moment in the winter of 1945. To his friend the Duchess of Portland Halifax wrote: 'My dearest Ivy, I am amused with you saying that some of the peers are apprehensive of being summoned to give evidence at Nuremberg.' He can't have been that amused though: 'Göring has requested me and Alex Cadogan to go and testify to how earnest a seeker of the peace he was up to the war.'[49] Of course Halifax declined.

While Chamberlain and Halifax took people like Brocket, Buccleuch-Queensbury, and Darnley seriously, Churchill made clear as early as September 1939 that he would not. One of his old friends was the Duke of Westminster,[50] a staunch anti-Semite, who had developed an interest in Nazi Germany through his relatives the Pless family. As a result Westminster supported German peace feelers in September 1939. To this effect he had written a memorandum which he read out to a selected group of British appeasers. The memorandum cannot be traced, but Churchill's reply to it makes clear what is was about. Though Churchill was not yet Prime Minister, he demonstrated to Westminster in no uncertain terms what he thought of his pro-German meddling:

> Dear Benny,
>
> It seems to me on reading it [Westminster's memo] that there are some very serious and bad things in it, the full bearing of which I feel you could not have properly apprehended. I am sure that pursuance of this line would lead you into measureless odium and vexation.... Very hard experiences lie before those who preach defeatism and set themselves against the will of the nation.[51]

Since Churchill was a friend of Westminster, the language he uses here shows how strongly he felt on this issue. Once he was in power he had to unite the Conservative party behind him, though, and did not start a revenge campaign against Halifax and former appeasers. He had made his point and they understood.

Psychological warfare is a key element in the work of security services. Go-betweens can become part of such warfare. Not even go-betweens themselves necessarily know whether their mission is genuine or not. Their instructions are on a 'need to know' basis. Ideally they should believe in it in order to carry it out well. The question, however, remains in many cases whether they are in fact sent off on a genuine mission or whether they are simply being sent off on a mission to test how determined the opposite side is.

This is exactly the dilemma when one looks at Max Hohenlohe's go-between work after the outbreak of war. He himself would claim for the rest of his life that the peace overtures he was instructed to make to the British were genuine. It is possible that he believed this. On the other hand he was a highly intelligent man who had already played a sinister double game in 1938. Ever since the Sudeten crisis Hohenlohe had built up Göring as the voice of peace. Göring was portrayed to the British as the 'moderate Nazi' the Allies could talk to. As we know today, it was correct that Göring had doubts about some of Hitler's decisions. But in the end, he always went along with them.

Coming to an arrangement with the British would have elevated Göring's position in Hitler's eyes and ousted Göring's old rival Ribbentrop. Göring dreamt a dream that Rudolf Hess would also dream and that ended quite dramatically with his doomed flight to Scotland. Hohenlohe and Göring failed long before Hess boarded his plane.

In October 1939 Hohenlohe started his overtures to the British. It was obvious to everyone involved that the first few months of the war were vital if an Anglo-German arrangement could be achieved. The emotional and financial costs had not yet amounted to much. Hohenlohe wanted to exploit this vacuum.

During the Runciman mission Hohenlohe had built up a particularly close relationship with Colonel Christie and they had prepared for all eventualities—even developing their own secret language. Henlein, the 'chicken', was no longer important, but the idea of chickens was never far away. The code name they now used for Germany was *chicken farm*. After the outbreak of war the *chicken farm* seemed in a tense state, or at least this was the impression Hohenlohe wanted to give Christie. In October 1939 he asked his British friend for a meeting.

He sent three telegrams to Christie from Berne. Christie passed them on immediately: 'I have reason to believe that the attached wire from Berne comes from Max Hohenlohe: he is a friend of mine who tried to be helpful in many talks between Henlein and myself in 1937–1938. VAN (Vansittart) knows him very well.... If it is not a trap it should mean that Hohenlohe has come out of Germany into Switzerland and wants to indicate that there are some possibilities of a new Government in Germany.'[52]

This was from now on the question. Were these possibilities serious?

During the months October 1939 to August 1940 Hohenlohe travelled several times to Switzerland. Papers in the Churchill Archives show in detail Hohenlohe's conversations with Colonel Christie. What Hohenlohe told Christie was quite daring. He claimed that he had talked to Göring and that if the peace terms were right, Göring was ready to sideline Hitler and the more radical elements within the Nazi party. This was a great teaser to which Christie naturally reacted excitedly. He was, however, not completely sure whether Göring would be a good alternative. He knew him well, after all, and thought him, despite all his rakish charm, to be as ruthless as Hitler. Still, the British kept sending Christie off for more meetings.[53] Again these meetings in Switzerland seem familiar. In the First World War, go-betweens had met in elegant Swiss hotels for secret peace feelers; now Hohenlohe and Christie continued this tradition. To the meeting in a Lausanne hotel, Christie brought along another expert on Germany who knew Hitler well: Conwell-Evans. Conwell-Evans had been the secretary of the Anglo-German

Fellowship and had arranged Lloyd George's visit to Hitler in 1936. To the Germans, Conwell-Evans was a known quantity, an appeaser they hoped to manipulate. In his 1947 interrogation by the Russians, Wilhelm Rodde (former aide to Ribbentrop and an Oberführer in the SS) even claimed that Conwell-Evans was one of Ribbentrop's agents:

> [Prof. Conwell-Evans] visited Germany very often and met with Ribbentrop not only in his office but in his apartment in Dahlem, near Berlin. I remember one instance in 1935, one of those Saturdays, not long before the Büro closed, Ribbentrop came to me in my office and asked what sums of money in English and American currency I had at my disposal. I gave him 300 Pounds Sterling and many Dollars. I put to you [his Soviet interrogator] that this money was given by Ribbentrop to Evans who left the following day for London, giving speeches in England in defence of the NSDAP.[54]

It is not clear to this day what Conwell-Evans actually was. He posed as an academic, but he was probably, like Christie, very close to the British intelligence services. Whether he used his work in the Anglo-German Fellowship as a cover or was genuinely pro-Hitler is hard to verify. He was definitely a very close friend of Christie and travelled with him often. At Lausanne Christie informed Hohenlohe that the British were adamant Hitler had to go, otherwise peace talks could not start. Hohenlohe indicated that this might be possible and described in great detail how divided the German leadership was. He wanted the British to believe in this 'group of critics' that could bring about regime change. Asked for more details about the opposition group Hohenlohe claimed to work for, he became rather vague. He was not willing to give names.

Apart from the hope of toppling the Führer, Christie wanted to know what would happen to Czechoslovakia and Poland in a peace agreement and Hohenlohe signalled that concessions could be made here too. He also stressed that there was another channel Göring was using for negotiations via Stockholm [Birger Dahlerus] and that several people could always be contacted—including the pro-German King of Sweden and the former British intelligence officer William Wiseman. It was the same Wiseman who Stephanie Hohenlohe had contacted in America.

It was agreed that Conwell-Evans should go to The Hague and wait for Hohenlohe to contact him if there were further developments. But then something happened to endanger this work. At the same time as the Hohenlohe–Christie channel was flowing, on 9 November 1939 the 'Venlo incident' took place: two British MI6 agents operating in the Dutch city of

Venlo had been given to understand that they were about to meet German opposition leaders. It was a trap and the agents were captured, giving away vital information about MI6. The Venlo incident was organized by Walter Schellenberg, who would become a close friend of Hohenlohe (though Hohenlohe claimed that he did not know him until 1942).

After this disaster for MI6 the Christie–Hohenlohe contacts were interrupted. The British now had reason to believe that Hohenlohe might not have genuine opposition contacts after all but posed another trap. Hohenlohe's promises that Göring would get rid of Hitler turned out to be misinformation. Hohenlohe suddenly backpedalled, claiming that Göring had never made such promises explicitly to him. Instead he had sent him off to ask Hitler whether he, Göring, should take over the peace negotiations with the British. At least this was Hohenlohe's new version. He also claimed he had actually gone ahead and been granted an audience with Hitler who had not made any commitments one way or the other.[55] How correct this version actually was is hard to verify. Hohenlohe probably invented the whole story for Christie. But it was not at all what Christie had hoped for. Nonetheless, they discussed details regarding a future constitution of Germany once Hitler was gone and also the future of Poland. In summary Hohenlohe demanded a signal from the British that they were ready for serious negotiations. He had not offered much himself, though, and could not seriously have expected to get much in return. The British had grown too cautious. A second Munich was not in sight.

Apart from Hohenlohe, Christie talked to several other Germans in February 1940: the former German Chancellor Joseph Wirth, the industrialist Fritz Thyssen, and his most important informant Johnny Ritter, rather obviously codenamed 'Knight' (a World War I air ace who had worked for Junkers and in 1935–38 was German air attaché in Paris). Even though the success in Poland seemed to have made Hitler untouchable in Germany, these men agreed with Hohenlohe on some points. They told Christie that the army was critical of the Führer and not interested in any further crusades. They also told him that there had been clashes between the army and the party. On 12 March 1940 Christie, together with Conwell-Evans, met Wirth and Ritter in Lausanne.[56] Wirth and Ritter claimed the German opposition also included generals. Ritter, however, 'felt personally uncertain as to whether the generals, even after being encouraged and fortified by the Prime Minister's speech . . . , would pluck up enough courage.'[57]

The signals that were reaching the British were therefore confusing. Hohenlohe himself seemed to be switching between posing as an opposition leader and a channel to Hitler. Eventually Christie told Hohenlohe that his superiors were seriously underwhelmed by what he had offered them so far. He put this into their code language, pretending to be a businessman who had to inform Hohenohe that his 'shareholders' (the British government) were not convinced by the 'proposal'. They had no trust 'in the business methods of the management and most of its co-directors' (Göring). In other words, they had developed serious doubts about Göring and other 'moderate' Germans as an alternative.

By then many people were booking Swiss hotel rooms. MI6 was a particularly frequent guest. Its agents needed as much information about the enemy as possible. Sir Stuart Menzies, chief of MI6, also wanted to know whether there was a genuine opposition in Germany and, if so, whether it would overthrow Hitler. Dusko Popov, who worked for Menzies as a double-cross agent, mentions in his memoirs a discussion with him on this subject. Menzies was interested in people he had identified as potential Hitler critics: Max Hohenlohe, Admiral Wilhelm Canaris [the head of military intelligence, the Abwehr], and two other Abwehr officers, Colonel Hans Oster and Hans von Dohnanyi.[58] Menzies was of the opinion that Canaris might become a leader of the opposition to Hitler. In the long term Menzies' interest in this group had a dangerous effect on Anglo-Russian relations. One of Menzies' agents, Kim Philby, was a mole, working for the Russians. He passed on Menzies' interest in Canaris. Philby had pointed out to Menzies that Admiral Canaris could be killed on a trip to Spain, but Menzies replied: 'I've always thought we could do something with the Admiral.' Philby concluded: 'It was only later that I learnt he was in touch with Canaris via a cut-out in Sweden.'[59]

To the Russians this information confirmed that the British might make peace with Germany. This was something that Stalin feared all along. It was in Russia's interest to hinder any such contacts.

Once Churchill became Prime Minister, the contacts had in fact already decreased. The appeasement minded were elegantly outmanoeuvred by Churchill. In the tradition of the civil service he moved several of them upstairs and sideways. He sent his old rival Halifax as ambassador to Washington and Samuel Hoare in the same capacity to Spain. These were important postings but hardly dangerous to the Prime Minister. The appeasers had lost their power base and the tide of the war also made contacts with the Germans more and more unlikely. The higher the human costs of the war, the more difficult a peaceful solution had become.

After Christie had lost interest in him, Hohenlohe tried to make contact with the new British ambassador to Switzerland, Sir David Kelly. Hohenlohe now claimed to have a direct message from Hitler: '[Hitler] does not wish to touch Britain or the British Empire (although a deal over one of the old German colonies would be helpful); nor to ask for any reparation.' Kelly's reaction was: 'knowing the vital importance of gaining time, I made a show of interest.'[60]

Hohenlohe had obviously dropped the pretence of Göring as an alternative to Hitler. In fact Göring had lost power at Hitler's court and this was well known to Hohenlohe. After the war he claimed he had given up on Göring because his old friend seemed not to help enough with his 'peace work'.

Despite Churchill being in power, Hohenlohe still had hopes of getting peace talks going. In his memoirs Sefton Delmer claims that Hohenlohe's reports had an effect in Germany. Delmer was in quite a good position to judge this. He had become part of a section in British Intelligence that specialized in black propaganda.[61] He was ideal for this job, since he knew members of the Nazi leadership well. As mentioned before, he also knew Hohenlohe, whom he suspected of being Ribbentrop's agent. Though Delmer was wrong about this, he was much closer to the truth when it came to what Hohenlohe passed on to Germany. Delmer knew that Hohenlohe still believed that there was a peace faction in Britain that could be encouraged, despite the fall of Chamberlain. One of Hohenlohe's sources was, according to Delmer, the Aga Khan.

In fact the Aga Khan had told Hohenlohe in Switzerland that Lord Beaverbrook was advocating a peace deal with Hitler. On 25 July 1940 Hohenlohe quoted this in a memorandum: 'Beaverbrook is the only man who has enough courage, the power and the standing to bring about a change in England even against Churchill, since Churchill has for a long time been in Beaverbrook's pay.'[62]

This was an allusion to the time Beaverbrook had kept Churchill financially afloat, paying generously for his articles. During his years in the political and financial wilderness, this support had been important to Churchill and to the building of his country retreat, Chartwell. And indeed Beaverbrook had for a long time hoped for a peace settlement. But Churchill had managed to win him over and the information was now dated. Delmer nonetheless believed that Rudolf Hess must have been aware of the Aga Khan report in which Beaverbrook was identified as an opponent of the war. It must have made sense to Hess. Together with Hitler, he had met Beaverbrook several times in Berlin between 1935 and 1939. As we know today, apart from Beaverbrook there were other signs that made Hess believe in a British peace party. His 'reception' in Scotland was naturally a let-down. The British security services handled the situation extremely badly. In fact a contemporary like Sefton Delmer already realized their mistakes at the time. He knew Hess well from his years as a reporter in Berlin and thought him to be a neurotic megalomaniac whose vanity had to be appealed to. If played rightly one could have used Hess as an excellent source. Instead he was confronted with the futility of his mission and clammed up completely. He only opened up for a moment when he was visited in captivity by Beaverbrook. Hess did not know that Beaverbrook was no longer interested in peace negotiations. They had in the past often discussed the Soviet threat and this was what Hess now brought up again: he wanted peace with Britain if Britain would help to attack Russia. It was a dream Hohenlohe had also helped to nurture.

After the war Max Hohenlohe would use his meetings with the British in 1939/40 to 'prove' his peace work. He would also tell the journalist Höhne in 1967 that he had sent 'warning messages to the Reich via a Vatican channel'. Indeed he was a master at spinning events to whatever was politically advantageous.

The UK National Archives website suggests that after 1941 Hohenlohe was used as a 'gentleman agent' by Admiral Canaris, head of the Abwehr. After Canaris' s fall, he 'was taken over as a "special informant" by Walter Schellenberg, who became head of foreign intelligence following the abolition of the Abwehr'. Like an unfaithful lover he had moved away from Göring and found new high ranking Nazi friends. After the war Hohenlohe claimed that he was impressed by Schellenberg because he had given him hope that a regime change could be achieved. According to Hohenlohe, Schellenberg's conclusion was that as long as Hitler was in power the Allies would not make peace with Germany. He also indicated that if Hitler was not going to go himself, he would have to be removed by force. According to his postwar version of events, Hohenlohe agreed with this wholeheartedly.

To work for Schellenberg, however, meant working for Himmler. There were at least two reasons for Max Hohenlohe to get involved with Himmler and his SD (he became agent number 144/7957): first, to protect his estates in the Sudetenland; and secondly, because being hooked up to Himmler potentially offered other rewards in the long run. After all it was now Himmler rather than Göring who might become a possible successor to the Führer. Hohenlohe did not of course admit to working for Himmler. He claimed that as a consequence of his conversation about overthrowing Hitler, he put Schellenberg in contact with the Americans. Indeed a meeting between a Schellenberg emissary and American intelligence officers took place in Lisbon in December 1942. Whether Hohenlohe really was the matchmaker for this meeting cannot be verified. But Schellenberg would have never decided to do this on his own initiative. He was obviously encouraged by Himmler to establish channels to the Americans. This means that at this early point in 1942/3 Himmler already had doubts whether the war could be won by Germany. But he was unsure how to proceed. Getting rid of Hitler and taking over himself was one option. His biographer Peter Longerich, however, claims that Himmler started his overtures to the Allies, much later in 'mid 1944'.[63] He then offered Jews in exchange for money or goods. This was, according to Longerich, not his main incentive. He was probably trying to get in contact with the Allies in order to end the war. Longerich also thinks that Himmler may have wanted to use the negotiations to play off the Russians against the Americans. John F. Waller has shown that several channels were becoming active in 1944:

> Strangely insensitive to the revulsion felt toward him by the West for atrocities he was known to have committed, but well aware of his fate if the Russians were to capture him upon Germany's ultimate capitulation, Himmler was sending out feelers to the Americans in Sweden and other neutral countries through a variety of go-betweens.[64]

Yet in fact Himmler started to build these channels much earlier, probably thinking of them as a future insurance policy. The Swedish channel became very active when he used Jacob Wallenberg (an uncle of the tragic Raoul Wallenberg). Jacob Wallenberg told an American OSS officer that 'cells were forming in Germany for the purpose of overthrowing Hitler'.[65] According to Jacob Wallenberg the only alternative to Hitler was Himmler. Schellenberg also made contacts for Himmler via the Swedish Red Cross and Count Bernadotte—using the traditional aristocratic channels reminiscent of the First World War.

Hohenlohe was Schellenberg and Himmler's Spanish channel and he naturally relished the idea, which introduced him to the new power brokers in Europe. Whether he switched to the Americans to save his skin or whether he did it for Himmler remains unclear—it was probably a bit of both.

The Americans did not mind talking to Hohenlohe. Their agenda was naturally to find out more about the alleged rift within the Nazi hierarchy. They even brought in their OSS chief Allen Dulles for this. Again Hohenlohe may have made this meeting of high ranking officials possible. He had known Dulles since 1923 and told Schellenberg: 'He is a tall, burly, sporting type of 45, healthy-looking with good teeth and a fresh simple open-hearted manner.'[66] Dulles was a partner in the American law firm that represented the business interests of Hohenlohe's wife. He was certainly more complex than was suggested by his 'open hearted manner'.

Hohenlohe met Dulles three times between January and April 1943, bringing along another officer from Himmler's department for western Europe. Also present at these meetings were the US ambassador, Leland Harrison, and Lieutenant-Colonel Duncan Lee. As Jonathan Haslam shows in his book on Soviet intelligence there was a certain irony in this, since these meetings were immediately leaked. Duncan Lee was secretly working for the Russians. He had been a Rhodes scholar at Oxford, where he was most probably recruited as a student (to this day the Oxford spy ring, unlike the Cambridge one, is mainly unidentified). Lee's Russian codename was rather oddly 'Koch', which means cook in German. Koch could certainly not have liked what was being cooked up by the old anti-Bolshevik Hohenlohe at these meetings. Hohenlohe suggested 'a cordon against Bolshevism and Panslavism' by 'expanding Poland to the East, maintaining the monarchy in Romania and a strong Hungary'. Dulles seemed to agree.[67]

Thus Hohenlohe was playing the old trump card with the Americans, the idea of a bulwark against the Russians. Hearing this—thanks to agent Koch—certainly did not encourage Stalin to trust his American allies.

The British noticed that Hohenlohe had moved to the Americans. When Hohenlohe was in Spain 'visiting relatives' it was Sir Samuel Hoare's brief to watch him. Hoare had been an appeaser before 1939 and become ambassador to Spain in 1940. In conversations with Spanish diplomats in 1940 the Duke of Windsor had praised Hoare highly. But Hoare knew which way the wind was blowing. His brief was to keep Spain out of the war, and he had given up his old appeasement friends once Churchill was secure. He had also changed his mind about Hohenlohe. His reports on him switched from positive to negative over the years. In 1942 he wrote to Foreign Secretary Eden:

Max Hohenlohe turned up. He met John [an unidentified colleague of Hoare] at a party and claimed that the position in Germany is intolerable. Hitler's relationship with generals intolerable. John made it clear that we were not at all interested in any proposals for peace. We intended to smash Hitler. Max seemed to accept this.[68]

By 1943 Hoare was writing that Hohenlohe wanted to move his family permanently to Spain:

Max and his kind are getting very nervous in Germany and he is [in Spain] to see whether there is any chance for peace talks.... John could not have been more resolute with him about peace. Max posed very much as the confidante of Göring and the anti-Hitler section in the country.[69]

Hoare was busy enough keeping an eye on the larger picture of a complicated intelligence scene. Neutral Spain was a hotbed of agents during the war. It was the ideal place to plant disinformation and Hoare had to spend most of his time figuring out who was behind which rumour. Hoare had many different 'contacts' who kept him informed. He made sure he covered the whole of Spain and did not just concentrate on Madrid. The Catalans were important for him too, and it was in Barcelona where he heard of another peace feeler. An influential businessman had told him that

a German industrialist of great importance had arrived in Barcelona and that he was anxious to start peace feelers. He claimed to represent Himmler and Speer... who, he declared, were dissociating themselves from Hitler and Goebbels.... The Himmler crowd had definitely come to the conclusion that as no one can, in their view, win the war, the best course is for the belligerents to make peace. I told [him] at once that we did not accept for a moment the conclusion of a stalemate and that we could not dream of starting peace talks with any one.

To Hoare this story about the 'Himmler crowd' sounded all too familiar. It reminded him of a conversation he had had with Max Hohenlohe:

You remember that some months ago I wrote to you about a similar suggestion that emanated from Max Hohelohe. It seems to me that the interest of the move attempted by the Alcalde's German friend consists in the fact that the proposal is on exact all fours with Max Hohenlohe's.[70]

He concluded that Max was certainly a German agent.

Officially, in his day job, Hohenlohe, however, posed as a representative of the Skoda car manufacturers in Spain. He now opened up his Spanish home for Nazis abroad and gave his old friend Reinhard Spitzy a nice job at Skoda. Spitzy's unofficial boss was Walter Schellenberg. Naturally Spitzy was happy about the arrangement and claimed in his memoirs that he took part in some of the conversations Max had with the OSS.

These American contacts meant much to Hohenlohe. In a postwar world, he wanted to be on the side of the winners. To make absolutely sure he would be associated with the right crowd, he also started an Austrian 'independence' group in January 1945. He suddenly remembered that he had once been an Austro-Hungarian subject. Though he now had a Liechtenstein passport and a SD number he simply turned himself into an Austrian patriot again. The British intelligence services were not fooled. On 8 January 1945 they reported:

> Source states that [an agent was in contact with] Count Seefried and Prince Hohenlohe through the new Austria group allegedly formed in Madrid. Source also states that he believes Hohenlohe is secretary to this new Austria group which has been outwardly formed for the purpose of pleading for Austrian independence: however, source's informant states that the group is in fact a secret German organisation which requires watching.[71]

This intelligence report on Hohenlohe also stated that he 'has many influential friends, including Lord Templewood [Samuel Hoare] and the Duke de Alba' and that he was 'very wealthy'. They were not very complimentary about his looks: 'Heavy build, large head, bloated face, fair hair going bald, blue eyes, large fat hands, dominating appearance, speaks Spanish, French, English and Czech. Holds German and Liechtenstein passports.'

By then the stresses of the war seem to have affected Hohenlohe's looks. If he had kept a picture of himself in the attic, it would have been truly hideous by 1945.

Prince Max Hohenlohe-Langenburg had started his career as a go-between in the Sudetenland but by 1940 had definitely turned into a German agent. He was an agent who did great damage. Because he had faked Göring's alleged opposition and exaggerated the influence of critics among the Nazi leadership, the British lost trust in the existence of a German resistance movement. When a more plausible opposition group around Count Stauffenberg actually emerged, they were sceptical. By then they were also locked in an alliance with the Russians who were hawkishly watching out for any contacts between Britain and Germany.

In the end Hohenlohe had played everyone. His greatest coup was to be remembered as 'a good Nazi'.

Conclusion

Did Go-Betweens Make a Difference?

In April 1945, when Carl Eduard Duke of Coburg was arrested by the Americans, he switched back into being an Englishman. He had enjoyed wearing Hitler's uniforms—the general's one in particular—but now had to dispose of them. Instead he put on an old hunting outfit, transforming himself into the epitome of a country gentleman. It was a wise choice, though not everyone was fooled by it. His American interrogators took an instant dislike to the Duke. They called him 'badly informed and arrogant'. One of them was the German émigré and novelist Stefan Heym. During an interview with Heym the Duke praised National Socialism and stressed that democracy was not a model for Germany since 'German people could not rule themselves'.[1] Asked about the concentration camps, he claimed that he was not responsible for them: 'ich bin nur ein kleiner Mann' (I am just a little man). He had obviously forgotten his nephew Waldeck-Pyrmont's 'dedicated work' for the concentration camp Buchenwald.

Heym was part of the American army's psychological warfare team. He found his interview with Coburg of such propaganda value that he used it for a radio programme which was broadcast on 17 April 1945:

> The Duke believed until recently that Germany would win the war. He thinks that Hitler did a wonderful job in Germany. Only trouble is that he 'overshot the mark'. Hitler should have managed his 'Drang nach Osten', by measures short of war. The method used in eliminating the Jews was harsh, but he thinks it was necessary to remove the Jewish influence from the German theatre, art, newspapers etc. When asked what he thought had been the percentage of Jews in Germany he replied: 'about ten per cent'.[2]

Heym and the other American officers had therefore asked the Duke if he would be ready to take part in a new German government. Coburg was only slightly surprised:

> The Duke looked at his wife and upon receiving her lively nod of approval said: 'yes of course'. He pointed out, however, that he would need 24 hours to name his colleagues. When asked from what group he would choose his co-workers, Carl Eduard replied: 'From the National Socialist Party.'

This sentence formed the highlight of Stefan Heym's radio programme. To the interviewer's delight the Duke even presented a list of 'demands':

> The United Nations should furnish Germany with raw materials so that it can rebuild its industries, become a great nation and thus be in a position to pay war damages: No one in Germany should be punished for war crimes because no German is guilty of any war crimes, says the Duke.[3]

This radio programme ensured that Carl Eduard's mental faculties were doubted. Yet he had simply stayed loyal to ideas he had acquired twenty years earlier.

It was ironic that Coburg stood by Hitler, who had given instructions for him to be killed. When Hitler issued a secret order that 'the Duke of Coburg should on no account fall into enemy hands' this was not meant in a caring way. We know that in 1945 Hitler gave the so-called Nero directive for German cities to be destroyed. He also issued similar orders to eliminate his secrets. These secrets were hidden in files and 'in' people. The German Foreign Ministry files for one had been transported to Marburg and were now ordered to be destroyed before the enemy could get hold of them. In the end the Americans were quicker and rescued them (including the Duke of Windsor's file).[4] It was also more complex for Hitler to get rid of people now. Ideally he wanted all his associates to commit suicide. His secretary, Traudl Junge, has described the pressure Hitler put on people in the bunker to kill themselves. He handed out cyanide capsules and made people swear an oath to commit suicide. Not everyone felt like doing it, though. While Goebbels famously obeyed him to the end, others took a different view. Carl Eduard never knew that Hitler wanted to get rid of him. Consequently he never disowned his 'Führer' and instead gave Heym this bizarre interview.

His 'Nibelungen-loyalty' was something Coburg started to regret when he was sent to an internment camp. He now hoped that the British royal family would help him out of his predicament. However, Coburg was not the only relative of the royal family who had got into trouble with the Allies. Other members of his peer group were also confronted with their Nazi pasts. The British royal family was swamped by German relatives pleading for help. Not all of them received it. Kaiser Wilhelm II's second wife Hermine and the Grand Duchess of Sachsen-Weimar were both captured by the Soviets. Queen Mary was approached for help and so was her son King George VI. However, Foreign Secretary Ernest Bevin's advice was clear: 'It is not thought desirable for His Majesty's Government to take any action in this matter. Any suggestion that we are hobnobbing with the German royal family would be eagerly seized on by the Russians or anyone else who likes to call us reactionary.'[5] This was understood, but in the end an exception was made for Carl Eduard. As usual it was his devoted sister Alice who tried to get him out of his latest 'scrape'. The Foreign Office was bombarded with letters from her, pressing for Carl Eduard's release from an American internment camp. An overworked official described how he had been approached by Alice's husband the Earl of Athlone for help:

> Athlone asked me to go and see him about his brother in law. They want to get him out of the internment camp to live with his wife in Coburg or Sweden. Of course I haven't the slightest idea what the man has done or whether it is possible, even were it desirable to alleviate his lot.[6]

Princess Alice also mobilized courtiers who used Balmoral and Buckingham Palace writing paper to put 'soft' pressure on the Foreign Office. But despite their deference to royalty, Foreign Office officials were not so easily intimidated by letterheads.

Together with a German lawyer, Alice now argued that her brother was suffering from cancer of the eye and arthritis and therefore had to be released on humanitarian grounds. In her memoirs she was outraged by the way her 'innocent' brother was treated:

> Because Charlie had belonged to the *partee*[7] and was head of the Red Cross and old comrades' association (though he had not fought in the war) the Americans put him in a camp . . . He found conditions almost unbearable.[8]

Alice tried to find better quarters for Coburg's wife and talked to German and American authorities who were 'all odious'. In her memoirs she explained to her grandchildren: 'In our efforts to do something for Uncle Charlie, Granpa (Alice's husband Athlone) and I humiliated ourselves by dining with the US Governor of Coburg, a Syrian by birth. We also called on and lunched with his successor, a Jewish-French American whom we did not think a suitable representative of his great country nor the sort of person one would select to instruct the Germans in democracy!'[9]

Alice never seemed to mind expressing her anti-Semitism in print. Despite her various prejudices, she was successful. In 1946 her brother was released from the camp. He still faced a denazification trial in 1947 and Alice made sure that this would go well too.

What Alice did next was impressive chutzpah. She completely white-washed her brother's Nazi career:

The Princess Alice spoke to me about the Duke the other day, she said that the latter—in his own estimation at any events—had done quite a lot to try to improve Anglo-German relations during the inter-war period in his capacity as President of the Anglo-German society, the German Red Cross and various ex-servicemen's associations. I gather that the Duke rather hoped that just as the Foreign Office had apparently [said] about Dr. Dirksen that the latter had in his capacity as Ambassador done his best to improve Anglo-German relations, so we would say something to this effect.[10]

However, the Foreign Office could hardly lie for her. By 20 August 1947 its research department had finally provided background information on the Duke that was, despite several gaps, damning:

[he] became one of the earliest sponsors of the Nationalist Movement. In 1919 he belonged to the staff of a Free Corps . . . and was district leader for Thüringen of the 'Brigade Erhardt' until 1926. He held a leading position in the Stahlhelm from 1926 to 1932 and in 1930 became a member of its Executive. During this time he was working for the Nazis and in 1932 was expelled from the Stahlhelm on account of his Nazi activities. . . . In 1933 he was made SA-Gruppenführer. His part in Nazi processions by the side of the local Nazi leader, Schwede, [foreman in the local gas works, later Gauleiter and Oberpräsident of Pomerania] was given much publicity by Nazi propaganda as a symbol of 'Volksgemeinschaft'. After being appointed Leader of the Nationalist Motor Sport Organisation in 1929, the Duke became Reichs Commissar for Voluntary Nursing and President of the German Red Cross.[11]

The rest of his many ranks and honours were then listed. Though his visit to the Far East was mentioned in this summary, his frequent visits to Britain and his US trips were not. In this regard the Foreign Office clearly remained protective of its own kind.

Alice apparently did not care much about such facts. She made sure that lots of the Duke's friends and aides attested to his 'peace work'.[12] By then Coburg's old ally Ribbentrop had been executed and could not be of use anymore, but Ribbentrop's successor at the German embassy in London, von Dirksen, testified to Carl Eduard's good works. Since many of the German diplomats had to hide as much as the Duke, they supported each other vigorously. Careers were being rewritten from May 1945 onwards and the years of lying had begun. With Alice's support, the Coburgs became masters at it. Carl Eduard's wife claimed in one interview that during the twelve years of National Socialism they had rarely entertained prominent Nazis because her husband was a 'very modest and shy man'.[13] And the Duke himself stated that 'on my foreign trips I have never made any propaganda for the NSDAP or National Socialism'.[14] The authorities wanted to believe him. He walked free.

Another go-between for Hitler, Stephanie Hohenlohe, also escaped sanction. After her American lover had died in 1955 she was wealthy, but still hungry for more. She had once described herself as Rothermere's 'ambassadress' and it had been a role she thoroughly enjoyed. At a time when women could not dream of ever becoming real ambassadors she had been treated like one in Hungary, Germany, and Britain. Her 'colourful' past now prevented her from ever being a political go-between again, but she used her old contacts to became something that was close to it—she became a 'fixer'. Hohenlohe now fixed famous interview partners for German journalists. The idea had come to her by chance. She rarely read books but she loved reading magazines including German ones and discovered that the German media was in need of good American contacts. She immediately provided them, first for Karl-Heinz Hagen who worked for the German magazine *Quick*, later for Henri Nannen's magazine *Stern*. Her vast network offered remarkably varied contacts—from old Nazis to American presidents. The way she had won over the latter was particularly ingenious.

In a former life, in the Vienna of the Habsburgs, Stephanie had been the under age lover of Count Joseph Gizycki. Gizycki had been tempestuously married to the journalist Eleanor Cissy Patterson, whose family owned an American media empire. He was now long dead, but his American daughter was very much alive. Stephanie got in touch with her, posing as an old friend of her father's. The daughter was useful for Hohenlohe since she was married to the American columnist Drew Pearson. Pearson was highly influential: his gossipy column 'The Washington Merry-Go-Round' appeared in over 600 newspapers all over America. As a result American presidents courted him and many people owed him favours. Pearson had already met Hohenlohe in the 1930s and he was now willing to open the doors of

Washington's inner circles to Stephanie.[15] They became an ideal team: she got Pearson an extra income, he secured interviews for her journalists. The first highlight came in September 1963 when Pearson arranged an interview with President Kennedy (the German magazine *Quick* paid Pearson $5,000 for the interview, and extended their generous contract with Hohenlohe). The Kennedy interview was a remarkable achievement and showed that human memory can be extremely short: Stephanie, who had been perceived by President Roosevelt and FBI chief Hoover as 'highly dangerous' in 1941, could twenty years later genuinely claim to have good White House contacts.

For many years Pearson and Hohenlohe did well out of their cheque book journalism. They helped each other to get scoops. When Hohenlohe needed an interview with Shah Reza Pahlawi, Pearson wrote her a glowing letter of recommendation:

> Princess Hohenlohe... has been a very great help to President Kennedy on his recent trip to Germany and has served in an unofficial capacity in helping to promote better relations for the United States in various parts of the world.[16]

Pearson was also helpful in arranging an interview for Hohenlohe with Kennedy's successor, Lyndon B. Johnson. Thanks to Hohenlohe and Pearson, the German journalist Hagen was received by Johnson in 1964. A year later Stephanie had worked out an even better deal with a rival German magazine (*Der Stern*) whose editor paid her and Pearson $20,000 for another interview with President Johnson. Hohenlohe then switched again and continued her lucrative work with another German publisher, Axel Springer. Springer, who founded the *Bild Zeitung*, the German equvialent of *The Sun*, was particularly devoted to her.

Death finally caught up with Stephanie in Geneva in 1972. She had been ill for some time and as usual was on her way to a party. By then she was 80 years old. According to her gravestone she died at the age of 67.[17]

Her fellow go-between Max Hohenlohe also rarely missed a party. His good contacts with the Americans had saved him from any prosecution after 1945. His sidekick Spitzy had also switched to the Allies, but his switch was not entirely smooth and after 1945 he had to go into hiding for a couple of years. He settled back in Austria in the 1950s, wrote his memoirs, and became a television celebrity.

Max Hohenlohe preferred to stay in Franco's Spain, just in case. He continued his jet set life in Marbella. Since politics were now out of the question, he focused on making money. After the war there was a lot of 'black money' around that needed to be laundered. Old Nazis liked investing it in safe havens like Franco's Spain. Hotel projects in Marbella were particularly popular. Hohenlohe seems to have been very 'helpful' in bringing them along. He is remembered to this day in tourist brochures as the man who discovered a beautiful spot—Marbella's Golden Mile:

> Sun, sea, and youthful energy: These are three things found in abundance throughout Spain's southern shores. The Marbella Golden Mile, which covers the coastline that stretches from western Marbella City to Puerto Banus, is an exclusive luxury development that takes full advantage of these and all the other benefits that make southern Spain's Andalusian community a favorite of those who seek both beauty and impeccable hospitality in any locality they choose to call home. Originally developed as a retreat for European nobles by Prince Max Egon zu Hohenlohe-Langenburg who, while touring the Mediterranean coast, discovered the area's unquestionable appeal after a problem with his automobile forced a stopover in the then small town of Marbella, the sandy, warm, and clean beaches of the Golden Mile continue to fascinate aristocrats, business leaders, and other celebrities of note.[18]

They did indeed. Only British diplomats tried to avoid Max Hohenlohe. After the war, the Foreign Office certainly did not want to be reminded of their previous on/off relationship with him. When a diplomat reported meeting him socially in Spain in 1953, London reacted tetchily. No further contact with Hohenlohe should be made since he had played a 'sinister role during the war'.[19]

Go-betweens such as Coburg, Max Hohenlohe, and Fürstenberg had been members of the old elite, determined to become the new elite. In an age of rapid change, they had defended their spheres of influence—on a regional, national, but most importantly international level. They were all deeply opportunistic. However, not all go-betweens described here were morally questionable figures. During the First World War some genuinely wanted to help end the war. Altruism certainly played a role with Lady Paget's and Lady Barton's work. Other go-betweens had their family's long-term interests at heart. General Paget, Ernst Hohenlohe-Langenburg, the Dowager Duchess of Coburg, Max von Baden, Hohenzollern-Sigmaringen, and the Parma brothers tried to act in their house's interest but also wanted to do the best for their country.

But were these people just footnotes in history or did their work really matter?

In his farce *Noises Off*, Michael Frayn shows a theatre company performing a mediocre play. The audience does not see much of the play itself, but is invited to follow the antics in the backstage area. Here the actors struggle in chaotic circumstances, trying to keep the show on the front stage going. They have to act silently—noises off—so as not to detract from the play. What happens backstage turns out to be much more dramatic (and hilarious) than at the front.

Unfortunately international relations do not offer many hilarious moments. Yet, if one wants to write it well, one cannot do this by focusing just on what appears on stage. Official documents do not reveal the whole story. One needs access to the backstage area, otherwise one misses out an important dimension. As this book has indicated, 'backstage' is indeed a closely guarded area. Politicians have no interest in their backstage methods being revealed. They prefer to keep the secrets of their trade to themselves. This includes the names of their go-betweens and the missions they send them on. The reason for this secrecy is obvious: they know only too well how the public would react. As we have seen, revelations about people like Fürstenberg (who was rumoured to 'control' Kaiser Wilhelm II) or Prince Sixtus of Bourbon-Parma (whose failed 'mission in 1917 damaged the Habsburgs' reputation) ultimately rebounded on their employers and fuelled dangerous conspiracy theories, as illustrated in the rather bizarre story of Noel Pemberton Billing's court case in 1918 (in Chapter 2).

Apart from conspiracy theories, one reason why go-betweens have been ignored is the fact that researching them can become a historian's nightmare.

Sources on missions are extremely difficult to find. When the Hungarian Prime Minister Gömbös says in a letter to Lord Rothermere in 1932, 'Everything else I have to say, the Princess [Stephanie Hohenlohe] will tell you herself,' one could despair about his discretion. But even when things are written down, these letters seem to get 'lost', like Horthy's letter to Chamberlain, which he accompanied with the words: 'I do not want to send it through official channels.' Frustrating indeed.

The lack of sources has therefore been a great challenge for this book. Since so many royal and aristocratic archives have closed their twentieth-century material to this day, backdoors had to be found.

But apart from the difficult access to sources, another reason why questions about go-betweens were never asked was because they were simply not seen as a distinctive method used by politicians. That these missions were carried out by aristocrats made the identification even more complicated. For a long time the study of aristocrats was an unfashionable (and therefore unfunded) subject in many countries. The fact that these aristocrats had a special European network and used it was therefore never understood. A further factor why they were ignored was also a sheer lack of interest among diplomatic historians. Go-betweens make writing about diplomacy even more difficult. They are an alternative to the official policy and that makes it harder to untangle decision making processes and map links of influence. They add another layer, sometimes a confusing one. Diplomatic historians have therefore not looked deeply into back channels or have simply buried them in their footnotes. But, as we have seen, it is indeed worth finding out more about them—even if this only gives us the tip of a much larger iceberg. Tantalizingly, there is certainly much that remains to be told, especially for the Cold War period, where go-betweens also seem to have played a decisive role.

In summary, what conclusions can we draw from the analysis of go-between missions in this book?

First, go-betweens were used by all kinds of governments—constitutional monarchies, semi-autocratic monarchies, and dictatorships, as well as democracies.

Second, for a long time the aristocracy had a monopoly of go-between work because of their international networks and the 'glamour factor' of old names which Marcel Proust described so well and which gave them an entrée to many antechambers.

Third, aristocratic women were valued as go-betweens as much as their men. Go-betweens like the Dowager Duchess of Coburg, Lady Barton, Lady Paget, and in the inter-war years Stephanie Hohenlohe, were taken seriously because they had something unique to offer. Whereas institutions today like the UN agonize about using women and how 'to match mediators to the mediated' this was completely understood by previous generations of politicians. To use women as go-betweens was perceived to be highly effective. First of all, they were less visible, i.e. less noticed as political messengers. When abroad they were therefore not necessarily on the radar of enemy intelligence services or journalists. Secondly, the rules of etiquette of the upper classes made it possible for female go-betweens to attain quick access. It was socially taboo to turn down an aristocratic lady who had requested an audience. The social repercussions could be dangerous. These women usually had a wide network of correspondents and could easily make it known that they had been treated badly. When they were received, they could often have a calming effect on their male dialogue partner. They were not perceived as a male rival might have been, but could act like wise, maternal figures.

Fourth, go-betweens were often used to float an idea or even to offer an alternative to the official policy. They were a politician's dream—off the books and off the record.

Fifth, at least for the period from 1900 to 1940, go-between missions in peacetime were ultimately more successful than in wartime. In wartime the missions were, apart from the Romanian case, failures. To record them therefore seems pointless at first. But they do offer us important insights into decision making processes and show that politicians tried many alternative policies. The rhetoric to the outside world had not much to do with what they were trying to carry out behind closed doors. Nothing was therefore as predetermined as it seemed. There was a variety of possible scenarios and politicians tried them. That go-betweens failed during the First World War was certainly not their fault. Ultimately their work was tilting at windmills. Too many players with too many different interests were now involved: allies who refused to cooperate or military leaders who were pursuing their own career agenda. Nevertheless, go-betweens were still a necessity, even in wartime. When embassies were shut down, go-betweens could work in the blackout that ensued. Fürstenberg's story also suggests that ways to get out of the First World War were being eagerly looked for at a relatively early stage of the conflict. In the case of the Fürstenberg circle, this was tried in 1916, long before the official appeals for peace by the Pope.

The papal peace initiative of 1917 was an official one, but even here a senior member of the Belgian clergy was getting involved behind the scenes (Cardinal Mercier, Archbishop of Mecheln and Primate of Belgium). And as this case demonstrates, aristocrats did not have a complete monopoly on such missions. Already before the First World War, bankers and businessmen, like Albert Ballin and Ernest Cassel, had tried to broker better Anglo-German understanding. Also when during the war the two opposing envoys to The Hague, the Austrian Count Ludwig Szechenyi and the British Sir Walter Townley, could not talk to each other directly, they used a journalist as a go-between.[20] This was a first sign of what was to come. Thirty years later journalists would work as regular go-betweens.

After 1918, people demanded more transparency in diplomatic relations. Yet despite Wilson's promises, there was no '*new* diplomacy'. Neither the front nor the back stage changed much. While proper diplomats on the front stage struggled to cope with a new breed of politicians who were driven by ideologies, backstage personnel thrived. Secret channels seem to have increased in the inter-war years. Democratic leaders used them as much as dictators. President Roosevelt, for example, constantly circumvented the State Department (his relationship with Secretary of State Cordell Hull was often tense, and they differed on most points). Instead the President sent junior officers for back channel negotiations regarding China. In Britain, Chamberlain and Halifax thought of Prince Hohenlohe in 1938 as their go-between to Henlein (while in fact he was Göring's). Furthermore, when in the summer of 1939 Chamberlain started his pretence of negotiations with the Soviet Union in the foreground, in the background he signalled to Germany via a go-between that he was not seriously committed to this policy. Once war broke out, British go-betweens were active sending out peace feelers. In 1939/40 Chamberlain was besieged by many eager establishment figures who wanted to offer their services. As on the German side, the people involved were well-connected aristocrats. Though Halifax has to this day been a genius in covering his tracks, circumstantial evidence shows that he was involved in such missions. Again, what was discussed 'backstage' differed considerably from what was acted out front of stage.

The true masters of the go-between game were, however, Hitler and Göring. Hitler distrusted his diplomats from the beginning of his reign and therefore preferred back channels. This was something already noted by his contemporaries, but has never been analysed in context. Especially during the years 1938–40 Hitler was directing two plays at the same time—the one on the front stage and an unofficial one played backstage, which was kept out of the files. His backstage play was, like Frayn's *Noises Off*, acted out as silently as possible. *Not* using diplomats was, despite (or perhaps because of) the chaos it created, often a highly successful tactic. The regular diplomats naturally despised their unofficial rivals. The number two at the German embassy in London, Prince Otto II von Bismarck, at first complained about the Duke of Coburg's secret visits to Britain. Later he learnt to accept this method. After all, one of his close friends, the go-between Max Hohenlohe, was involved in it too. The official ambassador to London, von Dirksen, described the unofficial Wiedemann mission of 1938 as Hitler's usual 'chaos', thereby pretending to miss the point. In truth Dirksen had learnt his lesson and knew how useful it was to be connected with a go-between like his close friend Stephanie Hohenlohe.

Go-betweens were helping Hitler to smooth over crises in the Rhineland and the Sudetenland. They were also doing their best to portray Germany during the backstage talks as a 'reasonable' power that needed to be better understood. Their high-level contacts and their persistent cultivation of appeasers certainly helped Hitler to get away with his violations of international law between 1936 and 1939.

We have also seen how go-betweens remained useful for Hitler well into the war. Bernd Martin, who studied German intelligence activities during the Second World War, came to the conclusion that Hitler's system of using 'special emissaries' was thriving during the early stages of the war.[21] Martin did not look at go-betweens in particular but he noticed that there were agents who were not part of the official intelligence services who were extremely busy during the 'phoney war'. In fact go-betweens could signal a completely different policy from the one conveyed to the public. For instance, during his first war speech on 19 September 1939 Hitler did not mention any precise peace offers. Behind the scenes, however, Göring had already sent off his Swedish go-between Dahlerus to contact London. Dahlerus was joined shortly afterwards by Max Hohenlohe who worked for Göring in Switzerland. Göring would not have dared to do this without Hitler's approval.

The go-between missions which Hitler and Göring launched show that they were carrying out a foreign policy which ran on many different levels, often far away from the public rhetoric.

That Hitler supported such missions also clarifies the Hess flight to Scotland. Hess got his timing wrong, but what he wanted to do was by no means unusual. He knew that Hitler had used back channels before and that if they worked well, as with the Sudeten question, the go-between was amply rewarded.

After 1945 aristocrats were no longer needed for go-between missions. Other classes had developed international networks and were dominating society. Furthermore the rise of the United States and the Soviet Union as adversaries with their very different kinds of elites forced the emergence of a new variety of go-betweens that could work above, below, and around normal diplomatic channels. Artifice thus replaced heredity as the organizational principle for oiling the wheels of international relations. Today go-betweens come from all walks of life. Though they are not aristocrats any more, the job itself has not changed. It is not a relic of the past. On the contrary.

We will never know how many unofficial channels existed in the twentieth century, let alone how many exist today. However, go-betweens are certainly back in fashion. Surveillance of all kinds of communications—phones, texts, emails—has nowadays become omnipresent. Confidentiality through electronic means can therefore never be guaranteed. *Not* to be recorded has become a luxury. This makes direct personal contact vital. If one wants to avoid being recorded, one needs a 'harmless' looking private individual who is discreet, has good contacts, and a good memory in order to discuss policies face to face.

This gives go-betweens a new role to play. They are the safest option for politicians in the twenty-first century. Despite all the demands for more transparency, go-betweens will always be with us.

Abbreviations

AOBS	Archiv der Otto-von-Bismarck-Stiftung. Friedrichsruh
BAB	Bundesarchiv Berlin-Lichterfelde
BAK	Bundesarchiv Koblenz
CCAC	Churchill Archives
DNVP	Deutschnationale Volkspartei (German National People's party)
FAS	Hausarchiv Hohenzollern-Sigmaringen
FCAC	Fürstlich Castell'sches Archiv, Castell
FFAD	Fürstlich Fürstenbergisches Archiv, Donaueschingen
FÖWA	Fürstlich Öttingen-Wallerstein'sches Archiv, Öttingen
GStAPK	Geheimes Staatsarchiv Preussischer Kulturbesitz, Berlin
HZA	Hohenlohe Zentralarchiv
NA	National Archives London
NSDAP/AO	Auslandsorganisation der NSDAP
OC	Organisation Consul
OSS	Office of Strategic Services
PA AA	Politisches Archiv des Auswärtigen Amtes
RA	Royal Archives Windsor Castle
SA	Sturmabteilung (Storm Troop)
SD	Sicherheitsdienst (Security Services)
SPD	Social Democratic Party
SS	Schutz-Staffel
STAWKB	Staatsarchiv Wertheim- Kloster Brombach
ULC	University Library, Cambridge
USPD	Unabhängige (independent) Socialist Party
WSC	Workers' and Soldiers' Council

Notes

INTRODUCTION

1. The pregnant Princess Marie Jose was married to the Italian Crown Prince Umberto.
2. 27 July 1940, Mackensen to German Foreign Ministry. German embassy Rome (Quirinal), Secret. Visas for members of the German Royal Houses and nobility, GFM33/791, NA. (791)
3. HW 1/3709, NA.

CHAPTER I

1. Martin Kilduff and Wenpin Tsai, *Social Networks and Organizations*, London, 2003, p. 5. See also Karina Urbach, 'Netzwerk', in Gerrit Walther and Michael Maaser (eds), *Bildung: Ziele und Formen, Traditionen und Systeme, Medien und Akteure*, Stuttgart, 2010.
2. The phrase Track II was coined by Joseph V. Montville, a former State Department diplomat.
3. See for this Verena Steller, *Diplomatie von Angesicht zu Angesicht. Diplomatische Handlungsformen in den deutsch-französischen Beziehungen 1870–1919*, Paderborn, 2011.
4. Vladimir Putin on 10 February 2007 at the Munich Security Conference.
5. Walter Demel, 'Der europäische Adel vor der Revolution: Sieben Thesen', in Ronald G. Asch (ed.), *Der europäische Adel im Ancien Regime. Von der Krise der ständischen Monarchien bis zur Revolution 1688–1789*, Cologne, 2001, 420.
6. Heinz Höhne, *The Order of the Death's Head: The Story of Hitler's SS*, London, 2001.
7. Thomas Mann, *Pariser Rechenschaftsbericht*, Berlin, 1926, cited in Anita Ziegerhofer-Prettenthaler, *Botschafter Europas. Richard Nikolaus Coudenhove-Kalergi und die Paneuropa-Bewegung in den zwanziger und dreißiger Jahren*, Vienna, 2003, 31.
8. Viscount Lymington, *A Knot of Roots: An Autobiography*, London, 1965, 146.
9. See also Georg Simmel, 'Zur Soziologie des Adels. Fragment aus einer Formenlehre der Gesellschaft', in Alessandro Cavalli and Volker Krech (eds), *Georg Simmel, Aufsätze und Abhandlungen, 1901–1908*, Frankfurt a. M., 1993.

10. Ibid.
11. Lord Hardinge to Sir Ralph Paget, 29 Nov. 1917. The private papers of Lord Charles Hardinge of Penshurst, Vol. 35, fos. 203f. University Library Cambridge (ULC).
12. Czernin to Baernreither in 1916, see *Der Verfall des Habsburgerreiches und die Deutschen. Fragmente eines politischen Tagebuchs 1897–1917*, ed. Oskar Mitis, Vienna, 1939, 267.
13. See for this: Bernd Martin, *Friedensinitiativen und Machtpolitik im Zweiten Weltkrieg 1939–1942*, Düsseldorf, 1974, 27.
14. See Oliver Bange on Willy Brandt's negotiations: 'The Stasi Confronts Western Strategies for Transformation 1966–1975', in J. Haslam and K. Urbach (eds), *Secret Intelligence in the European States System 1918–1989*, Stanford, Calif., 2013, 187.
15. Anna Keay, 'The Shadow King', in Philip Mansel and Torsten Riotte (eds), *Monarchy and Exile: The Politics of Legitimacy from Marie de Médicis to Wilhelm II*, London, 2011, 116.
16. Antonia Potter, 'In Search of the Textbook Mediator', in H. Martin, *Kings of Peace. Pawns of War*, New York, 2006, 100.
17. Ibid. 161.
18. Arno Mayer, *The Persistence of the Old Regime: Europe to the Great War*, New York, 1981.
19. Vansittart quoted in Patricia Meehan, *The Unnecessary War: Whitehall and the German Resistance to Hitler*, London, 1992.
20. See Angelika Linke, *Sprachkultur und Bürgertum. Zur Mentalitätsgeschichte des 19. Jahrhunderts*, Stuttgart, 1996, 3. Bo Strath (ed.), *Language and Construction of Class Identities*, Göteborg, 1990.
21. H. G.V. Studnitz, quoted in *Der Monat. Zeitschrift für Politik und geistiges Leben*, 9/100, Berlin, 1956, 43ff.
22. Ross McKibbin, *Classes and Cultures: England 1918–1951*, Oxford, 1998, 37.
23. See also James N. Retallack, *Germany in the Age of Kaiser Wilhelm II*, London, 1996.
24. Volker Stalmann, *Fürst Chlodwig zu Hohenlohe-Schillingsfürst 1819–1901. Ein deutscher Reichskanzler*, Paderborn, 2009.
25. Memorandum of Hohenzollern-Sigmaringen's conversation with Foreign Secretary Kühlmann, 4 Oct. 1917, Fürstlich Hohezollernsches Haus-und Domänearchiv, FAS, (Dep. 39), HS T18, Staatsarchiv Sigmaringen, FAS.
26. Monique de Saint Martin, *Der Adel. Soziologie eines Standes*, Konstanz, 2003, 35.
27. Julian Fellowes, *Snobs*, London, 2005, 57.
28. Alan S. C. Ross, *Linguistic Class-Indicators in Present-Day English*, London, 1953, 46.
29. P. G. Wodehouse, *Blandings Castle*, London, 1935.
30. Wolfgang Frühwald, 'Büchmann und die Folgen. Zur sozialen Funktion des Bildungszitates in der deutschen Literatur des 19. Jahrhunderts', in Reinhart Koselleck (ed.), *Bildungsbürgertum im 19. Jahrhundert. Teil II. Bildungsgüter und Bildungswissen*, Stuttgart, 1990, 197–220.

31. Aldous Huxley, 'Tillotson Banquet', in *Mortal Coils*, London, 1922.
32. Quoted in Karina Urbach, 'Adel versus Bürgertum. Überlebens- und Aufstiegsstrategien im deutsch-britischen Vergleich', in Franz Bosbach, Keith Robbins, and Karina Urbach (eds), *Geburt oder Leistung? Birth or Talent? The Formation of Elites in a British–German Comparison*, Munich, 2003, 25.
33. Michael Luke, *Hansel Pless: Prisoner of History*, London, 2002, 28.
34. Ibid.
35. Diary Victoria Bentinck, Bentinck Privatarchiv, Delden. Schloss Twickel TW 2012ff.
36. Daisy Pless, *Tanz auf dem Vulkan. Erinnerungen an Deutschland und Englands Schicksalswende*, Dresden, 1931, 14.
37. Aufzeichungen des Schloßverwalters Ebert 'Lebenslauf des Fürsten bis 1912', Papers of Karl Öttingen-Wallerstein, VIII, 19. 1b, No. 24, in Archiv der Fürsten Öttingen-Wallerstein, Harburg (FÖWAH).
38. Hans von Tresckow, *Von Fürsten und anderen Sterblichen. Erinnerungen eines Kriminalkommissars*, Berlin, 1922, 171.
39. HRH Prince Philip, Duke of Edinburgh, quoted in Jonathan Petropoulos, *Royals and the Reich: The Princes von Hessen in Nazi Germany*, Oxford, 2006, xix.
40. See for this envy: Rudolf Muhs, 'Geisteswehen: Rahmenbedingungen des deutsch-britischen Kulturaustausches im 19. Jahrhundert', in Rudolf Muhs, J. Paulmann, and W. Steinmetz (eds), *Aneignung und Abwehr. Arbeitskreis Deutsche England-Forschung*, Bodenheim, 1998, 44ff.
41. Nachlass Ernst II, LA A 7206, Staatsarchiv Coburg.
42. Pierre Bourdieu, 'Ökonomisches Kapital, kulturelles Kapital, soziales Kapital', in Reinhard Kreckel (ed.), *Soziale Ungleichheiten*, Göttingen, 1983. See also Monique de Saint Martin, *Der Adel: Soziologie eines Standes*, Konstanz, 2003.
43. F. Scott Fitzgerald, *The Great Gatsby*, ch. 9.
44. Randolph Trumbach, *The Rise of the Egalitarian Family: Aristocratic Kinship and Domestic Relations in 18th Century England*, New York, 1978, 7.
45. Peter N. Stearns and Carol Z. Stearns, 'Emotionology: Clarifying the History of Emotions and Emotional Standards', *American Historical Review*, 90/4 (October 1985), 828.
46. See for this technique Eva Giloi, *Monarchy, Myth, and Material Culture in Germany 1750–1950*, Cambridge, 2014 and Ewald Frie, *Friedrich August Ludwig von der Marwitz 1777–1837: Biographien eines Preussen*, Paderborn, 2001.
47. *Leipziger Neueste Nachrichten*, 22 April 1899. Quoted in Rainer Hambrecht, 'Eine Dynastie- zwei Namen. Haus Sachsen-Coburg und Gotha und Haus Windsor. Ein Beitrag zur Nationalisierung der Monarchien in Europa', in Wolfram Pyta and Ludwig Richter (eds), *Gestaltungskraft des Politischen. Festschrift für Eberhard Kolb*, Berlin, 1998, 291.
48. *Berliner Tageblatt* quoted ibid.
49. Alice, Countess of Athlone, *For my Grandchildren: Some Reminiscences of Her Royal Highness Princess Alice*, London, 1967, 84.

50. N. F. Hayward and D. S. Morris, *The First Nazi Town*, Aldershot, 1988.
51. Alice, Countess of Athlone, *Grandchildren*, 90.
52. Ibid.
53. Carl Eduard to Alice, 1 August 1902, Charles Duke of Saxe-Coburg and Gotha to his sister Alice Countess of Athlone, RA ACA/10, Royal Archives Windsor.
54. 9 November 1903. Ibid.
55. Glücksburg. 23 February 1905. Carl Eduard to Alice. RA ACA/10.
56. See for this Ulrike Grunewald, *Luise von Sachsen-Coburg-Saalfeld (1800–1831): Lebensräume einer unangepassten Herzogin*, Cologne, 2013.
57. Fritz Hesse thought that Coburg did not feel like an Englishman, but that he still spoke German with an English accent. Fritz Hesse, *Das Vorspiel zum Kriege* Leoni am Starnberger See, 1979, 28.
58. Robert Musil, *Der Mann ohne Eigenschaften*, 1930–41.
59. Holger Afflerbach, *Der Dreibund. Europäische Großmacht und Allianzpolitik vor dem Ersten Weltkrieg*, Cologne, 2002. Holger Afflerbach, 'Der Dreibund als Instrument der europäischen Friedenssicherung vor 1914', in Helmut Rumpler and Jan Paul Niederkorn (eds), *Der Zweibund 1879. Das deutsch-österreichisch-ungarische Bündnis und die europäische Diplomatie*, Vienna, 1996. Jürgen Angelow, *Kalkül und Prestige: Der Zweibund am Vorabend des Ersten Weltkrieges*, Cologne, 2000.
60. Peter Katzenstein, *Disjointed Partners: Austria and Germany since 1815*, Berkeley, 1976, quoted in Angelow, *Zweibund*, 331.
61. See for this group Heinz Gollwitzer, *Die Standesherren. Die politische Stellung der Mediatisierten 1815–1918. Ein Beitrag zur deutschen Sozialgeschichte*, Göttingen, 2nd edn 1964.
62. Aufzeichungen des Schloßverwalters Ebert 'Lebenslauf des Fürsten bis 1912', Papers of Karl Öttingen-Wallerstein, VIII, 19. 1b, No. 24, in: Fürstlich Öttingen-Wallerstein'sches Archiv der Fürsten Öttingen- Wallerstein und der Fürsten Öttingen-Spielberg, FÖWA.
63. Fürstin Therese Waldburg-Zeil to her husband, 24 November 1916, Nachlass Georg Waldburg-Zeil, Nr. 17 III, Archiv Waldburg-Zeil.
64. To piece together Fürstenberg's influence, a wide range of papers have been used (from his private archive in Donaueschingen, the archive Hechingen, the Generallandesarchiv Karlsruhe and the Staatsarchiv Sigmaringen and Staatsarchiv München Mikrofilmsammlung).
65. Fred Wille, *Rings um den Kaiser*, Berlin, 1913, 45.
66. R 1273, Königlich Preussische Gesandtschaft für Baden, Karlsruhe 4 October 1909, confidential: To Bethmann-Hollweg, Auswärtiges Amt, PA AA.
67. See Kathy Lerman, 'The Decisive Relationship: Kaiser Wilhelm II and Chancellor Bernhard von Bülow, 1900–1905', in John Röhl and Nicolaus Sombart, *Kaiser Wilhelm II. New Interpretations. The Corfu Papers*, Cambridge, 1982.
68. Prince Bernhard von Bülow, ed. F. von Stockhammer, London, 1931–2 (trans. F. A. Voigt), i. 149.

69. Volker Press, 'Das Haus Fürstenberg in der deutschen Geschichte', in Franz Brendle and Anton Schindling (eds), *Adel im Alten Reich. Gesammelte Vorträge und Aufsätze*, Tübingen, 1998, 165.
70. Victor von Fritsche, *Bilder aus dem österreichischen Hof- und Gesellschaftsleben*, Vienna, 1914.
71. Heinrich Prinz von Schönburg-Waldenburg, *Erinnerungen aus kaiserlicher Zeit*, Leipzig, 1929, 173.
72. Isabel V. Hull, *The Entourage of Kaiser Wilhelm II 1888–1918*, Cambridge, 1982. Ibid. 'Kaiser Wilhelm and the Liebenberg Circle', in John Röhl and Nicolaus Sombart (eds), *Kaiser Wilhelm II: New Interpretations. The Corfu Papers*, Cambridge, 1982.
73. Fürstenberg to Wilhelm II, 8 December 1906, Geheimes Staatsarchiv, BPH Rep. 53 J. Lit F Nr. 3.
74. 24 November 1908. Ibid.
75. Fürstenberg to his wife Irma, 31 March 1912, Fürstenbergarchive, FFAD.
76. Fürstenberg to Irma, 6 April 1908. Ibid.
77. Fürstenberg to Irma, 4 April 1912. Ibid.
78. 6 April 1912. Ibid.
79. 18 April 1908, Diary. Ibid.
80. Viktoria Luise, Herzogin von Braunschweig, *Im Glanz der Krone*, Göttingen, 1967, 227.
81. Fürstenberg to Oberamtsmann Dr Strauss, 16 March 1911 (copy, Fürstenbergarchive Donaueschingen).
82. Telegram, 24 November 1907, Großherzogliches Familienarchiv: Nachlass Friedrich Großherzog und Großherzogin von Baden, FA, Generallandesarchiv Karlsruhe.
83. Fürstenberg Diary, 17 April 1909, p. 10. Fürstenbergarchiv, Donaueschingen.
84. See William D. Godsey, *Aristocratic Redoubt: The Austro-Hungarian Foreign Office on the Eve of the First World War*, West Lafayette, Ind., 1999, 185 and 210f.
85. John C. G. Röhl, *Kaiser, Hof und Staat. Wilhelm II. und die deutsche Politik*, Munich, 1987, 93.
86. Wolfgang Mommsen, *War der Kaiser an allem schuld? Wilhelm II. und die preussisch-deutschen Machteliten*, Berlin, 2002.
87. Robert Scheu quoted in Gilbert Carr, 'Ein Heiratsbureau der Gedanken in der Wiener Jahrhundertwende. Zum kulturpolitischen Versuch Robert Scheus um 1900', in Jürgen Barkhoff, Hartmut Böhme, and Jeanne Riou (eds), *Netzwerke. Eine Kulturtechnik der Moderne*, Cologne, 2004, 198.
88. See for this, for example, Norbert Elias, *Die Höfische Gesellschaft. Untersuchungen zur Soziologie des Königtums und der höfischen Aristokratie*, Frankfurt a. M., 1983.
89. 15 April 1908, Tagebuch Fürstenberg, Donaueschingen.
90. Hull, *Entourage*, 153.
91. Joseph Maria Baernreither, *Der Verfall des Habsburgerreiches und die Deutschen. Fragmente eines politischen Tagebuchs 1897–1917*, ed. Oskar Mitis, Vienna, 1939, 119.

92. Fürstenberg to Wilhelm II, BHP Rep. 53 J. Lit F Nr. 3.
93. Ibid. 17 September 1907.
94. Baernreither diary entry 22 January 1913, Fragments of a political diary by Joseph M. Baernreither, ed. Joseph Redlich, London, 1930, 169f.
95. Fürstenberg to Jagow, 12 March 1913 (copy, Fürstenbergarchiv, Donaueschingen).
96. Fürstenberg to Paul Graf Almeida, 13 March 1913. Ibid.
97. Fürstenberg to ambassador Count Szögyenyi, 3 June 1913. Ibid.
98. Kaiserliche Deutsche Botschaft in Wien, 10 April 1913, Report to Bethmann-Hollweg; R 14303, PA AA.
99. 17 April 1908, Diary Fürstenberg, Donaueschingen.
100. 22 April 1909. Ibid.
101. 4 September 1909. Ibid. Lawrence Sondhaus, *The Naval Policy of Austria-Hungary 1867–1918: Navalism, Industrial Development, and the Politics of Dualism*, West Lafayette, Ind., 1994.
102. Ivo Lambi, *The Navy and German Power Politics 1862–1914*, London, 1984, 25.
103. 25 March 1911. Fürstenberg Diary, Donaueschingen.
104. Ibid.
105. Ibid.
106. 13 April 1908, Ibid.
107. Peter Winzen, *Das Kaiserreich am Abgrund. Die Daily Telegraph-Affäre und das Hale Interview von 1908*, Stuttgart, 2002.
108. Telegram, Wilhelm II to Fürstenberg, 16 November 1908, Fürstenberg Papers, Donaueschingen (FFAD).
109. In his memoirs Bülow described this as particularly frivolous. In fact he had sent the Kaiser off to Donaueschingen for recreation. Later Bülow claimed to have been shocked about Wilhelm II's trip during a time of crisis. Prince Bernhard von Bülow, ed by F. von Stockhammern, London 1931–2 (translated by F. A. Voigt), II. 353.
110. Wilhelm II to Max Egon Fürstenberg, 23 December 1908, Fürstenbergnachlass Donaueschingen.
111. Max Egon Fürstenberg to his wife, 1 April 1909, Ibid.
112. Prince Bernhard von Bülow, III. 25. Bülow was of the firm opinion that Fürstenberg had always intrigued against him. See also Bülow, II. 457 and 467.
113. Fürstenberg Diary, 31 March 1912, Donaueschingen.
114. Fürstenberg to Dr Rudolf Sieghan, 5 June 1913 (copy, Donaueschingen).
115. Baernreither diary entry 31 January 1913, Fragments of a political diary by Joseph M. Baernreither, ed. Joseph Redlich, London, 1930, 162.
116. 4 March 1913, ibid. 183.
117. Von Tschirschky to Jagow, 22 May 1914, quoted in Mommsen, *War der Kaiser*, 384.
118. Dumby in Oscar Wilde's *Lady Windermere's Fan* (1892).

CHAPTER 2

1. Aloys Löwenstein to his wife, 14 September 1914, LitD 761d., Staatsarchiv Wertheim.
2. July 1915, Duke of Portland to his Dutch relative Godard Bentinck, see Bentinck papers, Haus Amerogen, Reichsarchiv Utrecht, the Netherlands.
3. Linda Colley, *Britons: Forging the Nation 1707–1837*, London, 1992, 6.
4. See for this Karina Urbach, 'Zwischen Aktion und Reaktion. Die süddeutschen Standesherren und der Erste Weltkrieg', in Eckart Conze and Monika Wienfort (eds), *Adel und Moderne. Elitengeschichte im 19. und 20. Jahrhundert im europäischen Vergleich*, Munich, 2004.
5. Prinz Alain Rohan, Archiv für Sippenforschung, 6. Jg., Nr. 2, February 1929, 63.
6. Marie von Bunsen, *Die Welt in der ich lebte. Erinnerungen aus glücklichen Jahren 1860–1912*, Leipzig, 1929, 16.
7. Quoted in Diana Fotescu (ed.), *Americans and Queen Marie of Romania: A Selection of Documents*, Oxford, 1998, 121.
8. *Kölnische Zeitung*, 496, 20 June 1916.
9. Ibid.
10. Karl Kraus, *Die letzten Tage der Menschheit*, Part I.
11. Papers of Sir Francis Bertie (uncatalogued), deposited in Welbeck Archive (part of Ivy, Duchess of Portland Papers).
12. Grand Duke of Hesse, *Erinnertes. Aufzeichnungen des letzten Großherzogs Ernst Ludwig von Hessen und bei Rhein*, ed. Eckhart G. Franz, Darmstadt, 1983, 146f.
13. Fürstin von Pless, *Tanz auf dem Vulkan. Erinnerungen an Deutschlands und Englands Schicksalswende*, Dresden, 1930, 34.
14. Ibid. 171.
15. Max von Baden to Daisy Pless, 31 March 1916, Pless, *Vulkan*, 223.
16. Ibid. 80.
17. Victoria Bentinck, Diary. Archiv Twickel, Delden.
18. Diary entry 1 September 1914, Fürst Emich Leiningen Papers, Karton 7, Tagebücher 1910–1913, Leiningen Archive Amorbach.
19. 6 November 1917, Leiningen to his oldest son. Ibid.
20. Quoted in Fotescu (ed.), *Americans and Queen Marie of Romania*, 110.
21. Letter from 29 January 1936, death of George V. Ibid.
22. Prince Pless to his wife, 21 July 1916. Quoted in Pless, *Vulkan*, 244.
23. Carl Eduard to Alice, 27 November 1923, Charles Duke of Saxe Coburg and Gotha to his sister Alice Countess of Athlone. Athlone Papers, RA ACA/10.
24. Alice, Countess of Athlone, *Grandchildren*, 105.
25. Hesse, *Erinnertes*, 147.
26. Quoted in Angelika Püschel, 'Carl Eduard von Coburg', BA thesis in Staatsarchive Coburg, 25.
27. Alice, Countess of Athlone, *Grandchildren*, 160.

28. 3 August 1914, Diary entry Fürstenberg papers, FFAD.
29. Wilhlem II to Max Egon Fürstenberg, 14 August 1914. Ibid.
30. Letters by Baernreither to Fürstenberg, 20 November 1915, FFAD.
31. Telegram of the German embassy in Vienna, 30 June 1917, Auswärtiges Amt, R 8825, PA-AA.
32. Letter from the German embassy in Vienna, 9 November 1916, R 20107. Ibid.
33. Memorandum of a meeting on 24 October 1916 at Fürst Max Egon II Fürstenberg's in Vienna. Ten-page memorandum written by Baernreither. Envelope *Parliamentary Life*, July–December 1916, private papers Max Egon Fürstenberg, FFAD. A longer version is among Baernreithers papers: Joseph Maria Baernreither, *Der Verfall des Habsburgerreiches und die Deutschen. Fragmente eines politischen Tagebuchs 1897–1917*, ed. Oskar Mitis, Vienna, 1939, 263ff.
34. Alfonso XIII was from 1902 to 1931 King of Spain and died in exile in 1941.
35. Memorandum of a meeting on 24 October 1916 at Fürst Max Egon II Fürstenberg in Vienna, FFAD.
36. In the original German he calls him 'gemütlich'. Ibid.
37. Not all of them inherited the gene, though—the current King of Spain is Alfonso XIII's great-grandson.
38. Jose Maria Arin Arce, 'Alfons XIII', in Paul Hoser, Walter Bernecker, and Carlos Collado Seidel, (eds), *Die spanischen Könige*, Munich, 1997, 269ff.
39. See for this: Javier Tusell and Genoveva G. Queipo de Llano, *Alfonso XIII: El rey pólemico*, Madrid, 2001, 285.
40. Ibid. 288.
41. 8 April 1918, Fürstenberg to Clam-Martinic, copy, Fürstenberg papers, FFAD.
42. Telegram from Wedel to AA, Vienna, 18 February 1918, R 9004.
43. Wolfgang Steglich, *Die Friedenspolitik der Mittelmächte 1917/18*, Wiesbaden, 1964 (Habilitationsschrift 1963), 15.
44. Sarsina, Donna Francoise Aldobrandini, born Comtese de La Rochefoucauld 1844–1921.
45. Memorandum by Sir Hugh Whittal, Geneva, 14 April 1918, quoted in Steglich, *Die Friedensversuche der kriegführenden Mächte im Sommer und Herbst 1917. Quellenkritische Untersuchungen, Akten und Vernehmungsprotokolle*, Stuttgart, 1984, 77.
46. Joseph Maria Baernreither, *Der Verfall des Habsburgerreiches und die Deutschen. Fragmente eines politischen Tagebuchs 1897–1917*, ed. Oskar Mitis, Vienna, 1939, 192.
47. Ibid. 196.
48. Steglich, *Die Friedenspolitik*, 19.
49. Ibid. 49.
50. Quoted ibid. 49.
51. Ibid. 54.
52. In 2008 it became the Graduate Institute of International and Development Studies.
53. Milan Babík, 'George D. Herron and the Eschatological Foundations of Woodrow Wilson's Foreign Policy, 1917–1919', *Diplomatic History*, 35/5 (November 2011), 846.

54. 31 October 1918, German ambassador Wedel telegram. PA AA.
55. Max Fürstenberg, Vol. bb II/4 Letter to Emperor William, 17 August 1921 (copy), FFAD.
56. Queen of Romania to George V, 30 August 1916, Marie Queen of Romania, *The Story of my Life*, Vol. III London, 1935, 57.
57. Ibid. III, 424.
58. Quoted in Elizabeth Longford, *Victoria RI*, London, 1964. See also A. N. Wilson, *Victoria: A Life*, London, 2014.
59. Letter to his father Hermann Hohenlohe-Langenburg, 6 April 1894. Ernst Hohenlohe-Langenburg Papers, Hohenlohe Papers, HZA.
60. Barbara Jelavich, 'Romania in the First World War: The Pre-War Crisis, 1912–1914', *International History Review*, 14/3 (August 1992). The treaty was to be activated if Russia attacked one of the signatories.
61. Originally William as the older son should have become Crown Prince of Romania, but he renounced his right of succession in favour of his younger brother Ferdinand.
62. See for this Jagow to Hohenlohe, 11 June 1915, HZA.
63. Arrival in Romania on 14 July 1915. PA AA 6259. R 1872.
64. Lamar Cecil, 'Der diplomatische Dienst im kaiserlichen Deutschland', in Klaus Schwabe (ed.), *Das Diplomatische Korps 1871–1945*, Boppard, 1945, 23. See also Ralf Forsbach, 'Adel und Bürgertum im deutschen auswärtigen Dienst 1867–1950', in Franz Bosbach, Keith Robbins, and Karina Urbach (eds), *Geburt oder Leistung? Birth or Talent? The Formation of Elites in a British-German Comparison*, Munich, 2003.
65. That a proportionally large number of aristocrats were involved in such work during the First World War has so far been indicated only by the work of Wolfgang Steglich. In the 1960s Steglich researched the subject of peace feelers during the First World War. He did not distinguish between the unofficial and the official. What he did not notice was that many of the unofficial peace feelers he found were by internationally connected aristocrats. Steglich, *Die Friedenspolitik*. Ibid. *Die Friedensversuche*.
66. See for this Karina Urbach, 'Diplomat, Höfling und Verbandsfunktionär. Süddeutsche Standesherren 1880–1945', in Günther Schulz and Markus A. Denzel (eds), *Deutscher Adel im 19. und 20. Jahrhundert*, St. Katharinen, 2004, 360f.
67. Alois to his wife, 1916, Löwenstein papers, Wertheim.
68. Report Busche, Auswärtiges Amt, PA AA Vol. 6259.
69. Marie of Romania, *The Story of my Life*, 22.
70. Quoted in Hannah Pakula, *The Last Romantic: A Biography of Queen Marie of Roumania*, New York, 1986, 176.
71. Marie of Romania, *The Story of my Life*, III. 7.
72. Fürst Wilhelm Hohenzollern-Sigmaringen, Dep 39, HS1-80, FAS Hausarchiv Hohenzollern-Sigmaringen, FAS.
73. Ibid.
74. Ibid.

75. Jagow to Hohenlohe, 11 June 1915, in Nachlass Ernst II, Botschafter in Konstantinopel, HZA.
76. Ibid.
77. Ibid.
78. Marie of Romania, *The Story of my Life*, III. 25.
79. Marie of Romania, *The Story of my Life*, II. 323.
80. Marie of Romania, *Later Chapters of my Life: The Lost Memoir of Queen Marie of Romania*, ed. Diana Mandache, London, 2004, XXV.
81. See Fotescu (ed.), *Americans and Queen Marie of Romania.*
82. Ibid.
83. Marie of Romania, *The Story of my Life*, III, 26.
84. Ibid. 30.
85. Ibid. 26.
86. 'I knew that Alix had given this illness to her heir, and I dared not face such a risk for our family.' Marie of Romania, *The Story of my Life*, II. 323.
87. Marie of Romania, *The Story of my Life*, II. 327.
88. Ibid. III.31.
89. Ibid. 30.
90. It was a simple technique according to the Grand Duchess: 'I just received the enclosed letter from Nicky in answer to yours which I handed over to him.' Ibid. III. 36.
91. Quoted in ibid.
92. Jagow to Hohenlohe-Langenburg, 10 June 1916, Hohenlohe Papers, HZA.
93. HS 1 T9, 53, Nr. 176. Fürstlich Hohenzollerisches Haus und Domänearchiv, Depositium 39, HS T 10, Number 23, FAS.
94. HS 1 T9, 53, Nr. 176. Ibid.
95. Ibid.
96. Sophie Ruppel, 'Geschwisterbeziehungen im Adel und Norbert Elias' Figurationssoziologie—ein Anwendungsversuch', in Claudia Opitz (ed.), *Höfische Gesellschaft und Zivilisationsprozess. Norbert Elias' Werk in kulturwissenschaftlicher Perspektive*, Cologne/Weimar, 2005, 220.
97. Pakula, *Marie*, 197.
98. Hohenlohe's diary, 3 September 1916, Hohenlohe-Langeburg, HZA.
99. Luise was the daughter of Emperor William I.
100. 18 September 1916, Hohenlohe to Luise von Baden, copy, HZA.
101. 30 October 1916. Ibid.
102. 27 December 1916. Ibid.
103. Hohenzollern-Sigmaringen Papers, HS T 10 23, Staatsarchiv Sigmaringen, FAS.
104. Memo 6 November 1916. Ibid.
105. 24 September 1916, Marie to Nicky. Quoted in Marie of Romania, *The Story of my Life*, III. 66.
106. Marie of Romania, *The Story of my Life*, III. 150.

107. Ibid. 155.
108. Ibid. 151f.
109. Marie Dorothea Radziwill, *Briefe vom deutschen Kaiserhof, 1889–1915*, Berlin, 1936, 120.
110. Quoted in ibid.
111. Hesse, *Erinnertes*, 68.
112. Ibid. 98.
113. Mansel and Riotte, *Monarchy and Exile*, 6.
114. Antonio Niño, 'El rey embajador: Alfonso XIII en la política internacional', in Javier Moreno Luzón (ed.), *Alfonso XIII: Un político en el trono*, Madrid, 2003, 267.
115. Quoted in 'The Diary of George Huntington's Visit with Queen Marie at Cotroceni Palace, Bucharest 1925', in Fotescu (ed.), *Americans and Queen Marie of Romania*.
116. Stefan Gammelien, *Wilhelm II und Schweden-Norwegen 1888–1905*, Berlin, 2012.
117. Summary of Ernst Hohenlohe, who was the penfriend of Luise von Baden. 9 May 1918, Hohenlohe Papers, HZA.
118. Karina Urbach and Bernd Buchner, 'Houston Stewart Chamberlain und Prince Max von Baden', *Vierteljahrshefte für Zeitgeschichte* 2004.
119. While Matthias and Morsey have not realized this, Lothar Gall's short portrait of Baden was already indicating it. See Erich Matthias and Rudolf Morsey (eds), *Die Regierung des Prinzen Max von Baden*, Düsseldorf, 1962, xxix. Lothar Gall, 'Max von Baden (1867–1929)', in Wilhelm von Sternburg (ed.), *Die deutschen Kanzler. Von Bismarck bis Schmidt*, Frankfurt am Main, 1985, 137–43.
120. Quoted in Urbach and Buchner, 'Chamberlain', 123.
121. Quoted in Lothar Machtan, *Prinz Max von Baden. Der letzte Kanzler des Kaisers*, Berlin, 2013, 263.
122. W. N. Carlgren, *Neutralität oder Allianz. Deutschlands Beziehungen zu Schweden in den Anfangsjahren des Ersten Weltkrieges*, Stockholm Studies in History, Vol. 6, Stockholm, 1962, 213.
123. Ibid. 214.
124. Machtan, *Prinz Max von Baden*, 265.
125. See Patrick Vonderau, *Schweden und das nationalsozialistische Deutschland. Eine annotierte Bibliographie der deutschsprachigen Forschungsliteratur*, Stockholm, 2003.
126. See also Golo Mann, Introduction to Prince Max von Baden, *Erinnerungen und Gedanken*, Stuttgart, 1968, 76.
127. Quoted ibid.
128. Matthew Rendle, 'The Symbolic Revolution: The Russian Nobility and February 1917', *Revolutionary Russia*, 18/1 (June 2005), 23ff.
129. It was also rumoured that he supported another plan by the German Foreign Ministry to rescue the Tsar. This could not be verified though.
130. See Golo Mann, Introduction to Prince Max von Baden. *Erinnerungen und Gedanken*, 85.
131. Quoted ibid.

132. See for this a report of Wilhelm Hohenzollern-Sigmaringen about his visit to House Doorn from 10 to 17 August 1922. Staatsarchiv Sigmaringen Dep. 39 HS T 9 (KW) 53, FAS.
133. See for marriage contracts: Daniel Schönpflug, *Die Heiraten der Hohenzollern. Verwandtschaft, Politik und Ritual in Europa 1640–1918*, Göttingen, 2013.
134. Monika Kubrova, *Vom guten Leben. Adelige Frauen im 19. Jahrhundert*, Berlin, 2011.
135. Potter, 'In Search of the Textbook Mediator', 167.
136. 7 November 1917, Paget to her son, quoted in Steglich, *Die Friedenspolitik*, 109.
137. Lady Walburga Paget to Queen Maria Christine of Spain, 1 October 1917, The private papers of Sir Ralph Spencer Paget, Additional Manuscripts 51253, quoted in Steglich, *Die Friedenspolitik*, 103.
138. In her memoirs she did not mention her mission. Lady Walburga Paget, *Scenes and Memories*, London, 1923.
139. Sir Ralph Paget to Lord Hardinge of Penshurst, 26 October 1917, Steglich, *Die Friedenspolitik*, 105.
140. Christopher Clark, *The Sleepwalkers: How Europe Went to War in 1914*, London, 2013, 202.
141. Paget to her son, 7 November 1917, quoted in Steglich, *Die Friedenspolitik*, 108.
142. Ibid.
143. Ibid.
144. Ibid.
145. Ibid.
146. Steglich, *Die Friedenspolitik*, 6.
147. 5 August 1917, Austro-Hungarian Ambassador Prince Hohenlohe-Schillingsfürst to Austro-Hungarian Foreign Secretary Count Czernin, quoted in Steglich, *Die Friedenspolitik*, 98.
148. Steglich, *Die Friedenspolitik*, xlvii.
149. Paget to Queen of Spain, 1 October 1917, Steglich, *Die Friedenspolitik*, 103.
150. Ibid.
151. Steglich, *Die Friedenspolitik*, xlvii.
152. Hardinge to Lady Paget, 6 November 1917, quoted in Steglich, *Die Friedenspolitik*, 110.
153. Hardinge to Paget, 29 November 1917, Cambridge University Library, The Private Papers of Lord Charles Hardinge of Penshurst, Vol. 35, fos. 203–4, also quoted in Steglich, *Die Friedenspolitik*, 112.
154. Quoted in Steglich, *Die Friedenspolitik*, 108.
155. See for this the Home Office Files HO 144/1489/364780. Proceedings at the Central Criminal Court, Rex v. Noel Pemberton-Billing, 29, 30, 31 May and 1, 3, 4 June 1918. The Official Record. See also Karina Urbach, 'Das schwarze Buch. Kollektive Paranoia im Ersten Weltkrieg', in Andreas Fahrmeir and Sabine Freitag, *Mord und andere Kleinigkeiten*, Munich, 2001.
156. Philip Hoare, *Oscar Wilde's Last Stand*, London, 1997; Michael Kettle, *Salome's Last Veil*, London, 1977. Both authors believe in conspiracy theories.

157. Hoare, *Oscar Wilde's Last Stand*, 110.
158. Lady Cynthia Asquith, *Diaries 1915–1918*, New York, 1969, 446.
159. Quoted in Diana Souhami, *Mrs Keppel and her Daughter*, London, 1996, 10.
160. Souhami, *Mrs Keppel*, 113.
161. Ibid. 117.
162. Memorandum of Hohenzollern-Sigmaringen conversation with Foreign Secretary Kühlmann, 4 October 1917. Staatsarchiv Sigmaringen, HST 18, FAS.
163. Quoted in Souhami, *Mrs Keppel*, 113.
164. See for this Urbach, 'Das schwarze Buch', 176ff.
165. Asquith, *Diaries 1915–1918*, 447f.
166. Jesse Walker, *The United States of Paranoia: A Conspiracy Theory*, New York, 2013.

CHAPTER 3

1. Staffan Thorsell, *Mein lieber Reichskanzler! Sveriges kontakter med Hitlers rikskansli*, Stockholm, 2006, 210.
2. 6 January 1918, Waffenstillstandsverhandlungen, Hohenlohe to Luise von Baden, HZA.
3. 6 January 1918, Hohenlohe to Luise, ibid.
4. Quoted in Jonathan Haslam, ' "Humint" by Default and the Problem of Trust: Soviet Intelligence 1917 to 1941', in Haslam and Urbach (eds), *Secret Intelligence in the European States System*, 12.
5. Douglas Smith, *Former People: The Final Days of the Russian Aristocracy*, New York, 2012, 80.
6. Margarete (Mossy) von Hessen, 24 March 1917, to Daisy Pless, *Vulkan*, 288.
7. Löwenstein to his wife, May 1917, Löwenstein papers, STAWKB.
8. Ibid. 15 February 1918.
9. Marie of Romania, *The Story of my Life*, III. 427.
10. Marie of Romania, *Later Chapters of my Life*, 55.
11. Princess Löwenstein-Wertheim to her husband, No. 28, Family papers at Klatovy, Czech Republic.
12. Ibid. 25 July 1918.
13. Privatarchiv Oettingen Spielberg, Harburg, FÖWA.
14. Fürstenberg to his wife, Vienna, 19 January 1918, FFAD.
15. 7 October 1918, Box 27, Princess Löwenstein to her husband. Archive Klattau, Czech Republic.
16. Glassheim, *Noble Nationalists: The Transformation of the Bohemian Aristocracy*, Cambridge, Mass., 2005, 76.
17. Max Egon Fürstenberg to Hofrat Hoheness, 3 January 1920 (copy), Donaueschingen. He wrote a similar letter to Josefine Sauter, 27 March 1919: 'I can't go back to Bohemia because I am on a black list.' ACTA Briefe seiner Durchlaucht, 1916–1922, VOl bbII/4, FFAD.
18. Fürstenberg to William II, 17 August 1921. Ibid.

19. August 1921, Fürstenberg to William II. Ibid.
20. Fürstenberg to a friend (Lieber Alter!), 21 May 1919 (copy), Max Egon Fürstenberg Papers, ACTA, Briefe seiner Durchlaucht 1916–1922, Vol. bb II/4. Ibid.
21. 18 November 1918, Gustav Scanzoni von Lichtenfels letter to Max Egon, Fürstenberg Papers, ACTA, Briefe seiner Durchlaucht 1916–1922, Vol. bb II/4. Ibid.
22. Fürstenberg gave Lichtenfels 6,000 Marks as a down payment to avoid a scandal. Letter of Fürstenberg to Lichtenfels, 5 December 1918. Ibid.
23. Erich Leiningen to Ernst Löwenstein, 4 April 1919, Staatsarchiv Wertheim, Rep. 218 DK 12 Fasz 50, STAWKB.
24. Leiningen papers, Karton 7, 1 January 1919, Fürstlich Leiningsches Archive Amorbach.
25. Quoted in Luke, *Hansel Pless*, 66.
26. Wilhelm II to Max Egon Fürstenberg, Amerogen 27 January 1920. FFAD.
27. Castell to his wife, 24 October 1918, Friedrich Castell Nachlass, Castell'sches Hausarchiv, Castell, FCAC.
28. 17 April 1919, Hohenlohe to Luise von Baden, HZA.
29. Diary, Queen Marie of Romania, 21 June 1918, Marie of Romania, *The Story of my Life*, III. 388.
30. Prince H. Reuss XXXIII jüngere Linie to uncle Ernst Hohenlohe-Langenburg, 23 June 1918. HZA.
31. 4 October 1924, Ducky to her sister Alexandra (Sandra), ibid.
32. John J. Stephan, *The Russian Fascists: Tragedy and Farce in Exile, 1925–1945*, London, 1978, 2.
33. S. J. Taylor, *The Great Outsiders: Northcliffe, Rothermere and the Daily Mail*, London, 1996, 257.
34. Stephan, *Russian Fascists*, 3.
35. Haslam, Jonathan, *Near and Distant Neighbors: A New History of Soviet Intelligence, 1917–1989*, Oxford, 2015, pp. 18–21.
36. Andrew Barros, 'A Window on the "Trust": The Case of Ado Birk, *Intelligence and National Security*, 10/2 (April 1995), 273–93.
37. Hesse, *Erinnertes*, 88.
38. Co-author of Marie Alexandrovna's letter was her son-in-law Prince Ernst II Hohenlohe-Langenburg. See 19 May 1919, Ernst Hohenlohe papers, Briefe meiner Schwiegermutter nach England, Friedensvertrag betreffend. Papers of Fürst Enst II Hohenlohe-Langenburg, HZA.
39. Marie of Romania, *Later Chapters of my Life: The Lost Memoirs of Queen Marie of Romania*, ed. Diana Mandache, London, 2004, 53.
40. Diary entry 29 January 1936, I. Maiskii, *Dnevnik diplomata*, I, Moscow, 2006, 136.
41. Operation Blue Thread. Evacuation of relatives of UK Royal Family from Germany in an emergency. FO 369/5698.

42. Karina Urbach, 'Flirting with Hitler: Biographies of the German and British Nobility in the Interwar Years', *Bulletin of the German Historical Institute* (May 2007), 67.
43. Winston Churchill, 'Zionism versus Bolshevism', *Illustrated Sunday Herald*, 8 February 1920.
44. Ibid.
45. Jonathan Haslam, *Russia's Cold War*, New Haven, 2011, 10ff.
46. *Morning Post*, 13 January 1927. *The Times* described it as 'an attempt to organize the Orient against Western capitalist civilization'. *The Times*, 4 February 1925.
47. Cabinet Meeting 14 November 1920, quoted in Richard H. Ullman, *The Anglo-Soviet Accord: Anglo-Soviet Relations 1917–1921*, London, 1972, III. 412.
48. 'Let us continue to disinfect the world (of communism). It would be a great crusade, a thing worth doing, and it would have the beneficial result of bringing Europe together for common safety.': 'The Russian Epidemic', *Morning Post*. 3 March 1927.
49. In 1924 Northumberland spoke in the House of Lords about: 'The Labour and Socialist International'. See Parliamentary Debates, House of Lords, Vol. 56, columns 160–80 and 316–19; Lord Sydemham of Combe joined in. See Sydenham's speeches in 1921 'Bolshevik Propaganda—Legal Position to Cope with', Vol. 45, columns 104–42; 1922 'Bolshevik Propaganda—Position of Organized Associations', Vol. 51, columns 258–68; 1923 'Russia—Persecution of Church Dignitaries', Vol. 53, columns 454–5; 1924–5 'Russia—Soviet Missions' (centres of disturbances throughout the world); 'Hostile Propaganda, Centres of Attack on British Empire', Vol. 60, columns 114–38.
50. Taylor, *The Great Outsiders*, 272ff.
51. Ibid. 275.
52. President of the Council of Commissars Rykoff, defended the position of the Soviet Union: 'Soviet Relations with Britain', *Morning Post*, 20 April 1927, 11.
53. *Manchester Guardian*, 21 January 1927.
54. Quoted in Michael Horn, 'Zwischen Abdankung und Absetzung. Das Ende der Herrschaft der Bundesfürsten des Deutschen Reiches im November 1918', in Susan Richter and Dirk Dirbach (eds), *Thronverzicht: Die Abdankung in Monarchien vom Mittelalter bis in die Neuzeit*, Vienna and Cologne, 2014, 273.
55. Memo of Hohenzollern-Sigmaringen, Depositum 39 HS T 10 No. 25, FAS.
56. Hesse, *Erinnertes*, 8.
57. Marie of Romania, *The Story of my Life*, IV. 431.
58. Alice, Countess of Athlone, *Grandchildren*, 105.
59. Carl Eduard's grandson Prince Andreas, Duke of Coburg, handed over the running of his estate to his son Hubertus in 2011.
60. In the documentary I called Carl Eduard 'a big Nazi who got away with it'. Today, I would use stronger language.

61. Decisive are Carl Eduard's letters to his sister Alice in the Royal Archives Windsor, which are not fully accessible. The papers of Alice, Countess of Athlone include 41 items of which 26 are closed.
62. October 1919, Carl Eduard to his sister Alice, Countess of Athlone. RA ACA/10.
63. Ibid. 15 December 1919, Royal Archives, Windsor.
64. 15.11. 1928. Carl Eduard to his sister Alice, RA ACA/10.
65. Ibid.
66. Harald Sandner, *Hitlers Herzog. Carl Eduard von Sachsen-Coburg und Gotha*, Maastricht, 2010, 249.
67. Luke, *Hansel Pless*, 68. See also: Marcus Funck, 'Schock und Chance. Der preußische Militäradel in der Weimarer Republik zwischen Stand und Profession', in Forsbach (ed.), *Adel und Bürgertum*, 127–71; Marcus Funck, 'The Meaning of Dying: East Elbian Noble Families as "War Tribes" in the 19th and 20th Centuries', in Matt Berg and Greg Eghigian (eds), *Sacrifice and National Belonging in 20th Century Germany*, Arlington, Tex., 2001, 26–63. Marcus Funck, 'Ehre', in Eckart Conze (ed.), *Kleines Lexikon des Adels. Titel, Throne, Traditionen*, Munich, 2005, 70ff.
68. See for this Sandner, *Hitlers Herzog*, 182.
69. Ibid. 183.
70. Ibid.
71. Markus Josef Klein, *Ernst von Salomon. Eine politische Biographie*, Limburg, 1994, 97.
72. Sandner, *Hitlers Herzog*, 187.
73. Ludendorff quoted in a witness statement during the 1927 trial in Gießen. See Klein, *Ernst von Salomon*, 120.
74. Klein, *Ernst von Salomon*, 131.
75. Thirteen people were tried as accomplices of the Rathenau murderers (the killers Erwin Kern and Hermann Fischer had committed suicide by the time police surrounded their hideout). See for the involvement of Ehrhardt officers: Martin Sabrow, *Der Rathenaumord. Rekonstruktion einer Verschwörung gegen die Republik von Weimar*, Munich, 1994, 116.
76. Sandner, *Hitlers Herzog*, 187.
77. Hohenlohe to his aunt Luise of Baden, 3 September 1921, HZA.
78. Hohenlohe to his aunt Luise of Baden, 11 July 1922, ibid.
79. In the German original it is called 'Der Zug nach Coburg'. One could translate this literally with the 'Train to Coburg'—after all they did take the train to get there, but Zug in a military sense is a platoon and can therefore mean that a 'March to Coburg' had taken place. This would therefore be the more heroic version. Since Hitler shortly afterwards had a 'March to the Feldherrnhalle', he probably did not want to have two symbolic marches getting mixed up in the founding myth of the NSDAP. He therefore used the phrase 'Zug to Coburg' in *Mein Kampf*.
80. Speech quoted in Sandner, *Hitlers Herzog*, 280.

81. Ibid. 184.
82. *Goebbels Tagebücher*, Vol. III, Munich, 2001, 8 January 1937, 321.
83. Quoted in Sandner, *Hitlers Herzog*, 324.
84. Ibid.
85. 1 September 1923, Carl Eduard to his sister, RA ACA/10.
86. Ibid. 27 November 1923.
87. Quoted in Sandner, *Hitlers Herzog*, 193.
88. Though the Brigade Ehrhardt was officially dissolved in 1920, it continued under the name Bund Wiking. For Carl Eduard Coburg it obviously remained the Brigade Ehrhardt.
89. Carl Eduard to his sister, 27 November 1923, RA ACA/10.
90. Sandner, *Hitlers Herzog*, 193.
91. Hayward and Morris, *The First Nazi Town*, 62.
92. Quoted in Sandner, *Hitlers Herzog*, 205.
93. Anke Schmeling, *Josias Erbprinz zu Waldeck und Pyrmont. Der politische Weg eines hohen SS-Führers*, Kassel, 1993, 17.
94. Ibid. 29.
95. Ibid. 48.
96. Conze et al. (eds), *Das Amt und die Vergangenheit. Deutsche Diplomaten im Dritten Reich*, Munich, 2010, 57.
97. Duke of Coburg, Berlin, 3 December 1935. NS 10 149, BAB.

CHAPTER 4

1. Paul Sharp, 'Who Needs Diplomats? The Problem of Diplomatic Representation', *International Journal*, 52 (1997), 609–34.
2. Gerhard Weinberg, *The Foreign Policy of Hitler's Germany: Diplomatic Revolution in Europe 1933–36*, Chicago, 1970, 65.
3. Hans-Günther Seraphim, *Das politische Tagebuch Alfred Rosenbergs aus den Jahren 1834/35 und 1939/40*, Göttingen, 1956, 28.
4. Zara Steiner, *The Triumph of the Dark: European International History 1933–1939*, Oxford, 2011, 328.
5. Herbert von Dirksen, *Moskau, Tokio, London. Zwanzig Jahre deutscher Außenpolitik*, Stuttgart, 1949, 215ff.
6. Jonathan Petropoulos, *Royals and the Reich*, Oxford, 2006. See for Hesse's role also: Joanthan Steinberg, *All or Nothing: The Axis and the Holocaust 1941–43*, London, 2002.
7. Karina Urbach (ed.), *European Aristocracies and the Radical Right*, Oxford, 2007.
8. Apart from the period before 1914: Dominic Lieven, *The Aristocracy in Europe 1815–1914*, London, 1992 and Hans-Ulrich Wehler (ed.), *Europäischer Adel 1750–1950*, Geschichte und Gesellschaft, Sonderheft 13, Göttingen, 1990.
9. See for this Reisen und Staatsbesuche führender Persönlichkeiten, seating plans from 30 April 1939, 21 May and 6 July 1939, R 27159, PA AA.

10. Viktoria Luise, Herzogin von Braunschweig, *Im Glanz der Krone*, Göttingen, 1967, 162.
11. Richard Overy, *Goering: Hitler's Iron Knight*, London, 2011.
12. See for this also David Irving, *Göring*, Munich, 1987, 795.
13. Bella Fromm, *Blood and Banquets: A Berlin Social Diary*, London, 1942, 45.
14. Carin Göring to her mother, 28 February 1930. quoted in Irving, *Göring*, 132.
15. Berlin 27 March 1934, v. Plessen to Bismarck in London. Politische und kulturelle Propaganda in England Pol. 26 R 77171, Auswärtiges Amt Archiv, Berlin.
16. *Goebbels Tagebuch*, 1 February 1933. See also 31 March 1933 and 16 March 1933, 148 and 159, *Goebbels Tagebücher*, ed. Elke Fröhlich, Vol. 2/III: *October 1932 to March 1934*, Munich, 2006.
17. Politische und kulturelle Propaganda in England. Pol. 26 R 77171, PA AA.
18. R 27090 confidential reports to von Ribbentrop. Ibid. (Copy)
19. Diana Fotescu (ed.), *Americans and Queen Marie of Romania: A Selection of Documents*, Oxford, 1998, 130.
20. 10 December 1923, papers Hohenzollern-Sigmaringen, FAS.
21. Fromm, *Blood*, 34.
22. Sandner, *Hitlers Herzog*, 249.
23. Fromm, *Blood*, 137.
24. Jens Petersen, 'The Italian Aristocracy, the Savoy Monarchy, and Fascism', in Karina Urbach (ed.), *European Aristocracies and the Radical Right*, Oxford, 2007, 94.
25. Churchill's speech, 20 January 1927, in Rome. Quoted in HO 45/24893, NA.
26. Ex-Kaiser talks to *Evening Standard*. 'What Life is like at Doorn', *Evening Standard*, 19 December 1929, No. 32.872.
27. Letter of 16 May 1938, Dienststelle Ribbentrop R 27157, PA AA.
28. Otto II von Bismarck, to his mother Fürstin Herbert, Bismarck archive, Friedrichsruh, AOBS.
29. See for this Marie-Luise Recker, *England und der Donauraum 1919–1929. Probleme einer europäischen Nachkriegsordnung*, Stuttgart, 1976.
30. Baernreither to Fürstenberg, 25 February 1920, Fürstenberg Papers, FFAD.
31. Sigurd von Ilsemann, *Der Kaiser in Holland. Aufzeichnungen des letzten Flügeladjudanten Kaiser Wilhelms II*, I, Munich, 1968, 279.
32. Jeremy Noakes and G. Pridham, *Nazism 1919–1945*, ii: *Foreign Policy, Economy and Society—A Documentary Reader*, Exeter, 1984, 316ff.
33. Schriften des Vereins für Geschichte und Naturgeschichte der Baar und der angrenzenden Landesteile in Donaueschingen. XXI Heft 1940.
34. Fürstenberg to Bentheim-Tecklennburg, 6 July 1933. Donaueschingen, Sonstige Vereine. Acta. Verein der deutschen Standesherren, 1897–1939, Hofverwaltung, Vol. CX, Fasz. 1, FFAD.
35. See for this Stephan Malinowski, *Vom König zum Führer. Sozialer Niedergang und politische Radikalisierung im deutschen Adel zwischen Kaiserreich und NS-Staat*, Berlin, 2003, and also Heinz Reif, 'Adel im 19. und 20. Jahrhundert', *Enzyklopädie deutscher Geschichte*, Vol. LV, Munich, 1999.

36. 2 March 1939, Carl Eduard to his sister Alice, Athlone Papers, RA ACA/10.
37. Pauline Fürstin zu Wied, *Vom Leben gelernt*, Ludwigsburg, 1953. She was born Princess of Württemberg and attended several Reichsparteitage.
38. Quoted in Sandner, *Hitlers Herzog*, 280.
39. Ibid. 291.
40. Ibid. 220.
41. Hitler would use Carl Eduard as a go-between to Hugenberg again in November 1932.
42. Sandner, *Hitlers Herzog*, 233.
43. Her husband died before his grandfather the King. Her son Carl Gustav is the current King of Sweden.
44. *Coburger Zeitung Sondernummer!*, Wednesday 19 October 1932, 3. In Staatsarchiv Coburg, Bestand LAA, No. 13582.
45. Sandner, *Hitlers Herzog*, 274.
46. Ibid. 272.
47. Ibid. 280.
48. Reinhard Spitzy, *So haben wir das Reich verspielt: Bekenntnisse eines Illegalen*, Munich and Vienna, 1986, 408.
49. Peregrine Worsthorne, *In Defence of Aristocracy*, London, 2004.
50. Gregory D. Phillips, *The Diehards: Aristocratic Society and Politics in Edwardian England*, Cambridge, Mass., 1979.
51. Maurice Cowling, *The Impact of Hitler: British Politics and British Policy 1933–40*, Chicago, 1977, 265f.
52. Teilnachlass Fürst Alois Löwenstein-Wertheim No. 27 and No. 28. Klatovy, Czech Republic.
53. Cowling, *The Impact of Hitler*, 266.
54. Karina Urbach, 'Age of No Extremes? The British Aristocracy Torn between the House of Lords and the Mosley Movement', in Karina Urbach (ed.), *European Aristocracies and the Radical Right 1918–1939*, Oxford, 2007, 63.
55. Michael Bloch, *Operation Willi: The Plot to Kidnap the Duke of Windsor July 1940*, London, 1984, 54.
56. Letter Princess Löwenstein, 30 January 1936. Teilnachlass Fürst Alois Löwenstein-Wertheim Klatovy, Czech Republic.
57. An Apostle quoted in Philip Knightley, *Philby: KGB Masterspy*, London, 1988, 35.
58. Sandner, *Hitlers Herzog*, 243.
59. Alice, Countess of Athlone, *Grandchildren*, 223.
60. Interrogation of the German diplomat Carl August Clodius (1897–1952), 21 May 1946, Document 54 in V. Khristoforov et al. (eds), *Rossiya. XX Vek. Dokumenty. Tainy diplomatii tret'ego reikha. Germanskie diplomaty, rukovoditeli zarubezhnykh voennykh missii, voennyi i politseiskie attashe v sovetskom plenu. Dokumenty iz sledstvennykh del 1944/1945*, Moscow, 2011.
61. Nigel West and Oleg Tsarev, *Triplex: Secrets from the Cambridge Spies*, New Haven, 2009, 74.

62. Record of interrogation of Oberführer SS, Wilhelm Rodde, document 129, 31 March 1947, Khristoforov, *Rossiya*.
63. Alice, Countess of Athlone, *Grandchildren*, 209.
64. Ibid. 210.
65. Coburg to Alice, 15 April 1936. RA ACA/10.
66. John Julius Norwich (ed.), *The Duff Cooper Diaries 1915–1951*, London, 2005, 218.
67. Coburg had a more positive impression of the meeting with Duff Cooper. This was vehemently denied by Duff Cooper's son in a letter to *The Times* on 8 January 1963.
68. Chatham House Debate, April 1933. Christie and Bismarck, Christie Papers, CHRS 1/28 CCAC.
69. 22 August 1934, Otto II von Bismarck to Ministerialdirektor Dr Dieckhoff, Otto II Bismarck papers, Friedrichsruh, AOBS.
70. 4 September 1928, Früher regierende Familien, Pol. 11, No. 2, 77116, PA AA.
71. Otto II Bismarck to Diekhoff, 16 March 1934. AA report to Plessen, 4 April 1934, Bismarckarchiv Friedrichsruh, AOBS.
72. Lord Ronald Graham to German embassy, November 1934, Politische und kulturelle Propaganda in England, Pol. 26, R 77171, PA AA.
73. Letter from November 1934 and 13 November 1934 from Gesandtschaftsrat (envoy) Rüter, Pol. 26, R 77171, PA AA.
74. Diekhoff to Bismarck, 25 September 1935. Ibid.
75. See for this letter of Ann Marie Bismarck to Charles Higham. Charles Higham, *Mrs Simpsons: Secret Lives of the Duchess of Windsor*, London, 2004, 93.
76. Fritz Hesse, *Das Vorspiel zum Kriege. Englandberichte und Erlebnisse eines Tatzeugen. 1935–1945*, Starnberg, 1979, 28.
77. Ibid. 43.
78. Ibid. 27ff.
79. Weinberg gets it wrong. He thinks it was Max Hohenlohe who encouraged the speech. Weinberg, *The Foreign Policy of Hitler's Germany*, 215 n. 45.
80. Address given to the British Legion on 11 June 1935. See *The Times*, 12 June 1935.
81. Petropoulos, *Royals and the Reich*, 339.
82. Letter of Queen Marie of Romania to Ray Baker, in Fotescu (ed.), *Americans and Queen Marie of Romania*, 109.
83. Philip Ziegler, *King Edward VIII*, London, 2001, 179.
84. Quoted ibid. 179.
85. Ibid. 180.
86. From the Foreign Minister Colonel Juan Beigbeder to Franco, 25 June 1940 (encloses information from a secretary of the embassy, Bermejillo, who is known to be a friend of the Duke of Windsor). Record of conversation between Bermejillo and Duke of Windsor, 25 June 1940, Document 56, *Fundación nacional Francisco Franco, Documentos inéditos para la Historia del generalísimo Franco*, Vol. II-1, Madrid, 1993.

87. Astrid M. Eckert, *The Struggle for the Files: The Western Allies and the Return of German Archives after the Second World War*, Cambridge, 2014.
88. Memorandum from WSC to Prime Ministers of Canada, Australia, New Zealand, South Africa on the embarrassment caused by the Duke of Windsor to King George VI through his pro-Nazi activities on the Continent. CHAR 20/9A/34–8, CCAC.
89. Quoted in Petropoulos, *Royals and the Reich*, 201.
90. Ibid.
91. Ziegler, *Edward VIII*, 231f. See for Edward VIII also Denys Blakeway, *The Last Dance: 1936*, London, 2010.
92. Ibid. 474.
93. Telegram from German embassy, Washington Luther, reporting on Dunn, 21 January 1936. The telegram was marked: 'Seen by Führer and Reichskanzler, 23.1.36'. R 4311 1435, BAB.
94. Ibid.
95. Hoesch report (copy), Adjutantur des Führers, NS 10, BAB.
96. Report from Hoesch to AA (copy) 21 January 1936, R 43 II, 435, BAB.
97. Quoted in Fotescu (ed.), *Americans and Queen Marie of Romania*, 113.
98. Steiner, *The Triumph of the Dark*, 141.
99. Ibid. 142.
100. Ibid.
101. Duke of Windsor, *A King's Story: The Memoirs of HRH the Duke of Windsor*, London, 1951, 286f.
102. Hesse, *Das Vorspiel*, 43.
103. 15 April 1936, letter Carl Eduard to Alice, Athlone papers, RA ACA/A.
104. Ibid.
105. Quoted in Fotescu (ed.), *Americans and Queen Marie of Romania*, 128.
106. Confidential report Ribbentrop, R 27090–27091, PA AA.
107. Sandner, *Hitlers Herzog*, 325.
108. See for Anglo-German press relations: Dominik Geppert, *Pressefehden und Zeitungskriege: Öffentlichkeit und Diplomatie in den deutsch-britischen Beziehungen 1896–1912*, Munich, 2007.
109. October 1937, Confidential reports Ribbentrop, R 27090–27091, PA AA.
110. Sandner, *Hitlers Herzog*, 326.
111. Yuri Modin, *My Five Cambridge Friends*, London, 1994, 65.
112. National Archives website, summary of AGF's activities. <http://www.nationalarchives.gov.uk/releases/2003/may22/organisation.htm>.
113. Bericht unseres Vertrauensmannes in London, 11 December 1935, R 43 II 1434, BAB.
114. Hoesch report, R 43 II 1434, BAB.
115. Staatssekretär und Chef der Reichkanzlei to Joachim von Ribbentrop, 11 December 1935, R 43 II 1434, BAB.
116. There was a behind the scenes activity to coordinate the AGF with a German equivalent which would cement relations between Britain and Nazi Germany.

The DEG was founded in 1935 in Berlin by Ribbentrop. He had Hitler's support for the project and Goebbels was made an honorary member. A predecessor of the DEG was the Deutsch-Britische Gesellschaft, founded in 1932, before the Nazis came to power (the Russians always translate British as English, as one can see in the following quote of Rodde). See for the DEG: Ernst Ritter, Die erste deutsch-englische Gesellschaft (1935–1939), in Friedrich Kahlenberg (ed.), Aus der Arbeit der Archive, Boppard am Rhein 1989, p. 811ff.

117. Wilhelm Rodde (1893–1949) received business training in New York before the First World War. He joined the German army in 1914 and was awarded the iron cross 1st and 2nd class. He then joined the Freikorps Raben in 1919. He started a business in 1923 and went bankrupt in 1924. Rodde emigrated to Brazil and returned in 1931. He joined the NSDAP in February 1932 and joined the Büro Ribbentrop on 1 October 1934. He was in charge of its press affairs 1935–7. In July 1937 he joined the German Foreign Ministry. He became Generalkonsul in Winnipeg, Canada, later Gauwart, Gau Hamburg 1939. He died in Russian captivity in 1949.
118. Document 129, 31 March 1947, in Khristoforov et al. (eds), *Rossiya.*
119. Ernest W. D. Tennant, *True Account*, London, 1957, 201.
120. Document 129, 31 March 1947, in Khristoforov et al. (eds), *Rossiya.*
121. Ibid.
122. 'Germany in May by Sir Arnold Wilson MP', *English Review* (June 1934). Offprint sent to the German Foreign Ministry, R 77128, PA AA.
123. *None so Blind: A Study of the Crisis Years 1930–39. Based on the private papers of Group captain M. G. Christie, by T. P. Conwell-Evans*, London, 1947, p. XI.
124. Record of interrogation of Oberführer SS, Wilhelm Rodde, Document 129, in Khristoforov et al. (eds), *Rossiya.*
125. He does mention his friendship with Ribbentrop though. Ernest Tennant, *True Account*, London, 1957.
126. Carl Eduard to Alice, 2 March 1939. RA ACA/10.
127. Lawrence James, *Aristocrats: Power, Grace and Decadence*, London, 2009, 372.
128. Steiner, *The Triumph of the Dark*, 324.
129. Sandner, *Hitlers Herzog*, 337.
130. Quoted in David Faber, *Munich: The 1938 Appeasement Crisis*, London, 2008, 420.
131. 2 March 1939, Carl Eduard to his sister Alice, Athlone papers, RA ACA/10.
132. R 43 ii 428, BAB.
133. Rosenberg's memorandum about the visit, dated 25 July 1939, is among Stephanie Hohenlohes files, Hoover Archives.
134. Dirksen memo 2 August 1939, quoted by Elizabeth Wiskemann, *The Spectator*, 15 September 1949, 15.
135. Quoted in Haslam, *Near and Distant Neighbors: A New History of Soviet Intelligence, 1917–1989*, New York and Oxford, 2015, 103.
136. Conwell-Evans, *None So Blind*, 70.
137. Ibid. 199.

138. Burgess informed Moscow: 'All measures have been taken for Hermann Göring to arrive under secret cover in London on Wednesday 23rd' (of August 1939). Quoted in Haslam, *Near and Distant Neighbours*, 103.
139. See for this Sandner, *Hitlers Herzog*, 375.
140. Ibid. Sandner quotes a copy of the Russian Foreign Office report from 31 May 1940.
141. Dusko Popov, *Superspion. Der Doppelagent im Zweiten Weltkrieg*, Vienna, 1974, 80 and 117.
142. Alexander Shirokorod, Sekrety svergnutogo korolya in: Nezavisimoe voennoe obozrenie 8 Februar 2002. Shirokorod refers to secret memorandum No. K5/8175.
143. Interview with G. Sokolov published on 6 June 2014 in *Komsomolskaya Pravda*, under the headline 'Charl'z, natsistskogo rodstva ne ponyashchii'.
144. Petropoulos, *Royals and the Reich*, 350.
145. Peter Wright, *Spycatcher: The Candid Autobiography of a Senior Intelligence Officer*, Toronto, 1987, 223.
146. V. Popov, *Sovetnik Korolevy-Superagent Kremlya*, Moscow, 1995, 127.
147. 'Robert Huntington, a brother of the former Mrs. Vincent Astor, had once told her [the unidentified source] that he definitely had proof that Goering and the Duke of Windsor had entered into some sort of an agreement, which in substance was to the effect that after Germany won the war Goering, through control of the army, was going to overthrow Hitler and then he would install the Duke of Windsor as King of England.... She also told me again that there was no doubt whatever but that the Duchess of Windsor had had an affair with Ribbentrop, and that of course she had an intense hate for the English since they had kicked them out of England.' 2 May 1941, FBI Memorandum for the Director. See FBI files, the Vault (FOIPA), HQ 65-31113-22; HQ 65-31113-22.
148. The FBI files were released in 2003 and used for a Channel 4 documentary on the Duke of Windsor. For the Franco papers, see document 56, 25 June 1940. *Fundación nacional Francisco Franco, Documentos in inéditos para la Historia del generalísimo Franco*, Vol. II-1, Madrid, 1993.
149. Ibid.
150. Staffan Thorsell, *Mein lieber Reichskanzler! Sveriges kontakter med Hitlers rikskansli*, Stockholm, 2006, 181–6.
151. Ibid.
152. Quoted in Petropoulos, *Royals and the Reich*, 205.
153. Daniel B. Roth, *Hitlers Brückenkopf in Schweden. Die deutsche Gesandtschaft in Stockholm 1933–1945*, Berlin, 2009, 56.
154. Quoted ibid. 55.
155. Quoted ibid. 262.
156. Gerd R. Ueberschär and Winfried Vogel, *Dienen und Verdienen. Hitlers Geschenke an seine Eliten*, Frankfurt, 1999, 109 and 247.
157. Duke of Coburg, NS 10 149. BAB.

158. Rudolf Stoiber and Boris Celovsky, *Stephanie von Hohenlohe: Sie liebte die Mächtigen der Welt*, Munich, 1988, 141.

CHAPTER 5

1. KV 1696, 30 August 1939, National Archives London.
2. 15 November 1939, *Goebbels Tagebücher*, Vol. VII, Munich, 1998, 195, Elke Fröhlich (ed.), *Die Tagebücher des Joseph Goebbels*, III. 642.
3. Franz zu Hohenlohe, *Stephanie: Das Leben meiner Mutter*, Vienna, 1991.
4. Rudolf Stoiber and Boris Celovsky came closest to the truth in their version of events. In 1988 they published an unnoticed biography of Hohenlohe which became the base for Martha Schad's sensational and slightly confused 'Hitler's Spy Princess'. Martha Schad, *Hitlers geheime Diplomatin. Das Leben der Stephanie Hohenlohe*, Munich, 2002.
5. *Prager Monatsblatt*, 31 January 1938, in Stephanie Hohenlohe papers, Hoover Archives.
6. Marcel Proust, *The Captive & The Fugitive*, New York, 1913/1927.
7. 8 December 1933, *Goebbels Tagebücher*, 2/III, Munich, 2006, 332.
8. Stoiber and Celovsky, *Stephanie von Hohenlohe*, 55.
9. See for this Andreas Fahrmeir, *Citizenship: The Rise and Fall of a Modern Concept*, New Haven, 2008.
10. See Robert Evans, 'The Successor States', in Robert Gerwarth (ed.), *Twisted Paths: Europe 1914–1945*, Oxford, 2007.
11. Robert Gerwarth and John Horne, 'Fighting the Red Beast: Counter-Revolutionary Violence in the Defeated States of Central Europe', in Robert Gerwarth and John Horne (eds), *War in Peace: Paramilitary Violence in Europe after the Great War*, Oxford, 2012, 67.
12. See Andreas Oplatka, *Graf Stephan Szechenyi. Der Mann, der Ungarn schuf*, Vienna, 2004.
13. See Ignác Romsics, 'The Hungarian Aristocracy and its Political Attitudes in the Interwar Years', in Urbach (ed.), *Radical Right*, 187ff.
14. This party would later develop into the notorious Arrow Cross movement. A Széchenyi worked for its leader Ferenc Szálasi, and in 1939 won a seat in parliament. Ibid. 187ff.
15. Gerard Vernon Wallop Viscount Lymington (1898–1984) was Conservative MP for Basingstoke from 1929 to 1934. In 1943 he became the 9th Earl of Portsmouth.
16. Lymington, *Knot of Roots*, 160.
17. Count Pal Teleki, quoted in Judith Listowel, *This I have Seen*, London, 1943, 45.
18. Jim Wilson, *Nazi Princess: Hitler, Lord Rothermere and Princess Stephanie von Hohenlohe*, London, 2011.
19. Taylor, *The Great Outsiders*, 259. See also S. J. Taylor, *Reluctant Presslord: Esmond Rothermere and the Daily Mail*, London, 1999.
20. Hohenlohe, *Das Leben*, 77.
21. Ibid.

22. 4–5 November 1932, Hohenlohe papers, Hoover Archives, Stanford, Calif.
23. Draft memoir, Stephanie Hohenlohe, Hoover Archives, Stanford, Calif.
24. See for these versions Gordon Brook-Shepherd, *The Last Empress: Life and Times of Zita of Austria-Hungary, 1892–1989*, London, 1991.
25. Hohenlohe, *Das Leben*, 188.
26. Hohenlohe draft memoirs, Hoover Archives.
27. Rothermere to Hohenlohe, 29 July 1932. Hoover Archives.
28. See for this a report of Wilhelm Hohenzollern-Sigmaringen written after his visit to House Doorn, 10 to 17 August 1922. Dep. 39 HS T 9 (KW) 53 (Princely House), Staatsarchiv Sigmaringen, FAS.
29. Hohenlohe draft memoirs, 17, Hoover Archives.
30. Ibid.
31. Sefton Delmer, *Die Deutschen und ich*, Hanover, 1962, 146.
32. Correspondence Max Egon with House Doorn, 1929–39, FFAD.
33. Schlag auf Schlag, in *Spiegel*, 33 and 34, 23 August 1947.
34. Hohenlohe papers, Hoover Archives.
35. Taylor, *The Great Outsiders*, 299ff.
36. Report of Hohenzollern-Sigmaringen, Depositum 39 HST10 No. 25. Staatsarchiv Sigmaringen, FAS.
37. Faber, *Munich*, 196.
38. Note to the Führer, Ribbentrop, 31 October 1936, NS 10 91, BAB.
39. Hohenlohe, *Das Leben*, 95.
40. This OSS wartime report was declassified in 1969.
41. Hohenlohe draft memoirs, 17, Hoover Archives.
42. The interview was published in the April 1932 edition of Hearst's *International-Cosmopolitan*. Quoted in Peter Conradi, *Hitler's Piano Player*, London, 2011, 87.
43. Delmer, *Die Deutschen*, 148.
44. Hohenlohe papers, Hoover Archives.
45. Quoted in Conradi, *Piano Player*, 86f.
46. Hohenlohe papers, Hoover Archives.
47. Ernst Hanfstaengl, *Hitler: The Missing Years*, London, 1957, 55.
48. Quoted in Conradi, *Piano Player*, 55.
49. Delmer, *Die Deutschen*, 147n.
50. Quoted in Conradi, *Piano Player*, 80.
51. Ibid.
52. Interview Hanfstaengl with Dr Walter Langer 1943, quoted in Stoiber and Celovsky, *Stephanie von Hohenlohe*, 128.
53. 28 October 1941. Memorandum regarding: Princess Stephanie Hohenlohe Waldenburg, FDR Library, <http://docs.fdrlibrary.marist.edu/PSF/BOX3/A31A01.HTML>.
54. 2 April 1935, Rothermere to Hitler, Stephanie Hohenlohe papers, Hoover Archives.
55. 6 December 1935, Hoover Archives.
56. See for Mosley and the radical right: Martin Pugh, *Hurrah for the Blackshirts! Fascists and Fascism in Britain between the Wars*, London, 2005.

57. 28 October 1941, Memorandum regarding: Princess Stephanie Hohenlohe Waldenburg, FDR Library, <http://docs.fdrlibrary.marist.edu/PSF/BOX3/A31A01.HTML>.
58. Report of Günther Schmidt-Lorenz, 15 October 1933, R 43 II 1432a, BAB.
59. Hoesch to the AA, 6 June 1935, Pol. 11 R 77121, PA AA.
60. Judenfrage, letter of 24 February 1937, Pol 36 R 102827, PA AA.
61. Diana Guinness to Wiedemann, Wiedemann papers, N 1720/6 BAK.
62. Berlin 24 August 1937, Wiedemann to Diana Guinness. Ibid.
63. KV 1696 NA.
64. Ross McKibbin, *Classes and Cultures: England 1918–1951*, Oxford, 1998, 24.
65. Hohenlohe draft memoirs, 19, Hoover Archives.
66. *Time* magazine, 27 November 1939.
67. Fröhlich (ed.), *Goebbels Tagebücher*, Part I, 3/1 April. 1934–February 1936, 154.
68. See for this a report of Wilhelm Hohenzollern-Sigmaringen about his visit to House Doorn, Dep. 39 HS T 9 (KW) 53 (Princely House), FAS.
69. *Goebbels Tagebücher*, Vol. III, Munich, 2001, March 1936 to February 1937, 7 January 1937, 319.
70. Ibid.
71. 8 January 1937, 320.
72. *Goebbels Tagebücher*, Vol. IV, 27 May 1937, 152.
73. Ibid., 18 August 1937, 270.
74. Thank you letter from Wiedemann to Rothermere, 12 March 1937, N 1720/5, BAK.
75. Letter of Hitler to Hohenlohe in Wiedemann papers. Ibid.
76. Thank you note Stephanie Hohenlohe to Hitler, 12 January 1937, ibid.
77. Letter Wiedemann to Princess Hohenlohe, London 18 May 1937, N 1720/5, ibid.
78. Letter from Wiedemann, Adjudant des Führers, 10 June 1938. Ibid.
79. The FBI wrote a summary of their findings for President Roosevelt in October 1941. FDR Library, 28 October 1941, Memorandum regarding: Princess Stephanie Hohenlohe Waldenburg. <http://docs.fdrlibrary.marist.edu/PSF/BOX3/A31A01.HTML>.
80. FDR Library, ibid.
81. Hohenlohe, *Das Leben*, 193.
82. Stoiber and Celovsky, *Stephanie von Hohenlohe*, 186.
83. Ibid.
84. Malinowski, *Vom König*, 553ff.
85. Deutsch-Italienische Studienstiftung, 9 February 1940: An Herrn Obergebietsführer Nabersberg Dienststelle des Beauftragten der NSDAP für aussenpolit. Fragen im Stabe des Stellvertreters des Führers; R 27159 Reisen und Staatsbesuche führender Persönlichkeiten. PA AA.
86. Quoted in Fabrice D'Almeida, *High Society in the Third Reich*, London, 2008, 190.
87. Letter by Hauptmann Wiedemann, 3 November 1938, to the German Embassy, Paris, Count Johannes von Welcek, N 1720/5, BAK.

88. Wiedemann to the Preussisches Staatsministerium, Oberregierungsrat Normann, 1 December 1938. Ibid.
89. Wiedemann to Landesstatthalter Reiter, 21 April 1939. Ibid.
90. FBI file for President Roosevelt, FDR Library, 28 October 1941, Memorandum regarding: Princess Stephanie Hohenlohe Waldenburg, <http://docs.fdrlibrary.marist.edu/PSF/BOX3/A31A01.HTML>.
91. Steiner, *The Triumph of the Dark*, 329.
92. 22 February 1938, *Goebbels Tagebücher*, Vol. V, Munich, 2000, 171.
93. 3 April 1938. Ibid. 280.
94. Ibid. 14 May 1938, 303. See also Goebbels' comments on 28 May and 19 July 1938. Ibid. 321 and 387.
95. Hohenlohe draft memoirs, Hoover Archives.
96. Ibid.
97. Wiedemann letter to Lord Rotheremere, undated, N 1720/5, BAK.
98. Petropoulos, *Royals and the Reich*, 202.
99. Quoted in Faber, *Munich*, 196.
100. Steiner, *The Triumph of the Dark*, 579.
101. von Dirksen, *Moskau, Tokio, London*, 215ff.
102. Wiedemann papers, BAK. Also quoted in Steiner, *The Triumph of the Dark*, 580.
103. 'Mission Wiedemanns bei dem englischen Außenminister Halifax Juli 1938', Wiedemann papers, N 1720/3, BAK.
104. See for this the newspaper clippings in Stephanie Hohenlohe's collection. Hoover Archives.
105. C. A. Lyon, 'The most mysterious man in Europe', London, 31 July 1938. Ibid.
106. *Goebbels Tagebücher*, 23 July 1938, Vol. V.
107. 23 July 1938, Duff Cooper diary, 251f.
108. Ibid. 252.
109. *Daily Herald*, London, 1 July 1938, 'Hitler's dear Princess'. Press cutting in Hohenlohe File, newspaper clipping among Wiedemann papers, BAK.
110. See Spitzy, *Reich verspielt*, 160 and Hesse, *Das Vorspiel*, 101f. Also Dirksen, *Moskau, Tokio, London*, 215ff.
111. Hohenlohe draft memoirs, Hoover Archives.
112. Stephanie Hohenlohe to Hitler, 1 October 1938, Wiedemann papers, BAK.
113. Letter by Dr Wittmann, Budapest, 13 May 1938. Hoover Archives.
114. Letter of Wiedemann to Rothermere, undated, N 1720/5, BAK.
115. Letter Stephanie to Wiedemann, Wiedemann papers, ibid.
116. Second letter of Wiedemann to Rothermere, undated, probably November 1938, ibid.
117. Volker Ullrich, *Adolf Hitler. Biographie, Die Jahre des Aufstiegs 1889–1939*, Frankfurt am Main, 2013.
118. Interview Stoiber with Hanfstaengl, Stoiber and Celovsky, *Stephanie von Hohenlohe*, 121.
119. 13 April 1937, *Goebbels Tagebücher*, Vol. IV, Munich, 2000.
120. London, 12 February 1939, Putzi to Hitler, R 43 II 903c., BAB.

121. Hanfstaengl to Wittmer, 22 May 1939. Ibid.
122. MI5 memo written on 26 June 1939, KV 2/1696, NA.
123. Ibid. 26 June 1939.
124. Liddell got Wiedemann's first name wrong.
125. Nigel West (ed.), *The Guy Liddell Diaries*, I: *1939–1942*, London, 2005, 140.
126. *Time* magazine, 20 November 1939.
127. FO 371/65224 Delivery to the United Kingdom of twelve paintings from the Rothermere Collection found in Munich, FO 371/65224, NA.
128. FBI file quoted in Stoiber and Celovsky, *Stephanie von Hohenlohe*, 11f.
129. Susanne Meinl, *Nationalsozialisten gegen Hitler. Die nationalrevolutionäre Opposition um Friedrich Wilhlem Heinz*, Berlin, 2000, 268f.
130. West (ed.), *The Guy Liddell Diaries,* 8 April 1941.
131. Quoted in Stoiber and Celovsky, *Stephanie von Hohenlohe*, 265.
132. Wiedemann papers, BAK.
133. 28 October 1941, Memorandum regarding: Princess Stephanie Hohenlohe Waldenburg, FDR Library.
134. Ibid.

CHAPTER 6

1. Sefton Delmer, *Black Boomerang: An Autobiography*, Vol. II, London, 1962, 58.
2. Prince Max Egon Maria Erwin Paul Hohenlohe-Langenburg (KV 2/3289) 19/11/1937–25/08/1953, NA.
3. See also Ulrich Schlie, 'Max Egon Prinz zu Hohenlohe-Langenburg. Staatswissenschaftler, Großgrundbesitzer und Privat-Diplomat im Dritten Reich, 1897–1968', in *Lebensbilder aus Baden-Württemberg*, Stuttgart, 23 (2010).
4. I would like to thank Professor Bernd Martin for making photocopies of Höhne's questionnaire available. Hohenlohe wrote these replies to Höhne in February 1967.
5. Quoted in Schlie, 'Max Egon Prinz zu Hohenlohe-Langenburg', 445.
6. Ibid.
7. Glassheim, *Noble Nationalists*, 76.
8. Schlie, 'Max Egon Prinz zu Hohenlohe-Langenburg', 444. I disagree with Schlie's positive interpretation of Hohenlohe.
9. Ibid. 445.
10. Spitzy, *Reich verspielt*, 437.
11. See 13 June 1934, *Goebbels Tagebücher*, Vol. 3/1, 62.
12. Reinhard Spitzy, *So entkamen wir den Alliierten. Erinnerungen eines Ehemaligen*, Berlin, 1989. And Spitzy, *Reich verspielt*, 438.
13. See Jörg K. Hoensch, *Geschichte Böhmens. Von der slavischen Landnahme bis zur Gegenwart*, Munich, 1997.
14. Glassheim, *Noble Nationalists*, 83ff.
15. Eagle Glassheim, 'Genteel Nationalists: Nobles and Fascism in Interwar Czechoslovakia', in Urbach (ed.), *Radical Right*, 149ff.

16. See Interview with Count Jesko Dohna, Castell, March 2005.
17. Quoted in Glassheim, *Noble Nationalists*, 180.
18. Spitzy, *Reich verspielt*, 281.
19. Gerhard Weinberg, *The Foreign Policy of Hitler's Germany*, Chicago, 1970, n. 83.
20. Czecho-Slovaks: Political Relations with Allies, including alleged monarchical tendencies of the Czech aristocracy and of the British Legation in Prague. Confidental: 3 April 1919, FO 608/8/2. NA.
21. Memo by J. K. Roberts, 26 July 1940, FO 371/24407, NA.
22. Quoted in Steiner, *The Triumph of the Dark*, 557.
23. Ibid. 560.
24. Christie papers, 15 July 1938, CHRS 1/28 CCAC.
25. Andrew Roberts, *The Holy Fox: A Biography of Lord Halifax*, London, 1991, 103f.
26. Glassheim, *Noble Nationalists*, 179.
27. Ibid. 180.
28. Ibid. 178.
29. Ibid. 179.
30. *Daily Express* article in KV files. KV2/3289 Hohenlohe-Langenburg, Prince Max Egon, NA.
31. See for this Hohenlohe, *Das Leben*, 191.
32. Papers of Lord Vansittart of Denham, 1881–1957. Notes on Colonel Christie's conversation with Max Hohenlohe, Vansittart Papers, GBR/0014/VNST, CCAC.
33. Glassheim, *Noble Nationalists*, 180.
34. Quoted ibid. 182.
35. Steiner, *The Triumph of the Dark*, 589.
36. J. W. Brügel, 'Der Runciman Bericht', *Vierteljahrshefte für Zeitgeschichte*, 26 (1978), 652ff.
37. Ibid.
38. FO 371/21582 Pillage of Max Hohenlohe's castle, 29 September 1938: draft telegram, message from Sir R. Vansittart, FO 371/21582, NA.
39. Irving, *Göring*, 383. Andrew Roberts seems to think Max Hohenlohe was a good Nazi. Roberts, *Halifax*, 244f.
40. KV File Max Hohenlohe, NA.
41. Spitzy, *So entkamen wir den Alliierten*, 438.
42. Ulrich Schlie, *Kein Friede mit Deutschland: Die geheimen Gespräche im Zweiten Weltkrieg 1939–1941*, Munich, 1993, 103.
43. Quoted in Höhne, *The Order of the Death's Head*, 519.
44. KV2/3289 Hohenlohe-Langenburg, Prince Max Egon Maria Erwin Paul, NA.
45. St. S. England: Telegram Stohrer to AA, No. 499 13 February 1940, PPA AA.
46. See, for these letters, Prem 1 443, NA.
47. Diary entry 22 January 1940, in West (ed.), *The Guy Liddell Diaries*.
48. Chris Hastings, 'Lord Halifax Tried to Negotiate Peace with the Nazis', *Daily Telegraph*, 30 August 2008.
49. Halifax to Ivy 7th Duchess of Portland, 2 December 1945, Welbeck Private Archives.

50. See for the Duke of Westminster and his involvement with the Right Club: Richard Griffiths, *Patriotism Perverted*, London, 1998.
51. Churchill to Duke of Westminster, 13 September 1939, regarding Westminster's statement at a private meeting, 12 September 1939. CHAR 19/2A/22–3, CCAC.
52. Christie Papers, CHRS 1/28 CCAC.
53. Schlie, *Kein Friede*, 105.
54. 31 March 1947. V. Khristoforov et al. (eds), *Rossiya. XX vek. Dokumenty. Tainy diplomatii tret'ego reikha. Germanskie diplomaty, rukovoditeli zarubezhnykh voennykh missii, voennyi i politseiskie attashe v sovetskom plenu. Dokumenty iz sledstvennykh del 1944/1945*, Moscow, 2011, Document 129.
55. Notes of Christie, Christie papers CHRS 1/28. CCAC.
56. See for this Patricia Meehan, *The Unnecessary War: Whitehall and the German Resistance to Hitler*, London, 1992, 278.
57. Quoted ibid. 281.
58. Popov, *Superspion*, 80.
59. Knightley, *Philby*, 106.
60. See for this also Neville Wylie, *Britain, Switzerland, and the Second World War*, Oxford, 2003.
61. Delmer, *Die Deutschen*, 465.
62. Quoted in Delmer, *Black Boomerang*, II. 58.
63. Peter Longerich, *Heinrich Himmler*, Berlin, 2008, 728.
64. John H. Waller, 'Reichsführer Himmler Pitches Washington', in <www.cia.gov/library/center-for-the-study-of-intelligence/csi-publications/csi-studies/studies/vol46no1/article04.html>.
65. Ibid.
66. Quoted in Höhne, *The Order of the Death's Head*, 521.
67. Ibid. 523.
68. Sir Samuel Hoare to Anthony Eden, 1942, FO 954/27, NA.
69. Sir Samuel Hoare to Anthony Eden, 5 July 1943, ibid.
70. Ibid.
71. Hohenlohe KV file, National Archives London.

CONCLUSION

1. Radio programme 'Bunte Bühne für die Wehrmacht, 17th April 1945', in Peter Mallwitz (ed.), *Stefan Heym. Reden an den Feind*, Munich, 1986, 332.
2. Ibid.
3. Ibid.
4. See for this Denys Blakeway's programme on the Marburg Files. Archive hour, BBC Radio 4.
5. FO 1049/475, NA. Quoted in Petropoulos, *Royals and the Reich*, 468.
6. Miles Graham to Brian Robertson, Advanced Headquarters, Control Commission for Germany, 14 June 1946, NA.

7. It was odd that Alice, who spoke German well, suddenly could not spell 'Partei' properly. This means that she probably dictated her memoirs to a ghost writer.
8. Alice, Countess of Athlone, *Grandchildren*, 280.
9. Ibid. 281.
10. 28 August 1947, FO 371 64689, NA.
11. Confidential, Herzog von Sachsen-Coburg-Gotha, Carl Eduard George Albert, FO 371/64689, NA.
12. Correspondence regarding Duke of Saxe-Coburg und Gotha, 19 July 1946, Dr Langer, FO 1030/302, NA.
13. Quoted in Sandner, *Hitlers Herzog*, 294.
14. Quoted ibid. 281.
15. See for this Hohenlohe, *Das Leben*, 12.
16. Stephanie Hohenlohe papers, Hoover Archives.
17. Stoiber and Celovsky, *Stephanie von Hohenlohe*, 321.
18. <http://www.luxuryportfolio.com/browse~mnc/spain/malaga_(costa_del_sol)/marbella_golden_mile.cfm>.
19. Max Hohenlohe, KV 2/3289, NA.
20. See for this Steglich, *Die Friedenspolitik*, xciv.
21. Bernd Martin, *Friedensinitiativen und Machtpolitik im Zweiten Weltkrieg 1939–1942*, Düsseldorf, 1974, 27.

Archives and Bibliography

The thirty archives I have used in Britain, the United States, the Netherlands, the Czech Republic, and Germany have been extremely cooperative. I would like to thank in particular the staff at the Hoover Archives, Jesko Graf zu Dohna at Castell, Ulf Morgenstern at Friedrichsruh, Ralf Engel at the Bundesarchiv Lichterfelde, Derek Adlam at Welbeck Abbey, Andreas Wilts at Donaueschingen, and Lucie Storchova who helped me at Plzeň. Unfortunately the Royal Archives at Windsor restricted access to a degree unknown among other archives I consulted.

All translations from foreign languages are my own, except for the Russian sources, which Jonathan Haslam translated for me.

GERMAN ARCHIVES

1. Politisches Archiv des Auswärtigen Amtes (PA-AA), Berlin

Nachlass Dr. Leopold von Hoesch (1881–1936)

PA AA Vols. 6256ff Personalakte Fürst Hohenlohe-Langenburg; Berichte des Fürsten: R 16044ff.

R 3895 Fürst Wilhelm Hohenzollern-Sigmaringen

R 21 460ff Fürst Max Egon Fürstenberg

Dienststelle Ribbentrop

Abt. Pol. II/England Po 2, Vols 1–11; Po 36, Bd. 1

Abt. III, Pol.2/England, 2 volumes

Pol. 26/England Vol. 4; Pol. 29/England, Vol. 1

Pol. 11 R 77121 Personalien Staatsmänner

2. Geheimes Staatsarchiv Preußischer Kulturbesitz Berlin, Dahlem,

GStAPK

Kaiser Wilhelm II, Rep 53 GstA 1 HA Rep. 89 and 100.

(Letters Max Egon II Fürstenberg to Kaiser Wilhelm II: BHP Rep. 53J Lit F No. 3).

3. Bundesarchiv, Abteilung Berlin-Lichterfelde, BAB

R 43 NS 10:

Carl Eduard Herzog von Coburg II/428 and II/886 b

Ernst Hanfstängl (from England) II 903/c

Lord Londonderry II/1436

Lord Noel-Buxton II/1432 a

Prince Max Egon zu Hohenlohe-Langenburg II/895 a
Sir Oswald Mosley II/1432, II/1434
Sir Walter Runciman II/895 a

Adjutantur des Führers NS 10, letters from:
Herzog, Herzogin v. Windsor No. 18
Sir Walter Runciman No. 88
T. C. Moore No. 58
Unity Mitford No. 38
(Viscount) Lord Rothermere No. 295

4. Bundesarchiv Koblenz (BAK)
Fritz Wiedemann Papers N 1720

5. Hausarchiv Hohenzollern-Sigmaringen (FAS), Staatsarchiv Sigmaringen
Papers of Fürst Wilhelm von Hohenzollern-Sigmaringen, Dep. 39, HS 1 80ff and HS NZ 53,116b ff.

6. Fürstlich Waldburg- Zeil'sches Gesamtarchiv, Leutkirch
Papers of Fürst Georg Waldburg-Zeil (Nos. 16–67)
Papers of Fürstin Therese Waldburg-Zeil (Nos. 35–8)

7. Fürstlich Leiningsches Privatarchiv, Amorbach
Papers of Prince Emich Leiningen, 1866–1939 (Diaries Box 7 1910–1939)

8. Generallandesarchiv Karlsruhe
Großherzogliches Familienarchiv: Nachlass Friedrich Großherzog and Großherzogin Luise von Baden, FA Repertorien 2 Vol.
No. 141, correspondence with Hohenlohe-Langenburg

9. Fürstlich Castell'sches Archiv, Castell (FCAC)
HA I.d.VI- Fürst Friedrich Carl zu Castell-Castell (1864–1923)

10. Staatsarchiv Wertheim, Kloster Bronnbach (StAWtB)
Papers Alois zu Löwenstein-Wertheim-Rosenberg (1871–1952), Lit D 662ff.

11. Bismarckarchiv, Friedrichsruh, (AOBS)
Papers of Fürst Otto II von Bismarck

12. Staatsarchiv Bamberg
Papers Baron von Würtzburg AWM G 58 FII 2143ff.

13. Staatsarchiv Coburg
Coburger Zeitung, Bestand LAA, No. 13582.
Papers Ernst II von Sachsen-Coburg und Gotha, LA A 7044
Papers of Herzog Carl Eduard of Sachsen-Coburg und Gotha (up to 1920)

14. Archiv der Fürsten zu Fürstenberg (FFAD), Donaueschingen
Papers of Max Egon II Fürst Fürstenberg (1863–1941)

15. Archiv der Richard-Wagner-Gedenkstätte der Stadt Bayreuth
Letters of Max von Baden to Houston Stewart Chamberlain, 1914–19, HSC 247–55

16. Hohenlohe-Zentralarchiv Neuenstein (HZA)
Papers Ernst II von Hohenlohe Langenburg, 1863–1950; Büschel 61ff.

17. Burg Hohenzollern, Hechingen
Correspondence Fürst Max Egon Fürstenberg to Wilhelm II

18. Fürstlich Öttingen-Wallerstein'sches Archiv, (FÖWA)
VIII,19. 1b: Karl Friedrich Wolfgang Fürst zu Öttingen-Wallerstein (1877–1930)
Fürstin Öttingen-Spielberg papers (uncatalogued)

OTHER ARCHIVES

19. Hoover Institution Archives, Stanford University
Prinzessin Stephanie Juliana zu Hohenlohe-Waldenburg-Schillingsfürst papers

20. Statni oblastni archiv v Plzni pobocka Klatovy (State Archive Pilsen, Klatovy, Czech Republic)
Boxes No. 156, No. 606
Papers of Fürst von Hohenzollern-Sigmaringen
Papers of Princess and Prince Alois Löwenstein-Wertheim

21. British Library (BL) London
Paget Papers Add 51242

22. Archive of the Duke of Portland, Welbeck Abbey
Papers of William John Arthur Charles James Cavendish-Bentinck 6th Duke of Portland.
Ivy, 7th Duchess of Portland papers (includes some of the papers of Sir Francis Bertie)

23. Churchill College Archive Centre (CCAC), Cambridge
The Papers of Group Captain Malcolm Christie, CHRS 1/28
The Papers of Lord Vansittart of Denham, VNST
Sir Winston Churchill Papers, CHAR 19/2A/22–23, CHAR 20/9A/34–8

24. The National Archives London (NA)
MI5 files:
KV 5/3 Anglo-German Fellowship
KV 2 1696 and 1697 Alexander and Stephanie Hohenlohe-Waldenburg-Schillingsfürst

KV 2/3289 Max Egon Hohenlohe-Langenburg
KV 2 915 Fritz Hesse
KV 3 54 British Union of Fascists
Home Office:
HO 151 8; 173/3; 175/2; 181/3
HO 144/1489/364780 Proceedings at the Central Criminal Court, Rex v. Noel Pemberton-Billing, 29, 30, 31 May and 1, 3, 4 June 1918
War Office:
WO 32/5491; WO 32–5108ff.
Foreign Office:
Cecil Papers FO 800/195/98
FO 1020/2004 Greinberg und Hinterriss estates (alleged property of Duke of Saxe-Coburg-Gotha)
FO 371/64689 Denazification cases
FO 608 Czecho-Slovaks 1919

25. Rijksarchief Utrecht, Netherlands
Huis Amerongen Inv. No. 4325ff. (Bentinck Family Papers)

26. Private Archive Castle Twickel, Delden, Netherlands
Papers Victoria Maria Frederica Mechthild Bentinck, Gravin van Aldenburg-Bentinck (1863–1952). TW 2102ff.

27. Royal Archives, Windsor Castle
RA ACA/10: Charles Duke of Saxe Coburg and Gotha to his sister Alice Countess of Athlone

28. Hampshire County Council (Winchester)
Papers Viscount Lymington (9th Earl of Portsmouth). F 230–417

29. Archive of the University Library Cambridge
Stefan Heym papers
The private papers of Lord Charles Hardinge of Penshurst, vol. 35, fos. 203–4

30. Franklin D. Roosevelt Presidential Library:
28 October 1941 Memorandum regarding: Princess Stephanie Hohenlohe Waldenburg <http://docs.fdrlibrary.marist.edu/PSF/BOX3/A31A01.HTML>

31. FBI files, the Vault (FOIPA)
HQ 65-31113-22
HQ 65-31113-22

PRINTED SOURCES/NEWSPAPERS

Almanach de Gotha
Burke's Peerage

Ehrenkrook, Hans Friedrich v., *Genealogisches Handbuch der fürstlichen Häuser*, Vol. iii, 1955.

Europäische Stammtafeln

Fundación nacional Francisco Franco, Documentos in inéditos para la Historia del generalísimo Franco, Vol. II–1, Madrid, 1993.

Fotescu, Diana (ed.), *Americans and Queen Marie of Romania: A Selection of Documents*, Oxford, 1998.

Hansard. Parliamentary Debates, House of Lords 1920–39.

Khristoforov, V. et al. (eds), *Rossiya. XX Vek. Dokumenty. Tainy diplomatii tret'ego reikha. Germanskie diplomaty, rukovoditeli zarubezhnykh voennykh missii, voennyi i politseiskie attashe v sovetskom plenu. Dokumenty iz sledstvennykh del 1944/1945*, Moscow, 2011.

Morning Post, 1926 and 1927.

The Times, 1880–1939, London.

West, Nigel, and Tsarev, Oleg, *Triplex: Secrets from the Cambridge Spies*, New Haven, 2009.

Wiener High Life. Almanach der Wiener Gesellschaft, 1. Jahrgang 1905.

DIARIES/MEMOIRS/AUTOBIOGRAPHIES

Asquith, Lady Cynthia, *Diaries 1915–1918*, New York, 1969.

Athlone, Alice Countess of, *For my Grandchildren: Some Reminiscences of Her Royal Highness Princess Alice*, London, 1967.

Baden, Max von, *Erinnerungen und Dokumente*, Stuttgart, 1927 (new edition 1968 with an introduction by Golo Mann).

Baernreither, Joseph M., *Fragments of a political diary*, ed. Joseph Redlich, London, 1930.

Baernreither, Joseph Maria, *Der Verfall des Habsburgerreiches und die Deutschen. Fragmente eines politischen Tagebuchs 1897–1917*, ed. Oskar Mitis, Vienna, 1939.

Blücher, Evelyn Princess, *An English Wife in Berlin*, London, 1920.

Bülow, Bernhard von, *Memoirs (Denkwürdigkeiten)*, 4 vols, ed. F. von Stockhammer, trans. F. A. Voigt, London, 1931–2.

Bunsen, Marie von, *Die Welt in der ich lebte. Erinnerungen aus glücklichen Jahren 1860–1912*, Leipzig, 1929.

Conwell-Evans, T. P., *None so Blind: A Study of the Crisis Years 1930–39. Based on the Private Papers of Group Captain M. G. Christie*, London, 1947.

Czernin, Ottokar, *Über die Politik des Weltkrieges*, Vienna, 1918.

Delmer, Sefton, *Black Boomerang: An Autobiography*, vol. ii, London, 1962 (German edition: *Die Deutschen und ich*, Hanover, 1962).

Dilks, David (ed.), *The Diaries of Sir Alexander Cadogan 1938–45*, London, 1971.

Dirksen, Herbert von, *Moskau, Tokio, London. Zwanzig Jahre deutscher Außenpolitik*, Stuttgart, 1949.

The Duff Cooper Diaries 1915–1951, ed. John Julius Norwich, London, 2005.

Fritsche, Victor v., *Bilder aus dem österreichischen Hof- und Gesellschaftsleben*, Vienna, 1914.

Fromm, Bella, *Blood and Banquets: A Berlin Social Diary*, London, 1942.

Goebbels Diaries: Die Tagebücher von Joseph Goebbels, ed. Elke Fröhlich, vols 3–7, Munich, 1998–2006.

Hanfstängl, Ernst, *Hitler: The Missing Years*, London, 1957.

Hesse, Fritz, *Das Vorspiel zum Kriege*, Leoni am Starnberger See, 1979.

Hessen, Großherzog Ernst Ludwig, *Erinnertes. Aufzeichnungen des letzten Großherzogs Ernst Ludwig von Hessen und bei Rhein*, ed. Eckhart G. Franz, Darmstadt, 1983.

Hohenlohe, Franz, *Stephanie. Das Leben meiner Mutter*, Munich, 1991.

Ilsemann, Sigurd v., *Der Kaiser in Holland. Aufzeichnungen aus den Jahren von 1924–1941. Monarchie und Nationalsozialismus*, Munich, 1968.

Kelly, Sir David, *The Ruling Few*, London, 1952.

The Guy Liddell Diaries, i: *1939–1942*, ed. Nigel West, London, 2005.

Listowel, Judith, *This I Have Seen*, London, 1943.

Lymington, Viscount, *A Knot of Roots: An Autobiography*, London, 1965.

Maiskii, I., *Dnevnik diplomata*, vol. I, Moscow, 2006.

Paget, Lady Walburga, *Embassies of Other Days, and Further Recollections*, 2 vols, London, 1923.

Philby, Kim, *My Silent War: The Autobiography of a Spy*, London, 2003.

Pless, Daisy, *Tanz auf dem Vulkan: Erinnerungen an Deutschland und Englands Schicksalwende*, Dresden, 1931.

Popov, Dusko, *Superspion: Der Doppelagent im Zweiten Weltkrieg*, Vienna, 1974.

Radziwill, Marie Dorothea, *Briefe vom deutschen Kaiserhof, 1889–1915*, Berlin, 1936.

Romania, Marie Queen of, *The Story of my Life*, 3 vols, London, 1938.

Romania, Marie Queen of, *Later Chapters of my Life: The Lost Memoirs of Queen Marie of Romania*, ed. Diana Mandache, London, 2004.

Schönburg-Waldenburg, Heinrich Prinz v., *Erinnerungen aus kaiserlicher Zeit*, Leipzig, 1929.

Seraphim, Hans-Günther, *Das politische Tagebuch Alfred Rosenbergs aus den Jahren 1834/35 und 1939/40*, Göttingen, Berlin, Frankfurt am Main, 1956.

Spitzy, Reinhard, *So haben wir das Reich verspielt: Bekenntnisse eines Illegalen*. Munich, Vienna, 1986.

Spitzy, Reinhard, *So entkamen wir den Alliierten. Erinnerungen eines Ehemaligen*, Berlin, 1989.

Tavistock, Marquess of, *Fate of a Peace Effort*, London, 1940.

Tennant, Ernest, *True Account*, London, 1957.

Treschkow, Hans von, *Von Fürsten und anderen Sterblichen. Erinnerungen eines Kriminalkommissars*, Berlin, 1922.

Vanderbilt Balsan, Consuelo, *The Glitter and the Gold*, London, 1973.

Viktoria Luise, Herzogin von Braunschweig, *Im Glanz der Krone*, Göttingen, 1967.

Wied, Pauline, *Vom Leben gelernt*, Ludwigsburg, 1953.

Wilhelm II, *Aus meinem Leben*, Leipzig, 1927.

Wille, Fred, *Rings um den Kaiser*, Berlin, 1913.

Windsor, Duke of, *A King's Story: The Memoirs of HRH the Duke of Windsor*, London, 1998 (new edition).
Zedlitz-Trützschler, Robert v., *Zwölf Jahre am deutschen Kaiserhof*, Berlin, 1924.

SECONDARY SOURCES

Afflerbach, Holger, *Der Dreibund: Europäische Großmacht- und Allianzpolitik vor dem Ersten Weltkrieg*, Cologne and Vienna, 2002.
D'Almeida, Fabrice, *High Society in the Third Reich*, London, 2008.
Anderson, Benedict, *Imagined Communities*, London, 1983.
Angelow, Jürgen, *Kalkül und Prestige. Der Zweibund am Vorabend des Ersten Weltkrieges*, Cologne, 2000.
Asch, Ronald G. (ed.), *Der europäische Adel im Ancien Régime. Von der Krise der ständischen Monarchien bis zur Revolution (ca. 1600–1789)*, Cologne, 2001.
Babík, Milan, 'George D. Herron and the Eschatological Foundations of Woodrow Wilson's Foreign Policy, 1917–1919', *Diplomatic History*, 35/5 (November 2011).
Bange, Oliver, 'The Stasi Confronts Western Strategies for Transformation 1966–1975', in Haslam/Urbach (eds), *Secret Intelligence in the European States System 1918–1989*, Stanford, Calif., 2013.
Barros, Andrew, 'A Window on the "Trust": The Case of Ado Birk', *Intelligence and National Security*, 10/2 (April 1995), 273–93.
Blakeway, Denys, *The Last Dance: 1936: The year our lives changed*, London, 2010.
Bloch, Michael, *Operation Willi: The Plot to Kidnap the Duke of Windsor July 1940*, London, 1984.
Bosbach, Franz, Robbins, Keith, and Urbach, Karina (eds), *Geburt oder Leistung? Birth or Talent? The Formation of Elites in a British–German Comparison*, Munich, 2003.
Bourdieu, Pierre, 'Ökonomisches Kapital, kulturelles Kapital, soziales Kapital', in Reinhard Kreckel (ed.), *Soziale Ungleichheiten*, Göttingen, 1983.
Bourdieu, Pierre, 'Der Habitus als Vermittlung zwischen Struktur und Praxis (1970)', in Pierre Bourdieu, *Zur Soziologie der symbolischen Formen*, Frankfurt am Main, 4th edition 1991.
Breitman, Richard, 'A Deal with the Nazi Dictatorship? Himmler's Alleged Peace Emissaries in Autumn 1943', *Journal of Contemporary History*, 30/3 (July 1995), 411–30.
Brook-Shepherd, Gordon, *The Last Empress: Life and Times of Zita of Austria-Hungary, 1892–1989*, London, 1991.
Brügel, J. W., 'Der Runciman Bericht', *Vierteljahrshefte für Zeitgeschichte*, 26 (1978), 652ff.
Burleigh, Michael, *The Third Reich: A New History*, London, 2001.
Cannadine, David, *The Decline and Fall of the British Aristocracy*, New Haven and London, 1990.

Carlgren, W. N., *Neutralität oder Allianz. Deutschlands Beziehungen zu Schweden in den Anfangsjahren des Ersten Weltkrieges*, Stockholm Studies in History, Vol. 6, Stockholm, 1962.

Carr, Gilbert, 'Ein Heiratsbureau der Gedanken in der Wiener Jahrhundertwende. Zum kulturpolitischen Versuch Robert Scheus um 1900', in Jürgen Barkhoff, Hartmut Böhme, and Jeanne Riou (eds), *Netzwerke. Eine Kulturtechnik der Moderne*, Cologne, 2004.

Cecil, Lamar, 'Der diplomatische Dienst im kaiserlichen Deutschland', in Klaus Schwabe (ed.), *Das Diplomatische Korps 1871–1945*, Boppard, 1945.

Celovsky, Boris, and Stoiber, Rudolf, *Stephanie von Hohenlohe. Sie liebte die Mächtigen der Welt*, Munich, 1988.

Chickering, Roger, *Imperial Germany and the Great War, 1914–1918*, Cambridge, 1998.

Clark, Christopher, *William II: Profiles in Power*, London, 2000.

Clark, Christopher, *The Sleepwalkers: How Europe Went to War in 1914*, London, 2013.

Cole, Terence F., 'The Daily Telegraph Affair and its Aftermath: The Kaiser, Bülow and the Reichstag, 1908–1909', in John Röhl and Nicolaus Sombart (eds), *Kaiser Wilhelm II: New Interpretations. The Corfu Papers*, Cambridge, 1982.

Colley, Linda, *Forging the Nation 1707–1836*, London, 1996.

Conradi, Peter, *Hitler's Piano Player*, London, 2011.

Conze, Eckart, *Kleines Lexikon des Adels: Titel, Throne, Traditionen*, Munich, 2005.

Conze, Eckart, Frei, Norbert, Hayes, Peter, and Zimmermann, Moshe (eds), *Das Amt und die Vergangenheit. Deutsche Diplomaten im Dritten Reich*, Munich, 2010.

Conze, Eckart, and Wienfort, Monika (eds), *Adel und Moderne: Deutschland im europäischen Vergleich im 19. und 20. Jahrhundert*, Cologne, 2004.

Cowling, Maurice, *The Impact of Hitler: British Politics and British Policy 1933–1940*, London, 1977.

Demel, Walter, and Kramer, Ferdinand (eds), *Adel und Adelskultur in Bayern*, Munich, 2008.

Eckert, Astrid M., *The Struggle for the Files*, Cambridge, 2014.

Elias, Norbert, *Die Höfische Gesellschaft. Untersuchungen zur Soziologie des Königtums und der höfischen Aristokratie*, Frankfurt am Main, 1983.

Evans, Richard J. (ed.), *The Coming of the Third Reich: How the Nazis Destroyed Democracy and Seized Power in Germany*, London, 2004.

Faber, David, *Munich: The 1938 Appeasement Crisis*, London, 2008.

Fahrmeir, Andreas, *Citizenship: The Rise and Fall of a Modern Concept*, New Haven, 2008.

Fellowes, Julian, *Snobs*, London, 2005.

Field, Geoffrey George, *Evangelist of Race: The Germanic Vision of Houston Stewart Chamberlain*, New York, 1981.

Frie, Ewald, *Friedrich August Ludwig von der Marwitz 1777–1837: Biographien eines Preussen*, Paderborn, 2001.

Frühwald, Wolfgang, 'Büchmann und die Folgen. Zur sozialen Funktion des Bildungszitates in der deutschen Literatur des 19. Jahrhunderts'. in Reinhart Koselleck (ed.), *Bildungsbürgertum im 19. Jahrhundert*, ii: *Bildungsgüter und Bildungswissen*, Stuttgart, 1990.

Funck, Marcus, and Malinowski, Stephan, 'Masters of Memory: The Strategic Use of Autobiographical Memory by the German Nobility', in Alon Confino and Peter Fritzsche (eds), *The Work of Memory: New Directions in the Study of German Society and Culture*, Chicago, 2004.

Gall, Lothar, 'Max von Baden', in Wilhelm von Sternburg (ed.), *Die deutschen Kanzler. Von Bismarck bis Schmidt*, Frankfurt am Main, 1985.

Gammelien, Stefan, *Wilhelm II und Schweden-Norwegen 1888–1905*, Berlin, 2012.

Gerwarth, Robert, and Horne, John, 'Fighting the Red Beast: Counter-Revolutionary Violence in the Defeated States of Central Europe', in Robert Gerwarth and John Horne (eds), *War in Peace: Paramilitary Violence in Europe after the Great War*, Oxford, 2012.

Giloi, Eva, *Monarchy, Myth, and Material Culture in Germany 1750–1950*, Cambridge, 2014.

Glassheim, Eagle, *Noble Nationalists: The Transformation of the Bohemian Aristocracy*, Cambridge, Mass., and London, 2005.

Godsey, William D., *Aristocratic Redoubt. The Austro-Hungarian Foreign Office on the Eve of the First World War*, West Lafayette, Ind., 1999.

Gollwitzer, Heinz, *Die Standesherren. Die politische Stellung der Mediatisierten 1815–1918. Ein Beitrag zur deutschen Sozialgeschichte*, Göttingen, 2nd edn 1964.

Griffiths, Richard, *Patriotism Perverted*, London, 1998.

Grunewald, Ulrike, *Luise von Sachsen-Coburg-Saalfeld (1800–1831): Lebensräume einer unangepassten Herzogin*, Cologne, 2013.

Hambrecht, Rainer, 'Eine Dynastie—zwei Namen: "Haus Sachsen-Coburg und Gotha" und "Haus Windsor". Ein Beitrag zur Nationalisierung der Monarchien in Europa', in Wolfram Pyta and Ludwig Richter (eds), *Gestaltungskraft des Politischen. Festschrift für Eberhard Kolb*, Berlin, 1998.

Haslam, Jonathan, *Russia's Cold War*, New Haven, 2011.

Haslam, Jonathan, '"Humint" by Default and the Problem of Trust: Soviet Intelligence 1917 to 1941', in Jonathan Haslam and Karina Urbach (eds), *Secret Intelligence in the European States System 1918–1989*, Stanford, Calif., 2013, 187ff.

Haslam, Jonathan, *Near and Distant Neighbors: A New History of Soviet Intelligence, 1917–1989*, New York and Oxford, 2015.

Higham, Charles, *Mrs Simpsons: Secret Lives of the Duchess of Windsor*, London, 2004.

Hildebrand, Klaus, *Vom Reich zum Weltreich. Hitler, NSDAP und koloniale Frage 1919–1945*, Munich, 1969.

Hoare, Philip, *Oscar Wilde's Last Stand*, London, 1997.

Höhne, Heinz, *The Order of the Death's Head: The Story of Hitler's SS*, London, 2001.

Horn, Michael, 'Zwischen Abdankung und Absetzung. Das Ende der Herrschaft der Bundesfürsten des Deutschen Reiches im November 1918', in Susan Richter and Dirk Dirbach (eds), *Thronverzicht: Die Abdankung in Monarchien vom Mittelalter bis in die Neuzeit*, Vienna and Cologne, 2014.

Hoser, Paul, Collado-Seidel, Carlos, and Bernecker, Walter (eds), *Die spanischen Könige*, Munich, 1997.

Hull, Isabel V., *The Entourage of Kaiser Wilhelm II 1888–1918*, Cambridge, 1982.

Hull, Isabel V., 'Kaiser Wilhelm and the Liebenberg Circle', in John Röhl and Nicolaus Sombart (eds), *Kaiser Wilhelm II: New Interpretations. The Corfu Papers*, Cambridge, 1982.

Irving, David, *Göring*, Munich, 1987.

Jelavich, Barbara, 'Romania in the First World War: The Pre-War Crisis, 1912–1914', *International History Review*, 14/3 (August 1992).

Katzenstein, Peter, *Disjointed Partners: Austria and Germany since 1815*, Berkeley, 1976.

Keay, Anna, 'The Shadow King', in Philip Mansel and Torsten Riotte (eds), *Monarchy and Exile: The Politics of Legitimacy from Marie de Médicis to Wilhelm II*, London, 2011.

Kennedy, Paul, *The Rise of Anglo-German Antagonism 1860–1914*, London, 1980.

Kershaw, Ian, *Hitler 1936–1945: Nemesis*, London, 2001.

Kershaw, Ian, *Making Friends with Hitler: Lord Londonderry and Britain's Road to War*, London, 2005.

Kettle, Michael, *Salome's Last Veil*, London, 1977.

Kilduff, Martin, and Wenpin Tsai, *Social Networks and Organizations*, London, 2003.

Klein, Markus Josef, *Ernst von Salomon. Eine politische Biographie*, Limburg, 1994.

Knightley, Philip, *Philby: KGB Masterspy*, London, 1988.

Kocka, Jürgen, *Familie und soziale Platzierung*, Opladen, 1980.

Kubrova, Monika, *Vom guten Leben. Adelige Frauen im 19. Jahrhundert*, Berlin, 2011.

Lambi, Ivo, *The Navy and German Power Politics 1862–1914*, London, 1984.

Lerman, Kathy, 'The Decisive Relationship: Kaiser Wilhelm II and Chancellor Bernhard von Bülow, 1900–1905', in John Röhl and Nicolaus Sombart (eds), *Kaiser Wilhelm II: New Interpretations. The Corfu Papers*, Cambridge, 1982.

Lieven, Dominic, *The Aristocracy in Europe 1815–1914*, London, 1992.

Linke, Angelika, *Sprachkultur und Bürgertum. Zur Mentalitätsgeschichte des 19. Jahrhunderts*, Tübingen, 1996.

Longerich, Peter, *Heinrich Himmler*, Berlin, 2008.

Longford, Elizabeth, *Victoria RI*, London, 1964.

Luke, Michael, *Hansel Pless: Prisoner of History. A Life of H.S.H. Hans Heinrich XVII, 4th Prince of Pless*, London, 2002.

Lundgreen, Peter (ed.), *Sozial- und Kulturgeschichte des Bürgertums. Eine Bilanz des Bielefelder Sonderforschungsbereichs (1986–1997)*, Bürgertum. Beiträge zur europäischen Gesellschaftsgeschichte 18, Göttingen, 2000.

Machtan, Lothar, *Prinz Max von Baden. Der letzte Kanzler des Kaisers*, Berlin, 2013.

McKibbin, Ross, *Classes and Cultures: England 1918–1951*, Oxford, 1998.

Malinowski, Stephan, *Vom König zum Führer. Sozialer Niedergang und politische Radikalisierung im deutschen Adel zwischen Kaiserreich und NS-Staat*, Berlin, 2003.

Mallwitz, Peter (ed.), *Stefan Heym. Reden an den Feind. Karl Eduard von Sachsen-Coburg und Gotha*, Frankfurt am Main, 1990.

Mansel, Philip, and Riotte, Torsten (eds), *Monarchy and Exile: The Politics of Legitimacy from Marie de Médicis to Wilhelm II*, London, 2011.

Martin, Bernd, *Friedensinitiativen und Machtpolitik im Zweiten Weltkrieg 1939–1942*, Düsseldorf, 1974.

Martin, Harriet, *Kings of Peace, Pawns of War: The Untold Story of Peace-Making*, New York, 2006.

Matthias, Erich, and Morsey, Rudolf (eds), *Die Regierung des Prinzen Max von Baden*, Düsseldorf, 1962.

Mayer, Arno, *The Persistence of the Old Regime: Europe to the Great War*, London, 2010 (new edition).

Meehan, Patricia, *The Unnecessary War: Whitehall and the German Resistance to Hitler*, London, 1992.

Meinl, Susanne, *Nationalsozialisten gegen Hitler: Die nationalrevolutionäre Opposition um Friedrich Wilhelm Heinz*, Berlin, 2000.

Mitford, Nancy, 'Die englische Aristokratie', *Der Monat. Internationale Zeitschrift*, 9/97 (Berlin, 1956), 40–9.

Modin, Yuri, *My Five Cambridge Friends*, London, 1994.

Mombauer, Annika, *Helmuth von Moltke and the Origins of the First World War*, Cambridge, 2001.

Mommsen, Wolfgang, *War der Kaiser an allem schuld? Wilhelm II. und die preussisch-deutschen Machteliten*, Berlin, 2002.

Muhs, Rudolf, 'Geisteswehen: Rahmenbedingungen des deutsch-britischen Kulturaustausches im 19. Jahrhundert', in Rudolf Muhs, J. Paulmann, and W. Steinmetz (eds), *Aneignung und Abwehr. Arbeitskreis Deutsche England-Forschung*, Bodenheim, 1998, 44ff.

Niño, Antonio, 'El rey embajador. Alfonso XIII en la política internacional', in Javier Moreno Luzón (ed.), *Alfonso XIII. Un político en el trono*, Madrid, 2003, 239–76.

Noakes, Jeremy, and Pridham, G., *Nazism 1919–1945*, ii: *Foreign Policy, Economy and Society: A Documentary Reader*, Exeter, 1984.

Oplatka, Andreas, *Graf Stephan Szechenyi. Der Mann, der Ungarn schuf*, Vienna, 2004.

Overy, Richard, *Goering: Hitler's Iron Knight*, London, 2011.

Pakula, Hannah, *The Last Romantic: A Biography of Queen Marie of Roumania*, New York, 1986.

Petropoulos, Jonathan, *Royals and the Reich. The Princes von Hessen in Nazi Germany*, Oxford, 2006.

Phillips, Gregory D., *The Diehards: Aristocratic Society and Politics in Edwardian England*, Cambridge, Mass., 1979.

Popov, V. *Sovitnik Korolevy—Superagent Kremlya*, Moscow, 1995.

Press, Volker, and Brendle, Franz (eds), *Adel im alten Reich. Gesammelte Vorträge und Aufsätze*, Tübingen, 1998.

Pugh, Martin, *Hurrah for the Blackshirts! Fascists and Fascism in Britain between the Wars*, London, 2005.

Püschel, Angelika, 'Carl Eduard von Coburg', BA thesis deposited in Staatsarchive Coburg 2004.

Recker, Marie-Luise, *England und der Donauraum 1919–1929. Probleme einer europäischen Nachkriegsordnung*, Veröffentlichungen des Deutschen Historischen Instituts in London, 3, Stuttgart, 1976.

Reif, Heinz, 'Adel im 19. und 20. Jahrhundert', *Enzyklopädie deutscher Geschichte*, lv, Munich, 1999.

Rendle, Matthew, 'The Symbolic Revolution: The Russian Nobility and February 1917', *Revolutionary Russia*, 18 (June 2005).

Retallack, James N., *Germany in the Age of Kaiser Wilhelm II*, London, 1996.

Reynolds, K. D., *Aristocratic Women and Political Society in Victorian Britain*, Oxford, 1998.

Richter, Susan, and Dirbach, Dirk (eds), *Thronverzicht: Die Abdankung in Monarchien vom Mittelalter bis in die Neuzeit*, Vienna and Cologne, 2014.

Ritter, Ernst, 'Die erste Deutsch-Englische Gesellschaft (1935–1939)', in Friedrich Kahlenberg (ed.), *Aus der Arbeit der Archive*, Boppard am Rhein, 1989.

Roberts, Andrew, *The Holy Fox: A Biography of Lord Halifax*, London, 1991.

Röhl, John C. G., *Kaiser, Hof und Staat. Wilhelm II. und die deutsche Politik*, Munich, 1987.

Röhl, John C. G., *Wilhelm II.* 3 vols, Cambridge and Munich, 2001/2009.

Romsics, Ignác, 'The Hungarian Aristocracy and its Political Attitudes in the Interwar Years', in Karina Urbach (ed.), *European Aristocracies and the Radical Right. 1918–1939*, Oxford, 2007.

Ross, Alan S. C., *Linguistic Class-Indicators in Present-Day English*, London, 1953.

Roth, Daniel B., *Hitlers Brückenkopf in Schweden. Die deutsche Gesandtschaft in Stockholm 1933–1945*, Berlin, 2009.

Ruppel, Sophie, 'Geschwisterbeziehungen im Adel und Norbert Elias' Figurationssoziologie—ein Anwendungsversuch', in Claudia Opitz (ed.), *Höfische Gesellschaft und Zivilisationsprozess. Norbert Elias' Werk in kulturwissenschaftlicher Perspektive*, Cologne and Weimar, 2005.

Sabrow, Martin, *Der Rathenaumord. Rekronstruktion einer Verschwörung gegen die Republik von Weimar*, Munich, 1994.

Saint Martin, Monique de, *Der Adel. Soziologie eines Standes*, Konstanz, 2003.

Sandner, Harald, *Hitlers Herzog. Carl Eduard von Sachsen-Coburg-Gotha*, Maastricht, 2010.

Schad, Martha, *Hitlers geheime Diplomatin. Das Leben der Stephanie Hohenlohe*, Munich, 2002.

Schlie, Ulrich, *Kein Friede mit Deutschland: Die geheimen Gespräche im Zweiten Weltkrieg 1939–1941*, Munich, 1993.

Schlie, Ulrich, 'Max Egon Prinz zu Hohenlohe-Langenburg. Staatswissenschaftler, Großgrundbesitzer und Privat-Diplomat im Dritten Reich, 1897–1968', *Lebensbilder aus Baden-Württemberg*, Stuttgart, 2010, 23.

Schmeling, Anke, *Josias Erbprinz zu Waldeck und Pyrmont. Der politische Weg eines hohen SS-Führers*, Kassel, 1993.

Schönpflug, Daniel, *Die Heiraten der Hohenzollern. Verwandtschaft, Politik und Ritual in Europa 1640–1918*, Göttingen, 2013.

Sharp, Paul, 'Who Needs Diplomats? The Problem of Diplomatic Representation', *International Journal*, 52 (1997), 609–34.

Simmel, Georg, 'Zur Soziologie des Adels. Fragment aus einer Formenlehre der Gesellschaft', in Alessandro Cavalli and Volker Krech (eds), *Georg Simmel, Aufsätze und Abhandlungen, 1901–1908*, Frankfurt am Main, 1993.

Smith, Douglas, *Former People: The Final Days of the Russian Aristocracy*, New York, 2012.

Sondhaus, Lawrence, *The Naval Policy of Austria-Hungary 1867–1918: Navalism, Industrial Development, and the Politics of Dualism*, West Lafayette, Ind., 1994.

Souhami, Diana, *Mrs Keppel and her Daughter*, London, 1996.

Stalmann, Volker, *Fürst Chlodwig zu Hohenlohe-Schillingsfürst. Ein deutscher Reichskanzler*, Paderborn, 2003.

Stearns, Peter N., and Stearns, Carol Z., 'Emotionology: Clarifying the History of Emotions and Emotional Standards', *American Historical Review*, 90/4 (October 1985), 813–36.

Stedman Jones, Gareth, *Languages and Class: Studies in Working Class History, 1832–1982*, Cambridge, 1983.

Steglich, Wolfgang, *Die Friedenspolitik der Mittelmächte 1917/18*, Wiesbaden, 1964.

Steglich, Wolfgang, *Die Friedensversuche der kriegführenden Mächte im Sommer und Herbst 1917. Quellenkritische Untersuchungen, Akten und Vernehmungsprotokolle*, Stuttgart, 1984.

Steinberg, Jonathan, *All or Nothing: The Axis and the Holocaust 1941–43*, London, 2002.

Steiner, Zara, *The Triumph of the Dark: European International History 1933–39*, Oxford, 2013.

Steller, Verena, *Diplomatie von Angesicht zu Angesicht. Diplomatische Handlungsformen in den deutsch-französischen Beziehungen 1870–1919*, Paderborn, 2011.

Stephan, John J., *The Russian Fascists: Tragedy and Farce in Exile, 1925–1945*, London, 1978.

Stone, Dan, *Responses to Nazism in Britain, 1933–1939: Before War and Holocaust*, London, 2003.

Strath, Bo (ed.), *Language and Construction of Class Identities*, Göteborg, 1990.

Taylor, Sally J., *The Great Outsiders: Northcliffe, Rothermere and the Daily Mail*, London, 1996.

Taylor, Sally J., *The Reluctant Press Lord: Esmond Rothermere and the Daily Mail*, London, 1998.

Thorsell, Staffan, *Mein lieber Reichskanzler! Sveriges kontakter med Hitlers rikskansli*, Stockholm, 2006.

Trumbach, Randolph, *The Rise of the Egalitarian Family: Aristocratic Kinship and Domestic Relations in Eighteenth-Century England*, New York, 1978.

Tusell, Javier, and Queipo de Llano, Genoveva G., *Alfonso XIII: el rey pólemico*, Madrid, 2001.

Ueberschär, Gerd R., and Vogel, Wienfried, *Dienen und Verdienen. Hitlers Geschenke an seine Eliten*, Frankfurt am Main, 1999.

Ullman, Richard H., *The Anglo-Soviet Accord: Anglo-Soviet Relations 1917–1921*, London, 1972.

Ullrich, Volker, *Adolf Hitler: Biographie, Die Jahre des Aufstiegs 1889–1939*, Frankfurt am Main, 2013.

Urbach, Karina, 'Das schwarze Buch. Kollektive Paranoia im Ersten Weltkrieg', in Andreas Fahrmeir and Sabine Freitag (eds), *Mord und andere Kleinigkeiten*, Munich, 2001.

Urbach, Karina, 'Süddeutsche Standesherren und der Erste Weltkrieg', in Monika Wienfort and Eckart Conze (eds), *Adelsgeschichte als Gesellschaftsgeschichte. Deutschland im europäischen Vergleich im 19. und 20. Jahrhundert*, Munich, 2003.

Urbach, Karina, 'Adel versus Bürgertum. Überlebens- und Aufstiegsstrategien im deutsch-britischen Vergleich', in Franz Bosbach, Keith Robbins, and Karina Urbach (eds), *Geburt oder Leistung? Birth or Talent? The Formation of Elites in a British–German Comparison*, Munich, 2003.

Urbach, Karina, 'Age of no Extremes? The British Aristocracy between the House of Lords and the Mosley Movement', in Karina Urbach (ed.), *European Aristocracies and the Radical Right: 1918–1939*, Oxford, 2007.

Urbach, Karina (ed.), *Royal Kinship: Anglo-German Family Networks*, Munich, 2008.

Urbach, Karina, 'Flirting with Hitler: Biographies of the German and British Nobility in the Interwar Years', *Bulletin of the German Historical Institute* (May 2007), 64–75.

Urbach, Karina, and Buchner, Bernd, 'Houston Stewart Chamberlain und Prince Max von Baden', *Vierteljahrshefte für Zeitgeschichte* (2004), 121–77.

Urbach, Karina, and Haslam, Jonathan (eds), *Secret Intelligence and the International Relations of Europe in the 20thC*, Stanford, Calif., 2013.

Vonderau, Patrick, *Schweden und das nationalsozialistische Deutschland. Eine annotierte Bibliographie der deutschsprachigen Forschungsliteratur*, Stockholm, 2003.

Walker, Jesse, *The United States of Paranoia: A Conspiracy Theory*, New York, 2013.

Walther, Gerrit and Maaser, Michael (eds), *Bildung: Ziele und Formen, Traditionen und Systeme, Medien und Akteure*, Stuttgart, 2010.

Wehler, Hans-Ulrich (ed.), *Europäischer Adel 1750–1950*, Geschichte und Gesellschaft 13, Göttingen, 1990.

Weinberg, Gerhard, *The Foreign Policy of Hitler's Germany: Starting World War II, 1937–39*, vol. ii, Amherst, NY, 1993.

Wienfort, Monika, *Adel in der Moderne*, Göttingen, 2006.

Wilson, A. N., *Victoria: A Life*, London, 2014.

Wilson, Jim, *Nazi Princess: Hitler, Lord Rothermere and Princess Stephanie von Hohenlohe*, London, 2011.

Winzen, Peter, *Das Kaiserreich am Abgrund. Die Daily Telegraph Affäre und das Hale-Interview von 1908*, Stuttgart, 2002.

Worsthorne, Peregrine, *In Defence of Aristocracy*, London, 2004.

Wright, Peter, *Spycatcher: The Candid Autobiography of a Senior Intelligence Officer*, Toronto, 1987.

Wylie, Neville, *Britain, Switzerland, and the Second World War*, Oxford, 2003.

Ziegerhofer-Prettenthaler, Anita, *Botschafter Europas. Richard Nikolaus Coudenhove-Kalergi und die Paneuropa-Bewegung in den zwanziger und dreißiger Jahren*, Vienna, 2003.

Ziegler, Philip, *King Edward VIII*, London, 2001.

Picture Acknowledgements

1. Getty Images/Hulton Archive
2. Getty Images/Hulton Archive
3. Source: Wikimedia Commons <http://commons.wikimedia.org/wiki/File:Duckyandsisters.jpg?uselang=de>
4. Getty Images/Imagno
5. Wikipedia commons
6. Ullstein bild
7. Ullstein bild
8. Heinrich Hoffmann© 2015. Photo Scala, Florence/bpk, Bildagentur für Kunst, Kultur und Geschichte, Berlin
9. PA Images
10. Getty Images/Hulton Archive

Index